Appeasing Bankers

PRINCETON STUDIES IN
INTERNATIONAL HISTORY AND POLITICS

Series Editors
Thomas Christensen
G. John Ikenberry
Marc Trachtenberg

Appeasing Bankers

FINANCIAL CAUTION ON THE ROAD TO WAR

Jonathan Kirshner

PRINCETON UNIVERSITY PRESS

PRINCETON AND OXFORD

Published by Princeton University Press, 41 William Street, Princeton, New Jersey 08540
In the United Kingdom: Princeton University Press, 3 Market Place,
Woodstock, Oxfordshire OX20 1SY

Library of Congress Cataloging-in-Publication Data
Kirshner, Jonathan.
Appeasing bankers : financial caution on the road to war / Jonathan Kirshner.
p.   cm.   —   (Princeton studies in international history and politics)
Includes bibliographical references and index.
ISBN-13: 978-0-691-13144-3 (hardcover : alk. paper)
ISBN-13: 978-0-691-13461-1 (pbk : alk. paper)
1. War—Economic aspects. 2. Banks and banking—History—20th century.
3. Military history, Modern—20th century—Economic aspects. I. Title.
HB195.K56 2007
355.02'73—dc22
2007004163

British Library Cataloging-in-Publication Data is available

This book has been composed in Sabon

Printed on acid-free paper. ∞

press.princeton.edu

Printed in the United States of America

10 9 8 7 6 5 4 3 2 1

For Elie and Ari

Contents

Acknowledgments

Orson Welles once said, with mixed emotions, "And when it is finished, its title is going to be *When are you going to finish Don Quixote?*" In recent years I have heard the tone of his voice with increasing empathy. For a number of reasons, some much happier than others, this book has been a long time coming.

Support for this project was generously provided by the John M. Olin Institute for Strategic Studies at Harvard University, and I thank Steve Rosen for his faith in the work, which mattered. I also owe considerable thanks to Ann Townes at the Olin Institute. The book was completed at the Princeton Institute for International and Regional Studies, where Miguel Centeno and Susan Biddig provided an ideal and stimulating environment for the visiting fellows.

Over these years, this project has greatly benefited from comments and suggestions, in particular from participants at seminars at Dartmouth, Harvard, MIT, Princeton, University of California at Santa Barbara, and University of Southern California, where I presented various parts of the manuscript in progress. I have also benefited from the generosity of colleagues—David Asher, Richard Bensel, Allen Carlson, Phil Cerny, Jerry Cohen, Aaron Friedberg, John Ikenberry, Talbot Imlay, Isaac Kramnick, Jennifer Lind, Junichi Naito, Steve Rosen, Dick Samuels, and Hector Schamis—who shared their expertise on various draft chapters, often more than once. I would also like to thank Burt Diamond, Paul MacDonald, Livia Schachter, Geoff Wallace, Nick Winter, and three anonymous referees at Princeton University Press for exceptionally thoughtful and constructive suggestions. Chuck Myers did a terrific job both in dealing with me and in shepherding the book through the process at the press.

A handful of good friends have read too many versions of this book too many times—Rawi Abdelal, Tom Christensen, Matt Evangelista, Eric Helleiner, Peter Katzenstein, and Karl Mueller—whose suggestions and advice and relative sanity I have very much depended upon in completing this project. More generally, given my years at Cornell University, I would be remiss if I did not acknowledge the rewards of working across the hall from Peter Katzenstein, which are not easily overestimated. His influence is more evident in the vineyard than in the bottle, as it should be.

Above all, my greatest debt is to Esty, for walking down the avenue again.

Appeasing Bankers

CHAPTER 1

What Does Finance Want?

Is your money that good?
—*Bob Dylan*

Bankers dread war. More precisely, financial communities within states favor cautious national security strategies and are acutely averse to war and to policies that risk war. This general rule holds across time and place, in a wide variety of political and economic settings. This chapter explains why finance has these preferences. The chapters that follow probe and evaluate this argument, and consider its implications for contemporary international politics. The short answer is: finance wants macroeconomic stability. Because war is largely incompatible with macroeconomic stability, the financial community is especially leery of risking armed conflict. This disposition is an important influence in contemporary international relations and will remain so, especially for as long as financial globalization endures.

The principal argument of this book is that the caution of finance and its strong aversion to war are virtually universal traits; they are extraordinarily remarkable regularities that provide scholars of international relations with an important analytical tool for understanding world politics. The preferences of finance, especially since they are not felt with equal force in all states, affect the balance of power between states and influence the pattern of international conflict. Additionally, illustrating how the macroeconomic policy predilections of finance forge its foreign policy preferences enhances our understanding of the security strategies and choices that states embrace, by providing insights into how the definition of the national interest, and how best to advance that interest, is debated and contested by actors within societies.

For many inquiries, it would seem (and it often is) inappropriate to lump together a potentially diverse group of actors with occasionally divergent interests under the heading of finance. However, while acknowledging this, I argue that finance—meaning banks, the financial services sector, insurance companies, attendant financial institutions, various exchange markets (especially for currencies, bonds, and equities), and their allies and affiliates in government (almost always central banks and usually treasury departments)—share a deeply held set of preferences regarding the basic domestic macroeconomic environment in which they operate. Thus only two claims are in effect here: these actors share a basic disposition regarding the management of the economy, and this disposition, this package of policy preferences, represents strongly held first principles that reflect the fundamental material and institutional interests of the parties concerned. I do not assume that members of the financial community are in agreement on other issues; nor do I argue that finance acts in concert to advance its shared interests.

This basic disposition of the financial community is common across disparate countries and consistent over long periods of time. Finance, above all else, wishes to operate in a macroeconomic environment conducive to its interests. In a phrase, the ideal playing field is one of "macroeconomic stability."[1] In practice, this means low inflation and, just as important, policies designed to keep inflation low, robust and predictable real interest rates, stability in and maintenance of the value of the exchange rate and unfettered access to international financial centers abroad, balanced government budgets, modest government spending, low rates of taxation, and small and clearly sustainable levels of government debt.

WAR AND MONETARY DISORDER

The problem for finance is that war, and even policies that risk war, tends to undermine each and every one of these core preferences. War almost always results in inflation and the erosion of monetary discipline, gyrations in real interests (with negative real rates common as inflation outpaces nominal increases), exchange rate depreciation and instability, interruptions in international financial flows, and huge increases in government spending, partly offset by increased taxes but typically resulting in unbalanced budgets facilitated by expanding government debt and monetization (printing more money to pay the bills).

In the history of the United States, wartime inflation has been as American as apple pie. Indeed, militarized macroeconomic mayhem predates the establishment of the republic. Massachusetts racked up large debts and liberally issued paper money during King William's War (1689–97) and Queen Anne's War (1702–13). During the Seven Years' (French and

---

[1] As one astute reader pointed out, both "macroeconomic" and "stability" are used imprecisely here. There are many key macroeconomic variables, such as output, growth, and employment, which are not of paramount concern to the financial community. Also, an annual inflation rate of 40 percent would technically be more stable than rates that bounced around from 1 to 5 percent each year, yet finance would prefer the latter outcome. Thus the phrase "macroeconomic stability" should be understood simply as shorthand for the package of policy preferences and outcomes described here.

Indian) War many of the colonies resorted to the issue of paper notes to meet expenses, but even those that faithfully retained hard currency standards experienced wartime inflation. These difficulties, acutely felt at the time, proved to be but a warm-up for the collapse in the value of the Continental Currency during the Revolutionary War, which led to the once-common idiom "not worth a Continental."[2] Since independence, the American way of financing war has typically been to divide the effort between new debt, money creation, and some increases in taxes. A common consequence of this has been inflation and "debt that ultimately yielded large, negative returns to bond holders." Runaway inflation from the issue of greenbacks in the North and Confederate notes in the South during the Civil War is well established in American lore; but it was the War of 1812 that led to the first issue of circulating treasury notes, and the economic management of that conflict caused "very near[ly] a financial breakdown." In its wars of the twentieth century, America did not flirt as intimately with financial ruin, but the United States nevertheless emerged from its international conflicts carrying a legacy of inflation, larger government, and increased public debt.[3]

These wartime consequences and burdens do not pass unnoticed by the financial community. The costs and financial management of the Vietnam War weakened the dollar both at home, in the form of increased inflation, and abroad, by undermining the gold-dollar link at the foundation of the Bretton Woods international monetary regime (which collapsed in 1971). Even radical critics of U.S. foreign policy acknowledge that by 1968 the American financial community was very alarmed by the economic consequences of the war. Public statements by leading officers of major U.S. banks in a variety of venues linked the war with the problems of inflation,

[2] Robert J. Schiller, "The Invention of Inflation-Indexed Bonds in Early America" (NBER Working Paper 10183, December 2003), pp. 5–7, 11; Elmus Wicker, "Colonial Monetary Standards Contrasted: Evidence from the Seven Years' War," *Journal of Economic History* 45:4 (December 1985), pp. 872, 874, 876; Willard C. Fischer, "The Tabular Standard in Massachusetts History," *Quarterly Journal of Economics* 27:3 (May 1913).

[3] Lee E. Ohanian, *The Macroeconomic Effects of War Finance in the United States: Taxes, Inflation and Deficit Finance* (New York: Garland, 1998), pp. 3, 8 (quote), 12, 14, 62–63; Donald H. Kagin, "Monetary Aspects of the Treasury Notes of the War of 1812," *Journal of Economic History* 44:1 (March 1984), pp. 69, 77, 85–86; Charles J. Bullock, "Financing the War," *Quarterly Journal of Economics* 31:3 (May 1917), p. 360 (quote), 362, 366; Hugh Rockoff, "Price and Wage Controls in Four Wartime Periods," *Journal of Economic History* 41:2 (June 1981), pp. 381, 386; Arthur A. Stein, *The Nation at War* (Baltimore: Johns Hopkins University Press, 1978), pp. 57, 77; James L. Clayton, "The Fiscal Cost of the Cold War to the United States: The First 25 Years, 1947–1971," *Western Political Quarterly* 25:3 (September 1972), p. 389; George A. Lincoln, *Economics of National Security: Managing America's Resources for Defense* (New York: Prentice Hall, 1954), pp. 419, 421–22; Milton Friedman, "Price, Income, and Monetary Changes in Three Wartime Periods," *American Economic Review* 42:2 (May 1952), pp. 615, 618.

international monetary disorder, and attacks on the dollar; Federal Reserve chair William McChesney Martin warned that the management of the war economy had led to "an intolerable budget deficit and an intolerable deficit in our balance of payments."[4] While increasing dissent regarding the war could be heard from other members of the business community, it was finance whose interests felt the burdens of the war most directly and acutely.

What is remarkable about the American experience with wartime monetary upheaval is that it represents the rule, not the exception, across time and place. The association of war with macroeconomic instability is an enduring historical regularity, especially in the nineteenth and twentieth centuries, but with clear antecedents that stretch back throughout recorded history.[5]

From ancient times, debt, debasement (reducing the precious-metal content of coins in order to stretch the state's purchasing power), and even early experiments with paper currency and its debauchment were common features of war as money-starved governments resorted to what-

[4] Robert Buzzanco, "What Happened to the New Left? Toward a Radical Reading of American Foreign Relations," *Diplomatic History* 23:4 (Fall 1999), pp. 593–94, 595 (Martin quote); Helmut Kramer and Helfried Bauer, "Imperialism, Intervention Capacity, and Foreign Policy Making: On the Political Economy of the US Intervention in Indochina," *Journal of Peace Research* 9:4 (1972), pp. 291–92, 294; postrevisionist scholarship also describes the "intertwined . . . problems of the balance of payments, the Vietnam War, and the strength of dollar"; see Robert M. Collins, "The Economic Crisis of 1968 and the Waning of the 'American Century,' " *The American Historical Review* 101:2 (April 1996), pp. 401, 406 (quote), 415; Kevin Boyle, "The Price of Peace: Vietnam, the Pound, and the Crisis of American Empire," *Diplomatic History* 27:1 (January 2003), p. 71, and Francis J. Gavin, *Gold, Dollars and Power: The Politics of International Monetary Relations, 1958–1971* (Chapel Hill: University of North Carolina Press, 2004). See also Lawrence Klein, "The Role of War in the Maintenance of American Economic Prosperity," *Proceedings of the American Philosophical Society* 115:6 (December 1971), pp. 507–8, 511–12, 516.

[5] On the general relationship between war and macroeconomic distress, see R. Anton Braun and Ellen R. McGrattan, "The Macroeconomics of War and Peace," in *NBER Macroeconomics Annual 1993* (Cambridge, MA: MIT Press, 1993); Earl J. Hamilton, "The Role of War in Modern Inflation," *Journal of Economic History* 37:1 (March 1977); David Hackett Fischer, *The Great Wave: Price Revolutions and the Rhythm of History* (New York: Oxford University Press, 1996); Robert J. Barro, "Government Spending, Interest Rates, Prices and Budget Deficits in the United Kingdom, 1701–1918," *Journal of Monetary Economics* 20 (1987); Daniel K. Benjamin and Lewis A. Kochin, "War, Prices and Interest Rates: A Martial Solution to Gibson's Paradox," in Michael D. Bordo and Anna J. Schwartz (eds.), *A Retrospective on the Classical Gold Standard* (Chicago: University of Chicago Press, 1984); Herschel I. Grossman, "The Political Economy of War Debts and Inflation" (NBER Working Paper 2743, October 1988); Willard L. Thorp, "Postwar Depressions," *American Economic Review* 30:5 (February 1941); Henry Oliver, "War and Inflation Since 1790 in England, France, Germany and the United States," *American Economic Review* 30:5 (February 1941).

ever techniques they could call upon or invent to support their armies in the field. The Peloponnesian War forced Athens to debase its coins due to the "stress of the war and its consequences." (Arthur Burns compared the monetary disorder of that time to the terrible inflationary consequences of the First World War.) Some fifteen hundred years later, the stability of the unshakable Byzantine gold coin was lost to the financial strains of war; on the other side of the world, in the twelfth century, the Song dynasty in China resorted to paper currency to meet its mounting wartime expenditures; a century after that, the occupation of South China (with the fall of the Southern Song) was financed by a tenfold increase in the issue of paper money. The European wars of the late Middle Ages and the Renaissance, generally across the Continent but most notably involving Britain and France, were often long and expensive affairs that also led to considerable monetary disorder.[6]

In more modern times, especially with the more common use of paper currency and innovative forms of state finance, the relationship between war and macroeconomic distress became even more intimate. The Napoleonic Wars challenged state treasuries across the Continent: Spain borrowed heavily, expanded the issue of paper currency dramatically, and was left to wrestle with the consequences of inflation and depreciation. Even Britain, which avoided Spain's financial blunders, was forced to break with gold and borrow money to fight and endure its own inflationary episode. Ironically, France, having previously shredded its credibility as an international borrower as a result of the hyperinflation of the assignats that financed the French Revolution, suffered relatively less macroeconomic distress, though at the cost of a dramatic increase in domestic

---

[6] Arthur Burns, *Money and Monetary Policy in Early Times* (New York: Augustus M. Kelley, 1965 [1927]), pp. 377 (quote), 378, 365–66, 385, 392, 406; see also Thomas Figueira, *The Power of Money: Coinage and the Politics of the Athenian Empire* (Philadelphia: University of Pennsylvania Press, 1998), pp. 496–98, 508–11; Costas Kaplanis, "The Debasement of the 'Dollar of the Middle Ages,' " *Journal of Economic History* 63:3 (September 2003), pp. 768, 782, 795; Richard von Glahn, *Fountain of Fortune: Money and Monetary Policy in China, 1000–1700* (Berkeley: University of California Press, 1996), pp. 51, 60–61; Nathan Sussman, "Debasements, Royal Revenues, and Inflation in France during the Hundred Years' War, 1415–1422," *Journal of Economic History* 53:1 (March 1993), p. 45; Akira Motomura, "The Best and Worst of Currencies: Seigniorage and Currency Policy in Spain, 1597–1650," *Journal of Economic History* 54:1 (March 1994), pp. 105–6, 110, 117–18; Richard A. Kleer, " 'The Ruine of Their Diana': Lowndes, Locke, and the Bankers," *History of Political Economy* 36:3 (Fall 2004), pp. 533, 535; Harry A. Miskimin, *Money and Power in Fifteenth-Century France* (New Haven: Yale University Press, 1984), pp. 54–60; Carl Wennerland, "The Death Penalty as Monetary Policy: The Practice and Punishment of Monetary Crime, 1690–1830," *History of Political Economy* 36:1 (2004), pp. 134, 150.

taxation, including the introduction of an income tax.[7] Other wars left similar results. To help pay for the Crimean War, the Ottoman Empire expanded the production of the paper *kaime*, which in short order lost half of its value and generated considerable popular discontent. Throughout the second half of the nineteenth century, neighboring Greece suffered crisis-related spikes in defense expenditures that generated budget deficits, monetization, and inflation—its 1897 war with Turkey was financed by paper money creation and a further surge in inflation.[8]

Russia's troubled monetary history was deeply intertwined with its military adventures. From the late eighteenth century, Russia's ambitions as a great power brought about increased taxation but still did not raise enough revenue to avoid chronic budget deficits, financed by expanded emissions of paper money and foreign loans. Monetary instability accompanied the first Turkish war and the wars with Sweden, Poland, and Persia (and Turkey again) that followed. Contrapositively, the currency reform of 1839–43 was possible only after a decade of peace; this was washed away by the flood of rubles printed to finance the Crimean War (the money supply doubled during the conflict). The subsequent monetary rehabilitation of 1868–75 was set back by the military spending, monetization, inflation, and indebtedness caused by the war with Turkey in 1877–78, a pattern that was repeated during the Russo-Japanese War. As one scholar of Russian macroeconomic history concluded, "The [monetary] expansions of 1853–57, 1877–78, and 1905 resulted from budget deficits due to heavy expenditures for the Crimean, Balkan, and Japanese Wars, respectively."[9]

---

[7] Earl J. Hamilton, "War and Inflation in Spain, 1780–1800," *Quarterly Journal of Economics* 59:1 (November 1944), pp. 36, 53, 55, 57; Michael D. Bordo and Eugene N. White, "A Tale of Two Currencies: British and French Finance during the Napoleonic Wars," *Journal of Economic History* 51:2 (June 1991), pp. 303–4, 309–10, 314–15; Thomas J. Sargent and François R. Velde, "Macroeconomic Features of the French Revolution," *Journal of Political Economy* 103:3 (June 1995), pp. 474–518.

[8] Sevket Pamuk, "The Evolution of Financial Institutions in the Ottoman Empire, 1600–1914," *Financial History Review* 11:1 (2004), pp. 18, 25–26; Sevket Pamuk, *A Monetary History of the Ottoman Empire* (Cambridge: Cambridge University Press, 2000), pp. 142, 211, 214; Christopher Clay, *Gold for the Sultan: Western Bankers and Ottoman Finance, 1856–1881* (London: I. B. Tauris, 2000), pp. 47–49; Haim Gerber and Nachum T. Gross, "Inflation or Deflation in Nineteenth-Century Syria and Palestine," *Journal of Economic History* 40:2 (June 1980), p. 353; Sophia Lazaretou, "Monetary and Fiscal Policies in Greece, 1833–1914," *Journal of European Economic History* 22:2 (Fall 1993), pp. 291–92, 297–98.

[9] Olga Crisp, "Russian Financial Policy and the Gold Standard at the End of the Nineteenth Century," *The Economic History Review*, n.s., 6:2 (1953), pp. 156–57; Haim Barkai, "The Macro-Economics of Tsarist Russia in the Industrialization Era: Monetary Developments, the Balance of Payments, and the Gold Standard," *Journal of Economic History* 33:2 (June 1973), pp. 344, 345 (quote), 354, 357; William C. Fuller, *Strategy and Power in Russia, 1600–1914* (New York: Free Press, 1998), pp. 100–102, 269, 338–39, 405.

And, of course, no discussion of the macroeconomic consequences of war could be complete without reference to World War I, which overturned the preferences of finance one by one as if working its way methodically down a list—widespread suspension of convertibility, the disruption of international finance, ever greater government expenditures and accumulations of debt, more and more taxation, and finally an increasingly desperate expansion of the money supply when all other options were exhausted, leading to the complete collapse of the domestic and international European monetary order—which then contributed considerably to the crises of the interwar years.[10]

These pathologies have by no means been limited to the United States or to Europe and its periphery. South America's wars (more common before the remarkable long peace of the twentieth century, a puzzle worthy of further attention) visited the same macroeconomic consequences on their participants. War between Argentina and Brazil in the 1820s brought about a "monetary cataclysm" in Argentina; the Brazilian real lost half of its value. The real fared even worse during the War of the Triple Alliance (1864–70); while all of the combatants struggled with wartime inflation and Paraguay was left bankrupt and in ruins, Brazil, even in victory, faced the music of a fivefold increase in its money supply, generated to fight the war. The Pacific War (1879–83) caused monetization, inflation, depreciation, and a burdensome debt in Chile, and even more dramatic "intense monetary instability" in Peru, where inflation approached 800 percent.[11]

[10] T. Balderston, "War Finance and Inflation in Britain and Germany, 1914–1918," *Economic History Review*, n.s., 42:2 (May 1989), pp. 223, 237; Pierro Sraffa, "Monetary Inflation in Italy During and after the War," *Cambridge Journal of Economics* 17 (1993 [1920]), pp. 10–11, 14, 18–20; Boris Bakhmeteff, "War and Finance in Russia," *Annals of the American Academy of Political and Social Science* 75 (January 1918), pp. 192–93, 196–98; E. Dana Durand, "Currency Inflation in Eastern Europe with Special Reference to Poland," *American Economic Review* 13:4 (December 1923), pp. 593, 597; Hamilton, "The Role of War," p. 17; John Maynard Keynes, *The Economic Consequences of the Peace* (London: Macmillan, 1971 [1919]), pp. 148–57.

[11] Miguel Angel Centeno, *Blood and Debt: War and the Nation State in Latin America* (University Park: Penn State University Press, 2002), p. 132 (quote); I. Grinfeld, "Monetary Experiences of the Argentine Republic," *Political Science Quarterly* 25:1 (March 1910), pp. 110, 112–14; F. J. McLynn, "Consequences for Argentina of the War of the Triple Alliance 1865–1870," *The Americas* 41:1 (July 1984), pp. 89, 92; Norman T. Strauss, "Brazil after the Paraguay War: Six Years of Conflict, 1870–6," *Journal of Latin American Studies* 10:1 (May 1978), pp. 23, 35; Diego Abente, "Foreign Capital, Economic Elites and the State in Paraguay during the Liberal Republic (1870–1936)," *Journal of Latin American Studies* 21:1 (February 1989), p. 62; Vera Blinn Reber, "The Demographics of Paraguay: A Reinterpretation of the Great War, 1864–70," *Hispanic American Historical Review* 68:2 (May 1988), p. 316; Paul Gootenberg, "Carneros y Chuno: Price Levels in Nineteenth-Century Peru," *Hispanic American Historical Review* 70:1 (February 1990), pp. 6, 32 (quote); see

In every part of the world, and up to the present day, the song remains the same. Almost invariably, wherever and whenever there has been war, money has come under pressure, as seen in countless examples. Even Meiji Japan's successful wars of the 1890s and 1900s disrupted the country's finances and caused macroeconomic distress. China's unhappy decade of war after 1937 saw inflation jump to 27, 51, and 181 percent in the first three years of the fighting and then remained in triple digits. The financial economy was paralyzed; with negative real interest rates, banks were increasingly unwilling to engage in the business of lending.[12] In Korea the money supply doubled in 1951 and again in 1952; rampant wartime inflation was a problem throughout the peninsula. War rattled India's macroeconomic stability in the 1960s, and the Iran-Iraq War of the 1980s had similarly predictable effects. In the 1990s war between Armenia and Azerbaijan ensured the descent of both countries' currencies into hyperinflation.[13] History provides fewer messages with more clarity: war is an open invitation to macroeconomic disorder.

---

also pp. 28, 30 for Peruvian inflation caused by other nineteenth-century wars; Thomas F. O'Brien Jr., "Chilean Elites and Foreign Investors: Chilean Nitrate Policy, 1880–82," *Journal of Latin American Studies* 11:1 (May 1989), pp. 106–7, 111–12, 115, 118; Guillermo Subercaseaux, *Monetary and Banking Policy of Chile* (Oxford: Clarendon Press, 1922), pp. 92, 94, 199 (note also the civil war inflation of 1891 and defense spending increases due to border tensions with Argentina, disrupting plans for monetary reform in 1894, 1895, and 1898, pp. 101–2, 110, 133); see also Frank W. Fetter, *Monetary Inflation in Chile* (Princeton: Princeton University Press, 1931), pp. 32, 43.

[12] Hugh T. Patrick, "External Equilibrium and Internal Convertibility: Financial Policy in Meiji Japan," *Journal of Economic History* 25:2 (June 1965), pp. 198, 204; Guenther Stein, "Japanese State Finance," *Pacific Affairs* 10:4 (December 1937), pp. 393–95, 397; Choh-Ming Li, "Inflation in Wartime China," *Review of Economics and Statistics* 27:1 (February 1945), pp. 23, 27, 32; Andrew Chung Huang, "The Inflation in China," *Quarterly Journal of Economics* 62:4 (August 1948), pp. 563, 568–69, 572; Frank M. Tamaga, "China's Postwar Finances," *Pacific Affairs* 81:2 (June 1945), pp. 120, 122–24; Colin D. Campbell and Gordon C. Tullock, "Hyperinflation in China, 1937–49," *Journal of Political Economy* 62:3 (June 1954), pp. 237–39.

[13] Colin Campbell and Gordon Tullock, "Some Little-Understood Aspects of Korea's Monetary and Fiscal Systems," *American Economic Review* 47:3 (June 1957), pp. 336, 338–39; Youngil Lin, "Foreign Influence on the Economic Change in Korea: A Survey," *Journal of Asian Studies* 28:1 (November 1968), pp. 90–91, 92–93; Rahul Mukherji, "India's Aborted Liberalization—1966," *Pacific Affairs* 73:3 (Autumn 2000), pp. 376, 379; David Denoon, *Devaluation under Pressure: India, Indonesia, Ghana* (Cambridge, MA: MIT Press, 1986), p. 41; Abbas Alnasrawi, *The Economy of Iraq* (Westport, CT: Greenwood Press, 1994), pp. 80–81, 88, 98–99, and Thierry Gongora, "War Making and State Power in the Contemporary Middle East," *International Journal of Middle East Studies* 29:3 (August 1997), pp. 325, 327; Suzanne Godenberg, *Pride of Small Nations: The Caucasus and Post-Soviet Disorder* (London: Zed Books, 1994), pp. 73, 79, 270; Anders Åslund et al., "How to Stabilize: Lessons from Post-Communist Countries," *Brookings Papers on Economic Activity* 1 (1996), pp. 225, 232. For an illustration from Africa, see Ben Naanen, "Economy within an Economy: The Manilla Currency, Exchange Rate Instability and Social

THE ARGUMENT

The principal argument of this book is that because of the macroeconomic consequences of war, financial communities within countries will be among the most cautious elements when it comes to waging war or supporting foreign policies that risk war. Note that this is an *indirect* argument: finance is cautious about risking war because of war's economic consequences, not because of any inherent preferences about the particular international controversy in question or attitudes about the legitimacy of competing claims in a given international conflict. Rather, the financial community's aversion to armed conflict is a residual of its basic disposition in favor of macroeconomic stability. This is also a *relative* argument—the claim is not that finance always opposes war, but rather that, as a general rule, finance will be among the most cautious and reluctant to risk and initiate war.[14]

The aversion of finance to war has been noted by many others in the past, especially in the more distant past. The "mere hint" of international friction has been held responsible for unsettling money markets; French premier Jean-Baptiste Villèle (who served as his own finance minister) neatly captured the foundation of these sentiments in 1827, when, reluctant to celebrate the conclusion of a modest and successful military operation, he noted tersely, "Cannon fire is bad for good money." The interests of insurance companies are perhaps even more transparent in this regard. "War brings ruin," one advocate stated plainly. "The business of insurance is naturally allied with the forces that make for peace." Almost a century ago prominent financial observer Alexander Noyes explained that not only is the banking community inherently trepidant about war—as a "general rule . . . capital is slow to rush into war excitement"—but, further, no other actors in society were "fitted by instinct, training, disposition, and opportunity to insist that the government go slow in committing the country to a program of war." Years later, Karl Polanyi would assert that *haute finance* acted purposefully to prevent war from breaking out between Europe's great powers; he held that these efforts were crucial in facilitating the long peace of the nineteenth century.[15]

Conditions in South-Eastern Nigeria, 1900–48," *Journal of African History* 34:3 (1993), pp. 437, 442, 445.

[14] This construction (relative as opposed to absolute caution) does not undermine the falsifiability of the argument; however, as discussed later, it does influence the basis upon which the argument could be falsified.

[15] Hartley Withers, *The Meaning of Money* (London: Smith, Elder, 1909), p. 155 (first quote); André Jardin and André-Jean Tudesq, *Restoration and Reaction, 1815–1848* (Cambridge: Cambridge University Press, 1983), p. 69 (Villèle quote); David Starr Jordan, "War, Business and Insurance," *The Scientific Monthly* 1:2 (November 1915), p. 175 (quotes);

Despite the fact that these observations, and others like them, have been expressed in the past, there has been no systematic investigation into the proposition of the caution of finance on the road to war. Such an investigation is the purpose of this book. If financial caution is indeed a broad and general empirical regularity, then this book will contribute to an understanding of the behavior of states in world politics and of international relations more generally. Moreover, this finding generates an additional implication that I discuss in the concluding chapter: that the behavior of international financial markets can discourage states from embarking on the path toward war. The logic is as follows: if war unnerves finance, and if international financial markets reflect the cumulative sentiments of uncoordinated market actors, then finance (figuratively) will withdraw from, or at least be especially wary of, those states that seem to be approaching the precipice of armed conflict. The greater the significance of international finance, the more important this factor should be. By raising the opportunity costs that states face when considering a resort to arms, financial globalization can serve, ceteris paribus, to inhibit war; crucially, however, states will vary considerably in their sensitivity to such pressures. Thus, while the argument of this book is principally that bankers within states are more likely than others to favor appeasement, it also introduces the implication that international relations will at times be affected by the pressures states feel to appease the bankers.

No Theory of War: A Partial Equilibrium Approach

In the context of the discipline of international relations, this book is at the same time ambitious and modest in its reach. It is ambitious with regard to its strong claims of generalizability regarding financial caution across time and place—this proposition approaches a lawlike statement. On the other hand, it is comparatively modest in terms of expectations about what this argument can tell us about the specific behavior of states and about particular outcomes in international politics. The findings of this book are rich with implications for understanding state behavior and world politics, including the prospects for U.S. power, the implications of the rise of China, and the vulnerability of weak states to insurgent groups

---

Alexander D. Noyes, "International Arbitration and International Finance," *Journal of Political Economy* 30:3 (March 1912), pp. 256, 261 (quotes); Karl Polanyi, *The Great Transformation: The Political and Economic Origins of Our Time* (Boston: Beacon Press, 1957 [1944]), pp. 9–11, 14. See also Jacob Viner, "The Economic Problem," in George B. de Huszar (ed.), *New Perspectives on Peace* (Chicago: University of Chicago Press, 1944), pp. 89–90, 96–98; Lionel Robbins, *The Economic Causes of War* (New York: Macmillan, 1940), p. 58; and Roberto Rigobon, "The Effects of War Risk on U.S. Financial Markets" (NBER Working Paper 9609, April 2003), pp. 2, 11.

(these and other issues are explored in the conclusion). But it nevertheless holds a circumscribed view of what scholarship in international relations can hope to offer in terms of prediction.

In particular, this book has no theory of war. That is, I make no predictions about when war will occur. This requires some brief elaboration and justification because predicting war, with a greater or lesser emphasis on qualifying conditions, is explicitly or implicitly the ambition of an enormous body of literature in international relations, from all theoretical orientations and methodological approaches.[16] However, the position I adopt here is that from a practical standpoint, war is essentially not a predictable phenomenon.

There are three principal reasons why I am deeply skeptical of the enterprise of "predicting war" and thus why I avoid conditioning my analysis around such an approach in this book. First and most fundamentally is the enormous degree of complexity intrinsic to the causes of war, which involves a large number of explanatory variables, of which some are quite mercurial and idiosyncratic (the personal attributes of leaders is the most obvious example of this), and of which many are intricately interdependent rather than independent variables. Second is the lack of stability of these behavioral relationships over time, by which I mean that exactly the same set of circumstances that led to war in one period might not cause war in another, due to any number of factors, such as learning or a change in the normative environment. Third is the heterogeneity of the "dependent variable," that is, war. The U.S. invasion of Panama in 1989, China's attack on Vietnam in 1979, Great Britain's declaration of war on Germany in 1939, and Chile's decision to take on Bolivia and Peru in 1879 were all decisions by states to go to war, but in each case "war" had a very different meaning, purpose, and implication. In the business of "predicting war," lumping these cases together is problematic because it is likely that the paths to these different decisions followed distinct causal logics, but separating them out reduces for each category the number of

---

[16] See, for example, D. Scott Bennett and Allan C. Stam, *The Behavioral Origins of War* (Ann Arbor: University of Michigan Press, 2004), and Stephen Van Evera, *Causes of War: Power and the Roots of Conflict* (Ithaca: Cornell University Press, 1999). Bennett and Stam are very much in the business of prediction (see, for example, p. 157), although they are very attentive to the challenges and pitfalls of such an enterprise (see esp. chapter 2, "Comparative Hypothesis Testing and Some Limits to Knowledge," and pp. 165–66 on the challenge of generalizability). Van Evera is near the other end of the spectrum but nevertheless explores five principal hypotheses, in order to "apply them to explain history, infer policy predictions, and predict the future" (p. 3). Both works, it should be emphasized, are appropriately cautious; Bennett and Stam conclude, "There is no single story of war" and "In many ways we are as uncertain about the causes and likely timing of any individual war today as we were in 1942" (p. 201). Van Evera's strongest predictive claim is a negative one; in the "total absence" of his five factors, "war rarely occurs" (p. 255).

cases of an already rare phenomenon and opens a Pandora's box of controversies about definitions and classifications.

An example from economics illustrates further the formidable barriers to prediction in international relations. Even in the microeconomic field of consumer choice, where fewer and more pristine independent variables are at work and an enormous universe of data is available for study, and where it can be comfortably assumed that behavioral relationships are stable (such as elasticities of income and demand and the market sensitivity of complements and substitutes), "prediction" nevertheless refers to the average behavioral response of a large population making similar choices and not to predictions about the behavior of any one specific individual, which can vary broadly. This is perfectly satisfactory for consumer theory. Yet in international relations, the ultimate goal of the enterprise is capturing that markedly more elusive *individual* behavior (the behavior of a particular state) as opposed to the behavior of a hypothetical "average state"; thus, compared with consumer choice theory, predicting war and peace is a dramatically more ambitious enterprise in a vastly more challenging analytical setting.[17]

Even in economics, no less an authority than Alfred Marshall, who very much saw economics as a science, was profoundly skeptical of prediction, and this informed his approach to the discipline. Marshall nicely elucidated the problem of contingency in undermining the possibility of all but the most limited efforts at prediction:

Prediction in economics must be hypothetical. Show an uninterrupted game at chess to an expert and he will be bold indeed if he prophesies its future stages. If either side make one move ever so little different from what he expected, all the following moves will be altered; and after two or three moves more the whole face of the game will have become different.[18]

---

[17] On the challenge of complexity in international relations, and in particular with reference to the challenges of predicting the behavior of individual states, see Charles P. Kindleberger, "A Monetary Economist on Power Politics," *World Politics* 6:4 (July 1954), pp. 509–10, and Kindleberger, "Scientific International Politics," *World Politics* 11:1 (October 1958), p. 86; see also Jonathan Kirshner, "Rationalist Explanations for War?" *Security Studies* 10:1 (Autumn 2000), pp. 143–50.

[18] Alfred Marshall, "Fragments," in A. C. Pigou (ed.), *Memorials of Alfred Marshall* (London: Macmillan, 1925), p. 360 (quote); Alfred Marshall, *Principles of Economics*, 8th ed. (London: Macmillan, 1920), esp. book I, chapter 3, "Economic Generalizations or Laws," pp. 30–33. On the limits to prediction in economics, see also Frank H. Knight, " 'What Is Truth' in Economics?" *Journal of Political Economy* 48:1 (February 1940), pp. 29–31, and Andrew Rutten, "But It Will Never Be Science, Either," *Journal of Economic History* 40:1 (March 1980), pp. 139, 141–42. As it turns out, Marshall was no slouch in the business of predicting war: "I shall not live to see our next war with Germany; but you

These types of challenges are, if anything, more applicable to and less surmountable in the study of international relations and suggest that efforts should be redirected away from this goal. But this movement away from prediction is not as radical a turn as it might appear. It is not a retreat from—indeed it is wholly consistent with—rationalism, causality, generalizability, and falsifiability. One prominent international relations theorist, for example, renounced the goal of prediction—"We must give up the hope that a theory of international politics can have either the explanatory or the predictive power of a 'hard' science"—yet at the same time retained a vehement commitment to science.[19] This book eschews prediction in a similar spirit.

To draw on an analogy from economic theory once again, the approach here can be considered a "partial equilibrium" analysis. This approach, associated most famously with Alfred Marshall and his legacy in microeconomics, is the investigation of the behavioral properties of the price of one good, assuming the prices of all other goods are held constant, as opposed to a "general equilibrium" approach that aims to solve simultaneously for all prices in the economy at one time.[20] Transposing back to international relations, a "general equilibrium" perspective can be seen as one that seeks to predict war, while the partial equilibrium approach adopted here seeks to study and understand the behavioral properties of a particular variable in isolation.

This method of inquiry is greatly influenced by the work of Charles Kindleberger, who adapted the concept of partial equilibrium for studies of what he dubbed "historical economics." Kindleberger argued that "there is not one all purpose economic theory or model that illuminates economic history," emphasizing instead economics as a "toolbox" in which the practical economist is armed with a large set of theories (such as the law of one price, or Gresham's law) that are applicable to and provide insights into a variety of settings. Historical economics is an exercise in developing, honing (and possibly circumscribing or discarding) those tools, in particular by considering "how general are economic theo-

---

will, I expect"; Marshall to John Maynard Keynes, February 21, 1915, reprinted in Pigou, *Memorials*, p. 482.

[19] Morton A. Kaplan, "Problems of Theory Building and Theory Confirmation in International Politics," *World Politics* 14:1 (October 1961), pp. 6, 8, 11, 20 (quote), 21, 23–24; Morton A. Kaplan, "The New Great Debate: Traditionalism vs. Science in International Relations," *World Politics* 19:1 (October 1966), esp. pp. 1, 3, 12, 16, 19–20.

[20] Alfred Marshall, "Distribution and Exchange," *Economic Journal* 8 (March 1898), pp. 37–38, 40, 47–48; Alfred Marshall, *Principles*, pp. 36, 131, 366, 369; Alfred Marshall, "The Present Position of Economics (1895)," reprinted in Pigou, *Memorials*, p. 168; George Stigler, "The Place of Marshall's *Principles* in the Development of Economics," in John K. Whitaker (ed.), *Centenary Essays on Alfred Marshall* (Cambridge: Cambridge University Press, 1990), p. 5.

rems or laws, how well they fit case 2 if it is evident that they fit case 1 neatly."[21] Following Kindleberger, this book considers the preferences of the financial community in a variety of prewar settings in order to evaluate the "political theorem" of financial caution proposed here and to gain insight into its implications and behavioral characteristics.

Given this approach, evidence to falsify the thesis of this book would be found at the level of partial equilibrium (the preferences of finance) rather than at the level of general equilibrium (the occurrence of war). Since this is not a theory of war, variation in the pattern of armed conflict would neither support nor undermine the argument. Rather, contrary evidence would be found in instances where the financial community was among the most aggressive voices in society in prewar debates—those urging war or policies that risk or invite war. A modest number of such contrary examples could be considered exceptions to the general rule (and possibly even enhance our understanding of the factors that condition financial caution); however, if such instances were relatively common, they would provide powerful evidence against my central claim.

Appeasing Bankers in International Relations Theory

The argument of this book does not fit neatly into any of the main analytical perspectives of international relations theory. Because of this it is worthwhile to briefly consider the relationship between the appeasing bankers thesis and the principal approaches to the discipline. The purpose of this short discussion is not to rehearse, advance, or debate various controversies in the practice of international relations theory, but rather (as with the earlier discussion of prediction) to situate for the reader the argument of this book in order to clarify its objectives and help establish the criteria by which its contributions can be evaluated.

This book stands in obvious disagreement with much of the critical and Marxist-oriented literature on the causes of imperialism and war. In

---

[21] Charles P. Kindleberger, *Economic Laws and Economic History* (Cambridge: Cambridge University Press, 1989), pp. ix (quote), x, 127, 193; Charles P. Kindleberger, *Historical Economics: Art or Science?* (Berkeley: University of California Press, 1990), pp. 7, 9 ("toolbox"); Charles P. Kindleberger, *The Life of an Economist: An Autobiography* (Cambridge: Basil Blackwell, 1991), p. 194 (quote); see also Kindleberger, "Comparative Economic History," in Kindleberger (ed.), *Economic Response: Comparative Studies in Trade, Finance and Growth* (Cambridge, MA: Harvard University Press, 1978), p. 3, and Kindleberger, "Scientific International Politics," pp. 83–84. Kindleberger also explicitly rejects prediction and elaborates further that "historical economics, as I view it, believes in partial equilibrium . . . and looks for patterns of uniformity but is wary of insisting on identity" (*Historical Economics*, p. 4). On the role of economic history in honing economic theory more generally, see Donald N. McClosky, "Does the Past Have Useful Economics?" *Journal of Economic Literature* 14:2 (June 1976), esp. pp. 448–53, "Better Economic Theory."

particular, it holds the opposite perspective from John A. Hobson in his very influential work on imperialism. Hobson was not a Marxist, but his work shaped an important strand of neo-Marxist thought in this area, especially as articulated by Lenin, who was also greatly influenced by the distinct but complementary work of Rudolph Hilferding (and to a lesser extent by many others, including Rosa Luxembourg). Hobson's arguments are particularly noteworthy here because of his explicit emphasis on finance in particular as opposed to capitalism more generally (whereas increasingly in later generations of these arguments, finance, while still often exceptional, is intertwined with a consortium of capitalist interests). For Hobson, however (and for the argument of this book as well, if with very different implications), finance stands apart from the balance of the business community. Contra the appeasing bankers thesis, Hobson held that the "special interest of the financier" was the source of "war, militarism, and a 'spirited foreign policy,' " all of which derived from the need to secure private markets abroad that could serve as outlets for surplus capital. Hilferding reached similar conclusions, arguing that "finance capital needs [the] state . . . to pursue an expansionist policy and the annexation of new colonies."[22]

Hobson's arguments (and other writings in this vein) have been sharply criticized, and those challenges are especially damaging with regard to the evidence pertaining to the specific claims advanced by Hobson and others.[23] While acknowledging these shortcomings, the spirit of these argu-

---

[22] John A. Hobson, *Imperialism: A Study* (New York: James Pott & Company, 1902), pp. 56, 63 (quote), 66, chapter 6 ("The Economic Taproot of Imperialism"), 113 (quote), 380, 382–83; V. I. Lenin, *Imperialism: The Highest Stage of Capitalism* (New York: International Publishers, 1939 [1917]), pp. 15, 31, 47, 78–79, 84, 102–4; Keith Griffin and John Gurley, "Radical Analyses of Imperialism, the Third World, and the Transition to Socialism: A Survey Article," *Journal of Economic Literature* 23:3 (September 1985), pp. 1092, 1096–97; E. M. Winslow, "Marxian, Liberal and Sociological Theories of Imperialism," *Journal of Political Economy* 39:6 (December 1931), pp. 723–24, 726–28. Hilferding derived his conclusions from his efforts to establish a Marxist theory of money. Rudolph Hilferding, *Finance Capital: A Study on the Latest Phase of Capitalist Development* (ed. Tom Bottomore) (London: Routledge, Keegan and Paul, 1981 [1910]), pp. 311, 314, 317–18, 322–23, 330, 334 (quote), 335, 366. See also Harold James, "Rudolf Hilferding and the Application of the Political Economy of the Second International," *The Historical Journal* 24:4 (1981), esp. pp. 857, 868; and Wolfgang J. Mommsen, *Theories of Imperialism* (trans. P. S. Falla) (New York: Random House, 1980), pp. 17, 36–38, 41–43, 47.

[23] P. J. Cain, *Hobson and Imperialism: Radicalism, New Liberalism, and Finance, 1887–1938* (Oxford: Oxford University Press, 2002), esp. pp. 122–24, 235, 277–81; see also William Langer, "A Critique of Imperialism," *Foreign Affairs* 14 (1935–36), 102–19; D. K. Fieldhouse, "Imperialism: An Historical Revision," *Economic History Review*, n.s., 14:2 (1961), pp. 187–209; Benjamin J. Cohen, *The Question of Imperialism* (New York: Basic Books, 1973), pp. 44, 46, 58, 63–66; John R. Oneal and Frances Oneal, "Hegemony, Imperialism, and the Profitability of Foreign Investments," *International Organization* 42:2 (1988), pp. 347–73.

ments, however, still finds support among some scholars.[24] This book clashes with "financial imperialism" arguments more generally at the level of expectations about the preferences and motivations of finance and reaches the opposite conclusions about their implications for international relations.

Not only does the appeasing bankers thesis reverse Marxist expectations about finance and war, it also traffics in variables typically associated with liberal theory: the narrow interests of actors within societies and the role and consequences of market forces.[25] But despite these notable affinities, other departures from liberalism, regarding the national interest, the ambiguous role of "peaceful finance," and interdependence, disaffect the approach adopted here from important elements of liberal theory.

Of paramount importance is the role of the national interest. Stephen Krasner adroitly distinguished liberalism from statism on this basic foundation. For the former, "an inescapable implication of their position is that government policy is a reflection of whatever groups have power in society," but for the latter, "the objectives sought by the state cannot be reduced to some summation of private desires."[26] This approach, which reduces the national interest to some combination of particular interests, remains at the heart of contemporary liberal theory.[27] The perspective here takes as its point of departure the idealized statist conception of the national interest (albeit with some qualification, as discussed later).

A second important departure from liberalism concerns the tendency of liberal theory to suggest that the peaceful instincts it attributes to capitalists (or at least to merchants) is normatively a good thing. From the perspective of this book, this is not necessarily the case. Without advocat-

---

[24] See, for example, Gregory P. Nowell, "Imperialism and the Era of Falling Prices," *Journal of Post-Keynesian Economics* 25:2 (Winter 2002–3), pp. 317, 320, 325.

[25] On liberalism, see Andrew Moravcsik, "Taking Preferences Seriously: A Liberal Theory of International Politics," *International Organization* 51:4 (Autumn 1997), pp. 513–53.

[26] Stephen Krasner, *Defending the National Interest* (Princeton: Princeton University Press, 1978), pp. 30, 5–6 (quotes); see also pp. 10–12, 28, 36.

[27] See, for example, Gary Becker, "A Theory of Competition among Pressure Groups for Political Influence," *Quarterly Journal of Economics* 98:3 (August 1983), pp. 371–400; Peter Trubowitz, *Defining the National Interest: Conflict and Change in American Foreign Policy* (Chicago: University of Chicago Press, 1997); Benjamin O. Fordham, "Economic Interests, Party, and Ideology in Early Cold War Era U.S. Foreign Policy," *International Organization* 52:2 (Spring 1998), pp. 359–96; Jeffry Frieden, "Sectoral Conflict and Foreign Economic Policy, 1914–1940," *International Organization* 42:1 (Winter 1988), pp. 59–90. Additive of particular interests but with a greater emphasis on contingency are Peter Gourevitch, *Politics in Hard Times: Comparative Responses to International Economic Crises* (Ithaca: Cornell University Press, 1986), and Ronald Rogowski, *Commerce and Coalitions: How Trade Affects Domestic Political Alignments* (Princeton: Princeton University Press, 1989).

ing "war" as an abstract concept, there may nevertheless be times when an assertive foreign policy, or even the resort to arms, is in a state's best interest and is even proper. Yet even in these cases, finance will be reluctant to fight. The principal argument of this book is not that finance is "right" about foreign policy but rather, motivated by concerns for the domestic macroeconomic consequences, that finance seeks to avoid war. Sometimes that caution will be "wrong," undermine the national interest, and even threaten the security of the nation.

Finally, on questions of war and peace, liberal theory tends to lump finance with other capitalist or commercial interests, while this book is in the business of considering what is distinct and exceptional about the financial community.[28] This matters, for example, with regard to the relationship between interstate interdependence and war—an association that has been an important element of liberal theory but is held at arm's length by the analysis here.[29] Certainly, from a partial equilibrium perspective, the deductive logic of the liberal case is plausible (all other things held constant, increased levels of interdependence between two states will create a net disincentive for war between them). However, with my central emphasis on the indirect consequences of actors' macroeconomic preferences, as well as my self-conscious abstention from predicting war, the approach here is orthogonal to and agnostic regarding the relationship between interstate interdependence and war.[30] Beyond that, the emphasis on finance here actually suggests a modest and implicit challenge to liberal arguments based on the presumed pacific influences of capitalism and commerce.[31] The financial community has a strong and general interest

---

[28] It is common in analyses of foreign policy debates from various analytical perspectives to lump together the elements of a "free trade coalition"; see, for example, Steven E. Lobell, *The Challenge of Hegemony: Grand Strategy, Trade and Domestic Politics* (Ann Arbor: University of Michigan Press, 2003), pp. 21–23. However, the preferences of the financial community are often different from those of other business groups. See, for example, David E. Kaun, "War and Wall Street: The Impact of Military Conflict on Investor Attitudes," *Cambridge Journal of Economics* 14 (1990), pp. 439–40.

[29] Robert Keohane and Joseph Nye, *Power and Interdependence: World Politics in Transition* (Boston: Little, Brown, 1977); Moravcsik, "Taking Preferences Seriously," pp. 520–21, 528–30.

[30] On this issue, see Edward Mansfield and Brian Pollins, *Economic Interdependence and International Conflict: New Perspectives on an Enduring Debate* (Ann Arbor: University of Michigan Press, 2003); Gerald Schneider, Katherine Barbieri, and Nils Peter Gleditsch, *Globalization and Armed Conflict* (Lantham, MD: Roman and Littlefield, 2003); and Charles P. Kindleberger, *Foreign Trade and the National Economy* (New Haven: Yale University Press, 1962).

[31] See, for example, Joseph Schumpeter, "The Sociology of Imperialisms," in Richard Swedberg (ed.), *Joseph A. Schumpeter: The Economics and Sociology of Capitalism* (Princeton: Princeton University Press, 1991), and Christopher Way, *Manchester Revisited: Economic Interdependence and Conflict* (Ithaca: Cornell University Press, forthcoming).

in the preservation of peace. But there is no similar unambiguous and general compelling interest for capitalists, businesspeople, or even those engaged in international trade to fear war. While individual capitalists, businesspeople, or traders might find their narrow interests undermined by their home country's participation in a particular war, there is no reason why the interests of such actors would necessarily be harmed by any armed conflict in general; indeed, there are a good many wars in which particular elements of the business and commercial community might stand to gain handsomely. Thus, the bedrock foundations of financial caution contrast with and call attention to the absence of such a primordial disposition in business and commerce (although elements of these groups might be strongly opposed to particular conflicts). Moreover, this suggests (although it is not in the scope of this book to explore) that if the preferences of the financial community are withdrawn from the mix, the remaining influences of capitalism and commerce on war generally might be less apparent and instead more fluid, indeterminate, and contingent.

This book also has affinities with realism, most obviously with its baseline conception of world politics: states are the principal actors, and they pursue their security and self-interests in ways that are shaped by the context of anarchy and conditioned by the possibility of war (the prospects for which can vary considerably due to the intensity of the security dilemma and other factors).[32] However, this book also departs from realist orthodoxy, with two large steps away from characteristics that are common to many theories derived in a realist tradition: the primacy of structure (or systemic-level) analysis and the inviolability of a unique national interest.

Systemic-level analysis has captured the imagination of most realist thinkers, although one need not imply the other. Structural variables in international relations—the distribution of power between states and changes to the distribution of that power over time—are attractive, as they are parsimonious and generalizable. And for the analysis of international relations, they are important for understanding the environment in which states act.[33] Nevertheless, this book places much less emphasis on systemic-level analysis. Although valuable, and not to be dispensed with,

---

[32] The literature on realism is enormous and alive with active controversy. For an overview of the rich variety of theories in the realist tradition, see Michael W. Doyle, *Ways of War and Peace: Realism, Liberalism and Socialism* (New York: Norton, 1997), part 1.

[33] Kenneth Waltz, *Theory of International Politics* (New York: Addison-Wesley, 1979); Robert Gilpin, *War and Change in World Politics* (Cambridge: Cambridge University Press, 1981). Waltz's static approach aims to operate solely at the level of the system; Gilpin's dynamic theory is also systemic in terms of the framework of the theory, but his analysis ranges freely across all levels of analysis.

structural variables are largely indeterminate in explaining world politics.[34] As theories inspired by a microeconomic analogy of choice under market scarcity aver, the international system does indeed impose constraints on the states that constitute it in a way analogous to the manner in which the range of choices presented to consumers and firms is expressed by market forces that derive from the collective behavior of all participants but that are beyond the control of any particular actor. But even in the pristine world of microeconomics, with similar firms seeking singular goals (maximizing profits or market share), the deterministic implications of systemic market pressure (once again, on the "average" actor) are dependent on very strict assumptions of "perfect competition"—an environment characterized by a very large set of small actors that have no market power but instead are "price takers." As the idealized assumption of perfect competition is relaxed, market forces remain vital but individual choices become increasingly central to explaining behavior. In particular, large firms in oligopolistic settings, while certainly not unconstrained by market forces, nevertheless enjoy considerable discretion as to how they pursue their goals.

In international relations that range of freedom is at least an order of magnitude greater. States in world politics are much more like large oligopolists than small firms under perfect competition, and this is especially true for great powers whose behavior attracts the lion's share of the attention in international relations theory. Further, despite their common attributes, states are less similar to each other than are firms of the same industry, and despite a common desire for survival, states are more likely than firms to also harbor a broader range of goals selected from a larger set of possibilities. And even in the pursuit of the most narrow, common goal—survival—states will respond less predictably to the pressures of anarchy than firms will to market forces, because they can. Firms that make mistakes are more likely to be selected out of the system than states are when they pursue suboptimal national security strategies, due to the fact that, as Adam Smith observed, "there is a great deal of ruin in a nation."[35]

Structure thus informs importantly the environment in which all states act, but in that context all states, and especially great powers, enjoy considerable discretion with regard to how they pursue their goals and what sacrifices they make in the face of constraints. This is again the case with the essentially "structural" variable featured in this book—less salient in

[34] For a good discussion of this, see Joseph Nye, "Neorealism and Neoliberalism," *World Politics* 40:2 (January 1988), esp. pp. 235, 242, 245. My thinking on these issues has benefited greatly from exchanges at the National Intelligence Council's workshops, "Strategic Responses to American Preeminence," hosted by John Ikenberry.

[35] John Rae, *Life of Adam Smith* (London: Macmillan, 1895), p. 343.

most of the chapters but considered more closely in the concluding chapter: the degree of global financial integration. As mentioned earlier, given the preferences of the financial community, those preferences, as "expressed" by international market forces, act as a systemic disincentive to the initiation of war to an extent directly related to the relative size and significance of global financial markets (and to the relative importance of access to international finance to the state in question). While not a purely structural variable (as the degree of general openness or closure is the product of states' choices), the general level of global capital mobility reflects the choices of a few big states, and those choices are reinforcing; thus, as a practical matter, the large majority of states are presented with a common systemic pressure (the level of global capital mobility) over which they have little if any control.[36]

Financial globalization, as a systemic constraint, should not be conflated with interstate interdependence.[37] Additionally, in keeping with the partial equilibrium approach of this book, the observation that states face a common external pressure that raises (or lowers) uniformly the costs of pursuing policies that deviate from the preferences of the financial community is not deterministic. States always retain the ability to pursue policies at odds with international markets (and if they so choose, to restrict their own interactions with such markets). The point here is simply that those choices come with costs: the direct costs imposed by the consequences of international market reaction, and the opportunity costs of international financial options foreclosed.[38] These costs vary proportion-

---

[36] States, of course, can impose their own capital controls; the variable in question refers to the external environment. On capital mobility as a systemic constraint, see David Andrews, "Capital Mobility and State Autonomy: Toward a Structural Theory of International Monetary Relations," *International Studies Quarterly* 38 (1994), pp. 193–218. Andrews makes the case that capital mobility can be treated as a structural variable; on technical grounds, this is debatable; state choice fundamentally shapes the extent of capital mobility (though it may indeed be very difficult to recapture those forces once liberated), but states cannot choose, for example, the distribution of power between them. However, the contributions of Andrews's article stand regardless of this definitional issue.

[37] Interdependence refers to relations between two states, and theories of interdependence and war consider how these relations affect the prospects for war between them. Financial globalization is a general, systemic force that affects each state individually, and it affects each state's general calculations about the costs and benefits of war and ambitious national security strategies. Intense economic interdependence between two states can occur in the absence of globalized finance; states' national security strategies can be very sensitive to globalized finance unrelated to a particular bilateral economic relationship.

[38] The logic regarding the opportunity costs of disregarding the preferences of international finance is similar to the analysis of the opportunity costs of economic closure in Jeffry Frieden and Ronald Rogowski's "The Impact of the International Economy on National Economies: An Analytical Overview," in Robert Keohane and Helen Milner (eds.), *Internationalization and Domestic Politics* (Cambridge: Cambridge University Press, 1996), pp. 32–33.

ately with the extent of international financial integration and the relative size of international financial markets; thus in periods of "globalized finance," the costs of making the choice to deviate from the financial orthodoxy are relatively high. As discussed in the concluding chapter, international relations will be affected by the fact that particular states will be more or less sensitive to these costs.

This book also departs from the realist mainstream, and here the stakes are somewhat higher (as one can engage in broadly "realist" analysis without insisting on the primacy of structural variables in explaining behavior) by probing the concept of the "national interest." While I have rejected the liberal vision of a pluralist national interest in favor of the perspective that states as actors enjoy considerable autonomy and pursue broadly defined national interests, I emphasize that the national interest is malleable and contested, rather than always self-evident or unique.[39]

Realists have emphasized the tension between the national interest and economic interests, principally in considering the need to make departures from policies that maximize wealth and short-run economic growth in the name of national security.[40] But they have been less attentive to the contestation of the national interest and to the ways in which domestic economic conflicts can throw off-key the pursuit of the national interest. Anarchy does impose real (and dangerous) proscriptions against many policies states might choose. Nevertheless, there remains a plausible range of foreign policy orientations, quite distinct from one another, which could arguably be defined as "the national interest"—and various actors within societies will have distinct visions of what the national interest is and how it can best be served. These conflicts and competing visions are a central part of the analyses that follow.

The concept of a contested national interest has a constructivist flavor; moreover, when dealing with monetary politics, the role of ideology, not simply reducible to interests, always lurks in the background.[41] The

---

[39] On the centrality of the national interest for the realist tradition, see Hans Morgenthau, *In Defense of the National Interest* (New York: Knopf, 1951); George F. Kennan, *American Diplomacy, 1900–1950* (Chicago: University of Chicago Press, 1951); and Krasner, *Defending the National Interest*, p. 53.

[40] Jacob Viner, "Power versus Plenty as Objectives of Foreign Policy in the Seventeenth and Eighteenth Centuries," *World Politics* 1:1 (October 1948), esp. pp. 5, 10, 17; Robert Gilpin, "The Politics of Transnational Relations," *International Organization* 25:3 (Summer 1971), pp. 410, 403–4, 409; Michael Mastanduno, "Economics and Security in Statecraft and Scholarship," *International Organization* 52:4 (Autumn 1998), pp. 827, 842–43, 848; Jonathan Kirshner, "The Political Economy of Realism," in Michael Mastanduno and Ethan Kapstein (eds.), *Unipolar Politics: Realism and State Strategies after the Cold War* (New York: Columbia University Press, 1999).

[41] See, for example, Kathleen McNamara, *The Currency of Ideas: Monetary Politics in the European Union* (Ithaca: Cornell University Press, 1998); Jonathan Kirshner, "Ex-

preferences of finance are more than just beliefs; they are also held as an ideology. And the extent to which this ideology is in or out of favor *outside* the financial community, something that is not readily accounted for by liberal or realist approaches, matters greatly. However, the materialist roots of the argument here also cut against the grain of much that is central to the constructivist enterprise, such as culture, norms, and identity.[42]

Thus while the approach here has affinities with attributes of realism, liberalism, and constructivism, it also diverges from each and is an exemplar of none. Informed by the partial equilibrium approach championed by Kindleberger, this book is neither designed nor well suited to contribute to debates between dueling paradigms (beyond its contradiction of related Marxist theories) but is rather an example of what Katzenstein and Sil have dubbed "analytical eclecticism," and as such it "defies analytical capture by any one paradigm."[43] It can be situated with those works from a variety of perspectives that seek to explain the behavior of states by focusing on domestic groups and political competition between them,

---

plaining Choices about Money: Disentangling Power, Ideas, and Conflict," in Jonathan Kirshner (ed.), *Monetary Orders: Ambiguous Economics, Ubiquitous Politics* (Ithaca: Cornell University Press, 2003); Eric Helleiner, *The Making of National Money: Territorial Currencies in Historical Perspective* (Ithaca: Cornell University Press, 2003); Jacqueline Best, *The Limits of Transparency: Ambiguity and the History of International Finance* (Ithaca: Cornell University Press, 2005); Robert M. Fishman and Anthony M. Messina (eds.), *Year of the Euro: The Cultural, Social and Political Import of Europe's Common Currency* (Notre Dame: University of Notre Dame Press, 2006).

[42] For an excellent entrée into the burgeoning constructivist literature, see Peter Katzenstein (ed.), *The Culture of National Security: Norms and Identity in World Politics* (New York: Columbia University Press, 1996). On the malleability of the national interest, rooted in identity politics, norms, and culture, see Martha Finnemore, *National Interests in International Society* (Ithaca: Cornell University Press, 1996); Henry Nau, *At Home Abroad: Identity and Power in American Foreign Policy* (Ithaca: Cornell University Press, 2002); Rawi Abdelal, *National Purpose in the World Economy* (Ithaca: Cornell University Press, 2001); Peter Katzenstein, *Cultural Norms and National Security: Police and Military in Postwar Japan* (Ithaca: Cornell University Press, 1998).

[43] Peter Katzenstein and Rudra Sil, "Rethinking Asian Security: A Case for Analytical Eclecticism," in J. J. Suh, Peter Katzenstein, and Allen Carlson (eds.), *Rethinking Security in East Asia: Identity, Power, and Efficiency* (Stanford: Stanford University Press, 2004); Peter Katzenstein and Nobuo Okawara, "Japan, Asia-Pacific Security, and the Case for Analytic Eclecticism," *International Security* 26:3 (Winter 2001–2), p. 154 (quote); Rudra Sil, "Problems Chasing Methods or Methods Chasing Problems? Research Communities, Constrained Pluralism, and the Role of Eclecticism," in Ian Shapiro, Rogers M. Smith, and Tarek E. Masoud (eds.), *Problems and Methods in the Study of Politics* (Cambridge: Cambridge University Press, 2004); Samuel M. Makinda, "International Society and Eclecticism in International Relations Theory," *Cooperation and Conflict* 35:2 (2000), pp. 205–16; see also Stephen M. Walt, "International Relations: One World, Many Theories," *Foreign Policy* 110 (spring 1998), pp. 30, 34, 44.

and on the tensions that can exist between the pursuit of particular interests and the national interest.[44]

EVALUATING THE ARGUMENT

As mentioned earlier, evidence to support (or to undermine) the argument of this book will be found in the positioning of the financial community within societies in pre-war settings. Relative financial caution is consistent with the argument; episodes where finance is among those leading the charge toward war is powerful evidence against it. In this final section of this chapter, I discuss the logic behind the selection of the cases chosen for close scrutiny. First of all, the universe of potential cases is limited to prewar settings; that is, cases where war was discussed as a possibility and did occur.[45] Limiting potential cases to prewar settings ensures that we are indeed looking at pre*war* preferences, instances where we know for a fact that the risk of war was genuine because war did indeed occur. In theory the behavior of finance (and other actors) in crisis situations where war seemed likely but was ultimately avoided could also conceivably offer attractive insights. But such cases would too easily get bogged down in debates about how likely war actually was, or whether various actors were strategically posturing in these debates with the assumption that war would not occur. Limiting potential prewar settings to actual prewar settings sweeps aside these unnecessary controversies. (This methodological choice does risk giving the superficial impression that finance never gets what it wants. But as the cases make clear, this is simply not so.)[46]

[44] For examples of this type of work, see Benjamin Cohen, *In Whose Interest? International Banking and American Foreign Policy* (New Haven: Yale University Press, 1986); Rawi Abdelal and Jonathan Kirshner, "Strategy, Economic Relations and the Definition of National Interests," *Security Studies* 9:1/2 (1999–2000), pp. 119–56; Eckhart Kehr, "Anglophobia and Weltpolitik," in *Economic Interest, Militarism, and Foreign Policy* (Berkeley: University of California Press, 1977); Richard Rosecrance and Arthur Stein (eds.), *The Domestic Bases of Grand Strategy* (Ithaca: Cornell University Press, 1993); Steven E. Lobell, "War Is Politics: Offensive Realism, Domestic Politics and Security Strategies," *Security Studies* 12:2 (Winter 2002–3), pp. 165–96; Stephen David, *Choosing Sides: Alignment and Realignment in the Third World* (Baltimore: Johns Hopkins University Press, 1991); Jack Snyder, *Myths of Empire: Domestic Politics and International Ambition* (Ithaca: Cornell University Press, 1991).

[45] This does not raise the problem of sampling on the dependent variable, because the dependent variable in question is not the occurrence of war but the preferences of finance (and the positioning of the financial community within the prewar debate).

[46] Not surprisingly, finance sometimes wins and sometimes loses, and often it salvages something in defeat. As described in the chapters that follow, Japanese financiers got their way on foreign policy throughout the 1920s; France's problem was not that finance lost but

In the context of prewar settings, three additional attributes for possible cases are especially appealing. First, to test, as best as possible, the appeasing bankers hypothesis, the investigator should not know the preferences of the financial community regarding the prospects for war and peace in a particular case before embarking on the research. Second, recalling that the partial equilibrium approach of this book seeks to understand the behavior and contingent characteristics of the variable in question, each case has potentially more to offer the entire enterprise if it represents a relatively distinct setting. A heterogeneous set of cases promises to expand the range of conditions under which the behavior of the bankers can be evaluated; additionally, if we find that the preferences of finance are singularly consistent in diverse environments, this would provide further support for the main argument. Third, each case should bring something unique (and analytically valuable) to the table.

The cases in the chapters that follow meet these criteria extremely well. I avoided some cases because they failed to meet these criteria, even though they fit the argument remarkably well. In particular, this book avoids the entire pre–World War I setting, as well as the case of Britain in the interwar period. These prominent omissions merit brief attention here to quickly illustrate that they are entirely consistent with the argument of this book and to explain the basis of the decision not to consider them as full-blown case studies.

The behavior of financial communities within states in the period leading up to World War I fits precisely the argument of this book. Especially with regard to Great Britain, this will not come as a surprise to most readers. Paul Kennedy famously observed the fundamental tension between "strategy and finance" in this period and the incompatibility of the City of London's position as the world's financial hub with the prospects for confrontation and war with Germany.[47] It is worth noting, however, that if anything, this conventional wisdom understates the dread (and shock) with which the City viewed the approach and outbreak of war on the Continent and the extent to which finance hoped that Britain might

---

that it won so many battles in the interwar period. British finance won the day time and time again in the 1950s, 1960s and 1970s, so much so that finance-induced defense cuts came close to preventing the British from even attempting to retake the Falklands. Finally, and of course, in the universe of cases where war approached but did not occur, the preferences of finance likely contributed to some of those outcomes.

[47] Paul Kennedy, "Strategy *versus* Finance in Twentieth-Century Britain," *International History Review* 3:1 (1981), pp. 44–61; see also Paul Kennedy, *The Realities behind Diplomacy: Background Influences on British External Policy, 1865–1900* (London: Fontana, 1981), pp. 27, 68, 128, 137; David French, *British Economic Planning, 1905–1915* (London: George Allen and Unwin, 1982), pp. 13–14, 53, 67, 70, 91; Aaron Friedberg, *The Weary Titan: Britain and the Experience of Relative Decline, 1895–1905* (Princeton: Princeton University Press, 1988), pp. 89, 92–93, 99.

stay out of the conflict. Moreover, when push came to shove, with the breakdown of international payments that accompanied the outbreak of war, many of the City's leading commercial banks acted ignobly, covering their own positions and contributing to a financial crisis in Britain that was diffused only by cooler heads that prevailed at the Bank of England and the Treasury. As Keynes described at the time, with the outbreak of war, "the City was a very sick man, dazed and feverish, called in to prescribe for his own case," with the result that many of the captains of finance were "too much overwhelmed by the dangers, to which they saw their own fortunes and good names exposed, to have much wits left for the public interest and public safety."[48]

The reaction of the British financial community to the war was of a kind with the reaction of financial communities elsewhere, as belligerents suspended the convertibility of their currencies, markets panicked, and bankers were left scrambling to cover their positions in the wake of the unraveling of the intricate web of international financial flows. New York City's *Bankers Magazine* saw in the war "widespread disaster" for credit and banking and warned that "our own land, though suffering least of all, shall not be exempt" from the consequences. The very distinct perspective of the financial community on war was summarized in a subsequent editorial: "Among the countless brood of evils born of war few transcend unsound 'money' in their capacity to inflict injury upon the human race."[49] In Germany, bankers (while more prepared for the conflict than their British counterparts), on questions of war and peace, were also positioned within society as would be anticipated by this theory. The German financial community was, like its counterparts elsewhere, wary of uncertain adventurism and alarmed by the prospect of war and the threat

---

[48] Eyre Crowe of the Foreign Office wrote of "panic in the city," in a memo sent to Foreign Secretary Edward Grey on July 31, reprinted in G. D. Gooch and H. Temperley (eds.), *British Documents on the Origins of the War, 1898–1914* (London: HMSO, 1926–1938), vol. 11, *The Outbreak of War*, p. 228; see also the similar assessment of Chancellor of the Exchequer Lloyd George, *War Memoirs of David Lloyd George*, vol. 1, *1914–1915* (Boston: Little, Brown, 1933), p. 68; David Kynaston, *The City of London*, vol. 2, *Golden Years* (London: Chatto and Windus, 1995), pp. 600–611; "The Great Crisis," *Bankers Magazine* (*London*) 98 (September 1914), pp. 318 ("disastrous"), 321–22, 331, 337 ("catastrophe"); John Maynard Keynes, "War and the Financial System, August 1914," *The Economic Journal* 24 (September 1914), pp. 461, 464, 471–73, 484 (quotes); see also Keynes, "The City of London and the Bank of England," *Quarterly Journal of Economics* 29:1 (November 1914), pp. 48–71.

[49] "The Situation," *Bankers Magazine* 89:3 (September 1914), pp. 211 (quote), 212 (quote); "Unsound Expedients Generated by War," *Bankers Magazine* 89:4 (October 1914), p. 377 (quote). See also Jon Lawrence, Martin Dean, and Jean-Mouis Robert, "The Outbreak of War and the Urban Economy: Paris, Berlin, and London in 1914," *Economic History Review*, n.s., (August 1992), pp. 564–93.

of macroeconomic disruptions and instability. The relative caution of German finance was well known and often a source of frustration to the government. (Even Gerson Bleichröder, Bismarck's personal financial wizard, was known to fear war due to its financial consequences.) The approach of the Great War did little to alter this basic disposition. During the Agadir Crisis of 1911, it was widely believed that the German bankers tied the hands of their government in response to the financial distress exacerbated by the confrontation in 1911; this claim was almost certainly overstated, but it does accurately reflect the relative caution of the German financial community compared with other, more bellicose elements of German society in the years leading up to the war.[50] According to Kennedy, "Perhaps the most persistent economic lobby for good Anglo-German relations were the financial circles in the City of London and their equivalents in Frankfurt, Berlin and Hamburg." The relative political weakness of the financial community (and other elements in society wary of conflict) has been cited by others as a contributing cause of German aggressiveness in this era.[51]

Nevertheless, despite its fit to the theory, World War I is not chosen as a case for close study in this book, for two reasons. First and foremost, it would not offer a relatively pure test of the principal hypothesis, given the well-known preferences of finance in this setting. Second, a focus on the First World War would invite distraction and confusion over the issue of the relationship between interstate interdependence and war, which is not the focus of this book. While remaining aloof from this debate, it is relevant to note here that although the Great War is often used to ridicule the prophets of peaceful interdependence, Norman Angell and Ivan Bloch advocated rather than predicted peace, on the grounds that modern war

[50] See the reports prepared by Francis Oppenheimer, Britain's commercial attaché in Germany; reprinted in Gooch and Temperley, *British Documents;* "The German Financial Crisis" October 21, 1911, vol. 7, *The Agadir Crisis,* pp. 796–805, and "Germany's Financial Position," vol. 11, *The Outbreak of War,* pp. 205–7; M. Chase Going, "German War Finance," *Journal of Political Economy* 24:6 (June 1916), pp. 516–18, 542; Fritz Stern, *Gold and Iron: Bismarck, Bleichröder and the Building of the German Empire* (New York: Vintage, 1979 [1977]), pp. 68, 72, 308, 417, 429; Eckart Kehr, *Economic Interest, Militarism, and Foreign Policy: Essays on German Economic History* (Berkeley: University of California Press, 1977), pp. 7, 40, 70, 83–84; Gregor Schollegen (ed.), *Escape into War? The Foreign Policy of Imperial Germany* (New York: St. Martin's Press, 1990), p. 10; Fritz Fischer, *War of Illusions* (New York: Norton, 1975), pp. 22, 24, 121, 137, 199–201, 203, 357–60, 520–21; Niall Ferguson, *Paper and Iron: Hamburg Business and German Politics in the Era of Inflation, 1897–1927* (New York: Cambridge University Press, 1995), pp. 29, 91, 94, 99, 113–18.

[51] Paul Kennedy, *The Rise of the Anglo-German Antagonism, 1860–1914* (Boston: Allen and Unwin, 1980), pp. 47–48, 302 (quote), 303–5, 435–37, 459; Paul Papayoanou, "Interdependence, Institutions and the Balance of Power: Britain, Germany, and World War I," *International Security* 20:4 (Spring 1996), pp. 70–71.

was no longer a rational method by which states could hope to gain in an economic sense. Included in those arguments were accurate assessments regarding the costly financial disruptions that would (and did) accompany any such conflict.[52]

The position of British finance before World War II was also not chosen as a case for similar reasons (and also in support of the goals in case selection of heterogeneity across countries and periods and of analytical novelty). The struggles of the Treasury to manage Britain's fragile interwar finances and the pressure this placed on defense expenditures are well known, as is the great sensitivity of government to the need to maintain financial confidence as an integral component of British power. This imposed even greater restraint on government borrowing and spending and thus inhibited rearmament. As one study concluded, "The decision to limit defense expenditure . . . had its roots in economic assumptions shared by the Treasury and the financial community." These concerns regarding the spending, borrowing, and inflationary implications of an arms race with Germany for sound finance in Britain contributed to the policy of appeasement. Indeed, for Polanyi, "England's military unpreparedness was mainly a result of her adherence to gold standard economics."[53]

Not only did the City of London strongly favor the appeasement of Germany—and continued to do so right until the start of the war—the bankers directly participated in that aspect of the strategy known as "economic appeasement." Less infamous in history than its political counterpart, economic appeasement was an effort by the City, the Treasury, and the Bank of England to keep Germany integrated with the international financial system by granting one-sided economic concessions. The key-

[52] Norman Angell, *The Great Illusion: A Study of the Relation of Military Power in Nations to Their Economic and Social Advantage* (New York: G. P. Putnam and Sons, 1910), see esp. chapter 3, "The Great Illusion"; also pp. vi, 52 (on the consequences of "complex financial interdependence" for the costs and benefits of war), 54–56, 59–61, 372; Ivan S. Bloch, *Is War Now Impossible?* (Aldershot, England: Gregg Revivals, 1991 [1899]), pp. xlv, lxxix, 114, 347; see also Howard Weinrith, "Norman Angell and the Great Illusion: An Episode in Pre-1914 Pacifism," *The Historical Journal* 17:3 (September 1974), pp. 551, 556–57, 564, 568–59.

[53] Robert Shay, *British Rearmament in the Thirties: Politics and Profits* (Princeton: Princeton University Press, 1977), pp. 3–4, 23–26, 46–47, 75–78, 136–47, 159–62, 282–83, 288 (quote); G. C. Peden, *The Treasury and British Public Policy, 1906–1959* (New York: Oxford University Press, 2000), pp. 286, 288, 291, 298; Gustav Schmidt, *The Politics and Economics of Appeasement: British Foreign Policy in the 1930s* (New York: Berg, 1986), pp. 32, 347–56, 383–84; R.A.C. Parker, "Economics, Rearmament and Foreign Policy: The United Kingdom before 1939—a Preliminary Study," *Journal of Contemporary History* 10:4 (October 1975), pp. 637–69, 645; Bernd Jürgen Wendt, " 'Economic Appeasement': A Crisis Strategy," in Wolfgang Mommsen and Lothar Kettenacker (eds.), *The Fascist Challenge and the Policy of Appeasement* (London: George Allen and Unwin, 1983), pp. 161, 169; Polanyi, *The Great Transformation*, p. 246.

stone of this enterprise was the "standstill agreements," the provision by British banks of short-term credits to Germany in order to finance trade that would otherwise have been frozen by the standstill agreement of 1931. Economic appeasement was also aimed at empowering the German "moderates," such as the enigmatic president of the Reichsbank, Hjalmar Schacht, who had previously resigned as finance minister in part due to his concerns for the inflationary consequences of excessive defense spending. But the resolute commitment of the City to avoid war with Germany outlived any reasonable hope that the strategy was working. Despite coming under increased criticism from members of Parliament, the standstill agreements were renewed every year through 1938—and negotiations for their extension took place in May 1939—by which point Schacht had been removed.[54]

British finance was thus not only a leading advocate of appeasement but also, in both private and public capacities, an important practitioner of economic appeasement, which both reflected and reinforced its strong preference to avoid war at virtually all cost. Despite the fit of this case to the theory, it does not receive closer attention here; it has been ably and extensively studied elsewhere, and the case has relatively little to offer in terms of variation across countries, periods, and analytical themes.

In contrast, the cases that follow feature all of the attributes that I enumerated as ideal for evaluating the claims of this book. The United States before the Spanish-American War offers an excellent opportunity to compare the appeasing bankers hypothesis with Marxist arguments, since both Hobson and Lenin cited the war specifically as a supporting example. The relatively low military risks of the war for the United States also provide the opportunity to separate out a baseline disposition of "aversion to war" from "prudence" derived from concerns about the risks of military defeat. And the nature of the American economy at the time also makes it especially easy to isolate the preferences of the financial community. Japan in the interwar period presents a distinct setting and, with two specific turning points in its external ambition, provides an outstanding proving ground for the principal hypothesis of the book. The different choices of the 1920s and 1930s more generally also illustrate how various

[54] Scott Newton, *Profits of Peace: The Political Economy of Anglo-German Appeasement* (Oxford: Clarendon Press, 1996), pp. 58, 62, 65–66, 91, 93; Neil Forbes, "London Banks, the German Standstill Agreements, and 'Economic Appeasement' in the 1930s," *Economic History Review*, 2nd ser., 40:4 (1987), pp. 573, 583–84, 585–86; C. A. MacDonald, "Economic Appeasement and the German 'Moderates,' 1937–1939," *Past and Present* 56 (August 1972), pp. 105–8, 115, 121, 128; David Kynaston, *The City of London*, vol. 3, *Illusions of Gold, 1914–1945* (London: Chatto and Windus, 1999), pp. 441–46, 450–53; Paul Einzig, *Appeasement before, during, and after the War* (London: Macmillan, 1942), pp. 9–10, 15, 22, 76–77, 83.

actors within Japan had distinct visions of the national interest and how these very different conceptions were reflected in preferences about economic policy. France before World War II brings still further variation in terms of its political-economic setting. This case is also especially important in illustrating how the preferences of finance can be suboptimal, contributing to an overly cautious national security strategy.[55] The United States from the early cold war through the Korean War confronts the argument with a "hard case," given the economic, ideational, and international political setting of the time. The combination of dollar hegemony, postwar Keynesianism, and the early cold war suggests an extraordinarily permissive financial environment that would be uncharacteristically conducive to the financial community's supporting a more assertive national security posture. I chose British finance during the Falklands War as a potentially contrary case, designed to press against the limits of the argument; there were very good reasons why finance should have supported this war. Embedded in that chapter (chapter 6) as a "shadow case" is a consideration of the politics of the war in Argentina. The Falklands crisis is also especially attractive in that it presents a virtually unique laboratorylike setting: the crisis was long enough to allow for lengthy and vigorous debate, but short enough so that unlike any of the other cases, it was the single dominant political discussion in Britain and Argentina for the duration of the confrontation.

In sum, collectively the chapters that follow evaluate the principal hypothesis of this book (that of financial caution), illustrate the contestation of the national interest through the lens of the preferences of the financial community on the question of war, and highlight the costs and constraints often imposed by financial market forces. Chapter 7 ties these strands together to consider how and why this matters. It revisits the attributes of financial caution as a variable in international relations theory and explores the role of international financial markets as a systemic influence on the use of force. Drawing on theoretical arguments and informed by the insights the cases offer, the concluding chapter also enumerates the domestic, international, and ideological factors that contribute to the rela-

---

[55] Unlike all the other cases, interwar France does not offer a pure test of the principal hypothesis of the book. Prior to this book I was aware of the salience of French monetary orthodoxy in the interwar period, and although I had not previously explored the preferences of the French financial community before the Second World War, I was familiar with arguments that the fragility of the franc inhibited the assertiveness of France in responding to the rising German threat, in particular to the remilitarization of the Rhineland in 1936. (Jonathan Kirshner, *Currency and Coercion: The Political Economy of International Monetary Power* [Princeton: Princeton University Press, 1995], pp. 92–93.) However, given the other very attractive features of the case, and many other pure "tests" offered in all the other chapters, I made the decision that there was much to be gained by including the case.

tive influence of finance across different countries and periods. This in turn informs a discussion of the implications of appeasing bankers for contemporary international politics—the influence of the preferences of domestic financial interests and the role of financial globalization in shaping the capabilities, interests, and proclivities of the United States and China and in empowering and inhibiting other actors in world politics, from large states to transnational terrorist organizations.

CHAPTER 2

Ourselves Alone: Financial Opposition to the Spanish-American War

The Spanish-American War of 1898 provides an excellent starting point for an inquiry into the preferences of finance about questions of war and peace for three reasons. First, as noted in chapter 1, prominent theories argue almost exactly the opposite of what I postulate here—radical theories of imperialism and war that find "finance" as the "taproot" of these evils. Both Hobson and Lenin specifically refer to the Spanish-American War as an example of the consequences of the needs of finance capital.[1] Thus the case offers an opportunity to address head-on an important competing approach with contradictory expectations. Second, the war was, for the United States at least, a war of choice, and the road to war was not brief. As a result, the question of whether to initiate war with Spain over Cuba was debated at length, giving all sides ample opportunity to stand up and be counted for their preferences. Finally, it was also a war that posed very few risks for the United States (it was widely assumed that the United States would win the war); the question was more one of how difficult the victory would prove. Such circumstances provide a setting where the basis for opposition to war is pared down to first principles: those for peace are not afraid that the war will be lost; rather, they are against the very resort to arms.

The proximate cause of the war was a rebellion against Spanish rule on the island of Cuba, which began in February 1895.[2] The revolt was sparked by a decline in the island's economic fortunes that was exacer-

---

[1] J. A. Hobson, *Imperialism: A Study* (London: George Allen and Unwin, 1902), pp. 57, 75–76, 78; V. I. Lenin, *Imperialism: The Highest Stage of Capitalism* (New York: International Publishers, 1985 [1917]), p. 86.

[2] On the origins of the Spanish-American War, see John L. Offner, *An Unwanted War: The Diplomacy of the United States and Spain over Cuba, 1895–1898* (Chapel Hill: University of North Carolina Press, 1992); French Ensor Chadwick, *The Relations of the United States and Spain: Diplomacy* (New York: Charles Scribner's Sons, 1909); Thomas Hart Baker Jr., "Imperial Finale: Crisis, Decolonization and War in Spain, 1890–1898" (PhD diss., Department of History, Princeton University, 1976); Lewis L. Gould, *The Spanish-American War and President McKinley* (Lawrence: University of Kansas Press, 1982); see also Ivan Musicant, *Empire by Default: The Spanish-American War and the Dawn of the American Century* (New York: Henry Holt and Company, 1998), and David Traxel, *1898: The Birth of the American Century* (New York: Knopf, 1998).

bated by a modest tariff war between the United States and Spain (which reduced Cuban exports to its most important trading partner), but the uprising was long in coming and was essentially a revival of the unsuccessful rebellion of 1868-78. The conflict, ninety miles off the Florida coast, naturally caught the attention of the United States, which had business interests on the island. Spain's conduct of the war also created sources of conflict between the two powers—scores of citizen protection cases, personal and property compensation claims, and high-profile expulsions of American journalists—that inevitably complicated relations.[3]

The revolt was also widely popular in the United States, where the idea of rebels fighting to liberate themselves from European colonial domination resonated deeply with Americans. And these feelings were stoked by the activities of Cuban Americans vigorously promoting the cause in the United States. But President Grover Cleveland and his secretary of state, Richard Olney, wanted no part of the conflict. Their main goal was that the fighting and its disruptive effects come to a speedy resolution; privately, the administration had little confidence in the rebels and hoped Spain would quickly put down the insurrection. This was also the position of U.S. business interests that operated on the island, principally in sugar and tobacco cultivation.[4]

But Spain proved unable to crush the rebellion, and as the war continued, pressure on the Cleveland administration increased, especially in Congress, where, as Olney observed, members were "setting their sails to catch the popular pro-Cuban breeze." The general popularity of the rebel cause was further intensified by increasing sensational (and sensationalized) incidents on the island involving American citizens and property, but the president would not be moved, on three separate occasions issuing formal declarations of neutrality. As the war continued inconclusively into 1896, the administration quietly communicated to Spain that the United States was dissatisfied with the status quo and encouraged Spain to consider reforms in the nature of its imperial rule. In his final annual address, Cleveland noted that the United States could not allow the war to go on indefinitely, but despite the surge of pro-Cuban resolutions intro-

[3] Sebastian Balfour, *The End of the Spanish Empire, 1898–1923* (Oxford: Clarendon Press, 1997), p. 9; Offner, *Unwanted War*, p. 24; Chadwick, *Relations of the United States and Spain*, pp. 419–20, 427–29, 468–70, 489; Gould, *Spanish-American War*, p. 20.

[4] David S. Trask, *The War with Spain in 1898* (New York: Free Press, 1981), pp. 11–22; George W. Auxier, "The Propaganda Activities of the Cuban Junta in Precipitating the Spanish-American War, 1895–1898," *Hispanic American Historical Review* 19:3 (August 1939), pp. 286–305; Musicant, *Empire by Default*, pp. 77, 78, 80, 87; Offner, *Unwanted War*, pp. 2, 25.

duced in Congress, at no time did the president take any concrete measures to support the rebel cause.[5]

Cuba was not an issue in the election of 1896, which first and foremost was about the climactic battle of the standards, pitting the crusading Silverite William Jennings Bryan against William McKinley, the conservative stalwart of the gold-plated Eastern business establishment. McKinley's election suggested continuity not only in monetary matters but in foreign policy as well; the new president—a deeply religious man who had witnessed the horrors of battle firsthand when he served with distinction in the Civil War—was a dyed-in-the-wool pacifist. From the day of his inauguration, McKinley hoped to avoid war with Spain.[6]

Even in the context of this continuity, however, there were important sources of change. Although the new administration made no formal revisions to U.S. policy, McKinley and his men were more sympathetic to the rebels than their predecessors had been. More important, McKinley had inherited a deteriorating situation. The war dragged on unchanged into 1897, and its debilitating influence on business operations in Cuba led affected businessmen to increase their appeals that something be done to bring the unfortunate conflict to an end. Worse, the lingering stalemate suggested that even the brutal policies of Lieutenant General Valeriano Wyler would not win the war for Spain, and at the same time those policies did strengthen the case of those in the United States who demanded American intervention on humanitarian grounds.[7] Wyler, who had been appointed governor-general in early 1896 with a mandate to do whatever was needed to win the war, had earned the nickname "the butcher" *before* he was appointed governor-general, having built his reputation during the

[5] John A. S. Grenville and George Berkeley Young, *Politics, Strategy and Diplomacy: Studies in Foreign Policy, 1873–1917* (New Haven: Yale University Press, 1966), pp. 181–82, 184 (Olney quote), 192, 194, 197; Arthur Morford Barnes, "American Intervention in Cuba and the Annexation of the Philippines: An Analysis of the Public Discussion" (PhD diss., Cornell University, 1948), p. 41; Chadwick, *Relations of the United States and Spain*, pp. 433, 438.

[6] Gerald F. Linderman, *The Mirror of War: American Society and the Spanish-American War* (Ann Arbor: University of Michigan Press, 1974), pp. 10, 35. On the battle of the standards in the United States, see Richard Franklin Bensel, *The Political Economy of American Industrialization, 1877–1900* (New York: Cambridge University Press, 2000), chapter 6, "Political Administration and Defense of the Gold Standard," pp. 355–456; Gretchen Ritter, *Goldbugs and Greenbacks: The Antimonopoly Tradition in American Finance, 1865–1896* (Cambridge: Cambridge University Press, 1997), chapter 5, "The Battle of the Standards: The Financial Debate of the 1890s"; see also Hugh Rockoff, "The Wizard of Oz as a Monetary Allegory," *Journal of Political Economy* 98:4 (1990).

[7] Offner, *Unwanted War*, p. 41; Barnes, *American Intervention in Cuba*, pp. 94, 98, 117; Linderman, *Mirror of War*, p. 25.

1868–78 conflict and for his role in the repression of striking workers in Barcelona in 1888, 1890, and 1892. In Cuba, Wyler's signature policy was one of "reconcentration," whereby hundreds of thousands of people were forced from the countryside into fortified districts. The souls herded into these districts suffered unimaginably from inadequate health and sanitation; those who found shelter were crowded into old warehouses and abandoned buildings, and the rest spilled into the courtyards and streets. Those remaining in the countryside were assumed to be insurgents and shown no mercy, and Spanish patrols destroyed all crops and animals they encountered, lest they provide succor to the rebels.[8]

In this context, McKinley in September dispatched Stewart L. Woodford, his appointee as U.S. minister to Spain, to inform the Spanish government that if there was no positive movement toward peace by November 1, the United States would consider extending belligerent rights to the insurgents. Spain, flirting throughout the nineties with civil war and struggling with the financial burdens of the Cuban rebellion, had little appetite for a confrontation with the United States. Even without U.S. involvement, the war was increasingly costly to Spain; unable to secure new foreign loans, the government was forced to float domestic bonds at a very generous rate of interest to finance the fighting. Nevertheless, quitting Cuba was seen as a political impossibility; the public expected the rebellion to be crushed, and the empire, however modest, was thought to afford Spain a place among Europe's respected powers. Thus the government attempted to walk the tightrope of appeasing the Americans while retaining control of Cuba. In October the queen regent supervised the dissolution of the conservative government and the formation of a new liberal government under the leadership of Práxedes Mateo Sagasta. Wyler was recalled from Cuba, and new reforms were introduced on the island; plans were announced to phase in Cuba's "autonomy" under Spanish rule, beginning January 1.[9]

These accomplishments, though highly controversial in Spain's already charged political context, represented the high-water marks of McKinley's diplomacy, and in his December address to Congress, the president resisted demands that he recognize the rebels and instead indicated his willingness to give the Sagasta reforms time to succeed. But the first three months of the New Year would be punctuated by one event after another that would mark the descent to war. Antiautonomy and "Viva-Wyler"

[8] Philip S. Foner, *The Spanish-Cuban-American War and the Birth of American Imperialism, 1895–1902*, vol. 1, *1895–1898* (New York: Monthly Review Press, 1972), pp. 77, 111–12, 116–17; Baker, *Imperial Finale*, pp. 46, 195.

[9] Balfour, *End of the Spanish Empire*, pp. 7, 15–16, 19–20, 25; Offner, *Unwanted War*, pp. 54, 56, 70; Baker, *Imperial Finale*, pp. iii, 239, 248, 250; Chadwick, *Relations of the United States and Spain*, pp. 521, 527.

riots erupted in Cuba on January 12; some Spanish officers participated in the riots, reflecting the widespread hostility throughout the military toward the liberal government's policy of reform and appeasement. The riots not only indicated the limited room for maneuverability that the Spanish government enjoyed but also raised concerns in Washington that Madrid did not have the authority to fulfill the promises it made—and would make—regarding Cuba.[10]

These suspicions were bolstered when a private letter written by Enrique Dupuy de Lome, the Spanish minister in Washington, was stolen by a rebel sympathizer and subsequently published on February 9, 1898, in the *New York Journal*. The letter presented an extremely unflattering (if in some aspects accurate) portrait of President McKinley as an inherently political animal, as well as "weak and catering to the rabble . . . a low politician." Less inflammatory but perhaps more worrisome, the letter also contained passages that raised doubts about the sincerity of Spain's recent proposals regarding the key issues at stake—reform in Cuba and trade reciprocity with the United States. The embarrassing episode was well contained by both Washington and Madrid. McKinley kept his powder dry, de Lome resigned, and the appropriate apologies were issued. Although the inflammatory incident further embittered popular sentiment against Spain, within a week it seemed that the crisis had run its political course.[11]

But before the dust thrown by this incident had a chance to settle, on the evening of February 15, the U.S. battleship *Maine* exploded in Havana Harbor, with the loss of over 250 American lives. The president was awakened in the middle of the night with news of the disaster. As informed opinion at the time suspected and future studies would substantiate, an internal explosion almost certainly caused the loss of the ship. Nevertheless, the American public was all too ready to receive the common if unsubstantiated charge that sabotage or even a torpedo attack was to blame, and the incident raised public support for war with Spain to new heights. McKinley, determined to avoid war, tasked a commission to determine the cause of the *Maine* explosion, intensified diplomatic pressure, and searched for creative solutions to the impasse, even floating a scheme for Spanish suzerainty over Cuba which would leave the island essentially self-governing under titular Spanish rule and some sharing of customs revenue.[12]

---

[10] Musicant, *Empire by Default*, pp. 110, 115, 118; Offner, *Unwanted War*, pp. 86–87; Baker, *Imperial Finale*, pp. 288, 307, 310–11; Gould, *Spanish-American War*, pp. 31–32.

[11] Carlos Garcia Barron, "Enrique Dupuy de Lome and the Spanish American War," *The Americas* 36:1 (July 1979), p. 51 (quote); Linderman, *Mirror of War*, p. 26; Offner, *Unwanted War*, pp. 119, 122; Chadwick, *Relations of the United States and Spain*, p. 529.

[12] Gould, *Spanish-American War*, pp. 37–38; Offner, *Unwanted War*, p. 122; Trask, *War with Spain*, pp. 31, 35.

McKinley's boldest stroke, and his last great success, was his March 6 decision to ask Congress to appropriate $50 million from the federal surplus for national defense. The bill passed both the House and the Senate unanimously the next day. The measure allowed McKinley to prepare for war without making it and illustrated the breadth of national support for a more forceful policy. More than anything else, the ability of the Americans to effortlessly marshal such resources astonished the Spanish government. Woodford wrote to McKinley that "the ministry and the press are simply stunned" by the measure. Spain, then three years at war, was saddled with all of the financial ills associated with war making. Building throughout 1897, concerns for the very solvency of the state reached new heights in the last quarter of the year. The government was nearly bankrupt and had virtually exhausted its ability to borrow from either domestic or international sources. The rising costs of the war and the resort to inflationary measures to meet the financial strain were the most important causes of this distress. In the fall of 1897 the peseta dropped sharply on the international market, trading at 34.11 to the pound, down from 26.21 in 1890. The currency would fall to 43.66 in March and continue to depreciate throughout the spring. The passage of the $50 million appropriation led to a financial panic in Madrid; Bank of Spain stock in particular fell dramatically. (And when war with the Americans finally arrived, the lone hint of reticence to be found amid the widespread public rallying was the falling stock market; Spanish bonds also dropped to 29 percent of their issue value.)[13]

Tension built throughout March, but little changed, as Spain's limited room for maneuver, McKinley's silence and apparent passivity, and the intransigence of the (rarely consulted) Cuban rebels left the parties with few, if any, prospects for a peaceful settlement. Prowar fever and pressure on McKinley mounted with each passing week. A speech on March 17 by Senator Redfield Proctor upon his return from a visit to the island added further momentum—the senator, as a sober New England businessman, was everything most of the war agitators were not—and as such, his implicit prowar stance was taken seriously by those conservatives who tended to be tone-deaf to the din of the rabble-rousing populist-infused rhetoric that was sweeping the nation. The president was increasingly isolated, haggard, and distressed; his name was hissed in theaters, and posters of his image were torn from the walls and even burned in effigy

---

[13] Baker, *Imperial Finale*, pp. 223–24, 253–55; Offner, *Unwanted War*, pp. 129, 137–38, 192, 198; Balfour, *End of the Spanish Empire*, pp. 58, 97, 106, 168; quoted in Chadwick, *Relations of the United States and Spain*, p. 545 (quote).

by a mob in Virginia. McKinley resisted war well aware of his plunging popularity and even fearful for his personal safety.[14]

On March 24 the report of the navy board's investigation into the *Maine* disaster reached the White House; it attributed the loss of the ship to an external explosion. McKinley immediately issued diplomatic dispatches to Woodford in Madrid insisting that a path to Cuban independence be established and demanding a response by March 31; in the interim, the navy board's report was forwarded to Congress on March 28, accompanied by a characteristically dispassionate presidential message. But McKinley's ability to contain congressional pressure was reaching its end. The House of Representatives had been kept in line as a function of its large Republican majority and the iron rule of its powerful speaker, Thomas "Czar" Reed, but on March 29 more than forty Republican congressmen who favored a more aggressive posture caucused; the following day, the revolt attracted over one hundred Republicans who demanded that McKinley set a deadline for action. The congressional revolt was motivated by concerns for the upcoming fall elections, during which overwhelming popular support for the war would surely be exploited by Democrats and populists; indeed, with one exception, the dissident Republican caucuses were dominated by state delegations from the South and West, where Republicans were most vulnerable to such pressures in the upcoming elections. Several of the party's eminent national figures also warned that McKinley's antiwar stance was leading the party to electoral disaster.[15]

Spain's response arrived on March 31; McKinley huddled with his advisers and senior Republican officials, and they reached the conclusion that it was inadequate. The president prepared an April 4 message to Congress. Hopes that last-minute European diplomatic intervention, additional Spanish concessions, and time bought by the need to evacuate Americans from Cuba might just deliver a peaceful resolution allowed McKinley to delay his address twice; finally on Easter Sunday, April 10, McKinley held marathon sessions with his cabinet and congressional leaders for one last review. But the die was cast. Clarification of the Spanish concessions and the reaction to them in both Spain and Cuba made

---

[14] Linderman, *Mirror of War*, pp. 28, 37, 40; H. Wayne Morgan, *William McKinley and His America* (Syracuse: Syracuse University Press, 1963), p. 367; Grenville and Young, *Politics, Strategy and Diplomacy*, p. 243; Gould, *Spanish-American War*, pp. 40–41; Trask, *War with Spain*, pp. 31, 50, 56.

[15] Gould, *Spanish-American War*, p. 42; John Offner, "United States Politics and the 1898 War over Cuba," in Angel Smith and Emma Davila-Cox (eds.), *The Crisis of 1898: Colonial Redistribution and Nationalist Mobilization* (New York: St. Martin's Press, 1999), pp. 32–34; Linderman, *Mirror of War*, p. 34; Trask, *War with Spain*, p. 53; John A. Garraty, *Henry Cabot Lodge: A Biography* (New York: Alfred A. Knopf, 1953), p. 189.

clear that the underlying political problems fueling the confrontation would remain. And Speaker Reed and Vice President Garrett Hobart reported to McKinley that they could no longer hold back their respective houses of Congress. Finally the president yielded, but in truly McKinleyesque fashion. His seven-thousand word message read by a relay of clerks before the House of Representatives on April 11 was not a fiery declaration of war but a dispassionate request for the authorization to use force, and one that seemed to leave the door open for even further negotiations.[16]

The uninspiring message was roundly criticized by the interventionists, but it nevertheless gave the congressional hawks what they needed, and war was formally declared on April 25. In the end, the president's abhorrence of war was trumped by his political instincts, which would allow him to risk his own fate but not that of his party, and by his self-conscious unwillingness to lead—at no point would the White House be used as a bully pulpit. It is hard to improve Ernest May's assessment: McKinley "led his country unwillingly toward a war that he did not want for a cause in which he did not believe."[17]

The Path to War

That the United States would come into conflict with Spain over Cuba is hardly surprising. As one scholar observed, "What is puzzling about the Spanish-American War of 1898 is not why it happened, but why it was so long in coming."[18] The United States had a keen interest in Cuba since the days of the founding fathers, and again later when southern politicians

---

[16] Offner, *Unwanted War*, pp. 157, 159, 167–68, 177–78, 180–81; Baker, *Imperial Finale*, pp. 394, 396, 398; Barnes, *American Intervention in Cuba*, p. 252; Musicant, *Empire by Default*, pp. 177–78, 180–3; Morgan, *William McKinley and His America*, pp. 371–73.

[17] Ernest May, *Imperial Democracy: The Emergence of America as a Great Power* (New York: Harcourt Brace, 1961), p. 159. McKinley's reputation as a feckless and unprincipled leader has been contested by revisionist historians who have in general settled around the more moderate position that McKinley steered a steady and principled course throughout, limited by the difficulty of the challenges faced and his minimalist conception of the presidency. See Ernest May, *American Imperialism: A Speculative Essay* (Chicago: Imprint Publications, 1991), pp. xxi, xxiii; Brian P. Damiani, *Advocates of Empire: William McKinley, the Senate and American Expansion, 1898–1899* (New York: Garland, 1987), p. 17; Joseph A. Fry, "William McKinley and the Coming of the Spanish-American War: A Study of the Besmirching and Redemption of an Historical Image," *Diplomatic History* 3:1 (Winter 1979), p. 97; Paul S. Holbo, "Presidential Leadership in Foreign Affairs: William McKinley and the Turpie-Foraker Amendment," *The American Historical Review* 72:4 (July 1967), pp. 1321–35. For a strongly revisionist account of the entire McKinley presidency, see Kevin Phillips, *William McKinley* (New York: Times Books, 2003).

[18] Fareed Zakaria, *From Wealth to Power: The Unusual Origins of America's World Role* (Princeton: Princeton University Press, 1998), p. 155.

aspired to add it to the Union as a slave state. In the second half of the nineteenth century the United States emerged as the world's greatest industrial power, while Spain, having endured centuries of decline, retained political control of an island ninety miles off the U.S. coast, a distant vestige of its once great empire.[19] A war waiting to happen, the Spanish-American War was swift and U.S. victory decisive. On May 1 the Spanish navy was routed in Manila Bay. Two months later Spain's Atlantic fleet met a similar fate, and the battle on the ground in Cuba (where disease was a more formidable foe than the Spanish army) was effectively over on July 16.

While theories of international relations reveal much about the underlying reason for the conflict, its proximate causes are in greater dispute. The traditional explanation holds that public demand for action, fomented by the yellow press, forced war upon a reluctant McKinley and despite the opposition of the business community. There is clear evidence for this interpretation. In New York City William Randolph Hearst's *Journal* and Joseph Pulitzer's *World* pushed for war. The *New York Journal* not only published the de Lome letter but followed it with five days of first-page headlines on the story. The paper, with a circulation of eighty thousand in 1895 when it was purchased by Hearst, printed over one million copies for three days following the destruction of the *Maine*. Circulation increased further as war approached. The *Journal* thundered that if Spain was responsible for the *Maine* (as its headlines soon would assert), "no power from the White House to Wall Street will be able to restrain the American People."[20]

The popular-demand version of events fits snugly with studies that found business interests opposed to the war. Particularly influential was the work of Julius Pratt, who wrote that "business sentiment, especially in the east, was strongly anti-war." And there is little doubt that McKinley

---

[19] Although not a "hegemonic war," the Spanish-American conflict is easily understood through the lens of Robert Gilpin's dynamic structural perspective. Spain established the status quo at the height of its power. With the rise of the United States, a challenger to that order emerged. Given Spain's unwillingness or, perhaps more accurately, political inability to retrench in the light of the new realities of power, war was required to effect change and restore equilibrium. See Robert Gilpin, *War and Change in World Politics* (New York: Cambridge University Press, 1981), esp. pp. 10–11, 192–94. Several accounts of the war have stressed these changes in relative power. See May, *Imperial Democracy*, esp. pp. 6, 42, 269–70; H. Wayne Morgan, *America's Road to Empire: The War with Spain and Overseas Expansion* (New York: John Wiley, 1965), pp. 60–62; Charles S. Campbell, *The Transformation of American Foreign Relations, 1865–1900* (New York: Harper and Row, 1976), p. 278.

[20] Joseph E. Wisan, *The Cuban Crisis as Reflected in the New York Press (1895–1898)* (New York: Octagon Books, 1965), pp. 5, 26, 28, 382, 394 (quote from the February 17 *Journal*), 455, 458.

did not want war.[21] Upon closer inspection, however, there would appear to be a New York bias in arguments regarding both the yellow press and business opposition. This bias can too easily be exaggerated; the yellow press was a national phenomenon: papers throughout the nation relied upon the news services of the *Journal*, the *World*, and other prowar New York scandal sheets, creating a national conduit for the Gotham-based sensationalism; the *Atlanta Tribune*, *Chicago Tribune*, and *Kansas City Star* all pushed for war; in San Francisco, the *Chronicle* drew on the news services of the *New York Sun* and the *New York Herald*; and the *San Francisco Examiner* was a Hearst paper.[22]

Nevertheless, it is fair to conclude that newspapers from elsewhere in the country, which on balance still tended to favor war, were less sensational than their New York counterparts and were more likely to stress interest-based arguments. Moreover, the question remains open (and perhaps unanswerable) regarding the extent to which the money-hungry newsmen were creating public opinion or shrewdly cashing in on the pre-existing proclivities of their readers. (As noted, the rebel cause was broadly popular throughout the United States from the start of the uprising in 1895.) Additionally, critics of Pratt's definitive conclusion (especially by reputation) that business flatly opposed the war also noted his emphasis on eastern business groups; indeed it is possible to point to Pratt's own observation that business groups in the West and the Mississippi Valley, such as Chicago, St. Louis, and San Francisco, were "less opposed to war."[23]

Limitations on the weight that can be assigned to the yellow press and ambiguities regarding business sentiment outside the eastern establishment create room for explanations of the conflict that stress the influence of

[21] Julius Pratt, "American Business and the Spanish-American War," *Hispanic American Historical Review* 14:2 (March 1934), pp. 164 (quote), 169, 170; see also Julius Pratt, "The 'Large Policy' of 1898," *Mississippi Valley Historical Review* 19:2 (September 1932), and Pratt, *Expansionists of 1898: The American Acquisition of Hawaii and the Spanish Islands* (Baltimore: Johns Hopkins University Press, 1936). For the widespread acceptance of this interpretation, see, for example, the influential textbook by Thomas A. Bailey, *A Diplomatic History of the American People*, 10th ed. (New Jersey: Prentice Hall, 1980), pp. 451–64. See also Goran Rystad, *Ambiguous Imperialism: America's Foreign Policy and Domestic Politics at the Turn of the Century* (Stockholm: Esselte Studium, 1975), p. 13, on Pratt's influence. On the depth of McKinley's distress in late March and early April, see, for example, Traxel, *1898*, pp. 120–21; Morgan, *William McKinley*, pp. 370, 373.

[22] Marcus M. Wilkerson, *Public Opinion and the Spanish-American War: A Study in War Propaganda* (New York: Russell and Russell, 1932), pp. ii, 6, 53, 64, 119, 131; Foner, *Spanish-Cuban-American War*, p. 238.

[23] George W. Auxier, "Middle Western Newspapers and the Spanish-American War, 1895–1898," *The Mississippi Valley Historical Review* 26:4 (March 1940), pp. 523–24, 531; Howard Sylwester, "The Kansas Press and the Coming of the Spanish-American War," *The Historian* 31:2 (February 1969), pp. 251, 266; Philip S. Foner, "Why the United States

material interests. Two complementary lines of reasoning contribute to this argument, one that emphasizes underlying structural pressures, the other the demands of narrow economic interests. The first approach, associated most prominently with Walter LaFeber, places the timing of the conflict in the context of the severe depression of 1893–97. From this crisis, LaFeber argues, U.S. business and a growing number of political elites reached the conclusion that domestic overproduction required American manufacturers' access to secure and expanding foreign markets. The outward-looking National Association of Manufacturers (NAM), founded in 1895, spearheaded this movement. Business was, in this view, increasingly in favor of expansionism and the use of force to ensure such outlets—prosperity and domestic tranquillity depended on it.[24]

LaFeber's structural thesis has been challenged by postrevisionist scholars who question the relationship between the attitudes and rhetoric of some businessmen and the preferences and behavior of the general business community, and also the relationship between business preferences and American foreign policy.[25] William Becker and others argue that business interests that were most anxious about surplus production and who sought the ear of government represented a small and relatively weak minority. The giant U.S. firms, which accounted for about 80 percent of the nation's exports, were active and competitive abroad, suffered less during depressions, and saw little need to seek the support of the govern-

Went to War with Spain in 1898," *Science and Society* 32:1 (Winter 1968), pp. 45, 49, 51; Pratt, "American Business," p. 171.

[24] Walter LaFeber, *The New Empire: An Interpretation of American Expansion, 1860–1898* (Ithaca: Cornell University Press, 1963), esp. pp. 150, 172–75, 196–97; Walter LaFeber, *The Cambridge History of American Foreign Relations*, vol. 2, *The American Search for Opportunity: 1865–1913* (New York: Cambridge University Press, 1993), pp. 103–4, 112; see also Thomas J. McCormick, *China Market: America's Quest for Informal Empire, 1893–1901* (Chicago: Ivan R. Dee, 1967); Martin J. Sklar, "The N.A.M. and Foreign Markets on the Eve of the Spanish-American War," *Science and Society* 23:2 (Spring 1959), pp. 133–62; Foner, *Spanish-Cuban-American War*, pp. 298, 301; Foner, "Why the United States Went to War," p. 42; and Thomas G. Patterson, "The United States Intervention in Cuba, 1898: Interpretations of the Spanish-American-Cuban-Filipino War," *The History Teacher* 29:3 (May 1996), pp. 341–61.

[25] William H. Becker, *The Dynamics of Business-Government Relations: Industry and Exports, 1893–1921* (Chicago: University of Chicago Press, 1982); David M. Pletcher, "1861–1898: Economic Growth and Domestic Adjustment," in William H. Becker and Samuel F. Wells Jr. (eds.), *Economics and World Power: An Assessment of American Diplomacy since 1789* (New York: Columbia University Press, 1984); David M. Pletcher, *The Diplomacy of Trade and Investment: American Economic Expansion in the Hemisphere, 1865–1900* (Columbia: University of Missouri Press, 1998); Robert L. Beisner, *From the Old Diplomacy to the New, 1865–1900*, 2nd ed. (Wheeling, IL: Harlan Davidson, 1986), p. 21; Paul S. Holbo, "Economics, Emotion and Expansion: An Emerging Foreign Policy," in H. Wayne Morgan (ed.), *The Gilded Age*, rev. ed. (Syracuse: Syracuse University Press, 1970).

ment. Thus, while there certainly was talk of depression, overproduction, and foreign markets in the 1890s, it originated with smaller, inexperienced, and marginally profitable enterprises. In 1900 NAM, the largest and best-organized industry lobbying group, had only one thousand members, at a time when there were approximately eighty thousand manufacturing groups in the United States. Furthermore, powerful business interests of this era tended to deeply mistrust government—and in the unlikely event they would have sought out federal support, they would have found precious few resources upon which to draw. The State Department, underfunded and understaffed, had its hands full supervising the modest and undistinguished U.S. diplomatic and consular services spread thinly around the globe; the Commerce Department was not even established until 1903.[26] Finally, regardless of the ultimate resolution of this debate, it is very hard to apply the structuralist argument to the origins of the Spanish-American War. While undoubtedly big business was at the core of McKinley's political base, the president himself never registered a concern for foreign markets; nor would it have mattered in this war if he had—by the 1880s, Cuba was already an economic satellite of the United States, and that fact would not change whether the island was governed by the United States, Spain, or the Cubans themselves.[27] However, the work of both the revisionists and, tellingly, of their postrevisionist critics does support the view that some business interests by the mid-1890s favored the general concept of expansionist war, of which the Spanish-American War can be classified as an example.

The second materialist interpretation of the war tabulates the specific economic interests that stood to gain from the conflict and favored intervention to advance those interests. Pratt took for granted that sugar interests and other concerns with a direct business interest in Cuba would be prowar, given that the ongoing rebellion was disrupting trade and destroying foreign-owned assets on the island.[28] Trade between Cuba and the United States did fall dramatically, from over $96 million in 1894, the year before the revolt, to $65, $47, and $26 million respectively in the following three years. More than fifty businessmen from the Mobile, Alabama, area sent a petition to President McKinley in January 1898. Referring to the "tremendous losses inflicted upon American commerce," the businessmen noted that "steps so far taken . . . have not sufficed" and urged McKinley that "prompt and efficient measures" must be taken by

[26] Becker, *Dynamics of Business-Government Relations*, pp. viii–ix, 15, 19, 32, 40–41, 182–83; Pletcher, "Economic Growth and Diplomatic Adjustment," pp. 125–27, 129; Zakaria, *From Wealth to Power*, pp. 11, 120–22.

[27] Morgan, *William McKinley*, p. 331; Offner, *Unwanted War*, p. 228; Pletcher, "Economic Growth and Diplomatic Adjustment," p. 153.

[28] Pratt, "American Business," pp. 171–72, 176–78.

the United States to "restore to us a most valuable commercial field." Other business groups, such as those from Missouri, also pushed for war—their exports of flour and grain to the Island were distressed, and St. Louis was a hub for the distribution of Cuban tobacco, coffee, and sugar. The Kansas City Board of Trade and the St. Louis Merchants' Exchange demanded action. As early as December 1895—notably, even before the arrival of General Wyler—Missouri senators Francis Crockrell and George Vest introduced the first of many resolutions urging that the United States recognize the Cuban belligerency.[29]

More broadly, by calling attention to specific business interests that sought war or, like some in shipbuilding and the steel industry, who thought that they would benefit from it, revisionist scholarship does make the case that business opposition to war was not monolithic. The business community did not speak with one voice but made individual assessments of its interests and preferences. In this estimation, it is appropriate to conclude that business was divided on whether to seek war with Spain, with numerous prowar voices to be found in the West and Midwest.[30]

In sum, considerable scholarship does support the contention that it is an oversimplification to broadly assert that "business opposed the Spanish-American War." But it is equally clear that economic interests did not represent a significant driving force behind the decision to go to war, and that *in aggregate and on balance*, business attitudes are well represented by the resolution passed unanimously by the New York Chamber of Commerce—on April 7, very late in the day—castigating the resort to war and endorsing the president's continued search for a peaceful resolution.[31] This

---

[29] Tom Edward Terrill, "An Economic Aspect of the Spanish-American War," *Ohio History* 76:1–2 (Spring 1967), p. 74; Tennant S. McWilliams, "Petition for Expansion: Mobile Businessmen and the Cuban Crisis, 1898," *The Alabama Review* 28:1 (January 1975), pp. 60–61; Foner, *Spanish-Cuban-American War*, p. 231. Ruby Weedell Waldeck, "Missouri in the Spanish American War," *Missouri Historical Review* 30:4 (July 1936), pp. 369–71, 373. Another proponent of U.S. intervention was the Cigarmakers International Union, which was supported by the American Federation of Labor. Much of the labor force that participated in Florida's expanding cigar production had come from Cuba, and union leaders sought to cultivate their support and hoped to establish a union tradition in an independent Cuba. John C. Appel, "The Unionization of Florida Cigarmakers and the Coming of the War with Spain," *Hispanic American Historical Review* 36:1 (February 1956), pp. 38–49.

[30] LaFeber, *New Empire*, pp. 385–86; LaFeber, *American Search for Opportunity*, p. 141; Barnes, *American Intervention in Cuba*, p. 299; see also Nancy Lenore O'Connor, "The Spanish-American War: A Re-Evaluation of Its Causes," *Science and Society* 22:2 (Spring 1958). O'Connor also sees a "strong split over business opinion," and reports that the machine tools and electrical equipment industries expected to benefit from war; pp. 136, 138, 130–32. That the business community was not monolithic in its opposition to war is acknowledged by the postrevisionists; see, for example, Pletcher, "Economic Growth and Diplomatic Adjustment," p. 166.

[31] Barnes, *American Intervention in Cuba*, pp. 305–6, 309.

remains the best indicator of underlying business preferences in this case, even accounting for the facts that many business interests, especially in the South and Midwest, did favor war and that an increasing number of businessmen did come around to support the resort to arms in late March.[32] In any event, it is not necessary for purposes of this book to establish a unicausal explanation for the Spanish-American War. Clearly, the war was widely popular, and some material interests favored a confrontational policy as well. Of immediate concern here is the position of finance within the heterogeneous U.S. business community, and the way in which the financial concerns perceived their interests as war approached.

The Depth and Basis of Financial Opposition

The financial community strongly opposed the war. These sentiments were plain from the beginning. In December 1896 pro-Cuban sentiment in Congress boiled over as the Senate Foreign Relations Committee voted to recognize the independent republic of Cuba. A brief war scare swept through the country; the stock market plunged, and the bankers mobilized. "The financial interests," wrote Senator Henry Cabot Lodge, "rose in wrathful opposition," and at this early stage, "financial interests had their way." The crisis was resolved when the Cleveland administration made clear that it would not act on such a resolution even if it was passed by both houses of Congress.[33]

---

[32] A focus on increasing business support for war at the last minute—as well as the debate over the "Reick telegram" of March 25, in which the city editor of the *New York Herald* reported to Washington a shift in the City's business opinion—tends to obscure rather than clarify the causes of the Spanish-American War. Those businessmen who came to favor war in late March and beyond did so in the context of the overwhelming popular demand for war, a demand not of their making. In this setting, some of those previously opposed to war decided that if war was to come, it was better for business to end the uncertainties and get it over with; even more important, as discussed earlier, were the increasing concerns that McKinley's pacifism would lead to an electoral disaster in the fall, and the economic policies of the Democratic Party would be even more damaging to business than the costs of the war. In both cases, absent the loud, exogenous demand for war, these businessmen would not have shifted from their underlying antiwar positions. See Louis L. Gould, "The Reick Telegram and the Spanish-American War: A Reappraisal," *Diplomatic History* 3:2 (Spring 1979), pp. 194, 198–99; Pletcher, *Diplomacy of Trade and Investment*, pp. 345, 353; LaFeber, *American Search for Opportunity*, p. 142; Barnes, *American Intervention in Cuba*, pp. 126, 152–53; Offner, *Unwanted War*, pp. 31, 228; G. Wayne King, "Conservative Attitudes in the United States toward Cuba (1895–1898)," *The Proceedings of the South Carolina Historical Association* (1973), p. 95.

[33] Henry Cabot Lodge, *The War with Spain* (New York: Harper and Brothers, 1899), pp. 19, 20; Walter Karp, *The Politics of War: The Story of Two Wars Which Forever Altered the Life of the American Republic (1890–1920)* (New York: Harper and Row, 1979), pp. 67, 75, 79; Chadwick, *Relations of the United States and Spain*, pp. 483, 485, 487.

While often wrapped in the noble sentiments of their rhetoric, it was interest that motivated the preferences of finance. War would bring an increase in government spending, risk inflation, and, most important, threaten the sanctity of the gold standard. Financing the war might either force the nation to suspend the gold standard, as it had done in the Civil War, or require the monetization of silver. This latter possibility represented an extremely sensitive issue. Hard money interests would appear to have ended the war of the standards with their decisive victory in the 1896 election, but the gold bugs counted themselves lucky in that contest and were vigilant against anything that might threaten monetary orthodoxy. When the *Maine* exploded in Havana Harbor, McKinley had been president for less than a year, and the echoes of the battle of the standards still rumbled throughout the American heartland. The off-year elections of 1897 were seen as a victory for the Democratic Party, and William Jennings Bryan interpreted the results as reviving the hopes for silver.[34]

Individual bankers, such as J. P. Morgan, opposed the Spanish-American War, as did John F. Dryden, the president of the Prudential Insurance Company, and McKinley's Treasury secretary, Lyman Gage, who found the president's dispassionate, equivocating "war message" of April 11 too provocative.[35] Even LaFeber, who counted "many pro-war voices" in the business community, observed that "in the money-capitals of the Northeast, more pacifism appeared," a sentiment reflected by the way the stock market would invariably fall in response to rumors of war in the fifteen months leading to the commencement of hostilities.[36] But the breadth and depth of the opposition that resonated throughout the community can be

[34] Offner, *Unwanted War*, pp. 15, 76; Grenville and Young, *Politics, Strategy and Diplomacy*, pp. 162, 233–34; see also Willard Fisher, "The Silver Question in the United States of America," *Economic Journal* 7 (March 1897), p. 117, and Bensel, *The Political Economy of American Industrialization*, chapter 6. It is important to note that the preferences of finance do not necessarily yield the optimal policy. Abandoning the gold standard, sound money champions Friedman and Schwartz have argued, "might well have been highly preferable to the generally depressed conditions of the 1890s." Milton Friedman and Anna Schwartz, *A Monetary History of the United States, 1857–1960* (Princeton: Princeton University Press, 1963), p. 111. See also Rockoff, "The Wizard of Oz as a Monetary Allegory."

[35] Ron Chernow, *The House of Morgan: An American Banking Dynasty and the Rise of Modern Finance* (New York: Atlantic Monthly Press, 1990), p. 80; and Jean Strouse, *Morgan: American Financier* (New York: Random House, 1999), pp. 369–70; See also, for example, Alexander Dana Noyes, *The Market Place: Reminiscences of a Financial Editor* (New York: Greenwood Press, 1938), pp. 157–59; Barnes, *American Intervention in Cuba*, p. 310 (on Dryden); and Offner, *Unwanted War*, p. 184 (Gage).

[36] LaFeber, *American Search for Opportunity*, p. 141; on the stock market, see, for example, Pletcher, *Diplomacy of Trade and Investment*, p. 336; Barnes, *American Intervention in Cuba*, pp. 123, 296; Musicant, *Empire by Default*, p. 95; see also reports in *The Commercial and Financial Chronicle*, for example, May 15, 1897; May 22, 1897; November 6, 1897; March 5, 1898; and April 9, 1898.

seen most clearly in the pages of the daily, weekly, and monthly publications that were widely recognized as the industry's mouthpieces: The *Wall
Street Journal*, the *Commercial and Financial Chronicle*, and *The Banker*.

The *Wall Street Journal*, which did not have a formal editorial column
at this time, nevertheless reported the news from the perspective of the
financial community. The common theme of the paper's coverage was
reports of the crisis coupled with market analyses that stressed the positive
correlation between perceived increases in the likelihood of war and economic and financial distress. In reporting the destruction of the *Maine*,
the *Journal* immediately concluded that it was "not at all likely" the work
of the Spanish government, though it "[will] undoubtedly be made the
occasion for intemperate speeches in Congress." Weeks before war was
declared, the *Journal* was still holding out hope that conflict could be
avoided. On March 29, under the banner "Peace with Honor," it reported
the statement of "one of the most clear minded and determined" senators
in support of McKinley's continued efforts to find a peaceful resolution
to the crisis.[37]

In April the *Journal* continued to reflect Wall Street's anxiety about the
possibility of war and the eagerness of investors to seize upon any rumor
of peace. Despite "the willingness of the market to respond to anything
like favorable news," however, its analysis grew increasingly resigned,
conceding that "the general tendency of the news was against the market." Nevertheless, even in the weeks following McKinley's war message,
the paper dutifully reported the continued market sentiment against war
and cringed at the likely consequences, such as the prospects for new taxes
to fight it.[38]

The *Commercial and Financial Chronicle* was the most persistent and
passionate advocate of peace. The paper steadfastly opposed U.S. involvement in the Cuban situation, reassured its readers that war would not
occur, and warned that if it were to occur, the conflict would be more
costly and difficult than was commonly anticipated. In early 1897, the
paper criticized the "agitators" pressing for U.S. involvement in Cuba.
Later that year it would argue that the need to curb government spending
should inform a more conciliatory U.S. posture toward Spain. In December the *Chronicle* insisted that the removal of Governor-General Wyler
"makes intervention by this country in the Cuban imbroglio a diplomatic
and logical impossibility." With the brutal Wyler recalled and given
Spain's renewed efforts to bring the conflict to a close, "it would be in

---

[37] *Wall Street Journal*, February 17, 1898, p. 3; March 29, 1898, p. 1.
[38] *Wall Street Journal*, April 8, 1898, pp. 1, 2 (second quote); April 9, 1898, p. 2; April
12, 1898, p. 1; April 21, 1898, p. 2 (first quote); April 23, 1898, p. 2.

the highest degree undiplomatic and improper to attempt any interference under present conditions."[39]

Almost every week, from the explosion of the *Maine* through the commencement of hostilities, the *Chronicle* ran a lengthy antiwar editorial. Under headings such as "Cuba and American Self-Control," "The Real Cuban Situation," and "Why War Is Improbable," the paper rallied the anti-interventionist troops. The *Chronicle* argued that Spain was probably not responsible for the *Maine*, and then remarkably staked out an even more antiwar posture, stating that even if the American warship had been destroyed by a deliberate torpedo attack, it would be "as unjust as it is absurd" to assume that this would require war. Rather than "forcing Congress into unprecedented naval appropriation," the explosion "ought to inspire our legislators and committees with redoubled caution." For the *Chronicle*, the $50 million for defense that Congress subsequently provided to the president (which, as noted earlier, stunned the Spanish government and was McKinley's last successfully played diplomatic card) only "added somewhat to the uneasy feeling."[40]

In mid-March the paper summarized and defended the financial perspective on warfare. The United States and Spain had nothing to gain and much to lose. "There are those who choose to exhibit indignation because what they call the 'money power' stands repeatedly in the way of war," the *Chronicle* noted. "We believe that in the present instance the influence of these conservative interests has been very great, and rejoice that we have been able to exert it." More broadly, it concluded: "The lesson of the nineteenth century, from opening to close, is that the most unsatisfactory means of settling an international controversy is by the gage of war."[41]

The approach to war saw no retreat in the paper's editorial policy. As March turned to April, the *Chronicle* insisted, somewhat implausibly, that great public sentiment for war "is in very large measure an illusion." Two days before McKinley's request to Congress for war authorization (which was five days *after* the date originally announced by the president for what was widely understood to be his war message), the *Chronicle* blasted the "extremists" and "reckless agitators" who had "resolved on war for its own sake." In contrast, the prevailing opinion on Wall Street was "that there is no real cause for war." The paper held out until the end, indeed, until after the end, editorializing against intervention one week later (in the interim between the president's request and the congressional machi-

[39] *Commercial and Financial Chronicle*, February 27, 1897, p. 394; November 20, 1897, p. 948; December 4, 1897, pp. 1049 (first quote), 1050–1, 1051 (second quote); also November 13, 1897, p. 896.

[40] *Commercial and Financial Chronicle*, February 19, 1898, pp. 358, 360, 361–62; February 26, 1898, pp. 400, 401; March 5, 1898, pp. 446, 448; March 12, 1898, p. 490.

[41] *Commercial and Financial Chronicle*, March 12, 1898, pp. 493–94.

nations and posturing before the formal and overwhelming adoption of the measure) and "still hopeful the worst may be averted."[42]

Finally, financial opposition to the war was also illustrated less passionately, but plainly and succinctly, by *The Banker*. In its March edition, the periodical raised concerns about the "almost geometrical progression" in the costs of war and worried that the gold standard might be suspended should war arise. Indeed the first ten paragraphs of its lead (antiwar) editorial address the currency question and the costs of war before Spain is even mentioned. America needed "to place the finances of the country on a sound basis" and refrain "from engaging in war without the greatest provocation." Given the unsettled nature of the financial system and the economy more generally ("just now recovering" from the 1893–97 recession), the country "can ill afford to stand the ruin and disaster which are the inevitable concomitants of armed conflicts."[43]

As war approached in April, *The Banker* seemed to acknowledge (in a way that the *Chronicle* would not) the building momentum for war. In a last-ditch effort for a peaceful resolution, the magazine raised the long-dormant idea of purchasing Cuba from Spain. Tellingly, it elaborated a scheme by which the purchase would be made entirely with silver bullion, even though this would entail taking both a loss on the exchange (the government would part with the silver at a lower price than it originally paid for it) and the loss of seigniorage presently enjoyed by the federal government from the issue of silver certificates. Even though "this purchase of Cuba would not by any means be a profitable one for the United States," it was still preferable to a war that "would no doubt be more costly." Moreover, the purchase would allow the United States to "get rid of its entire stock of silver," which would afford "the entire removal of the silver bugbear."[44]

Throwing silver at the Cuban problem would have killed two birds for the banking community, but the opponents of high finance saw the situation conversely. From this corner emanated another material interest, more aggressive and transparent than those from industry who favored war for economic gain. Not surprisingly, this was most obvious in Nevada, which was both in economic distress and dominated by big silver. McKinley's timidity derived from the fact that he was "bound hand and foot to the money power," explained Senator William Stewart of Nevada.

---

[42] *Commercial and Financial Chronicle*, April 2, 1898, pp. 639–41; April 9, 1898, pp. 682, 685–86, 693; April 16, 1898, pp. 731, 732. See also March 19, 1898, p. 544; March 26, 1898, pp. 590, 592, 593; April 23, 1898, pp. 782, 784; and *Commercial and Financial Chronicle Quotation Supplements*, April 2, 1898, p. 5; May 7, 1898, p. 5.

[43] *The Banker* 56:3 (March 1898), pp. 345–47, 348, 358.

[44] *The Banker* 56:4 (April 1898), pp. 520, 517–18.

But war "would not be an unmitigated evil," he argued, if it would "force the United States . . . to create legal tender money without regard for the material upon which it is printed or stamped." The *Silver Knight-Watchman* concurred, asserting that the benefits from the forced monetization of silver would easily surpass the "evil of any war."[45]

These predilections were not isolated. LaFeber reports that "arguments were stuffed into the *Congressional Record* by Populists who hoped that war with Spain would force the impoverished United States Treasury to coin silver," and these sentiments were echoed in the bimetallist press. Populist papers in Kansas saw the war as an opportunity to advance the soft money agenda, reflecting the broader trend throughout the South and Midwest, where agrarians favored war on the grounds that it would stimulate inflation; in the West, "pro-silver areas were among the most vocal supporters of intervention and war." In sum, as *The Nation* argued, "those who desired cheaper money were among the Agitators for war."[46]

This, of course, did not go unnoticed by the financial community. The *Commercial and Financial Chronicle* had linked prowar agitation with soft money advocates as early as January 1897, and in May of that year it complained that "unceasing mischief-makers composing the silver faction" hoped to "irritate a war with Spain." The *Chronicle* insisted, of course, that "situated as our currency, the Government revenue and business affairs are, no course could be more reckless." In 1898 the paper would continue to call attention to its view that many who supported war "do not at all care for Cuba: they are only interested in the establishment of a free-silver standard, a plan which they think war would advance."[47]

---

[45] Paul S. Holbo, "The Convergence of Moods and the Cuban-Bond 'Conspiracy' of 1898," *The Journal of American History* 55:1 (June 1968), pp. 59 (Stewart quotes), 61; Joseph A. Fry, "Silver and Sentiment: The Nevada Press and the Coming of the Spanish-American War," *Nevada Historical Quarterly* 20:4 (Winter 1977), pp. 223, 225, 228 (*Silver Knight-Watchman*). Fry also observes that New York's *World* and *Journal* were Democratic papers, and that Hearst not only supported Bryan and free silver but had substantial holdings of silver mines (p. 233). See also Mary Ellen Glass, *Silver and Politics in Nevada, 1892–1902* (Reno: University of Nevada Press, 1969), p. 132. On the elements of the prosilver coalition more generally, see Francis A. Walker, "The Free Coinage of Silver," *Journal of Political Economy* 1:2 (March 1893), pp. 163, 165–66, 178.

[46] LaFeber, *New Empire*, pp. 290 (quote), 385; Sylwester, "The Kansas Press," p. 258; Fry, "Silver and Sentiment" (quote), p. 233; Barnes, *American Intervention in Cuba*, p. 298 (*The Nation*); see also William E. Leuchtenberg, "The Needless War with Spain," in Allan Nevins (ed.), *Times of Trial* (New York: Knopf, 1958), p. 183; Pletcher, *Diplomacy of Trade and Investment*, p. 329; Holbo, "Presidential Leadership in Foreign Affairs," p. 1323.

[47] *Commercial and Financial Chronicle*, January 9, 1897, p. 54; May 22, 1897, p. 974; February 12, 1898, p. 308 (in response to the agitation surrounding the publication of the de Lome letter). On April 2 the paper reprinted a very lengthy antiwar letter written by Edward Phelps, former U.S. minister to England, with the admonition that "no one should

Viewed along this dimension, the debate over the war could be seen as revisiting the 1896 election, but with McKinley this time on the losing side, with the popularity of the war diminishing and distilling his broad electoral coalition down to its narrowest money-lending base. William Jennings Bryan, who would again be his party's standard-bearer in 1900, was more than happy to define the politics along these lines, commenting, "The sufferings of [Cuba's] people cannot be ignored unless we, as a Nation, have become so engrossed in money-making as to be indifferent to distress." And Democrats routinely charged that McKinley's pacifism was a function of the fact that he was in the hip pocket of the antiwar financial community, or even that the president was conspiring with European financiers to prevent Cuban independence and avoid war. But as with much of national politics in the 1890s, the battle lines were drawn more sharply on money than on party. Many in the silver press, especially in the Midwest, saw the war with Spain over Cuba as a continuation of the crusade for silver against the money interests of Wall Street and their British allies. Gold Democrat Cleveland had been similarly pilloried for letting his Wall Street connections rather than the will of the American people dictate his (passive) Cuba policy; and silver Republicans in Congress were a constant source of difficulty for McKinley, including six Republican senators who had opposed his election. In late March, when meeting with the dissident Republican congressmen, the president urged just a little more time to allow for Spain's response to his final ultimatum. "I don't believe a word of it," one congressman responded, "Wall Street doesn't want a war and you are doing their bidding."[48]

This view was widely held by those who favored war. The Hearst papers leveled this charge directly at Mark Hanna, the Ohio business magnate widely perceived as the kingmaker, if not puppet master, behind McKinley's throne, who was burned in effigy alongside the president by prowar demonstrators. According to the *Silver Knight-Watchman*, it was not that the opponents of war "loved Free Cuba less, but they loved Hanna's administration and bondholders more"; other editorialists concurred, blasting "the goldite oligarchy" that opposed war. One did not need to be prosilver, it should be stressed, to recognize that the bankers

---

omit to read it carefully." According to Phelps, "Every man who voted for Bryan and free silver is shouting today for war with Spain, and for the same reason" (pp. 644–47). See also February 22, 1898, p. 154, and *The Quotation Supplement*, March 3, 1898, p. 5.

[48] Offner, *Unwanted War*, pp. 153 (Bryan quote), 169, 42 (silver Republicans); J. Stanley Lemmons, "The Cuban Crisis of 1895–1899: Newspapers and Nativism," *Missouri Historical Review* 60:1 (October 1965), pp. 64, 69, 70–71, 74; see also John Hingham, "Anti-Semitism in the Gilded Age: A Reinterpretation," *Mississippi Valley Historical Review* 43:4 (March 1957), p. 574. Holbo, "Economics, Emotion and Expansion," pp. 219–20; Barnes, *American Intervention in Cuba*, p. 124; Musicant, *Empire by Default*, p. 175 (quote).

viewed the Cuban question through the lens of financial stability. On March 26 Hanna was publicly confronted by an angry Theodore Roosevelt at a well-attended Washington dinner. Then assistant secretary of the navy, the future president, an expansionist who anxiously sought war as an exciting adventure that he thought would be good for the national character, would later write in his memoirs, "The Big financiers and the men generally who were susceptible to touch in the money nerve, and who cared nothing for National honor if it conflicted even temporarily with business prosperity, were against the war." Roosevelt's patron, Republican senator Lodge of Massachusetts, heard more than his share of antiwar advocacy, not only in the form of frantic telegrams from his constituents in the financial community but also from the pen of his own personal financial adviser, Henry L. Higginson. Nevertheless, Lodge, like Roosevelt, was disdainful of "the powerful financial interests of the Eastern cities . . . [who] exerted their great force to stop every forward step along the inevitable path" to war.[49]

The Consistency of Financial Caution

While there were prowar voices in the business world, the U.S. financial community was steadfastly opposed to the Spanish-American War, a pacifism that was not a function of deeply held principles about international politics but derived from concerns about how war might affect macroeconomic conditions and thus their narrow economic interests. This attitude was not a peculiar artifact of the Cuban situation but a reflection of underlying preferences. This can be seen through a brief review of another crisis from the same decade, the 1895 Venezuela Boundary Dispute between the United States and Great Britain. This less consequential episode was a dress rehearsal of the alignment of interests and domestic political conflict that would play out in 1898.

The crisis began over the formal definition of the border between eastern Venezuela and the British colony of Guiana.[50] In 1842 the British

[49] Wilkerson, *Public Opinion and the Spanish-American War*, p. 110; Linderman, *Mirror of War*, p. 7; Holbo, "Convergence of Moods," p. 70 (*Silver-Knight Watchman*, editorial quotes); Edmund Morris, *The Rise of Theodore Roosevelt* (New York: Modern Library, 2001), p. 635; Theodore Roosevelt, *An Autobiography* (New York: Macmillan, 1919), p. 228; Lodge, *War with Spain*, p. 32 (quote); Garraty, *Henry Cabot Lodge*, pp. 182, 186, 188.

[50] See Paul R. Fossum, "The Anglo-Venezuelan Border Controversy," *Hispanic American Historical Review* 8:3 (August 1928), pp. 299–329; John M. Dobson, *America's Ascent: The United States Becomes a Great Power, 1880–1914* (DeKalb: Northern Illinois University Press, 1978), esp. pp. 74–85; Walter LaFeber, "The Background of Cleveland's Venezuelan Policy: A Reinterpretation," *American Historical Review* 66:4 (July 1961), pp. 947–67; Jennie A. Sloan, "Anglo-American Relations and the Venezuela Boundary Dispute," *His-*

declared a boundary that had never been accepted by Venezuela, but with the region unexplored and unsettled, the issue remained on the back burner. Over time, however, and with the discovery of gold in the disputed region and each side seeking to control the strategic Orinoco River, the dispute heated up. Britain preferred to resolve the conflict through bilateral negotiations, whereas the Venezuelans sought international arbitration as a means of mitigating their relative weakness. The United States, perceiving a new pattern of British aggressiveness in the hemisphere following recent incidents involving Brazil and Nicaragua, interceded, nominally on behalf of Venezuela but principally to assert regional dominance (at no time did the United States consult with the Venezuelan government regarding the affair). The Cleveland administration, initially slow to act, was aroused by public support and bipartisan pressure from the leaders of the foreign policy establishment. Secretary of State Richard Olney, evoking the Monroe Doctrine, sent a bellicose message for U.S. Ambassador Thomas Bayard to deliver to the British government. Olney's July 20 missive, the "twenty inch gun," as it was approvingly referred to by Cleveland, lectured Britain that "the U.S. is practically sovereign" and its law "fiat" on the continent and demanded that the dispute be settled by arbitration.[51]

Prime Minister Salisbury, skeptical of how the Monroe Doctrine could apply to a boundary dispute, essentially ignored the message. Finally on November 26 Salisbury's response reached Washington; the condescending note coolly and comprehensively dismissed the Americans' claims, categorically challenging both the right of the United States to intervene in the matter and the exaggerated interpretation of the Monroe Doctrine.[52] Cleveland was furious, and on December 17, 1895, he delivered a special

panic *American Historical Review* 18:4 (November 1938), pp. 486–506; also A. E. Campbell, *Great Britain and the United States, 1895–1903* (London: Longmans, 1960), pp. 11–48; H. C. Allen, *Great Britain and the United States: A History of Anglo-American Relations (1783–1952)* (London: Odhams Press, 1954); Campbell, *Transformation of American Foreign Relations*, pp. 194–221.

[51] Grenville and Young, *Politics, Strategy and Diplomacy*, pp. 129, 164; T. Boyle, "The Venezuela Crisis and the Liberal Opposition, 1895–96," *The Journal of Modern History* 50:3 (supplement), p. 1190; Beisner, *From the Old Diplomacy to the New*, pp. 109–10. For Olney's note, see United States Department of State, *Foreign Relations of the United States [FRUS] 1895*, part 1 (Washington, DC: U.S. Government Printing Office, 1896), pp. 545–62.

[52] On Salisbury, and the British perspective more generally, see Andrew Roberts, *Salisbury: Victorian Titan* (London: Weidenfeld and Nicholson, 1999), pp. 615–17, 628, 632–33, 710; R. A. Humphrey, "Anglo-American Rivalries and the Venezuela Crisis of 1895," *Transactions of the Royal Historical Society*, 5th ser., 17 (1967), pp. 133, 147–48, 155–56; also David Steele, *Lord Salisbury: A Political Biography* (London: UCL Press, 1999), pp. 330–33; Aubrey Leo Kennedy, *Salisbury, 1830–1903: Portrait of a Statesman* (London: J. Murray, 1953), pp. 257–63.

message to Congress that clearly threatened the use of force in support of America's demands. The public rallied around the president; Britain, on the other hand, with an eye toward European power politics, saw nothing to be gained by a confrontation with the United States. Any doubts the prime minister might have harbored about the need to resolve the matter gracefully were erased by the implications of the December 31 Jameson Raid in South Africa and Kaiser Wilhelm's congratulatory "Kruger Telegram" that followed on January 3; in the end the Venezuelan dispute was settled by arbitration as the United States had demanded.[53]

Assertive diplomacy was broadly popular in the United States, but as would be the case in 1898, the business community was divided. In this instance, however, the cleavage between finance and industry was more profound, since outside of the New York financial community the private sector supported and almost unanimously urged a very aggressive stance.[54] Bradstreet's survey of leading merchants and manufacturers in twenty American cities showed strong support, reflecting business opinion throughout the South, Midwest, and West. Business groups in Pittsburgh, Buffalo, Baltimore, Trenton, Kansas City, St. Paul, Milwaukee, and Indianapolis also fully supported Cleveland's confrontational policy. They were joined in their praise by journals such as *The American Manufacturer*, *The Manufacturer's Record*, and *The Bulletin of the American Iron and Steel Association*.[55]

[53] Campbell, *Great Britain and the United States*, pp. 11, 13, 15–16, 24, 27; Joseph J. Mathews, "Informal Diplomacy in the Venezuelan Crisis of 1896," *Mississippi Valley Historical Review* 50:2 (September 1963), pp. 196, 197; James Bryce, "British Feeling on the Venezuela Question," *North American Review* 162 (February 1896); William Lyne Wilson, *The Cabinet Diary of William L. Wilson, 1896–1897* (ed. Festus P. Summers) (Chapel Hill: University of North Carolina Press, 1957), pp. 4, 5, 7; Boyle, "Venezuela Crisis," pp. 1191, 1193–95; Grenville and Young, *Politics, Strategy and Diplomacy*, pp. 168, 200; John M. Oven IV, *Liberal Peace, Liberal War: American Politics and International Security* (Ithaca: Cornell University Press, 1997), p. 169; Zakaria, *From Wealth to Power*, pp. 148–52 (note that Zakaria reports a more cautious reaction by the American public, p. 151). For Salisbury's note and Cleveland's message, see *FRUS 1895*, part 1, pp. 563–76, 542–45; see also *FRUS 1896* (Washington, DC: U.S. Government Printing Office, 1897), pp. 240–55.

[54] Walter LaFeber, "The American Business Community and Cleveland's Venezuelan Message," *Business History Review* 34 (Winter 1960). LaFeber argues that "industrialists and merchants almost unanimously backed the President." In studies that show business opposition, "every businessman who is quoted . . . is a banker from New York" (pp. 401–2, 402 n. 46). Accordingly, the opposition of the *New York Times* reflected Wall Street's concerns; Owen, *Liberal Peace, Liberal War*, p. 166; Campbell, *Great Britain and the United States*, p. 16.

[55] LaFeber, "American Business Community," pp. 394–95, 399–401; LaFeber, *New Empire*, pp. 272, 274, 275; Pletcher, *Diplomacy of Trade and Investment*, pp. 319–20; C. Tsehloane Keto, "The Aftermath of the Jameson Raid and American Decision Making in Foreign Affairs, 1896," *Transactions of the American Philosophical Society* 70:8 (December 1980), p. 16.

The financial community, on the other hand, was bitterly opposed to threatening or risking war with Britain. As one prominent financial journalist described, "downtown New York was explosive in its wrath" as the market "plunged downward in panicky fashion." Although the market would soon recover, financial hostility did not abate. Secretary Olney's brother wrote from New York to report that "there is an undercurrent of sentiment among bankers and businessmen of considerable strength, that censures" Cleveland's message. Another insider, fresh from dinner with leading financiers such as J. P. Morgan and the president of the New York Stock Exchange, told a friend "they all believed . . . that we were on the eve of a financial cataclysm."[56]

The *Wall Street Journal* (which, as noted, had no formal editorial column) reported the immense popularity of the president's message on both Tuesday, December 17, and Wednesday the eighteenth, but by the next day, it ran a story called "The Real Sentiment." Here, the *Journal* noted that while none of the respondents wanted to appear unpatriotic in public and therefore refused to be quoted, its survey of the financial community found that "practically everybody asked regrets the stand taken by the President and expresses disgust over the whole incident." On Friday direct quotes from the "vigorous opposition" emerged. President Williams of the Chemical Bank called the president's message "wicked," and other bankers proclaimed their opposition to the "most ill advised" action, describing the message as a "calamity." One bank president added plainly: "I am opposed to the position assumed. The Monroe Doctrine does not apply." The *Commercial and Financial Chronicle* saw the matter in exactly the same way. "In our view President Cleveland's message to Congress on the Venezuelan question must be considered in every way unfortunate," the paper editorialized. "It is not at all obvious that the Monroe Doctrine . . . is applicable."[57]

Averse to conflict in general, picking a fight with Britain—the center of European and international finance—seemed especially misguided to

---

[56] Noyes, *Market Place*, p. 121 (quotes); Ada Matthews, "New York Bank Clearings and Stock Prices, 1866–1914," *Review of Economics and Statistics* 8:4 (October 1926), p. 186; Grenville and Young, *Politics, Strategy and Diplomacy*, pp. 168–69; see also New York reactions in Charles Tansill, *The Foreign Policy of Thomas F. Bayard, 1885–1897* (New York: Fordham University Press, 1940), p. 727; LaFeber, *New Empire*, p. 271 (Olney letter); Alfred P. Dennis, *Adventures in American Diplomacy, 1896–1906* (New York: E. P. Dutton, 1928), pp. 31–33, 35; Royal Cortissoz, *The Life of Whitelaw Reid*, vol. 2, *Politics—Diplomacy* (New York: Charles Scribner's Sons, 1921), pp. 201, 202 ("cataclysm").

[57] *Wall Street Journal*, December 17, 1895, p. 1; December 18, 1895, p. 1; December 19, 1895, p. 1; and December 20, 1895, p. 1; *Commercial and Financial Chronicle*, December 21, 1895 (quotes); see also December 28, 1895.

American financiers. Such a confrontation could easily cause the withdrawal of vital European lending, destabilizing domestic banks and threatening the economy. Thus the *Commercial and Financial Chronicle* suggested that if President Cleveland hoped "to bring out in strongest relief the financial weakness of the United States he could not have hit on a better device for doing it than his earlier message to Congress on the Venezuelan question." This source of distress also calls attention to the fact that the risk of war not only threatens sound money but can also interfere with unfettered access to and relations with international financial markets, another issue of great concern to the financial community.[58]

Also present in this crisis, though less salient, was the undercurrent of monetary conflict and hostility toward the banking community's timidity, a dominant theme in the period before the Spanish-American War. Some of those who supported an aggressive stance against Britain over Venezuela hoped that war or policies that risked war might force the monetization of silver or even the issue of unbacked paper notes. This too was recognized by the bankers, and the *Wall Street Journal* explicitly raised fears for the gold standard and the possibility that the conflict might be used as an excuse for the free coinage of silver. Senator Stewart of Nevada went further, asserting, "War would be a good thing, even if we did get whipped, for it would rid us of English bank rule."[59]

Republicans Henry Cabot Lodge and Theodore Roosevelt also favored a confrontational stance against the British, not because they had a financial stake in the conflict, but because they were spoiling for a fight. (Figuratively, that is; they sought American assertiveness and confrontation but were not eager for war with Britain; nor did they expect it.) Well before Cleveland's congressional message put the dispute on the front page, Lodge plainly oversold the controversy in order to rally public support. England's actions were "a direct violation of the Monroe Doctrine," he wrote, and "the time has come for decisive action." As he would soon be again with regard to the Spanish-American confrontation over Cuba, Lodge was contemptuous of the "frightened complaints of the bankers" who trembled at the prospect of conflict and exchanged sharp letters with his financial adviser, Higginson, on the subject. Roosevelt shared both

[58] *Commercial and Financial Chronicle*, December 21, 1895 (quote); Cortissoz, *The Life of Whitelaw Reid*, pp. 201–2; Garraty, *Henry Cabot Lodge*, p. 161. On the importance of ties between the New York and London financial communities, see Bensel, *Political Economy of American Development*, pp. 83–85, 88–91, 356, 453–54.

[59] See Nelson Blake, "Background of Cleveland's Venezuela Policy," *American Historical Review* 47:2 (January 1942), pp. 261, 265; also LaFeber, "The American Business Community," p. 400; *Wall Street Journal*, December 21, 1895, p. 1; Musicant, *Empire by Default*, p. 33 (Stewart); Karp, *Politics of War*, pp. 38, 41, 45.

Lodge's preferences and his assessments, complaining that "the antics of the bankers, brokers and anglo-maniacs are humiliating to a degree."[60]

The Venezuela Boundary Dispute illustrates again that finance's caution regarding questions of war and peace reflects a basic disposition that derives from a concern for macroeconomic stability, rather than from an assessment of the merits of or international political risks associated with a particular international dispute. The same disposition informed the preferences of finance over the Cuban situation as well. The Spanish-American War was an extremely popular, relatively painless war that in broad stroke is easily understandable from the perspective of power politics. Yet it was opposed, vituperatively and in virtual isolation, by the financial community. The uniform and passionate opposition of finance stood out even in comparison with the more heterogeneous sentiments of the broader business community. And not even swift and easy victory in that conflict would temper finance's caution. While noting that the Treasury had emerged from the Spanish-American War in even better condition than it had entered it, as the century turned, McKinley's treasury secretary, Lyman Gage, sounded a cautionary note about the fragility of finance. Referring to the gold standard, he wrote, "Disturb the confidence in any manner, raise doubt either as to the purpose or power of the government in the direction in question, and the whole credit structure is shaken to its center." The Venezuela Boundary Dispute, he noted, offered a "striking example" of how "the possibility of war with a great world power subjected the Treasury's gold to attack and put all trade and industry at a stand-still."[61]

"The financial classes are lovers of peace, yet they are obliged more than any to bear the burdens and losses of war." These words (especially the second clause), from a lead editorial that appeared in *The Banker* two years before the Spanish-American War, explain why finance is so cautious. Aside from the obvious risk to sound national finance, there was the "immense costliness of modern naval and military equipment," which would "magnify the burden of taxation" and result in unsustainable levels of "accumulated national debts." Instead of war, the editorial urged, all states should agree to settle international disputes through arbitration. This would allow for the reduction of "the immense standing armies" now in existence. "Under arbitration the so called strong Government would have less reason for its existence; their power need not exceed

---

[60] Henry Cabot Lodge, "England, Venezuela, and the Monroe Doctrine," *North American Review* 160:463 (June 1895), pp. 653, 655, 657 (quotes); Garraty, *Henry Cabot Lodge*, pp. 156, 161 (quote), 162–63; Leuchtenberg, "Needless War with Spain," p. 171 (Roosevelt quote).

[61] Lyman Gage, "Condition and Prospects of the Treasury," *North American Review* 168:511 (June 1899), pp. 651, 647.

what was necessary to maintain internal order." This contraction of the state would reduce the risk of socialism or anarchy, "for these arise from a poverty caused largely by excessive taxation."[62]

What is remarkable about these sentiments—for sound money, small government, and low taxes, as well as the need to subordinate virtually all other goals to these sacred trusts—is the extent to which they are held in financial communities from every corner of the globe throughout the modern era. As I will demonstrate further in the following chapters, wherever they are found, bankers see international relations first through the lens of macroeconomics—with all eyes on the price level, interest rates, exchange stability, sustainable debts, and modest public interference in the business of finance. From this perspective, in the normal course of events, low inflation trumps high politics.

[62] *The Banker* 52:3 (March 1896), pp. 289–91.

CHAPTER 3

Meet the New Boss: The Rise of the Military and the Defeat of Finance in Interwar Japan

The case of interwar Japan offers an excellent testing ground for the principal hypotheses of this book. Two attributes of this case are especially promising. First, the period is neatly bifurcated—Japanese foreign policy was relatively cautious during the first half of this period, 1920–30, and then increasingly aggressive in the second half, 1931–41. What was the role of finance in this era, in terms of its foreign policy preferences and participation in debates about grand strategy? Second, in the more assertive period, there are two distinct turning points—1931 and 1937, when Japan markedly increased its ambition and expanded the war in China. Where was finance at these critical junctures? If the basic hypotheses of this book are correct, we would expect to find that the financial community was in favor of the more cautious policies of the 1920s (ideally, explicitly for macroeconomic reasons) and that finance stood opposed to the two bouts of expansion in the 1930s. Remarkably, this is exactly what happened, and the case of interwar Japan not only offers an especially clear test of the principal arguments of this book but provides strong support for those arguments.

Scholars of international relations have debated whether Japan's foreign policy became "overexpansionist" in 1931 or 1937.[1] For current purposes, however, the issue is not which of these two points represented the "wrong turn," the point at which Japanese expansionism became inefficient and self-defeating. Rather, what is important is the observation that there were two moments in the 1930s when Japanese foreign policy clearly became more ambitious. Whether or not that expansionism made strategic sense is not of present concern. What is of concern is the position and preferences of the financial community and its role in the disposition of foreign policy. Specifically, this chapter will evaluate the contention that Japanese foreign policy in the 1920s was associated with the strong

---

[1] See Charles Kupchan, *The Vulnerability of Empire* (Ithaca: Cornell University Press, 1994), on 1937, pp. 277, 299; and Jack Snyder, *Myths of Empire: Domestic Politics and Political Ambition* (Ithaca: Cornell University Press, 1991), on 1931, p. 115; more generally, see also W. G. Beasley, *Japanese Imperialism, 1894–1945* (Oxford: Oxford University Press, 1987), and Louise B. Young, *Japan's Total Empire: Manchuria and the Culture of Wartime Imperialism* (Berkeley: University of California Press, 1998).

political influence of finance, and that *each* expansion of foreign policy assertiveness in the 1930s, in 1931 and 1937, was associated with a defeat of financial interests. The analysis here will explore the disparate visions of Japan's national interest, as seen in the contrasting choices made in the 1920s and 1930s, and will assess the argument that certain choices were possible only following the resolution of domestic political conflicts along specific lines.

In considering a theory that features a prominent role for particularistic economic interests within Japan, and, more narrowly, to evaluate an argument about the distinct preferences of "finance," it is necessary to address issues that arise as a result of the particular attributes of the Japanese political economy. Specifically, can the interests of finance be distinguished and isolated, especially given the importance of the *zaibatsu* in the Japanese economy? These massive commercial entities, such as Mitsui and Mitsubishi, brought under one company name both important industrial and banking concerns.

Yet even when accounting for the zaibatsu, we can still see distinct divisions between financial interests and those of other actors. First, there were many important financial institutions, such as the Industrial and Hypothec Banks and the Yokohama Specie Bank, that were closely associated not with the zaibatsu but with the government. At the same time, large segments of the Japanese economy, such as the agricultural sector (which accounted for well over half of Japanese employment in 1920), had no connection with finance whatsoever. Further, in some industries, such as textiles, the influence of the zaibatsu was limited, and in others, such as the electric and chemical industries, newer zaibatsu (such as Nippon and Mori) emerged, and these did not have their own banking institutions. Finally, by the end of the First World War, firms within the traditional zaibatsu received little long-term capital from their banking brethren. Rather, more and more of the lending done by zaibatsu banks was to outsiders, allowing for clearer functional divisions and distinctions between industry and finance even within the traditional zaibatsu.[2]

Perhaps most important, even with the distinct attributes of the Japanese political economy, the Japanese banking establishment acted in a way that was quite similar to its counterparts abroad. The leaders of the Bank of Japan, the Ministry of Finance, and other public and private financial institutions throughout the country exhibited the easily recognizable profes-

[2] Kozo Yamamura, "The Japanese Economy, 1911–1930: Concentration, Conflicts, and Crises," in Bernard S. Silberman and H. D. Harootunian (eds.), *Japan in Crisis: Essays on Taisho Democracy* (Princeton: Princeton University Press, 1974), pp. 312–16, 319; William W. Lockwood, *The Economic Development of Japan: Growth and Structural Change, 1868–1938* (Princeton: Princeton University Press, 1954), p. 516.

sional ethic and culture shared by bankers all over the world. Consider, for example, Matsukata Masayoshi, appointed minister of finance in October 1881. Matsukata first put modern Japan's financial affairs in order, overseeing the establishment of the Bank of Japan and the creation of silver convertible notes. In his memorandum of March 1, 1882, which outlined the need for a central bank, he wrote that for the domestic economy, "there is nothing of greater importance" than a "sound financial policy." He also argued that "the most urgent financial measure to be taken is to relieve the country of the evils of an inconvertible currency."[3]

Matsukata achieved all of the goals he set for national policy, bringing stability to public and private finance in Japan by eliminating inflation, balancing the budget, and successfully defending the silver parity rate of the currency. But this came at a price, known as the Matsukata deflation, during which the fall in wages, commodity prices, and land values was accompanied by increased farm foreclosures, growing urban bankruptcies, and reduced national economic growth. Indeed, these policies caused "severe depression in some sectors of the economy."[4] Such measures did, however, represent the interests of the financial community, which in the last twenty years of the century had formed powerful organizations to advocate its policy preferences.[5]

THE 1920s: INTERNATIONALISM, PARTY GOVERNMENT, AND FINANCIAL RESTORATION

The 1920s represented the height of the influence both of political parties and financial circles in Japan. With regard to political economy, the main project of the decade was financial restoration, that is, the reestablishment

[3] Hiroshi Shinjo, *History of Yen: 100 Years of Japanese Money-Economy* (Tokyo: Kinokuniya Bookstore, 1962), p. 41 (first quote); Tamaki Norio, *Japanese Banking: A History, 1859–1959* (Cambridge: Cambridge University Press, 1995), p. 58 (second quote). Matsukata's policies were "classical in their orthodoxy"; Hugh T. Patrick, "External Equilibrium and Internal Convertibility: Financial Policy in Meiji Japan," *Journal of Economic History* 25:2 (June 1965), p. 198. Although Matsukata's monetary theory was orthodox, his overall economic vision was more nationalist; see Eric Helleiner, *The Making of National Money* (Ithaca: Cornell University Press, 2002), pp. 86–87.

[4] On the Matsukata deflation, see Raymond W. Goldsmith, *The Financial Development of Japan, 1868–1977* (New Haven: Yale University Press, 1983), esp. pp. 27–28; Tamaki, *Japanese Banking* ("severe depression"), p. 69; Patrick, "External Equilibrium," pp. 199–200.

[5] In 1880 there were already "bank assemblies" representing financial interests in Osaka and Tokyo; by 1900 they appeared in Yokohama, Kobe, and Nagoya. William Miles Fletcher III, *The Japanese Business Community and National Trade Policy, 1920–1942* (Chapel Hill: University of North Carolina Press, 1989), p. 17.

of the gold standard. The financial community, of course, favored a return to gold, but the goal of restoration was widely popular in Japan for a number of reasons, including international prestige. In the words of one scholar, the adoption of the gold standard in 1897 was seen as marking "Japan's appearance on the world stage."[6]

While the gold standard had wide support in principle, there was considerable debate over when to lift the embargo against gold exports, the measure that would reestablish the convertibility of the yen into gold.[7] Japan ultimately tacked toward restoration, navigating through variable political and stormy economic winds. Regarding the former, political power in Japan passed back and forth between two major parties, of which only one was committed to early restoration. The resulting stop-and-go pattern of economic policy was amplified by a series of economic crises that buffeted Japan in the 1920s and interrupted the normal course of economic policy, requiring the introduction of emergency measures. But the gold standard was restored by the end of the decade, and the period, viewed as a whole, was marked by financial prudence. Total government expenditures increased from ¥1.4 billion in 1920 to ¥1.6 billion in 1930, a very modest absolute increase that represented a large decline in terms of percentage of national product.[8]

The Japanese Political Economy after World War I

World War I treated Japan quite well. Allied with the winning side but a virtual noncombatant, Japan's economy thrived. Industrial production increased dramatically as allied governments demanded munitions, while neutral states turned to Japan for goods that they once purchased from the combatants. With this relief from pressures on the balance of trade that traditionally plagued the economy, Japan was also able to play the role of creditor, extending loans to Britain, France, and Russia. Japan's economic robustness during the war was illustrated by its retention of the gold standard longer than any other state, leaving finally on September 2, 1917, two days after the U.S. departure. In retrospect, however, although real GNP rose almost by 40 percent from 1914 to 1919,

---

[6] Tamaki, *Japanese Banking*, p. 85. To stay on the gold standard, the Bank of Japan maintained relatively high interest rates from 1897 to 1911 (p. 92).

[7] Fletcher, *Japanese Business Community*, pp. 27, 54–57; Masato Shizume, "Economic Developments and Monetary Responses in Interwar Japan: Evaluation Based on the Taylor Rule," Institute for Monetary and Economic Studies, Discussion Paper 2002-E-7 (Bank of Japan, July 2002), pp. 7, 11.

[8] Jerome B. Cohen, *Japan's Economy in War and Reconstruction* (Minneapolis: University of Minnesota Press, 1949), p. 4; G. C. Allen, *Japanese Industry: Its Recent Development and Present Condition* (New York: Institute of Pacific Relations, 1939), pp. 86–87.

clouds were visible on the horizon. Wartime inflation surged in the last few years of the conflict, and the Japanese financial system rested on fragile foundations.[9]

Such concerns were less obvious at the time; the wartime boom created a financial cushion for Japan, and the country was able to enjoy relatively easy monetary policy during the war, with little apparent consequence. But with the end of the war and its attendant set of extraordinary economic circumstances, Japan's position deteriorated, with renewed pressure on trade and payments. Monetary policies were reversed and interest rates raised, but this did not prevent the arrival of the first postwar economic crisis, precipitated by Black Monday on March 15, 1920, when Japan's securities and commodities markets collapsed.[10]

Despite remarkable growth during the war, then, the postwar economy was widely perceived to be in disarray, although opinions differed as to how best to restore order. This coincided with the emergence of the first of the "true party cabinets" in 1918. For the next fifteen years competitive party politics would characterize Japanese national governance, and two parties dominated that process, the Seiyukai and the Kenseikai. (The smaller Kenseikai would eventually merge with a number of other parties to form the Minseito.) The parties represented different core constituencies, but they shared, at least, an investment in the democratic process; both parties had to finesse relationships with formidable antidemocratic forces in the bureaucracy and the military. The Seiyukai, whose origins and traditional power base were in rural and agricultural districts, preferred a policy of government spending on public works projects such as railways in order to enhance national economic strength. The Kenseikai, on the other hand, reflected more closely the preferences of the financial community, favoring reduced government spending, tax reductions, and balanced budgets. From this perspective, economic strength would result from putting Japan's financial house in order.[11]

[9] Victor S. Clark, "Prices and Currency in Japan," *Quarterly Journal of Economics* 34:3 (May 1920), pp. 432, 436; G. C. Allen, "The Recent Currency and Exchange Policy of Japan," *The Economic Journal* 35:137 (March 1925), pp. 72–75; Kozo Yamamura, "Then Came the Great Depression: Japan's Interwar Years," in Herman van der Wee (ed.), *The Great Depression Revisited: Essays on the Economics of the Thirties* (The Hague: Nijhoff, 1972), p. 183; Lockwood, *Economic Development of Japan*, p. 38; Shinjo, *History of Yen*, p. 106.

[10] Nakamura Takafusa, *Economic Growth in Prewar Japan* (New Haven: Yale University Press, 1983), p. 35; Lockwood, *Economic Development of Japan*, p. 258; Goldsmith, *Financial Development of Japan*, p. 82; Tamaki, *Japanese Banking*, p. 140.

[11] Robert Karl Reischauer, *Japan: Government—Politics* (New York: Thomas Nelson and Sons, 1939), p. 103; Peter Duus, *Party Rivalry and Political Change in Taisho Japan* (Cambridge, MA: Harvard University Press, 1968), pp. 4, 147; Taichiro Mitani, "The Establishment of the Party Cabinets, 1889–1932" (trans. Peter Duus), in Peter Duus (ed.), *The*

Parties, Politics, and Economic Crises

The effects of Black Monday did not chase the ruling Seiyukai from power, and in fact the party won an impressive victory in the elections of May 1920. Thus, despite the fact that many in the banking community, such as Inoue Junnosuke, then head of the Bank of Japan, called for austerity measures and an early return to the gold standard, the Seiyukai policy of a relatively modest "positive" economic policy was sustained into the start of the 1920s. But disappointing economic performance, highlighted by persistent balance-of-payments problems and external specie drain, continued.[12] The government endured until internal political conflict contributed to the resignation of the cabinet in June 1922.

The five-year rule of the Seiyukai was followed by several years of nonparty and coalition cabinets. The Bank of Japan and the Finance Ministry still pressed for an early restoration of the gold standard, and in September 1922 the finance minister announced that the deflationary policies required to provide the foundation for such a move would be continued. But both November and December of that year were punctuated by banking panics and general business unrest, forcing a reversal of the deflationary policies.[13] Renewed movement toward financial retrenchment in 1923 was also reversed by the consequences of the great Kanto earthquake of September of that year. The devastating earthquake destroyed much of central Tokyo, killing more than one hundred thousand people and destroying over half a million buildings. This not only dealt a major blow to the real economy but heightened demand for imports and government spending to support reconstruction, which did not represent the path to restoration in the short run. On the contrary, the expansion of credit via emergency "earthquake bills" contributed further to the underlying weakness in the financial system.[14]

Cambridge History of Japan, vol. 6, *The Twentieth Century* (Cambridge: Cambridge University Press, 1988), pp. 59, 61; Gordon M. Berger, "Politics and Mobilization in Japan, 1931–1945," also in Duus (ed.), *Cambridge History of Japan*, vol. 6, pp. 98–99, 101. Hiroshi Shinjo, "History of Yen—Its Developments in the Japanese Economy (2)," *Kobe Economic and Business Review* 6 (1959), p. 5.

[12] W. Miles Fletcher, "Japanese Banks and National Economic Policy, 1920–1936," in Harold James, Hakan Lindgren, and Alice Teichova (eds.), *The Role of Banks in the Interwar Economy* (Cambridge: Cambridge University Press, 1991), p. 253; Robert A. Scalapino, *Democracy and the Party Movement in Prewar Japan* (Berkeley: University of California Press, 1953), pp. 220, 281.

[13] Scalapino, *Democracy and Party Movement*, p. 223; Shinjo, *History of Yen*, pp. 108–9; Nakamura, *Economic Growth*, p. 153; Yamamura, "Great Depression," pp. 186–87.

[14] David L. Asher, "Convergence and Its Costs: The Failure of Japanese Economic Reform and the Breakdown of the Washington System, 1918–1932" (PhD diss., St. Anthony's College, Oxford University, 2002), pp. 170, 172, 174, 176, 182; Allen, "Recent Currency

For the following nine months, Japan was governed by a series of "transcendent" nonparty cabinets, until, in June 1924, a new coalition cabinet was formed, headed for the first time by a representative of the Kenseikai.[15] While both parties supported a return to the gold standard in principle, it was in 1924, with the arrival on the scene of the Kenseikai as a viable governing party (as opposed to the voice of dissent), that the differences between the parties became more consequential. This would contribute further to the stop-and-go pattern of economic policy in the next eight years. The Seiyukai continued to support a more activist spending policy, especially on railroads, harbors, roads, and bridges, which would benefit rural areas. The Kenseikai was more closely associated with urban financiers, who stressed balancing budgets and paying close attention to the balance of payments.[16]

The economic strategy of the Kenseikai was plainly stated by its finance minister, Hamaguchi Osachi (Yuko), who had gained prominence in 1920 with his repeated attacks on government spending and inflation. In an address he delivered in July 1924, Hamaguchi insisted it was of "vital importance that we carry out a retrenchment and readjustment of government finance." The basis for future economic development required that Japan "cultivate the excellent customs of self-denial and frugality."[17] In September the party produced a budget that would have cut ¥280 million, or 17 percent, from the previous year's budget. However, this proposal still had to survive both the cabinet and the house, where the Seiyukai remained influential. This, along with the opposition of powerful sectors of the bureaucracy (which faced the brunt of the spending cuts), pared the final reduction to ¥91 million, a still notable 6 percent of the budget.[18]

In July 1925, the coalition cabinet fell apart as its Seiyukai participants resigned. An all-Kenseikai cabinet was established, increasing the momentum for a return to the gold standard. Especially given Britain's return to gold just a few months earlier, expectations were that Japan would do the

---

and Exchange Policy," pp. 66, 80; Michael A. Barnhart, *Japan and the World Since 1868* (London: Arnold, 1995), p. 78; Shinjo, *History of Yen*, p. 113.

[15] Reischauer, *Japan*, pp. 103, 140; Mitani, "Establishment of the Party Cabinets," pp. 55–57.

[16] Nakamura Takafusa, *Lectures on Modern Japanese Economic History, 1926–1994* (Tokyo: LTCB International Library Foundation, 1994), pp. 27–28.

[17] Duus, *Party Rivalry and Political Change*, p. 194 (quotes), see also pp. 193, 188; Riccardo Faini and Gianni Toniolo, "Reconsidering Japanese Deflation during the 1920s," *Explorations in Economic History* 29 (1992), p. 122; Mark Metzler, "Woman's Place in Japan's Great Depression: Reflections on the Moral Economy of Deflation," *Journal of Japanese Studies* 30:2 (2004), pp. 324, 326.

[18] Duus, *Party Rivalry and Political Change*, pp. 195–96, 198; Scalapino, *Democracy and Party Movement*, p. 229.

same. However, once again, financial fragility undermined those efforts, with the emergence of yet another banking panic.[19] The government attempted to address the issue of the general financial soundness of the Japanese banking system with legislation that would force greater concentration in the industry. New regulations, such as higher capital requirements, would force smaller banks to either merge or go out of business. It was recognized that the ultimate return to the gold standard might well be accompanied by gold outflows at first, and this might add further to financial fragility in the short run. As a result, the Ministry of Finance saw little alternative to a wholesale housecleaning of the banking industry.[20]

But efforts to strengthen the banking system did not arrive in time to prevent a major banking panic in March 1927. The closing of the Watanabe Bank of Tokyo on the fifteenth incited runs on a number of other large banks. The underlying weaknesses in the banking system, traceable to both the great earthquake and the subsequent reconstruction boom, were revealed, and the entire financial structure of the country trembled. Only the imposition of a bank holiday and the generous infusion of liquidity by the Bank of Japan stabilized the situation. Before the dust settled, the Bank of Japan had lost almost half of its gold reserves, which fell from ¥800 to ¥425 million.[21]

The crisis contributed to the fall of the government in April 1927 and marked the end of three years of cabinets dominated by the Kenseikai Party, which was transformed into the Minseito Party.[22] The return of the Seiyukai and its "positive" economic policies saw an expansion of spending and the postponement of plans to return to the gold standard. But it did not lead to an improvement in domestic economic conditions, partly due to global economic factors. Two years later the dance partners changed hands again, and the Seiyukai cabinet resigned, returning the Minseito Party to power in July 1929. With Hamaguchi as prime minister, the party announced its intention to restore the gold standard, once and for all. The gold embargo was lifted in January of the following year, representing the culmination of the financial project that dominated the

---

[19] Yamamura, "Great Depression," pp. 189, 191; Scalapino, *Democracy and Party Movement*, p. 233; Shinjo, *History of Yen*, p. 115.

[20] Shiro Yabushita and Atasushi Inoue, "The Stability of the Japanese Banking System: A Historical Perspective," *Journal of the Japanese and International Economies* 7 (1993), pp. 388, 393–94; Nakamura, *Japanese Economic History*, pp. 31–32.

[21] Tamaki, *Japanese Banking*, p. 151; Asher, "Convergence and Its Costs," pp. 184, 189–90, 204–5; Yabushita and Inoue, "Japanese Banking System," pp. 396, 405; Nakamura, *Japanese Economic History*, pp. 33–34; Lockwood, *Economic Development of Japan*, pp. 43, 517; Fletcher, "Japanese Banks," p. 256; Cohen, *Japan's Economy*, p. 4.

[22] On the politics of the transformation of the Kenseikai into the Minseito, see Duus, *Party Rivalry and Political Change*, pp. 231–35.

political agenda of the 1920s. In the words of one scholar, "Normalcy, as the bankers defined it, had been restored."[23]

Distributional Conflict over Policy

The preceding discussion of Japan's serpentine path to financial stability runs the risk of oversimplifying some important domestic political conflicts that were taking place at the time. On the one hand, it is important to note that the two dominant parties agreed on much, including the overall goal of restoring the gold standard. They disagreed on tactics and timing, but each recognized the issue as the most important one of the decade. Neither one seriously considered altering the par rate, a tactic that would have sidestepped some of the important problems associated with going back on gold. Focusing solely on the policy changes that occurred as power oscillated between the parties also obscures other continuities in economic policy. The Bank of Japan, representing the traditional preferences of finance, raised interest rates successively after the war, holding the discount rate high and steady at 8 percent through both the postwar depression and the 1923 earthquake.[24]

On the other hand, there were profound political-economic divisions within Japanese society at this time, differences that were not obviously reflected in the overall performance of the economy. Focusing on macroeconomic aggregates almost always obscures fundamental political conflict, and this is particularly true for the Japanese case.[25] The fortunes of important sectors of the Japanese economy, such as finance and agriculture, as well as other important groups, such as the military, varied dramatically in the 1920s.

The Japanese economy expanded by more than one-third over the course of the decade. Such a rate of growth represents a good economic performance, both from a global historical perspective and compared with other nations at the time. Yet, Japan's economic performance during the period was considered dismal. This was partly due to the fact that growth had been and would be much higher in the preceding and following decades. But it was mostly because of the way that economic growth was distributed during the 1920s. Agriculture, in particular, suffered terri-

---

[23] Scalapino, *Democracy and Party Movement*, pp. 235, 287–88; Nakamura, *Japanese Economic History*, p. 35; Fletcher, "Japanese Banks," p. 257 (quote).

[24] Hugh T. Patrick, "The Economic Muddle of the 1920s," in James William Morley (ed.), *The Dilemmas of Growth in Prewar Japan* (Princeton: Princeton University Press, 1971), pp. 226, 232, 234; also Goldsmith, *Financial Development of Japan*, p. 82.

[25] For a discussion of how the analysis of aggregate economic data can obscure political analysis, see Jonathan Kirshner, "The Political Economy of Low Inflation," *Journal of Economic Surveys* 15:1 (2001), pp. 41–70.

bly during this time. In the second half of the decade, the real income of the average farmer fell by over 30 percent, a staggering decline. Since by 1930 agriculture still accounted for half of Japan's employment, for a very large segment of Japanese society, life was "hard and miserable."[26]

However, to focus on the agricultural sector alone is to tell only part of the story. Prices of agricultural products fell in absolute terms, but they also fell relative to the prices of other sectors' products. This deterioration in the terms of trade not only magnified the true nature of agricultural poverty but also serves as a reminder of the heterogeneous character of Japanese economic performance in the 1920s. If incomes were falling in the agricultural sector, which accounted for about one-sixth of the gross national product, then incomes must have been rising, on average, in the rest of the economy, at a rate even higher than the average national rate.

Rural depression, combined with industrial consolidation, contributed to the emergence in the 1920s of a "dual structure" in the economy, characterized by increasing disparities in both the scale of production and the distribution of wealth.[27] Developments in the financial sector were representative of the urban economic setting: strong economic performance and dramatic industrial concentration. The 1920s were good to high finance: the financial sector as a whole outperformed the real side of the economy, and the economic stresses of the decade, combined with aggressive legislation designed to force concentration in the industry, allowed the big banks to shed hundreds of competitors. More than half of the banks in Japan did not meet the new regulatory standards of the New Bank Act of 1927.[28]

These differential experiences further clarify the basis of some of the disputes between the political parties in the 1920s. Despite changing considerably over the years, the Seiyukai's political base remained agrarian. Thus, while the Minseito and its core constituents could advocate deflation in order to restore orthodoxy, this was, of course, not the logical preference for actors who were suffering a severe depression.[29]

While agriculture was an unintended victim of the quest to restore financial order, however, the military was an explicit target. The clash be-

[26] Nakamura, *Economic Growth*, p. 156; Lockwood, *Economic Development*, pp. 63, 465; Faini and Toniolo, "Reconsidering Japanese Deflation," pp. 127–28; Nakamura, *Japanese Economic History*, p. 12 (quote).

[27] Yamamura, "Concentration, Conflicts and Crises," pp. 300, 311, 328; Patrick, "Economic Muddle," pp. 215–17, 220; Nakamura, *Economic Growth*, pp. 13–14, 142, 227.

[28] Goldsmith, *Financial Development of Japan*, p. 77; Fletcher, "Japanese Banks," pp. 258, 260; Tamaki, *Japanese Banking*, pp. 155, 158; Nakamura, *Economic Growth*, p. 205.

[29] On the partisan consequences that resulted from differences in the parties' constituencies, see Scalapino, *Democracy and Party Movement*, pp. 277, 282; also Duus, *Party Rivalry and Political Change*, p. 219.

tween the armed forces and the financial elite was the starkest political confrontation of the era. Economic and foreign policies were intimately intertwined in Japan in the 1920s.[30] The conciliatory Shidehara diplomacy, named after the foreign minister of the Kenseikai and Minseito who dominated policy in 1924–27 and 1929–31, went hand in hand with the economic agenda of financial interests. Cooperation with the western powers allowed reduced military expenditures and thus balanced budgets; it also ensured access to international finance and foreign markets. Confrontation with the West would have the opposite effects.

The Finance Ministry was determined to balance the budget, and from its perspective, reducing military expenditures offered the best opportunity for savings. The ministry, which was one of Japan's most powerful from 1920 to 1936, recognized the link between reduced military spending and a return to the gold standard. With its position at the center of the budget process, it would remain the most important check on the influence of the military on foreign policy, resulting, in the words of one analyst, in "frequent and violent clashes between the military and the Finance Ministry over foreign and economic policies."[31]

In the 1920s, finance won these battles more often than not. As noted previously, government spending was held in check during this decade, rising only from ¥1.4 billion to ¥1.6 billion over the course of the twenties. This was accomplished largely at the expense of the military, whose share of those expenditures fell from 47.8 percent in 1920 to 28.4 percent in 1930. As early as January 1921, Hamaguchi, then a Kenseikai representative in the Diet, took to the floor to explicitly link Japan's participation in naval arms-reduction talks with the need to reduce the burdensome level of military spending at the time. In 1922 the Japan Trade Council called for cuts in military spending in order to curb overall government spending, and the most vocal advocates of early restoration of the gold standard were typically the loudest voices for reduced military spending as well. The Washington Naval Conference that commenced in November 1921 and led to the treaty of 1922 advanced that agenda.[32]

The early to mid-1920s represented the high point of liberal internationalism in Japanese foreign policy. Military spending had increased tre-

---

[30] The argument here emphasizes sectoral interest, not ideological conflict. For a discussion of the relationship between economic and foreign policy with an emphasis on the influence of liberal internationalism in Japan, see Kato Shuichi, "Taisho Democracy as the Pre-Stage for Japanese Militarism," in Silberman and Harootunian, *Japan in Crisis*, esp. p. 220.

[31] Yamamira Katsuro, "The Role of the Finance Ministry," in Dorothy Borg and Shumpei Okamoto (eds.), *Pearl Harbor as History: Japanese-American Relations, 1931–1941* (New York: Columbia University Press, 1973), pp. 287, 288 (quote).

[32] Sterling Tatsuji Takeuchi, *War and Diplomacy in the Japanese Empire* (Chicago: University of Chicago Press, 1935), p. 277; Fletcher, *Japanese Business Community*, pp. 33, 38–39; Cohen, *Japan's Economy*, p. 4. For more on the Washington Naval Conference, see

mendously during World War I; that successful experience was followed by the disastrous and protracted Siberian adventure that began as part of the allied intervention in the Russian civil war. Given pressures at the time for financial housecleaning, the military's huge budgets and unpopular Siberian escapade created a ripe political environment for defense cuts. This played into the hands of the financiers such as Bank of Japan governor Inoue Junnosuke. Inoue, along with like-minded international bankers such as Morgan chief executive Thomas Lamont and Benjamin Strong (the powerful governor of the Federal Reserve Bank of New York), saw in the naval arms-reduction talks a broader "Washington System" that would integrate Japan as a prominent hub in a larger, harmonious international financial order.[33]

With the ascension of the Kenseikai to power in 1924, the program of financial and thus military retrenchment took another step further. Over the strong objections of the military, additional spending cuts were enacted and the army was forced to dissolve four divisions. Pressure on the armed forces was relieved somewhat with the return to power of the Seiyukai in 1927, due to the party's closer ties to both agriculture and the military. But the return of the austerity-minded Minseito in 1929 did not bode well for the armed forces, especially after the party won the 1930 elections on a platform of "economy, disarmament, purification of politics, reform of China policy, and removal of the gold embargo."[34]

The interdependency between finance and politics in Japan in the 1920s meant that the military (as reflected in table 3.1), along with agriculture, were the big losers of the decade. It is not surprising that these two groups would come to view finance as their common foe. The military sought to cultivate support in the rural districts and recognized villages there as core elements of its political constituency. The army produced its own schemes for public works projects targeted to promote rural employment and publicly vilified the "decadent capitalist" as undermining traditional Japanese values. The crisis in agriculture served to promote radicalism in the armed

---

Ian Nish, *Japanese Foreign Policy in the Interwar Period* (Westport, CT: Praeger, 2002), pp. 33–43.

[33] Asher, "Convergence and Its Costs," pp. 117–18, 130, 132–34, 226, 234; Leonard A. Humphreys, *The Way of the Heavenly Sword: The Japanese Army in the 1920s* (Stanford: Stanford University Press, 1995), pp. 25, 44–45, 60–61; Shin'ichi Kitaoka, "The Army as a Bureaucracy: Japanese Militarism Revisited," *The Journal of Military History* 57:5 (October 1993), p. 76; Mitani, "Establishment of the Party Cabinets," p. 93.

[34] Michael A. Barnhart, *Japan Prepares for Total War: The Search for Economic Security, 1919–1941* (Ithaca: Cornell University Press, 1987), p. 25; Reischauer, *Japan*, pp. 103, 139; Scalapino, *Democracy and Party Movement*, pp. 229, 234–36, 237 (quote). In exchange for the massive personnel cuts, the army was able to extract the compromise that some of the savings would be earmarked for military modernization. See Kitaoka, "Army as Bureaucracy," p. 77 (and p. 78 on the 1929 cuts); see also Humphreys, *Heavenly Sword*, pp. 90, 92 (and p. 179 on the compromises of the 1920s more generally).

TABLE 3.1
Military Expenditures, 1920–30 (¥ million)

1920	940	1926	437
1921	842	1927	494
1922	693	1928	519
1923	530	1929	497
1924	487	1930	444
1925	448		

Source: Patrick, "The Economic Muddle," p. 249.

forces, especially among younger officers who had only recently left their homes in the farming villages. Not only did the army have a sensitivity to the plight of agriculture, it also had tangible concerns about the very health and morale of the conscripts who by necessity would form the basis of the national defense. The deepening of the depression at the dawn of the new decade only served to heighten these tensions.[35]

THE 1930s: TWO DEFEATS OF FINANCE

The restoration of the gold standard and, just as important, the introduction of policies associated with its restoration and required for its maintenance represented the triumph of financial interests in Japan. But the return to gold was fundamentally mistimed, coinciding with the deepening international depression. This served to further intensify the tension between finance and other sectors within the domestic political economy. The 1930s witnessed two dramatic expansions of Japanese military adventures. Each was associated with a major defeat for financial interests and the policy preferences that they held in place. By the end of the period, the military was in control of Japanese society, and financial influence was at its nadir.

The Restoration of Gold and Its Discontents

As mentioned earlier, the resignation of the Seiyukai cabinet led to the return of the Minseito to power in July 1929. Hamaguchi, as prime minis-

[35] R. P. Dore and Tsutomu Ouchi, "Rural Origins of Japanese Fascism," in Morley, *Dilemmas of Growth*, pp. 197, 203; Tsutomu Ouchi, "Agricultural Depression and Japanese Villages," *The Developing Economies* 5:4 (December 1967), pp. 618, 620; Humphreys, *Heavenly Sword*, pp. 98, 176; see also Richard J. Smethurst, *A Social Basis for Prewar Japanese Militarism: The Army and the Rural Community* (Berkeley: University of California Press, 1974), esp. pp. xxi–xxix, 69–76.

ter, presided over a party and a cabinet that had pledged themselves to a platform six months earlier calling for economic austerity, improving relations with China, multilateral arms control, and the restoration of the gold standard. Thus the return of the Minseito was accompanied by the return of Foreign Minister Shidehara and his internationalist diplomacy.[36]

The new finance minister was Inoue Junnosuke, one of the most influential figures in Japanese financial circles. Inoue had previously been the president of the Yokohama Specie Bank (1913–19), had served as the governor of the Bank of Japan (1919–23 and 1927–28), and had also served as finance minister (1923–24). Inoue was a strong proponent of a return to the gold standard. He was, however, under no illusion regarding the costs of such a move, which would require a painful contraction of economic activity. But, he added, short-term sacrifices to put the financial house in order were better than the alternative, "a recession whose end is completely unseen."[37] He wrote:

> So now you know my views and can appreciate the consequences, as I see them, of removing the embargo. It is not a cheerful picture—it may well be even less cheerful than you had expected—but the fact remains that the existence of the embargo is in itself irregular, anomalous, a financial monstrosity—you cannot get away from that. The existence of the embargo infringes on every canon of sound finance and is throwing the entire economic machinery of this country out of gear: come what may, it is the duty of the nation to spare no effort to get rid of it and return to the gold standard.[38]

Returning to gold required a "drastic retrenchment" of the economy in order to reduce prices, which was necessary to restore the yen to its prewar exchange rate. This would put an additional strain on many Japanese firms that were only marginally competitive in international markets. This, too, was understood by members of the financial community, who thought that a pruning of the weaker branches of Japanese industry would leave those robust firms that survived in a better position to expand Japan's exports. Inoue discarded the 1929 budget that had already been passed and produced a new budget, which "radically cut" government spending. He instructed the Bank of Japan to raise interest rates and even engaged in a speaking tour to urge reduced consumption and increased

---

[36] Nakamura, *Japanese Economic History*, p. 35; Metzler, "Moral Economy of Deflation," p. 326.

[37] Quoted in Fletcher, "Japanese Banks," p. 256. For a brief biographical sketch of Inoue, see Masataka Matsuura, "Analysing the Relationship between Business and Politics in Prewar Japan: Some Thoughts on the *Zaikai*" (Discussion Paper JS/00/381, Suntory Center, London School of Economics, February 2000), pp. 32–33.

[38] Junnoskue Inouye, *Problems of the Japanese Exchange, 1914–1926* (trans. E. H. de Bunsen) (Glasgow: Robert Maclehose, 1931), p. 153.

savings, part of a massive public relations campaign to promote "public and private retrenchment" that featured thousands of public lectures and the distribution of millions of pamphlets. With the strong support of the major banking organizations, Inoue lifted the gold embargo on January 1, 1930, paving the way with an engineered recession.[39]

The economic downturn that followed, however, was more severe than anticipated. The return to gold had the misfortune of coming on the heels of the crash of the New York stock market, which turned out to be a turning point in the deepening of the international depression rather than the transient phenomenon that Inoue assumed it would be. With the international slump came reduced export opportunities for Japanese products and a continued fall in agricultural prices. Broad sectors of the economy were negatively affected, once again with agriculture leading the way. Average household income fell like a stone: to ¥650 in 1931, from an already low ¥1,326 in 1929.[40]

But finance was unrepentant and unyielding, having waited so long for the chance to restore financial orthodoxy. Inoue stuck to his guns, maintaining currency convertibility and raising interest rates further, into the teeth of the depression. Government spending was cut yet again, settling at ¥1.477 billion in 1931, down from ¥1.815 billion in 1928. Inoue's policies were strongly supported in financial circles. Financiers retained the view, articulated by Sobun Yamamuro, the director of the Mitsubishi Bank, that "adjustment could not be achieved without great hardships; good medicine is bitter to the taste."[41]

Financial support for the gold standard was retained even after Britain closed its gold window in September 1931, which was quite a blow, since the European restorations of the twenties had helped nudge Japan back toward gold. In October and November, Inoue defended his policy both rhetorically and with two further interest rate hikes. This was accompanied in early November by public statements of support from members of the financial community. Even after Japan abandoned the gold standard (about which more later), Inoue and his allies did not give up the cause. Inoue made the issue the centerpiece of his campaign in the elections of

[39] Nakamura, *Japanese Economic History*, pp. 37 (quotes), 38, 40; Metzler, "Moral Economy of Deflation," pp. 332, 343; Fletcher, *Japanese Business Community*, pp. 53, 56, 60–61.

[40] G. C. Allen, "The Political and Economic Position of Japan," *International Affairs* 13:4 (July–August 1934), pp. 547–48; Nakamura, *Japanese Economic History*, pp. 38, 41; Yamamura, "Great Depression," p. 198.

[41] Sobun Yamamuro, "Economic Depression and the Gold Embargo," *Contemporary Japan* 1:1 (June 1932), p. 53; Shinjo, *History of Yen*, p. 119; Nakamura, *Japanese Economic History*, pp. 39, 49.

February 1932.[42] Mitsubishi Bank's Sobun Yamamuro also continued to offer a spirited defense, writing that devaluation and suspension of convertibility were permissible only in "extreme circumstances" and insisting "it is a fact that the financial situation of Japan was by no means critical prior to the recent suspension of the gold standard." Prompt restoration was essential, and until that time, "retrenchment must continue to be the watchword in public as well as private finance."[43]

Ultimately and, given international economic pressures, perhaps inevitably, Japan would be forced to cut the tie between the yen and gold. But more important, the efforts to sustain convertibility revealed that the divergence between the interests of finance and those of other important groups in Japanese society had reached a critical level. As one Seiyukai official commented,

> When I think quietly of the opinions of Prime Minister Hamaguchi or Finance Minister Inoue, it seems that they consult only the interest of big bankers or big businessmen and do not pay extensive and close attention to the benefit of the public.[44]

The most important source of dissent from financial orthodoxy came not from the public, however, but from the military, which once again had perceived its interests to have been sacrificed on the altar of high finance.

Strategy versus Finance at the London Conference and After

The "Ten Big Political Principles"—Hamaguchi's policy statement accompanying the return of the Minseito to power in 1929—has been correctly interpreted as a combination of the Shidehara diplomacy and Inoue's tight financial policy.[45] But this interrelationship was more than just an alliance of interests. The Shidehara diplomacy did not require financial orthodoxy; rather, from this perspective the two policies went harmoniously hand in hand. But financial orthodoxy *did require* the Shidehara diplomacy. The professed interests of finance could not be advanced without it. While there was some ideological support within Japan for liberal internationalism,[46] finance was the principal material interest supporting

---

[42] Fletcher, "Japanese Banks," pp. 262–63; Fletcher, *Japanese Business Community*, pp. 66–67, 69–70.

[43] Yamamuro, "Economic Depression and the Gold Embargo," pp. 58, 61; Yamamura, "Great Depression," pp. 199–200.

[44] Quoted in Chu Yukio, "From the Showa Economic Crisis to Military Economy: With Special Reference to the Inoue and Takahashi Financial Policies," *The Developing Economies* 5:4 (December 1967), p. 580.

[45] See, for example, Yukio, "From Showa Economic Crisis," p. 574.

[46] See Shuichi, "Taisho Democracy," p. 220.

this style of foreign policy. Reversing the Shidehara diplomacy thus required the defeat of finance.

This became increasingly clear in 1930, when disarmament issues returned to the center of the political stage. The Hamaguchi cabinet was strongly in favor of advancing arms control and reduction, along the lines established by the Washington Naval Treaty of 1922. It saw the further reduction of military expenditures as necessary both for its direct effect on sound finance (helping to balance the budget) and for the indirect effect of maintaining cooperative relations with the United States and Britain: continued access to the international financial system. This was seen as a prerequisite for establishing and maintaining the convertibility of the yen. For many military leaders, on the other hand, the Washington Naval Conference system represented the institutionalization of their political defeat within Japan, and they sought its abolition.[47]

The London conference was designed to revisit the naval armament issues addressed in the Washington treaty. Hamaguchi and Shidehara were strongly in favor of reaching a new arms accord, but the military opposed this. The arms reductions of the 1920s had not been forgotten. When the army lost four divisions in 1925 to the budget ax, for example, it saw the standing army reduced from 18 to 14 divisions, even though the army's own estimate was that 21 divisions were needed—and this itself represented a reduction from its earlier estimate of 25. If anything, the military was looking for a restoration of the spending that it had grown accustomed to before the emphasis on financial prudence became the touchstone of all fiscal policy.[48]

Despite the concerns of the military, the Minseito cabinet decided to participate in the London conference. Even the proponents of arms control, however, thought that Japan's share of world naval forces should be increased. The Washington Naval Treaty had set a tonnage ratio for the United States, Britain, and Japan at 5:5:3, respectively. It was agreed that Japan should insist on a revision of this ratio to 10:10:7, and these were the instructions that the Japanese representatives brought to the conference. However, the conference quickly deadlocked on this issue.[49] The

[47] Takashi Ito, "Conflicts and Coalitions in Japan, 1930: Political Groups and the London Naval Disarmament Conference," in Sven Groenings, E. W. Kelley, and Michael Leiserson (eds.), The Study of Coalition Behavior (New York: Holt, Rinehart and Winston, 1970), p. 168; Nish, Japanese Foreign Policy, p. 47; Yamamura, "Concentration, Conflicts and Crises," pp. 290–91.

[48] James B. Crowley, Japan's Quest for Autonomy: National Security and Foreign Policy, 1930–1938 (Princeton: Princeton University Press, 1966), p. 87; Berger, "Politics and Mobilization," pp. 102, 105.

[49] One reason why the London conference was called was to apply arms control to an additional class of warships, heavy cruisers. The Washington Naval Treaty had focused on battleships. On the London conference, see Takeuchi, War and Diplomacy, esp. chapter 25.

conference appeared to be headed toward an unsuccessful resolution when an American and a Japanese delegate reached the Reed-Matsudaira compromise. Under this agreement, the treaty would not stipulate the 10:7 ratio (rather, the language of the treaty suggested a ratio of 10:6.975), but the Americans would modulate their cruiser production so that only in 1938, with the construction of the final ship allowed under the treaty, would that ratio be exceeded. Thus Japan would enjoy a de-facto 10:7 ratio until that time, and it was expected that a new round of naval arms-control talks would occur as early as 1935 and result in a new agreement that would supersede the London pact and become effective well before 1938, when the 10:7 ratio would be violated.[50]

The proposed Reed-Matsudaira compromise set off a heated political debate in Japan. The 10:7 principle had attracted broad popular support. The navy was strongly opposed to the compromise, and the opposition Seiyukai Party, with its traditional ties to the military and sensing a political opportunity, also took up the cause against the treaty. But Foreign Minister Shidehara argued that the treaty was necessary, given the importance of international cooperation and the need for the government to reduce military expenditures. Since, in the words of one analyst, the Hamaguchi cabinet "represented most faithfully the interests of the finance capitalists," it "sought to bring about naval disarmament even at the cost of making a concession to America's demands."[51] After considerable political turmoil, the government was able to force passage of the treaty. But it did so over the unanimous objections of the navy general staff, and a military establishment that held the opinion that national security had been compromised for the sake of balanced budgets and adherence to the gold standard, that is, sacrificed to financial orthodoxy.[52]

The passage of the treaty marked the final breaking point in the tensions between the military and finance. In 1930 Hamaguchi presented a balanced budget that further cut military spending. On October 2, 1930, the London Naval Treaty was ratified. On November 14 Hamaguchi was shot by a rightist supporter of the military, who was agitated by the London treaty and the hardships visited by the depression. The prime minister would live with his wounds until April of the following year, but he was forced to resign in favor of Wakatsuki Reijiro. Changing the man did not change the party, and in 1931 the Finance Ministry announced plans for

[50] Crowley, *Japan's Quest for Autonomy*, p. 64; Nish, *Japanese Foreign Policy*, p. 68.

[51] Crowley, *Japan's Quest for Autonomy*, pp. 57, 62, 64, 80; Takeuchi, *War and Diplomacy*, p. 333; Shinobu Seizaburo, "From Party Politics to Military Dictatorship," *The Developing Economies* 5:4 (December 1967), p. 672 (quote).

[52] Nish, *Japanese Foreign Policy*, pp. 68–69; Patrick, "Economic Muddle," p. 263; Ito, "Conflicts and Coalitions," p. 174; Shuichi, "Taisho Democracy," p. 233.

additional reductions in the military budget, proposing cuts of ¥15 million for the army and ¥13 million for the navy.[53]

The army had seen enough. On September 18, 1931, it precipitated the Mukden Incident, in which Japanese agents sabotaged the South Manchurian railway and blamed Chinese forces. This event was used as a pretext to expand Japan's military operations in China. With troops fanning out in the field, the army then demanded the funds to support them. As one analyst noted, "A government less devoted to sound finance and less determined to have it . . . might have looked with favour on adventures in China." But this government was so devoted, and protests came from its ministers, including Shidehara, who was concerned for the international implications, and Inoue, who thought such adventures a waste of money that would threaten financial stability. But the military was not asking for permission, and it pressed ahead with its expansion of the Manchurian conflict.[54]

Close on the heels of Mukden came the October Incident, a coup planned by midlevel army officers who hoped to eliminate the political barriers to further expansion of the Manchurian conflict. Although this plot was thwarted, it served to further heighten domestic political tension. Prime Minister Wakatsuki, searching for a way out of the crisis, proposed the formation of a coalition cabinet with the opposition Seiyukai. But Inoue and Shidehara were strongly opposed, arguing that the government should not waver from the trajectory of its traditional policies. Wakatsuki then retreated, alienating those who had come to favor a shift to coalition government. The confusion led to the collapse of the cabinet and the resignation of its ministers on December 10, 1931. The Minseito government that had restored financial orthodoxy to Japan was removed from power.[55]

The First Defeat of Finance and the Takahashi Recovery

With the collapse of the Minseito government, the Seiyukai formed a new cabinet under the leadership of Inukai Tsuyoshi, and in February 1932

---

[53] Stephen S. Large, "Nationalist Extremism in Early Showa Japan: Inoue Nissho and the Blood-Pledge Corps Incident, 1932," *Modern Asia Studies* 35:3 (2001), pp. 547–58; Nish, *Japanese Foreign Policy*, p. 70; A. Morgan Young, *Imperial Japan, 1926–1938* (Westport, CT: Greenwood Press, 1974 [1938]), pp. 59, 72.

[54] Young, *Imperial Japan*, pp. 77 (quote), 84; Crowley, *Japan's Quest for Autonomy*, p. 82; see also p. 251; Nish, *Japanese Foreign Policy*, pp. 74–76. Kupchan argues that the London treaty "set the stage" for the Mukden Incident, an effort by the military to assert its autonomy in the wake of its defeat over the agreement. *Vulnerability of Empire*, p. 306; see also Allen, "Political and Economic Position," p. 349.

[55] Humphreys, *Heavenly Sword*, pp. 123, 137, 179; Nakamura, *Japanese Economic Growth*, p. 49.

the public endorsed the new government by handing the Seiyukai a resounding victory at the polls. The reversal of Minseito policies, on the other hand, took place on the very first day, as Inukai appointed the venerable Takahashi Korekiyo to be his finance minister. Takahashi had been a leading figure in the party for two decades, serving repeatedly as finance minister in numerous Seiyukai cabinets; he also served for eight months as prime minister in the early 1920s. (Oddly enough, Takahashi had been a mentor to and patron of Inoue, and although their economic philosophies diverged sharply, the two men remained friendly.) As his first act, Takahashi banned the export of gold and suspended the convertibility of the yen.[56]

This, however, was but Takahashi's first measure, for the worldly finance minister, who had spent some time in the United States, had lost a fortune chasing silver in Peru, and had raised money for his country in London during the Russo-Japanese War, was arguably a proto-Keynesian. He was not only familiar with some of Keynes's writings but had himself written, quite early on, about the concept of the multiplier. Takahashi did not simply intend to take Japan off the gold standard; he intended to break completely with economic orthodoxy and introduce new policies designed to lift the economy out of the depression.[57]

[56] Nakamura, *Japanese Economic Growth*, pp. 49–50; Asher, "Convergence and Its Costs," pp. 225, 278–79. On Takahashi, see Ippei Fukuda, "Korekiyo Takahashi: Japan's Sage of Finance," *Contemporary Japan* 1:4 (March 1933); Richard J. Smethurst, "The Self-Taught Bureaucrat: Takahashi Korekiyo and Economic Policy during the Great Depression," in John Singleton (ed.), *Learning in Likely Places: Varieties of Apprenticeship in Japan* (Cambridge: Cambridge University Press, 1998), pp. 228–32; Richard J. Smethurst, "Takahashi Korekiyo's Economic Policies in the Great Depression and Their Meiji Roots" (Discussion Paper JS/00/381, Suntory Center, London School of Economics, February 2000), pp. 2–3. Asher offers a somewhat more negative assessment of Takahashi than most other accounts, taking him to task for failing to contain dangerous asset bubbles as finance minister in the early 1920s and painting him as more of an economic nationalist ("Convergence and Its Costs," pp. 164–68, 229, 231).

[57] There is a modest debate over whether and to what extent Takahashi could have been influenced by Keynes. On the one hand Takahashi was clearly familiar with and influenced by Keynes's writings on monetary affairs and his opposition to Britain's return to the gold standard at prewar parity. On the other hand, Takahashi's discussion of the multiplier does predate the publication of Kahn's influential paper on that subject (R. F. Kahn, "The Relation of Home Investment to Unemployment," *The Economic Journal* 41:162 [June 1931], pp. 173–98), as well as Keynes's most famous writings from the early and mid-1930s (for the relevant Keynes sources, see Jonathan Kirshner, "Keynes, Capital Mobility, and the Crisis of Embedded Liberalism," *Review of International Political Economy* 6:3 [Autumn 1999], pp. 313–37). On Keynes and Takahashi, see Dick K. Nanto and Shinji Takagi, "Korekiyo Takahashi and Japan's Recovery from the Great Depression," *American Economic Review* 72:2 (May 1985), pp. 372–73; Eleanor M. Hadley, "The Diffusion of Keynesian Ideas in Japan," in Peter A. Hall (ed.), *The Political Power of Economic Ideas: Keynesianism across Nations* (Princeton: Princeton University Press, 1989), esp. pp. 292–96; Smethurst,

This would involve a fundamental reversal of the Hamaguchi-Inoue economic project. Takahashi not only ended the gold standard but encouraged the devaluation of the yen. Government spending was increased, and much of this was deficit spending, financed by bonds underwritten by the Bank of Japan. The statutory note limit for the Bank of Japan, which had been fixed at ¥120 million in 1897, was raised to ¥1 billion. Interest rates were lowered, and loans extended to agricultural villages. All of these policies stimulated capital flight, and the government responded first with the Capital Flight Prevention Act in June 1932 and subsequently with the Foreign Exchange Control Act of March 1933. The latter measure placed the foreign exchange market firmly under the control of the Finance Ministry, further reducing constraints on its policies regarding the note issue and interest rate policy.[58]

Each of these measures represented a direct blow to financial interests. As described in chapter 1, and seen clearly in the preferences expressed by Japanese bankers and the Inoue policies, financiers desire balanced budgets, high interest rates, high and stable exchange rates, and unfettered intercourse with international financial markets. Each of these was jettisoned by the Takahashi program. Many of these changes are illustrated in table 3.2.

The Takahashi program was remarkably successful, and the Japanese economy emerged quickly from the depression, with the gross national product growing at over 4 percent annually from 1932 through 1936. All sectors of the economy enjoyed the benefits of the recovery, but the big winners were manufacturing interests, especially in the heavy and chemical-related industries. Conditions improved in the agricultural sector as well, especially with regard to production, though in general the rate of increase in consumption still lagged behind the pace of economic expansion.[59]

The politics of government spending also reversed those of the preceding era. The main increases in government spending from Takahashi's budget came in the form of defense spending and special expenditures for

"Takahashi Korekiyo's Economic Policies," pp. 4, 6; Metzler, "Moral Economy of Deflation," pp. 339–40.

[58] N. Skene Smith, "Some Observations on the Last Eighteen Months in Japan," *Economic Journal* 43: 170 (June 1933), pp. 260–62; Yukio, "From Showa Economic Crisis," pp. 581, 588; Shinjo, *History of Yen*, pp. 120, 124; Young, *Imperial Japan*, p. 184; Tamaki, *Japanese Banking*, pp. 166–67; Nakamura, *Japanese Economic History*, pp. 58–59.

[59] Myung Soo Cha, "Did Takahashi Korekiyo Rescue Japan from the Great Depression?" *Journal of Economic History* 63:1 (March 2003), pp. 128, 136; Goldsmith, *Financial Development of Japan*, pp. 107–8. The Japanese recovery fits the pattern that follows Eichengreen's argument regarding the gold standard, the introduction of expansionary measures, and recovery. See Barry Eichengreen, *Golden Fetters: The Gold Standard and the Great Depression, 1919–1939* (New York: Oxford University Press, 1992).

TABLE 3.2
The Takahashi Reversal

	Gov. spending	New gov. bonds	Interest rates	$/¥
1930	1,588	110	5.1	.49375
1931	1,477	210	6.6	.49375
1932	1,950	830	4.4	.37000
1933	2,255	880	3.7	.31250
1934	2,163	870	3.7	.30375
1935	2,206	790	3.3	.29125
1936	2,287	720	3.3	.29500

Sources: Nakamura, *Economic Growth*, pp. 237, 242; Nakamura, *Modern Japanese History*, p. 60; Shinjo, *History of the Yen*, p. 118. Denominations are in ¥ million. Interest rates are Bank of Japan year-end discount rate on commercial bills; the exchange rate is the year's highest rate.

farm relief. These represented the cornerstones of the new policies. No sector of the economy saw faster expansion than the military, and much of the unbacked note expansion was necessary to support military operations on the Asian mainland. Emergency rural relief, introduced as a new item in the budget, represented an explicit shift in government policy from an emphasis on urban areas to rural ones (at least for the first few years) and was of both practical and symbolic significance.[60]

The financial community was not untouched by the new prosperity. But its members continued to harbor grave reservations about the Takahashi program. Deficits expanded, interest rates fell, and inflation crept upward, though modestly at first. It was difficult to argue against success, however, and the voices of opposition were muted as the economy expanded,[61] but they were not silenced. Despite the performance of the economy, financiers maintained the view that the policies that had engineered the recovery would ultimately prove disastrous, given sustained unbalanced budgets and permissiveness regarding inflation.[62] Moving into the middle of the

[60] Nakamura, *Economic Growth*, pp. 236–37; Young, *Imperial Japan*, p. 177; Nanto and Takagi, "Korekiyo Takahashi and Japan's Recovery," pp. 370–72.

[61] Fletcher, "Japanese Banks," pp. 263–65; Nakamura, *Japanese Economic History*, pp. 60–61.

[62] On these concerns and the reactions of finance in general, see, for example, Aiichi Nishinoiri, "The Budgetary Dilemma," *Contemporary Japan* 2:3 (December 1933), esp. p. 436; and Shigeyoshi Hijikata, "The 1935–6 Budget and After," *Contemporary Japan* 3:4 (March 1935), esp. p. 551.

decade, their concerns, both political and economic, seemed increasingly justified. The national debt doubled, reaching ¥13 billion, or almost two-thirds of national income in 1937. That increase was facilitated by further increases in the unbacked note issue, which was expanded from ¥1.4 billion to ¥2.3 billion over the same period. Banks saw their autonomy slip away, as artificially low interest rates, which eased the burden of government debts, no longer reflected the market interplay between supply and demand. The Bank of Japan and the commercial banking system, churches of the low-inflation faith, became at the same time the conduits of government-induced inflation. As one study concluded, "the banks increasingly lost the possibility of determining their own lending or liquidity policies and became executors of government instructions."[63]

This defeat of finance took place in an increasingly explosive domestic political setting. The tensions of the 1920s within Japanese society had been strained to the breaking point by the end of the decade, as seen in the 1930 assassination of Hamaguchi. These stresses would not be relieved by a simple transfer of power between political parties, because the cleavages ran deep. While the military, for example, would prefer the Seiyukai to the Minseito, for the armed forces the parties were more clearly defined by their similarities as a type of political entity than they were by their particular policy differences. For many, party government and indeed ascendant capitalism itself were departures from traditional Japanese society.[64]

Japanese politics became increasingly radicalized in this era. During the election campaign of February 1932, Inoue, campaigning for a return to the gold standard, was assassinated by a young militant—who, like many of his associates, was an urban refugee from the rural depression. Inoue had understood the risks. According to Takahashi, as Inoue returned to the Finance Ministry in 1929, he urged confidants, "If I am assassinated, immediately carry out the lifting of the gold embargo." As William Lockwood has argued, he "paid with his life not so much for the damaging economic consequences of deflation as for his courageous opposition to Army expansionism on the continent," but clearly the latter was a necessary consequence of the former. The divisions reflected by these contrasting constellations of policy preferences were profound. Indeed, Inoue's assassins at one point planned to kill twenty of Japan's political and financial leaders, figures such as Ikeda Seihin, head of the Mitsui Bank. Ikeda, who had served as finance minister and would become governor of the Bank of Japan, opposed the China war and sought international cooperation to

---

[63] Tamaki, *Japanese Banking*, p. 169; Allen, *Japanese Industry*, p. 91; Goldsmith, *Financial Development of Japan*, pp. 114, 118 (quote).

[64] Mitani, "Establishment of Party Cabinets," pp. 95–96; Berger, "Politics and Mobilization," pp. 107–9, 114–15.

resolve the conflict. Though deeply shaken by the plot against him (and increasingly cautious in its wake), Ikeda ultimately escaped attack. Others were less fortunate. On March 5 Dan Takuma, the liberal internationalist director general of Mitsui, was gunned down outside the entrance of the Mitsui Bank. Finally, on May 15, 1932, Prime Minister Inukai himself was assassinated by a group of young military officers.[65]

The attack on the Seiyukai prime minister serves as a reminder that the young officers saw themselves at war with the entire civilian political elite in Japan, not any political party. The assassins cited the ratification of the London Naval Treaty as the principal impetus to their action. Ten days after the murder of Inukai, the cabinet resigned and the era of party government came to an end. But civilian officials serving in military-led cabinets still retained considerable influence over the next five years.[66]

Among the most powerful of these ministers was Takahashi, who directed the course of Japanese finance until 1936. At first, the armed forces were quite pleased with his policies, which is not surprising, as military spending more than doubled under his guidance in the first half of the 1930s. But as the economy approached full employment, Takahashi and his closest adviser, Bank of Japan governor Fukai Eigo, became cautious about pressing ahead with additional expansionist policies. In July 1935 Takahashi warned of the dangers of "evil inflation," and, with the endorsement of financial leaders ringing in his ears, he proposed reductions in government spending and bond issues.[67] Financial prudence had found a new champion. And regardless of whether it was under the guidance of the dogmatic Inoue or the pragmatic Takahashi, the constraints of walking down the path of orthodoxy remained the same.

The Second Defeat of Finance

Takahashi had engineered and introduced the policies that represented the defeat of financial interests in Japan. But once in office, he who had slain the financial dragon would ultimately come to represent its interests.

---

[65] Asher, "Convergence and Its Costs," p. 274 (quote); Lockwood, *Economic Development of Japan*, p. 64 (quote); Matsuura, "Analysing the Relationship between Business and Politics," pp. 35, 37, 39; Metzler, "Moral Economy of Deflation," pp. 327–28; Large, "Nationalist Extremism," pp. 533, 552–53, 555.

[66] Ben-Ami Shillony, *Revolt in Japan: The Young Officers and the February 26, 1936 Incident* (Princeton: Princeton University Press, 1973), pp. 3, 7, 11; Scalapino, *Democracy and Party Movement*, p. 243; Reischauer, *Japan*, p. 157; Berger, "Politics and Mobilization," pp. 116–17; Nish, *Japanese Foreign Policy*, pp. 82–83.

[67] Fletcher, "Japanese Banks," p. 265 (quote); Nakamura, *Japanese Economic History*, p. 62; Nishinoiri, "Budgetary Dilemma," p. 436; Nanto and Takagi, "Korekiyo Takahashi and Japan's Recovery," p. 373.

TABLE 3.3
Military Expenditures, 1930–39 (¥ million)

1930	444	1935	1,043
1931	462	1936	1,089
1932	705	1937	3,299
1933	886	1938	5,984
1934	953	1939	6,495

Source: Patrick, "Economic Muddle," p. 249.

Given the structural power of the Finance Ministry, the diminished influence of other civilian politicians and institutions in general, and the enormous respect that he commanded throughout Japanese society, Takahashi became "the representative of the financial world in the Government," who was "able to exercise some control over the militarist activities."[68] This became a problem for the armed forces relatively quickly, since, as mentioned previously, Takahashi was a proto-Keynesian pragmatist, not an unlimited expansionist. Once the economy approached capacity, he became increasingly wary of unbalanced budgets and concerned that additional pump priming would be expressed in inflation, not increased output. What ultimately distinguished Takahashi from others in the financial community was not a disinterest in the establishment of sound finance. Rather, it was his view that a robust economy would allow for financial orthodoxy, and not vice versa, as finance had been preaching.[69]

As seen in table 3.2, Takahashi's revolutionary increases in government spending leveled off under his guidance by the end of 1933. Military spending (as seen in table 3.3) continued to increase, but at a slower rate, and finally leveled off in his last two years at the helm, 1935 and 1936. Takahashi, the proto-Keynesian, had pushed government spending (and other policies) as a means to lift Japan's economy out of depression. Given the political realities of the 1930s, military spending offered the path of least resistance to this goal. However, as the economy approached, in his estimation, full employment, Takahashi, the finance minister, became much more cautious, sensitive to the risk of inflation and overheating of the economy. At this point, putting the brakes on military spending came easily—having spent his life in finance, Takahashi had never

---

[68] Reischauer, *Japan*, p. 172 (quotes); Allen, *Japanese Industry*, p. 98.

[69] Yosahio Kamii, "Industrial Recovery in Japan: Its Causes and Social Effects," *International Labour Review* 35:1 (January 1937), p. 36; Kamekichi Takahashi, "The Fiscal Policy of Finance Minister, Dr. Baba," *Contemporary Japan* 5:1 (June 1936), p. 25.

been much of a fan of the military and was even less enchanted with military adventurism.[70]

Military spending would have increased even more slowly had Takahashi won all of his political battles. But while the finance minister increasingly clashed with the armed forces, neither side was satisfied with the outcome. The Finance Ministry became the only important source of resistance to the military in Japan, wrestling over both the 1933 and the 1934 budget.[71] In 1934, when the Saito government resigned, the army made it clear that it would support for prime minister only a candidate who would not retain Takahashi as finance minister in the new cabinet. Takahashi was thus not included in the original Okada cabinet, but the robust octogenarian returned to head the ministry when the younger man who replaced him fell ill and died within four months.[72]

Clashes between the military and Takahashi intensified and were regularly reported in the press. In 1934 the Finance Ministry resisted army plans to enhance the government's power to direct economic activity within Japan.[73] In 1935 and 1936 the battle to control military spending came to a head. On July 31, 1935, Takahashi argued that increased military spending would lead only to a fruitless arms race. On November 26 he stated that greater defense spending would lead to costly inflation. The following day, responding to the army's call for more arms, he responded:

[70] Takahashi nursed ambitions that Japan would be recognized as a great power, but throughout his career he was wary of the armed forces and of "excessive" military spending. In 1913, as finance minister, he fought the army's plan to create two new divisions; in 1915 he opposed the "21 demands" imposed on China; indeed, over the years he consistently broke with his own party (the Seiyukai) on China policy and was strongly opposed to adventurism on the continent. Takahashi had been a consistent critic of military spending, writing in 1916 that although Japan must have the capacity to defend itself, military spending must not exceed financial capacity. Takahashi also resisted the unfortunate Siberian operation and sought defense cuts in the early 1920s. See Smethurst, "Self-Taught Bureaucrat," pp. 232–33; Smethurst, "Takahashi Korekiyo's Economic Policies," p. 10; Cha, "Did Takahashi Korekiyo Rescue Japan?" p. 147; Humphreys, *Heavenly Sword*, p. 46. Note also that Takahashi's return to "sound finance" was consistent with Keynes's prescriptions as well; as Keynes wrote, "The boom, not the slump, is the right time for austerity at the treasury"; John Maynard Keynes, "How to Avoid a Slump," *The Times*, January 12–14, 1937, reprinted in Donald Moggridge and Elizabeth Johnson (eds.), *The Collected Writings of John Maynard Keynes* (London: Macmillan, 1971–89), 21:384–98, 388 (quote).

[71] Guenther Stein, "Japanese State Finance," *Pacific Affairs* 10:4 (December 1937), pp. 398–400; Barnhart, *Japan Prepares for Total War*, pp. 35–36, 105; Kamekichi Takahashi, "Fiscal Policy of Finance Minister," p. 26.

[72] Young, *Imperial Japan*, pp. 268–69, 280.

[73] The army was successful in establishing the Cabinet Investigative Bureau. "Only the very conservative ministries, such as finance, opposed the army's ideas." Takahashi in particular was "aghast at the expense of the army's plans to remake the entire Japanese economy." Barnhart, *Japan and the World*, p. 105.

"I have stretched what little money I have to approve an appropriation of ¥100 million each for the Army and the Navy. I can hardly offer more." In January he added that the failure of disarmament talks should not lead to increased naval expenditures. Rather, he announced, with the achievement of economic recovery, government policies should be directed at controlling inflation.[74]

Takahashi, like his wayward protégé Inoue before him, understood the risks involved in his efforts. He told an acquaintance, "At my age I have no future," and this made it easier for him to confront the military. "I entered the government again . . . thinking that this is my last chance to serve. I am prepared to die now." Indeed, from the military's perspective, there was eventually little difference between Takahashi and Inoue. The finance minister's call for fiscal restraint, moreover, was not appreciated in the rural sectors of the economy. Conditions had improved in agricultural communities, but the recovery there lagged behind that of other sectors, and life in the villages remained arduous. Political tensions remained high as the returns from the elections of February 1936 (which had been called by the Seiyukai and attracted over 80 percent of the electorate) revealed a major victory for the Minseito.[75]

Days later, on the morning of February 26, 1936, fourteen hundred troops led by junior officers seized the center of Tokyo. The young officers not only hailed from the rural sectors of Japan but were seething with anger regarding civilian control over military finances (for which the London Naval Treaty still served as a potent symbol). The eighty-two-year-old Takahashi was murdered in his sleep to shouts of "Traitor!" and "Heavenly Punishment!" Also among those assassinated was former prime minister Saito. Prime Minister Okada escaped death only because his brother-in-law was mistakenly killed in his place. The coup, apparently successful at first, ultimately failed when it was opposed by the general staffs of both the army and the navy.[76] But the political consequences of the incident and the practical and symbolic implications of the murder of Takahashi were profound. His tenure as finance minister started with the first defeat of finance, at his hands, and ended with the second defeat of finance, with his death.

[74] Shillony, *Revolt in Japan*, pp. 30, 87–88; Yukio, "From Showa Economic Crisis," p. 588; Cohen, *Japan's Economy*, p. 8; Takafusa Nakamura, "Depression, Recovery and War, 1920–1945" (trans. Jacqueline Kaminsky), in Duus, *Cambridge History of Japan*, p. 477.

[75] Smethurst, "Takahashi Korekiyo's Economic Policies," p. 18 (quote); Kamii, "Industrial Recovery in Japan," p. 50; Reischauer, *Japan*, p. 171; Berger, "Politics and Mobilization," p. 118.

[76] Shillony, *Revolt in Japan*, pp. ix, 11, chapter 6, p. 135 (quote), 167; Berger, "Politics and Mobilization," pp. 119–20; Kitaoka, "Army as Bureaucracy," pp. 81–82; Nish, *Japanese Foreign Policy*, pp. 107–8.

While civilians still served as cabinet officials and in the Diet, the military now dominated Japanese politics, and there was little counterweight to its political power. The military installed yes-man Baba Eiichi as the new minister of finance, and a carnival of spending followed. Bursting from the constraints of financial prudence, military spending tripled in 1937, with additional huge increases in the following years (see table 3.3). Total government spending also skyrocketed, increasing by two and a half times, to ¥5,521 million in 1937, and then on to ¥8,084 and ¥8,952 million in 1938 and 1939. Government debt and the note issue also expanded dramatically. Consumer prices, which had increased at an annual rate of about 2.5 percent during the Takahashi era (1932–36), increased by approximately 8, 10, and 12 percent respectively in the following three years. Wholesale prices jumped by over 20 percent in 1937 alone, reflecting the strains on national economic capacity.[77]

Once again, as with the first defeat of finance, the new policies regarding spending, borrowing, and monetary policy were the opposite of those favored by the financial community. Baba's policies "shocked the financial world." Beyond the new economic policies, banks faced greater government regulation. Financial consolidation, which had favored the big banks in the 1920s, was taken to new extremes, this time over the strong objections of the bankers. The number of banks in Japan ultimately fell from 424 in 1936 to 186 in 1941.[78]

Despite the fact that "reaction in Japanese financial circles was quite severe and criticism of Baba's policies was vehement," there was little that could be done to stop the new measures. Takahashi's old ally Fukai spoke publicly of the need for reduced consumption and warned of the danger of inflation. His attempts to slow the growth of military spending were ineffectual, however, and he resigned as governor of the Bank of Japan in January 1937. He maintained the view that the "chief concern" of the Bank of Japan should be to "ensure confidence in . . . our currency by putting a check on monetary inflation."[79]

[77] Nakamura, *Japanese Economic History*, pp. 77–79; Cohen, *Japan's Economy*, p. 5; Goldsmith, *Financial Development of Japan*, pp. 109–11; inflation rates are calculated from p. 110. See also Kurt Bloch, "Far Eastern War Inflation," *Pacific Affairs* 13:3 (September 1940), pp. 331–32, 335; and Frank M. Tamagna, "The Financial Position of China and Japan," *American Economic Review* 36:2 (May 1946), pp. 619–20.

[78] Fletcher, "Japanese Banks," pp. 265 (quote), 266. See also Gordon Mark Berger, *Parties Out of Power in Japan, 1931–1942* (Princeton: Princeton University Press, 1977), p. 112; Nakamura, "Depression, Recovery and War," pp. 480–81. Even the most optimistic Japan watchers were taken aback by Baba's policies; see Elizabeth Boody, "Politics and the Yen," *Far Eastern Survey* 6:11 (May 26, 1937), pp. 120–22.

[79] Nakamura, *Economic Growth*, pp. 266–67 (first quote); on Fukai, see Eigo Fukai, "The Recent Monetary Policy of Japan," in Arthur D. Gayer (ed.), *The Lessons of Monetary*

A final glimmer of hope for the financiers could be found in the elections of April 1937, the last competitive elections in Japan until after the Pacific War. The political parties drew strong support in the election, suggesting that alternatives to military rule were still plausible. But the army's expansion of the China war with the attack at the Marco Polo Bridge on July 7, 1937, effectively ended whatever remained of the ability of civilian politicians to circumscribe the ambitions of Japan's military leaders.[80]

The military could not dictate the laws of economics, however; it could only react to them. Takahashi had understood that the recovery in Japan would create pressures, such as those on the balance of payments, that would require deft management. This was one motivation behind his restraint in the middle of the decade. But when Baba, under military orders, floored the economic accelerator, these problems quickly became critical. Not surprisingly, given the political environment, the attempted solutions came once again at the expense of financial interests.

While economic recovery was certainly welcome in Japan, the fact that the Japanese economy was growing comparatively quickly meant that imports were likely to rise faster than exports. The devaluation of the yen (by 40 percent against both the dollar and sterling, even after their respective devaluations), although it promoted exports by making them less expensive abroad, was a double-edged sword. For Japan, a resource-poor state, many of its imports were essential for expanding industrial production. Yen devaluation made those imports more expensive. In the first six years of the decade, the terms of trade turned dramatically against Japan: in 1936 the ratio of export to import prices was 74 percent of what it had been in 1930.[81]

The balance of trade had thus presented problems throughout the period. The trade deficit had crept upward during the Takahashi era, from ¥21.5 to ¥56.2 to ¥110.7 million in 1932–34. The trade account registered a surplus in 1935 before slipping back to a deficit of ¥70.7 million in 1936. But the post-Takahashi policies shattered whatever trade equilibrium existed, and the deficit exploded to ¥607.7 million in 1937. Such a deficit could be covered only through the shipment of gold abroad, and in 1937 gold left Japan "on a previously unheard of scale." The ¥866

Experience: Essays in Honor of Irving Fisher (London: George Allen and Unwin, 1937), esp. p. 395 (quote).

[80] Scalapino, *Democracy and Party Movement*, pp. 385–87; Reischauer, *Japan*, pp. 178–81; Shillony, *Revolt in Japan*, pp. 210–12; Nish, *Japanese Foreign Policy*, pp. 116–17, 120.

[81] Laurence Phillips Dowd, "The Impact of Exchange Policy on the International Economy of Japan during the Period 1930–1940," *Kobe Economic and Business Review* 4 (1957), pp. 26, 53–54; Kamii, "Industrial Recovery in Japan," pp. 38–39; Lockwood, *Economic Development of Japan*, p. 69.

million in gold that was sent abroad in that year was more than the entire gold reserve Japan held at the start of the decade.[82]

Japan's external economic position was unsustainable. As one analyst noted, "Under ordinary circumstances" such a crisis "would trigger a round of fiscal and financial belt tightening." Of course this solution, which would have certainly been a welcome relief to the financial community, was incompatible with the military's plans and was not seriously considered. On the contrary, the reaction was to attempt to insulate the economy from market forces to allow for a continued divergence from financial orthodoxy. Trade would be brought directly under government control. September 1937 saw the passage of the Temporary Funds Adjustment Law and the Temporary Import-Export Grading Measures Law. While there had been other important regulatory laws introduced earlier in the decade, such as the Foreign Exchange Control Law discussed earlier, the new measures were qualitatively different. These measures essentially detached the financial and commodities markets from the influence of economic forces and laid the groundwork for command control of the Japanese economy. Under the government's direction, imports were slashed by about 30 percent, and the immediate payments crisis was thus alleviated.[83]

With the outbreak of the wider China war in the summer of 1937 and the economic regulations that followed in the fall, the Finance Ministry completed its transition from pivotal policy-maker to subordinate administrator, executing the instructions of others. Seeking ultimately to retain even that role—functional control over financial affairs—the ministry had lost not only its influence but its relevance. It was not kept apprised of military planning and learned only through private sources of preparations for war against the United States.[84]

The story of Japan's expansionist foreign policy leading up to the Pacific War is relatively well known. But these policies were contested, and com-

---

[82] Dowd, "Impact of Exchange Policy," p. 57 (quote); Cohen, *Japan's Economy*, p. 13; Allen, *Japanese Industry*, pp. 99, 101.

[83] Nakamura, *Japanese Economic History*, p. 81 (quote), 82, 89; Nakamura, *Economic Growth*, p. 288; Cohen, *Japan's Economy*, pp. 12–13. On the increasing regulation of the economy, its preference by the military and the opposition of finance, see Fletcher, *Japanese Business Community*, pp. 131–34; Reischauer, *Japan*, p. 184; Kupchan, *Vulnerability of Empire*, pp. 307–8. A summary of additional economic controls introduced from the end of 1937 to the start of the Pacific War can be found in Nakamura, *Economic Growth*, pp. 302–10. For an illustration of how those controls adversely affected one member of the financial community, see Makoto Kasuya, "Securities Markets and a Securities Company in Interwar Japan: The Case of Yamaichi," in Makoto Kasuya (ed.), *Coping with Crisis: International Financial Institutions in the Interwar Period* (Oxford: Oxford University Press, 2003), pp. 215, 224.

[84] Yamamira, "Role of the Finance Ministry," pp. 289, 300.

peting foreign policy visions were articulated and advocated. This chapter illustrated these contrasting visions of the national interest, and how the foreign policy vision of finance, which held sway in the twenties, was rooted in its macroeconomic policy preferences. The entire episode also provided an excellent opportunity to test this book's argument about the position of the financial community in national security debates within societies—specifically, that finance favors a cautious, nonprovocative grand strategy—and more broadly, to explore the relationship between financial interests and foreign policy. From this perspective, the case of interwar Japan offers both fresh and important insights. The first part of the period illustrates the close relationship between the political influence of the financial sector and the practice of cautious foreign policy, providing strong support for the general argument of this book. The second part of the period offers an opportunity to come at the question from a different angle: what were the politics of finance in the context of two specific bouts of international adventurism? Here the evidence again provides strong support for this book's central thesis, illustrating how each of the major advances in Japan's external ambition was associated with major internal political defeats for the financial community. Regardless of why Japan raised the stakes in both 1931 and 1937, or whether the decisions to do so were based on sound strategy, they would not have been possible without the defeat of finance in those political struggles.

CHAPTER 4

Interwar France: Your Money or Your Life

Armed Robber: Your money or your life!
Jack Benny (after a long pause): I'm thinking, I'm thinking.

In the cases considered so far, financial interests have, as anticipated, been among the most cautious voices with regard to the formation of grand strategy and the pursuit of policies that risk or embrace war. As this pattern holds, one possible reaction might be that finance is not "cautious" but rather "right"—perhaps if the advice of finance were simply heeded, the world would be a less violent place. Most obviously, while bankers in interwar Japan blundered horribly in their application of deflation—the wrong medicine at the wrong time—Japan's bid to conquer Asia, and all that it entailed, would not have been thinkable before the financiers were removed from the scene.

But even if caution is often best, or at least good, it is not the right policy all the time. Sometimes caution can be overcaution and result in an underresponsive foreign policy and grand strategy. This is illustrated by the experience of interwar France, where the stranglehold of orthodox policies associated with the preferences of the financial community suffocated the economy, leaving the military to atrophy. In this instance, removing financiers from the scene would have resulted in a more vigorous and clearly better preparation for France as it faced the German challenge.

This case also illustrates, again, how different interests within societies can have different conceptions of the national interest, and that these contrasting visions are in accord with underlying preferences about macroeconomic policy management. It is necessary, however, to place this case in context. Removing the yoke of financial orthodoxy would have dramatically and consequentially lightened France's load as it faced the great challenge to its survival, but it would not have been a panacea. France's failure to meet the German challenge—a challenge to France's very existence—cannot be explained by economic factors alone. Interwar France was a deeply and profoundly troubled society. Some elements looked, and not just with nostalgia, to the mid-nineteenth century (if not earlier). Others pressed for a new and radically different (and vaguely specified and utopian) France. Each interpreted the world increasingly through the eyes of this great domestic conflict, and this accounts for the basic contours of French foreign policy more than any other single factor.[1]

The discussion of France will proceed in two parts. First, the political conflicts over the right to run the country and manage the economy will be reviewed. These fights are important in showing the central role monetary conflict played in understanding France's interwar political economy and in turn its grand strategy. The financial community fought relentlessly and vigorously in support of monetary orthodoxy, at the expense of all other national priorities, including national security. This was especially consequential, because in the words of one keenly observant analyst at the time, in France "the rentier class ha[d] more political influence than in any other country."[2]

Second, the discussion will focus explicitly on how those political conflicts affected France's security. Especially as France entered the Great Depression, the pursuit of monetary orthodoxy undermined France's security in three monumental ways. First and most generally, it sapped the strength of the economy as a whole. The economy performed dismally in the 1930s, eroding the industrial base from which military strength would necessarily draw. Second, as deflationary policies contracted government revenue, budgets came under constant pressure, leading to cuts in defense spending and preventing aggressive rearmament. Finally, fears for the fragility of the franc conditioned the assessment of foreign policy choices and inhibited French leaders from rising to the challenge in crises, even if they had been inclined to respond assertively. All of these problems were alleviated, but not eliminated, with the political defeat of finance at the ballot box and the arrival of the Popular Front government in 1936; the rearmament and devaluations the Socialists introduced illustrate both how oppressive the burden of orthodoxy had been on French security policy and how, even in opposition, finance could still inhibit efforts for a more robust national security strategy.

Finally, as always, it is necessary to be clear about what claims are being evaluated in this chapter and what are not. Monetary orthodoxy may have contributed to but did not cause the defeat of France in World War

---

[1] For a broad overview of French society and politics from this perspective, see William L. Shirer, *The Collapse of the Third Republic: An Inquiry into the Fall of France in 1940* (New York: Simon and Schuster, 1969); see also Eugen Weber, *The Hollow Years: France in the 1930s* (New York: Norton, 1994). Accounts such as these are sometimes criticized as presenting an overly deterministic account of the failure of interwar France. Anthony Adamthwaite, for example, argues that contingency and choice played a much greater role in determining France's fate; see his *Grandeur and Misery: France, 1914–1940* (London: Arnold, 1995); even this account, however, paints a very distressing picture of the health of French interwar society.

[2] Paul Einzig, *The Economics of Rearmament* (London: Kegan Paul, 1934), p. 94.

II; and certainly it cannot explain the catastrophic collapse of French military resistance in the spring of 1940.[3] Rather, two propositions are evaluated here: first, that the foreign policy preferences of the financial community in interwar France fit the pattern anticipated by the principal hypothesis of this book; second, that France would have been better off, as the Second World War approached, had it not labored under the constraints imposed by the orthodox policies championed by finance.

POLITICAL AND ECONOMIC CONFLICT IN FRANCE: FINANCIAL ORTHODOXY, DOMESTIC POLARIZATION, AND THE EROSION OF FRENCH POWER

France's dilemma after World War I is well known. Nominally victorious in the conflict, France emerged from the war deeply shaken. The western war was fought largely in the heart of the country's industrial center, which was devastated, not to mention the lost generation of young men who had been asked to sprint into machine-gun fire. Germany, defeated, still seemed to have history on its side, growing ever larger as France's population stagnated.[4] France financed the war largely by borrowing, and even more would be needed to finance reconstruction.

The wartime borrowing (only one-sixth of the war had been paid for through taxation) had set the franc, cut loose from gold at the outset of hostilities, on an inflationary path. Prices were at three and one half times their prewar level. As all the European currencies floated freely in markets after the war, France had two choices: recognize the new gold value of the franc and restore convertibility relatively quickly, or aim, as the British did, to restore convertibility at the prewar level. The second solution was possible, in theory. It resonated with France's traditional concerns, monetary stability and national prestige. It was also, in the words of one study, "rather like bringing the piano to the stool." The difficulties associated with stabilizing the franc would dominate the agenda until 1926.[5]

[3] For an entrée into the voluminous and active debate over the defeat of France, see Ernest May, *Strange Victory: Hitler's Conquest of France* (New York: Hill and Wang, 2000).

[4] Charles Kindleberger, *Economic Growth in France and Britain, 1851–1950* (Cambridge, MA: Harvard University Press, 1964), pp. 69, 79; Weber, *Hollow Years*, p. 251; Adamthwaite, *Grandeur and Misery*, pp. 65, 67, 91.

[5] Jean-Pierre Patat and Michel Lutfalla, *A Monetary History of France in the Twentieth Century* (trans. Patrick Martindale and David Cobham) (London: Macmillan, 1990), pp. 21, 32 (quote); Tom Kemp, *The French Economy, 1913–39: The History of a Decline* (London: Longman, 1972), pp. 58, 61–62, 73, 75; see also James Rogers, *The Process of Inflation in France, 1914–1927* (New York: Columbia University Press, 1929), pp. 89–139; Jean Bouvier, "The French Banks, Inflation and the Economic Crisis, 1919–1939," *Journal of European Economic History* 13:2 (Fall 1984), pp. 29–80.

The French political landscape was characterized by three centers of gravity, represented by political parties, though none easily fit the traditional definition of "party." The center of power rested with the Radical Party, which invariably participated in interwar governing coalitions and was in fact best described as conservative. "Radical" was a vestige of the fact that the party was forged by turn-of-the-century issues—support for democracy, a strong advocacy for (and execution of) the separation of church and state, and support of private property, especially small holdings. But by the 1920s, of course, these were not radical positions. And while the large party was home to members from a spectrum of political leanings, its base rested squarely on the shoulders of the peasants of rural France. On most practical questions then, and especially on economic ones, the party was quite conservative.[6]

To the right of the radicals were a number of political organizations— various associations and federations—whose ambivalence about democracy left them resistant to calling themselves "parties." Often labeled conservative, they were in fact reactionary, with some clearly proto-Fascist and antiparliamentary elements sponsoring paramilitary organizations. The most important parliamentary group among the reactionaries was the Republican Federation. The federation, fiercely nationalist and staunchly Catholic, opposed the increased taxes and progressive social legislation that seemed to accompany twentieth-century parliamentary democracy. Champions of strong defense and assertive foreign policy in the 1920s, in the 1930s the members of the federation, and the French Right as a whole, increasingly saw domestic change as the gravest threat to their way of life and feared war would be accompanied by social upheaval.[7]

To the left of the radicals stood the Socialist Party and, to their left, the Communists. While the Socialists participated at times as a junior partner in radical-led coalition governments, they were essentially a party of opposition until the victory of the Popular Front in 1936. As such, for much of the period their criticism outweighed their positive program, which, when studied, did not always appear coherent. The foreign policy of the Left was the mirror image of the Right. Pacifist, internationalist, and pro-disarmament into the early 1930s, the emergence of fascism in Europe

---

[6] Peter J. Larmour, *The French Radical Party in the 1930s* (Stanford: Stanford University Press, 1964), pp. 8–9, 18, 32, 63–64; John Eldred Howard, *Parliament and Foreign Policy in France* (London: Cresset Press, 1948), p. 158; Julian Jackson, *The Politics of Depression in France, 1932–1936* (Cambridge: Cambridge University Press, 1985), pp. 18–19.

[7] William D. Irvine, *French Conservatism in Crisis: The Republican Federation of France in the 1930s* (Baton Rouge: Louisiana State University Press, 1979), pp. xiii, xviii, 152, 159–60, 166, 196; Shirer, *Collapse of the Third Republic*, pp. 277–78, 324.

raised the back of the French Left, and it was increasingly the more assertive with regard to defense and foreign policy as the 1930s wore on.[8]

Battle Lines Drawn

Problems associated with the management of the franc dominated the first years following the war. There were rounds of speculation, especially immediately after the war; efforts at deflation, typically in response; and instability that derived from international crises, such as France's disastrous occupation of the Ruhr.[9] But the stark politics underlying macroeconomic management were not revealed until May 1924, when the Radical Party, under the leadership of Edouard Herriot, formed a coalition government with the Socialists, an association known as the Cartel des Gauches. No Socialist held any cabinet post—although the party was willing to participate in the coalition, its members were not yet ready to be implicated in the policy decisions of the radical government. Yet this development was viewed with great apprehension by financial markets and France's conservatives in general. They were deeply suspicious of any government that might lean, however modestly, to the left, and did not sit passively when faced with what they considered a political crisis.[10]

The period of the cartel governments, May 1924 through July 1926, was characterized by financial and political instability. But it was also accompanied by solid real economic performance.[11] Much of the financial instability had political origins, and almost all of the political instability was attributable to financial distress. In this period, lasting less than twenty-seven months, there were five different cartel cabinets, as one after another was forced out by events. The year 1925 saw seven finance minis-

[8] On the Socialist Party, see Julian Jackson, *The Popular Front in France: Defending Democracy* (Cambridge: Cambridge University Press, 1988); Helmut Gruber, *Leon Blum, French Socialism, and the Popular Front: A Case of Internal Contradictions,* Cornell Western Societies Program, 17 (1986).

[9] See Patat and Lutfalla, *Monetary History of France,* p. 33; Rogers, *Inflation in France,* pp. 237–43; Stephen Schuker, *The End of French Predominance in Europe* (Chapel Hill: University of North Carolina Press, 1976); Robert Ailber, "Speculation in the Foreign Exchanges: The European Experience, 1919–1926," *Yale Economic Essays* 2:1 (1961), pp. 171–245, esp. 199–219.

[10] Martin Wolfe, *The French Franc between the Wars, 1919–1939* (New York: Columbia University Press, 1951), p. 35; Eleanor Lansing Dulles, *The French Franc, 1914–28: The Facts and Their Interpretation* (New York: Macmillan, 1929), p. 180. Dulles notes here that "the link between politics and finance was becoming constantly more close." See also Beth Simmons, *Who Adjusts? Domestic Sources of Foreign Economic Policy during the Interwar Years* (Princeton: Princeton University Press, 1994), pp. 143, 157.

[11] Wolfe, for example, writes that the performance of French trade and industry "give[s] us a strangely different impression from that received in the agitated domain of fiscal and monetary history." *The French Franc,* p. 53.

ters alone, which could only exacerbate the interrelated problems of depreciation, capital flight, and waning public confidence.[12]

Throughout the period, France's powerful rentier class flexed its muscles, until it was finally able to chase the cartel from power. While some of the capital flight that occurred could be attributed to skepticism about the cartel's policies and its lack of a clear plan of action, financial interests and the Bank of France used their economic power to influence politics.[13] The first confrontation occurred between the Herriot government and the Bank of France in April 1925. For some time, the bank had printed notes beyond the legal limit but withheld this information from its biweekly reports while privately warning the government of the problem. When the government and the bank clashed over tax policy, the bank revealed its ace. On April 7 the Herriot cabinet approved a capital levy proposal, and two days later, the bank's report made clear that the note circulation was above the legal limit. The following day, April 10, the senate passed a vote of no confidence, and Herriot resigned.[14]

But removing the man did not remove the governing coalition, and conflicts continued to simmer. With renewed depreciation of the franc toward the end of 1925, high finance apparently decided that it had seen enough of Finance Minister Joseph Caillaux, who, it should be noted, represented the conservative wing of the Radical Party and was a strong proponent of monetary orthodoxy. Nevertheless, a renewed "flight from the franc," largely from within France, forced Caillaux's resignation in October. According to Eleanor Lansing Dulles, "there is no doubt that hidden maneuvers and speculation of financiers helped to make his position untenable." Finance offered both carrots and sticks. Afterward, the *New York Times* reported on November 2, 1925, "intervention in the franc market . . . was carried out by banks apparently desirous of obliging the new Premier."[15]

The carousel of French politics found Caillaux back at his old post within eight months, and he had the pleasure of firing Bank of France

[12] Kemp, *The French Economy*, pp. 78–79.

[13] See Dulles, *The French Franc*, pp. 50, 412, on the power of finance; see also Donald G. Wileman, "What the Market Will Bear: The French Cartel Elections of 1924," *Journal of Contemporary History* 29:3 (July 1994), pp. 486–87, 498. Simmons, in *Who Adjusts*, pp. 157–58, 171, stresses the importance of capital flight but emphasizes economic over political motives; see also Harold James, "Financial Flows across Frontiers during the Interwar Depression," *Economic History Review* 45:3 (1992), pp. 597–98.

[14] Gregory Carl Schmid, "The Politics of Financial Instability in France, 1924–1926" (PhD diss., Department of Political Science, Columbia University, 1968), p. 33; Alessandro Prati, "Poincaré's Stabilization: Stopping a Run on Government Debt," *Journal of Monetary Economics* 27 (1991), pp. 219–21.

[15] Dulles, *The French Franc*, pp. 181, 183 (quote), 354 (*New York Times*); also Wolfe, *The French Franc*, p. 39.

governor Georges Robineau, who had never fully cooperated with any of the cartel governments, and replaced him with Emile Moreau. But a final franc crisis that had been brewing in France came to a head the following July. The franc, which had risen as high as 85 to the pound in 1924, and which had fallen to 130 at the end of 1925, collapsed in the summer of 1926. At 173.25 to the pound on June 26, it fell to 193.50 on July 8 and reached 240 less than a fortnight later. Herriot was called upon to form a new government as the slide continued. He was informed by Moreau, however, that the Bank of France had reached the limit of its willingness to assist the government, and Herriot's new government quickly lost a vote of no confidence. Raymond Poincaré was then called upon to form a government of "national unity" (excluding Socialists and Communists), but in practice, Poincaré's return to the premiership signaled the end of the cartel experiment and the resumption of conservative rule. There would be no further talk of a capital levy; instead, changes to the tax code shifted the burden away from high-income earners. Capital that had fled the country quickly returned. "The firm stance of the Bank of France," Moreau would write in his diary, "contributed a great deal to this outcome." Herriot would reach a similar conclusion but from a different perspective. Convinced that he had been undone by the "Wall of Money," he lamented that "in a debtor state, a democratic government is a slave."[16]

The very return of Poincaré was enough to stop the fall of the franc and end the financial crisis. The modest policies enacted had little real effect, and as noted, the productive side of the economy was in good shape anyway. What Poincaré brought was confidence. He instilled confidence in the man in the street to be sure, but more important, he enjoyed the enthusiastic support of the financial community in general and the Bank of France in particular. The entire episode underscores the power of these actors within French society at the time.[17]

---

[16] Schmid, "Financial Instability in France," p. 40 (Crises of 1926, Herriot quote); William Adams Brown, *The International Gold Standard Reinterpreted, 1914–1934* (New York: National Bureau of Economic Research, 1940), pp. 438, 442–43; Jackson, *Politics of Depression*, pp. 9–10; Emile Moreau, *The Golden Franc: Memoirs of a Governor of the Bank of France: The Stabilization of the Franc (1926–1928)* (trans. Stephen Stoller and Trevor Roberts) (Boulder, CO: Westview Press, 1991), p. 42.

[17] The extent to which the restoration of confidence ended the financial crisis was remarkable. In the words of one scholar, "The mere presence of this financial conservative helped stem the hysteria." Richard F. Kuisel, *Capitalism and the State in Modern France* (Cambridge: Cambridge University Press, 1981), p. 74. This view is universally held; see Pierre-Cyrille Hautcoeur and Pierre Sicsic, "Threat of a Capital Levy, Expected Devaluation and Interest Rates in France During the Interwar Period," *Notes D'Etudes et de Recherche*, 50 Banque de France (January 1998); also Dulles, *The French Franc*, pp. 418 (who also reports this as Schumpeter's position, p. 420); Kemp, *The French Economy*, p. 80; Patat and Lutfalla, *Monetary History of France*, p. 52; Wolfe, *The French Franc*, p. 44.

Finance, the Bank of France, and the Poincaré Stabilization

At the center of the French financial community stood the Bank of France. The bank, a private institution and functioning commercial bank, had always been immensely powerful. Even in the nineteenth century, the bank "never hesitated to oppose or checkmate" the government's policies, especially when those policies leaned to the left. After the Great War the power of the bank to impose its will only increased. The only check the government had over the bank was its ability to appoint (and dismiss) the governor and the two assistant governors. But political leaders were quite reluctant to exercise this option, and even when new governors were appointed, the governors' loyalties tended to rest with the bank, not the government.[18]

The unique structure of the Bank of France had much to do with this. While the bank had 40,000 shareholders, only the 200 largest shareholders had the right to vote. These powerful oligarchs appointed the fifteen regents and three auditors who, along with the governor and assistant governors, managed the affairs of the bank. In accordance with bank rules, the governor was required to have a stake in the bank similar to the 200—thus collectively they would provide each new governor with 100 shares of the bank. This was worth two million francs, or over $130,000, a considerable fortune at the time. Further, retired governors typically served on the boards of other shareholder companies. Thus, more often than not, "the regents had the governor in their pocket."[19]

Finance was not shy about taking on the government in public. During the financial crises of the cartel governments, one regent stated explicitly that the bank would not provide the government with any more assistance until a more conservative government was in place. The bank also used its funds to finance planted stories in newspapers that supported its position or attacked those of its adversaries.[20]

But what exactly did finance want? Not surprisingly, all of the usual suspects regarding inflation, interest rates, budgets, and exchange stabil-

[18] Georges Boris, "Reforming the Bank of France," *Foreign Affairs* 15:1 (October 1936), pp. 156, 157 (quote); Margaret G. Myers, "The Nationalization of Banks in France," *Political Science Quarterly* 64:2 (June 1949), p. 190.

[19] Alexander Werth, *The Twilight of France, 1933–1940* (edited and introduced by D. W. Brogan) (New York: Howard Fertig, 1966 [1942]), p. 108. The power of the so-called 200 families became an important rallying point in French politics. Even those who dismiss this as rhetoric concede it is "an indisputable fact" that a "financial and industrial oligarchy of a sort with considerable political influence has existed." Malcolm Anderson, "The Myth of the 'Two Hundred Families,' " *Political Studies* 13:2 (June 1965), p. 178.

[20] Boris, "Reforming the Bank," p. 159. Moreau discusses these press campaigns in his memoirs; see Moreau, *The Golden Franc*, pp. 358, 376–77, 379, 384, 386, 389, 511.

ity. Additionally, the financial powers in interwar France longed for a return to tradition and stability—political and economic—as they understood it. Allergic to taxes, skeptical of monetary reform, and rooted to a vision of the past, this gave a French twist to the standard orthodox package. In practice, this meant support for the immediate stabilization of the franc and the prompt restoration of the gold standard, and unflinching spending cuts to ensure a balanced budget. The interconnections between these programs cannot be overestimated; it was accepted as an article of faith that the franc rested on the foundation of the balanced budget.[21] And it was through these lenses that the financial community viewed issues of international politics. The only positive program on the agenda was the establishment of Paris as an international financial center that would rival London. This, of course, put a premium on the need to ensure the international reputation of the franc.[22]

In the person of Raymond Poincaré, finance had found a politician with whom it could work. The Poincaré stabilization featured cuts in government spending that eliminated the deficit and produced surpluses, higher interest rates, and a consolidation of government debt. The franc continued its recovery, appreciating throughout the year. These all contributed to a recession that lasted about a year but that was followed by two years of recovery, 1928–29. The economic downturn caused by deflation and the appreciation of the franc led to the decision to stabilize the currency at 124 to the pound (25 to the dollar) in December 1926 in order to prevent additional appreciation. The stabilization of the franc at 124 had two important consequences. First, it left the franc somewhat undervalued, which would help French exports and increase the likelihood that the new rate could be defended indefinitely.[23] Second, at one-fifth of prewar parity, it represented, in the eyes of finance, an enormous sacrifice. While Moreau orchestrated the stabilization, he did so over the objections of many of the most influential regents of the Bank of France, such as

---

[21] Kenneth Mouré, *Managing the Franc Poincaré: Economic Understanding and Political Constraint in French Monetary Policy, 1928–1936* (Cambridge: Cambridge University Press, 1991), p. 121; Wolfe, *The French Franc*, p. 83; Kuisel, *Capitalism and the State*, p. 79.

[22] Moreau hoped that the Paris market "would become one of the premier markets of the world"; *The Golden Franc*, p. 525. He also competed aggressively with the Bank of England over financial influence in eastern Europe; see pp. 430–473. See also Mouré, *Managing the Franc*, pp. 130, 132–34, 135; Robert Boyce, "Business as Usual: The Limits of French Economic Diplomacy, 1926–1933," in Boyce (ed.), *French Foreign and Defense Policy, 1918–1940: The Decline and Fall of a Great Power* (London: Routledge, 1998), p. 110; Margaret G. Myers, *Paris as a Financial Center* (London: P. S. King and Son, 1936), pp. 4, 135.

[23] Patat and Lutfalla, *Monetary History of France*, p. 54; Kemp, *The French Economy*, pp. 81, 97.

François de Wendel and Edouard Rothschild, who favored a higher rate, such as the psychologically appealing 100 francs to the pound. From the perspective of finance, then, the 1920s were a decade of inflation and devaluation, and this experience only stiffened their resistance to even the hint of any future retreat from orthodoxy.[24]

While there was some initial caution, and the bank would never shrink from asserting itself, the financial community came to work closely with Poincaré, and finance in general came to work closely with the conservative government. The recovery of 1928 produced surpluses that allowed for increased government spending, and at the same time the stability of the franc allowed for the formal restoration of the gold standard in late June. Poincaré's relationship with finance was more than friendly. During the 1928 elections, Moreau wrote:

> At Mr. Poincaré's request, I went to deliver 500,000 francs in banknotes to the Minister of the Interior, Mr. Albert Sarraut, to aid the government in supporting its candidates. . . . I advised [Sarraut] not to be overly generous towards the voters during the first two or three years of the new legislature and to wait with tax reductions until the eve of the 1932 elections.[25]

Riding the crest of economic expansion, especially on the heels of the recent instability, the elections of 1928 provided a decisive victory for Poincaré, and in the late 1920s—for one desperate moment—France was arguably secure, prosperous, and confident.

The Depression and the Gold Standard

In 1929 health matters would force Poincaré from the political scene. But as much of the world headed toward depression, France embarked on an ambitious five-year plan to spend its accumulated treasury surpluses. By 1931, however, the depression finally reached France; while it was not as severe there as it was in other countries, it lingered for a much longer period than it did elsewhere. Debate over the management of the economy and successive rounds of financial crises dominated French politics. From 1932 to 1936, orthodox solutions prevailed, but for the most part they were self-defeating. The money supply was allowed to contract continually during this period. And in the four years from 1932 to 1936, government spending was cut by 20 percent, from 50 to 40 billion francs. At the

---

[24] H. Clark Johnson, *Gold, France and the Great Depression, 1919–1932* (New Haven: Yale University Press, 1997), pp. 75, 78, 105, 140; Kenneth Moure, *The Gold Standard Illusion: France, the Bank of France, and the International Gold Standard, 1914–1939* (Oxford: Oxford University Press, 2002), pp. 129, 132, 133, 136; Simmons, *Who Adjusts?* pp. 160, 172–73; Moreau, *The Golden Franc*, pp. 134, 166, 168, 171.

[25] Moreau, *The Golden Franc*, entry of 25 April 1928, p. 478.

TABLE 4.1
The Depression in France

Year	Production index	M2 (Change)	Exchange rate F/ $	F/ £
1931	88.9	−7.9%	25.50	123.94
1932	68.8	−0.6%	25.44	87.36
1933	76.7	−6.4%	25.62	86.12
1934	71.0	+0.7%	16.06	81.28
1935	67.4	−5.5%	15.19	74.34

Sources: William H. Wynne, "The French Franc, June 1928–February 1937," *Journal of Political Economy* 45:4 (August 1937), p. 501 (production index, 1929 = 100); Patat and Lutfalla, *Monetary History of France,* p. 73 (M2); League of Nations, *Statistical Yearbook, 1935/6* (Geneva: League of Nations, 1936), p. 235 (exchange rates); Wolfe, *The French Franc,* p. 213 (dollar rate).

same time government debts increased by 64 billion francs, as the deflation and austerity cut economic activity and tax revenues.[26] The French economy was chasing its tail.

Perhaps because the depth of the depression was not so severe in France or because of the divisions within French society, the political system produced a paralysis that triumphed over creativity. The Radical Party ducked for cover; once assured of the agricultural protectionism and price supports that its rural base demanded the party was content to follow its conservative economic instincts on all other matters. Farther to the right, the conservatives preached orthodoxy and more orthodoxy. Their prescription can easily be called economic anorexia—the belief that if the economy could just get one bit slimmer still, everything would be fine. And since they were not the ones who actually went hungry,[27] they could not or would not understand how anyone could disagree with this logic. The Socialists on the other hand, if well intentioned, did not offer a coherent alternative. They opposed deflation and austerity budget cuts; instead they proposed increased spending and reflation. At the same time, they supported the gold standard, which simply would not have been sustainable if their other policies were enacted.[28]

The Bank of France, and the French Right in general, saw themselves as the guardians of the franc and financial orthodoxy (and private prop-

[26] Jackson, *Politics of Depression,* pp. 23, 218; Kemp, *The French Economy,* p. 99; Patat and Lutfalla, *Monetary History of France,* p. 72.

[27] Deflation allowed the rentier to give up his cake and eat it too.

[28] See Alfred Sauvy, "The Economic Crisis of the 1930s in France," *Journal of Contemporary History* 4:4 (October 1969), esp. pp. 24, 33; also Simmons, *Who Adjusts?* pp. 261–62; Kuisel, *Capitalism and the State,* pp. 96–98; Irvine, *French Conservatism,* pp. 80–81.

erty and social order). With regard to the franc, however, more often than not their repeated exhortations fell on receptive ears, for an instinctive, almost mystical commitment to gold was ingrained in French society. Thus, the debate over orthodoxy focused on spending and economic expansion, rather than the value of the franc and its link to gold. But the gold standard was a cancer at the heart of the French economic system. The undervalued franc had contributed to France's economic expansion in the late 1920s. After devaluation of the pound in 1931 and the dollar in 1933, however, the franc was suddenly overvalued, and this hurt French exporters as well as the tourist trade.[29] Much worse, and following the pattern Barry Eichengreen described, adherence to the gold standard prevented France from introducing the policies necessary to escape the depression. States on the gold standard that attempted to expand their economies would undermine the credibility of their commitment to gold and stimulate capital flight. They would then be required to reverse policy and raise interest rates if they were to retain the capital necessary to remain on the gold standard. And as other states abandoned gold, such pressures would only mount on those who remained.[30] Pressure on the franc routinely provided the major impetus for new rounds of deflation and budget cuts in the 1930s, and this prolonged the depression in France.[31]

Politics and Economic Conflict in the Depression

In the wake of the depression, the elections of May 1932 returned the Radicals to power, under the leadership of Herriot. The party formed an alliance with the Socialists, this time called the Union des Gauches. But the shadow of the cartel loomed over the union, and there were many familiar echoes of the past, in particular, the pattern of financial crises contributing to seemingly constant collapse and re-formations of the cabinet. This even though Herriot, once bitten, was quite shy about challenging the financial community. His cabinet excluded left-wing politicians, and the finance and budget positions were given to conservatives, choices that were lauded by the financial press.[32]

---

[29] Robert Murray Haig, "The National Budgets of France, 1928–1937," *Proceedings of the Academy of Political Science* 17:4 (January 1938), pp. 26, 29; Kemp, *The French Economy*, pp. 100, 103; Weber, *The Hollow Years*, pp. 29, 49–50.

[30] See Barry Eichengreen, *Golden Fetters: The Gold Standard and the Great Depression, 1919–1939* (New York: Oxford University Press, 1992).

[31] Mouré, *Managing the Franc*, pp. 17–18, 22, 27; Kemp, *The French Economy*, p. 102; "France's Economic Problem," *The Economist*, April 27, 1935, pp. 943–45; "France and the Franc," *The Economist*, December 21, 1935, pp. 1264–65.

[32] Sauvy, "The Economic Crisis," p. 22; Patat and Lutfalla, *Monetary History of France*, p. 68; Jackson, *Politics of Depression*, p. 53.

But despite the fact that, much to the dismay of the Socialists, the Radicals pursued the orthodox remedies to the depression—price deflation and budget cuts—finance was no less suspicious of the union than it was of the cartel. The Bank of France used its influence to press for an even more dedicated application of the orthodox medicine and to ensure that Socialists were kept at arm's length from the successive Radical cabinets that were formed. The bank also continued its aggressive (and secret) press campaign, planting stories in favor of deflation and further budget cuts, and even running bogus stories on the negative effects of the U.S. devaluation on the American economy.[33]

The depression left the government especially vulnerable to high finance. Despite sustained efforts at retrenchment, falling revenues ensured that the budget would always be out of balance, and thus the government always needed to borrow or, more commonly, to have its bonds underwritten in order to finance the shortfall. Thus, as one scholar of this period concluded, "When the financiers were discontented, the market for Treasury bonds suddenly dried up, the Bank of France placed conditions on advances to the Treasury's account, and gold began fleeing the country." In January 1933 such pressure was applied in order to keep Socialist ministers out of the new Daladier cabinet. It resumed in the autumn of the same year after the Daladier government fell, and then abated once again when Camille Chautemps was finally able to form a government, after meeting with leading financial figures to assure them of his commitment to further spending cuts.[34]

Radical governments continued to struggle, barely treading water. They were also squeezed by pressure from both sides. On the Left, increasing discontent from the Socialists over economic policy threatened the sustainability of the governing coalition. And seemingly nothing could satisfy the Right, out of power but clamoring for even more aggressive efforts at contraction. The back of the fragile government was finally broken in February by the Stavisky scandal and the violent street riots that followed.[35] The implication of Radical deputies in the financial scandal, news of which broke on January 3, 1934, led to protests and increasingly large street riots on January 22, 23, and 27, finally forcing the resignation of the Chautemps government. Daladier was then called back in an effort to form a new government. The riots, however, continued, led by hun-

<hr />

[33] Boris, "Reforming the Bank," p. 159; Wolfe, *The French Franc*, pp. 105, 107, 112.

[34] Larmour, *The French Radical Party*, p. 136.

[35] Alexandre Stavisky was a swindler who sold worthless municipal bonds in Bayonne. On the run from the authorities, he died under mysterious circumstances, amid charges that a number of prominent Radical politicians were implicated in his schemes. The events were seized upon by right-wing opponents of the government. For colorful details, see "Distraction from the Scandal," *Time*, March 12, 1934.

dreds of young men associated with the right-wing leagues and paramilitary organizations (but ultimately joined in the streets by Communists who shared their distaste for republican government). Things came to a head on February 6, when, on the streets of Paris, some 40,000 rioters clashed with the police, leaving 17 dead and over 2,000 wounded. Daladier and his associates, after considering more aggressive countermeasures (such as declaring a state of siege and arresting the riots' leaders), fearing for the preservation of the republic, chose to resign instead. A new coalition government (excluding the Communists and Socialists) was formed, and political leadership passed back to the conservatives.[36]

But the conservative leaders faced the same basic economic dilemma that plagued the union, and the same medicine would not work, regardless of who dispensed it. The conservative Doumergue government, focused almost exclusively on the budget deficit, introduced additional budget cuts and further deflationary measures. But this led, once again, to falling tax revenues and a further decline in economic activity. In November the Radical Party ousted Gaston Doumergue and replaced him with the more moderate Pierre Etienne Flandin.[37]

Flandin attempted to bring the economy around, however modestly, stating that deflation was "almost completed," since, he asserted, a rise in world prices mitigated the need for additional reductions in the French price level. It was also impossible to imagine that the budget could be cut any further, and in fact Flandin ordered some increases in spending and an expansion of credit. He also fired Bank of France governor Clément Moret and replaced him with Jean Tannery, in the hope that the new governor might be more independent of the regents, who were openly critical of Flandin's policies. Finance responded with its familiar trump card. Capital fled the nation, the franc came under pressure, and the government was in need of financial support.[38]

The bank, however, would not offer assistance to the government, nor would it act promptly to stem capital flight without a price—new spending cuts. Flandin resisted, but pressure only increased. In March Belgium abandoned the gold standard, placing renewed pressure on the franc, and in April, it became clear that the government would be unable to meet its debt obligations due to mature on June 15 without the support of the Bank of France. François de Wendel, perhaps the most influential regent, gave a speech in April that outlined a deflationary program demanded by the bank. Flandin held out for as long as he could, but a new financial

---

[36] Shirer, *Collapse of the Third Republic*, pp. 204, 208–9, 219–20, 223. See also Shirer's entire compelling eyewitness account on pp. 199–230; Weber, *The Hollow Years*, pp. 141, 147, 150; Adamthwaite, *Grandeur and Misery*, pp. 164–65.

[37] Sauvy, "The Economic Crisis," p. 23; Jackson, *Politics of Depression*, pp. 81, 88, 92.

[38] Jackson, *Politics of Depression*, pp. 93, 95–96; Mouré, *The Gold Standard*, p. 217.

crisis developed in May—the worst since 1926—and 1.5 billion francs in gold fled the country in the week of May 20–24. In the wake of the resignation of his finance minister (who had routinely undercut him from the right, anyway),[39] Flandin took over the portfolio himself and finally asked for special powers to bring about the budget cuts demanded by the bank. But the government was defeated on May 31, paving the way for one final effort at "superdeflation."[40]

From the perspective of the Left, the Bank of France went out of its way to make sure that Flandin's efforts at expansion would fail and provoked the final crisis of the franc. On the other hand, two leading authorities of the period argue that this is a myth. Both Kenneth Mouré and Julian Jackson stress fundamental problems with Flandin's policies themselves. The basic problem is that, following Barry Eichengreen's argument discussed earlier, efforts at expansion were incompatible with the gold standard. Thus Mouré and Jackson can conclude that the bank did not proactively force the failure of Flandin's efforts.[41]

But this overstates the case in the opposite direction. As Paul Einzig has argued, the bank pursued a policy of "passive resistance," designed to force "drastic deflationary measures" on the government. Ultimately Flandin faced a choice of either national bankruptcy or submission to the "dictation of the Financial interests behind the Bank of France." The bank also remained passive during the financial crisis, allowing gold to flow from France without raising interest rates—that is, until the day after Flandin agreed to the bank's demands.[42] Thus, while it is true that finance did not actually push Flandin overboard, it did lean over the railing, with life preserver in hand, and shout questions about how cold the water was. The bank could easily have saved Flandin, but it withheld the support that it would provide to others. For this reason, while denying the simple financial-conspiracy myth, Jackson can acknowledge a "central role" to the bank in the crisis, "sabotaging Flandin's credit policy" and making "further spending cuts inevitable."[43]

---

[39] The minister, Lars Germain-Martin, consistently pressed Flandin for reductions in spending and a resumption of deflation. In March he told the influential and conservative Senate Finance Committee that budget cuts were necessary to save the franc but that he did not have the authorization to enact them. Jackson, *Politics of Depression*, p. 102.

[40] Jackson, *Politics of Depression*, p. 99; Werth, *Twilight of France*, p. 44; Wolfe, *The French Franc*, pp. 113–14; Wynne, "The French Franc," p. 510.

[41] Mouré, *Managing the Franc*, p. 149; Jackson, *Politics of Depression*, pp. 99–100.

[42] Paul Einzig, *Bankers, Statesmen, and Economists* (London: Macmillan, 1935), pp. 212, 213; Einzig states plainly that the new deflation was "dictated by the Bank of France," p. 222. Also Boris, "Reforming the Bank," p. 161; Werth, *Twilight of France*, pp. 44–46.

[43] Jackson, *Politics of Depression*, p. 104. Mouré also admits that the Bank did not like Flandin, that it attempted to extort deflation, and that Tannery was not averse to using his interest-rate policy to pressure the government. *Managing the Franc*, pp. 148–49.

In the week following the fall of the Flandin government, three separate attempts were made to form a new government. None managed to last more than a couple of days, as the bank made clear that it would support only a government that was granted special plenary powers and used those powers to impose sweeping budget cuts. Finally, on June 7 a government under the leadership of Pierre Laval was formed and was granted special powers. Laval introduced 549 decree laws, the centerpiece of which was a virtually across-the-board 10 percent cut in government expenditure, designed to save almost ten million francs. Laval, who to a large extent was carrying out the deflationary program outlined by De Wendel in his April speech, was offered the assistance that the bank had denied Flandin and the fleeting cabinets of the first week in June.[44]

The Laval government enjoyed the close cooperation and support of the Bank of France. The bank was now willing to rediscount government paper, and by September it held over two million francs' worth of new government debt. The bank also provided advances to the government and looked the other way as the 1936 budget was balanced solely by a creative juggling of the books. Nor did the bank deny the fact that it was providing to Laval what it would not to Flandin, explaining in its own publications that the bank's support for the government depended on whether the economy was managed as the bank saw fit.[45]

But even the bank could not save a losing policy. Nor could anyone deny that orthodoxy had been allowed to take its best shot. But "superdeflation" did not deliver the goods. The value and stability of the franc seemed assured, but businesses suffered, with further losses in the export sectors and tourism industry. It was also increasingly clear that as France remained mired in the depression, other countries were recovering. The grip of orthodoxy finally started to slip a bit; devaluation was, finally, at least debatable in respectable circles, and Laval did not even ask for an extension of plenary powers when they expired in October. But what is amazing is that deflation was tried for so long. As Martin Wolfe argues, France's obsession with money orthodoxy can be explained only by political factors, "the powerful political position of the French rentiers," and

---

[44] Jackson, *Politics of Depression*, pp. 104–5; Werth, *Twilight of France*, pp. 45–46; Boris, "Reforming the Bank," p. 161; "France and Stabilization," *The Economist*, July 20, 1935, p. 112.

[45] Jackson, *Politics of Depression*, pp. 108–9; Boris, "Reforming the Bank," p. 162. Einzig notes that the bank still limited the Treasury's supply of cash to ensure its continued dependence on the bank; *Bankers, Statesmen, and Economists*, p. 213. See also Mouré, *Managing the Franc*, pp. 146, 150, 154–55. Mouré paints a more sympathetic portrait of the bank than is presented here. He argues, for example, that the bank "felt itself compelled to interfere in government policy to obtain the conditions necessary for the defense of the franc" (p. 155).

French politicians "more concerned with protecting the purchasing power of their constituents' investments than with correcting the strangulating effect of the overvalued franc."[46]

The Popular Front and the End of Orthodoxy

The failure of sustained efforts at deflation, and especially of the Laval superdeflation, finally shifted the terrain of French politics. The Popular Front—a political alliance between the Radicals and the Socialists and Communists—was forged by a common opposition to further deflation. The elections of 1936 provided a decisive victory for the Popular Front, with strong returns in favor of the Socialists and for the left wing of the Radical Party. On June 4 Leon Blum became France's first Socialist premier.[47] This unprecedented event ushered in an era marked by both continuity and change. The change was a dramatic and unambiguous about-face: the deflationary episode was ended, and the budget was no longer the focus of the government's attention. This mattered, and it was all for the good. The money stock grew by 35 percent over the next three years, and there was a 20 percent increase in industrial production over the same period. Economic growth also improved. On the other hand, much about France was quite familiar. Economic conflict and financial crises plagued the leftist government, and Blum, failing to receive emergency powers, was forced to resign one year after taking office. Successive Popular Front governments (including a second one under Blum's leadership) came and went, each tending to be a bit more conservative in an effort to restore economic stability. This created a stop and go pattern of economic activity—retrenchment in 1938 led to slower growth than in the fatter years of 1937 and 1939.[48]

The Socialists recognized that financial interests would attempt to obstruct their economic program. Thus one of the first measures the new government took was a major reform of the Bank of France. The reform eliminated the regents and replaced them with twenty councillors, of whom only two were appointed by the bank's shareholders. The governor was no longer required to hold shares of the bank, and he received his full salary three years past the end of his tenure, during which time he could

[46] Wolfe, The French Franc, pp. 118–20, 132, 137, 133, 134 (quotes); Jackson, Politics of Depression, pp. 109–10; "A Desperate Defense," The Economist, August 17, 1935, pp. 313–14; "Deflation in France," The Economist, September 21, 1935, p. 553.

[47] Sauvy, "The Economic Crisis," p. 26; Larmour, The French Radical Party, pp. 171, 202.

[48] Patat and Lutfalla, Monetary History of France, pp. 81, 83; Wolfe, The French Franc, pp. 156, 169.

not be employed in the private sector. The reform passed by a vote of 444–77, with 55 of those in opposition from the Republican Federation.[49]

But reforming the bank did not end the opposition of the financial community. Although the government was no longer its hostage, there was no simple about-face in the bank's preferences or in its basic policy prescriptions, and capital flight and the resistance of the Right in general to the Popular Front program were significant problems. That said, there is also no escaping the fact that the Socialists' economic program was essentially incoherent, and this contributed to a self-defeating spiral. Much of the blame has been placed on the ill-timed insistence on the forty-hour workweek, with enforced pay raises and increased vacation, policies that could not help but put pressure on the balance of payments and thus the franc, stimulating further capital flight.[50]

Something had to give, and ultimately it was the franc, which was devalued in September, the final nail in the coffin of orthodoxy.[51] The devaluation was a long time in coming and contributed to improved economic conditions in France. However, as noted, other problems remained, and although the French economy turned the corner and generally improved in the final three years before World War II, it continued to lurch from one financial and political crisis to the next. The spell of orthodoxy was broken, but much of the damage had been done by the gutting of the economy in the middle of the 1930s. And even in the late 1930s, finance, though down, was not out.

FINANCIAL ORTHODOXY AND FOREIGN POLICY

The suffocating grip of financial orthodoxy, rooted in politics, weakened France considerably in the 1930s. Still, there is no doubt that, as mentioned earlier, one cannot begin to understand French foreign policy without an appreciation for the profound domestic divisions that plagued the Third Republic. Almost all individual positions on foreign policy debates or ex-

---

[49] Boris, "Reforming the Bank," p. 155. The bank was also prohibited from using its funds to engage in political activities, pp. 162–64. Myers, "Nationalization of Banks," p. 200; Werth, *Twilight of France*, p. 107; Irvine, *French Conservatism*, p. 92.

[50] Charles P. Kindleberger, *The World in Depression, 1929–39*, rev. ed. (Berkeley: University of California Press, 1986), pp. 251–54; M. Kalecki, "The Lesson of the Blum Experiment," *Economic Journal* 48 (March 1938), p. 39 (note that Kalecki puts a more positive spin on the Popular Front's program and suggests political motives for the capital flight); Jackson, *Politics of Depression*, pp. 203–7; Kemp, *The French Economy*, p. 124; Kuisel, *Capitalism and the State*, p. 120.

[51] On the devaluation debate, see Mouré, *Managing the Franc*, pp. 237, 241, 245, and chapter 6; Jackson, *Politics of Depression*, chapter 8.

ternal matters, such as those regarding the Spanish Civil War, the meaning of European fascism, and relations with the Soviet Union, could be derived from domestic politics and policy preferences regarding internal issues.[52] And these divisions hardened positions on economic issues, which, if anything, tended to tighten the screws of orthodoxy even further.[53] But there is also no doubt that the persistence of orthodoxy was an important and independent source of French weakness, and had France broken with orthodoxy sooner, it would have been better prepared for its confrontation with Germany. As Jackson argued, at stake in the debate over economic policy in France "was ultimately the balance of power in Europe."[54]

The grip of financial conservatism in France weakened the republic in three ways. First, it caused the depression to linger while the economies of other states, including Germany, recovered. This contracted the economic base that would provide the necessary foundation of any defense effort. In August 1938, the month before the Munich crisis, the index of industrial production in France reached its interwar low; between 1929 and 1938 industrial production increased by 20 percent in Britain and 16 percent in Germany but fell by 24 percent in France. Orthodoxy sustained and deepened the depression, which "enfeebled France and contributed to the collapse of 1940."[55] Second, the continual insistence by the financial community that the government—any government—above all else balance the budget could not help but put constant pressure on defense spending. Even at those times when defense spending was not cut, this demand presented an immediate and imposing constraint. Third, and not unrelated, the Bank of France regarded the commitment to maintaining the convertibility of the franc into gold at the level established in 1928 as a sacred trust. As a result, policies such as the threat of military mobilization, which might lead to new expenditures or stimulate capital flight, were resisted, undercut, or simply understood to be impossible. Thus while the balanced budget reduced France's material capabilities, concern for the franc not only exacerbated the depression but also sapped the strength and assertiveness of French foreign policy.[56]

[52] Anthony Adamthwaite, *France and the Coming of the Second World War, 1936–1939* (London: Frank Cass, 1977), pp. xiii, 42; Howard, *Parliament and Foreign Policy*, pp. 145, 157; Irvine, *French Conservatism*, pp. xx, 152, 160, 166.

[53] Tom Kemp, "The French Economy under the Franc Poincaré," *The Economic History Review* (2nd ser.) 24:1 (February 1971), p. 98; Kindleberger, *Economic Growth*, pp. 109, 205, 329; "France's Dilemma," *The Economist*, November 30, 1935, pp. 1058–59.

[54] Jackson, *Politics of Depression*, p. 2.

[55] Talbot Imlay, *Facing the Second World War: Strategy, Politics and Economics in Britain and France, 1938–1940* (Oxford: Oxford University Press, 2003), p. 25; Adamthwaite, *Grandeur and Misery*, pp. 141 (quote), 142; Mouré, *The Gold Standard*, p. 245.

[56] Haim Shamir, *Economic Crisis and French Foreign Policy, 1930–1936* (Leiden, Netherlands: E. J. Brill, 1989), pp. 16–17, 26, 44; Kemp, "The Franc Poincaré," p. 99.

The Inescapable Mathematics: Budgets and Defense

Even in the flush years of the Poincaré surpluses, the Finance Ministry protested increases in military expenditure. In an era of plenty, however, there were few hard choices, and spending was increased virtually across the board. But as the twenties gave way to the thirties and the economy slowed, the black ink that had marked France's budgets turned red. And until the arrival of the Popular Front, the struggle to balance the budget dominated the political agenda, except in those instances when it was displaced by concerns for the convertibility of the franc. Of course, since a balanced budget was seen as a prerequisite for monetary stability, concerns for the franc only increased pressure on government spending.[57]

Defense spending was gutted in an effort to balance the budget. The relationship was obvious by fiscal year 1930–31. Maxime Weygand, chief of the General Staff of the French army, was able to secure only 690 million francs for his six-year program to modernize France's armed forces, which had a projected overall price tag of 9 billion francs (or roughly 1.5 billion annually). And this was just the beginning. From 1930 to 1933, defense spending was cut by 25 percent—in fact military spending at the 1930 level would not be reached until 1937. Between 1933 and 1938, German defense spending would practically triple France's, and during roughly the same period (1934–38, already two years after the start of the German rearmament effort), real military spending in Germany would increase by 470 percent, in France, 41 percent. Even Britain, often criticized for its sluggish response to the German threat, increased defense spending by 250 percent in real terms over this period.[58]

In 1933 budget constraints led to a contraction of the army—500 officers and 28,000 soldiers were let go from the service. Responding to complaints from the navy about its budget cuts, Finance Minister Henry Cheron wrote: "The present circumstances require that we save the national finances in order to save the value of the currency . . . this too is, in the very highest degree, a question of national defense."[59] Measures to reduce military spending were proposed with such regularity it was reported that General Weygand was reluctant to leave Paris out of fear that

---

[57] Wolfe, *The French Franc*, p. 75; Mouré, *The Franc Poincaré*, p. 39; Adamthwaite, *Grandeur and Misery*, p. 149.

[58] Shamir, *Economic Crisis*, p. 44; Adamthwaite, *Coming of the Second World War*, p. 165; Barry Posen, *The Sources of Military Doctrine: France, Britain and Germany between the World Wars* (Ithaca: Cornell University Press, 1984), p. 20.

[59] Martin S. Alexander, "In Defense of the Maginot Line: Security Policy, Domestic Politics and Economic Depression in France," in Robert Boyce (ed.), *French Foreign and Defense Policy, 1918–1940: The Decline and Fall of a Great Power* (London: Routledge, 1998) p. 178 (quote).

TABLE 4.2
Military Spending in Germany and France

	France (billion francs)			Germany (billion marks)		
Year	National income	Military expenditure	% of GNP	National income	Military expenditure	% of GNP
1930–31	332	15.1	4.3	–	–	–
1931–32	312	12.9	4.1	58	.8	1
1933	259	11.7	4.5	59	1.9	3
1934	237	10.2	4.3	67	4.1	6
1935	221	10.4	4.7	74	6.0	8
1936	239	14.4	6.0	83	10.8	13
1937	304	20.8	6.8	93	11.7	13
1938	347	28.4	8.2	105	17.2	17
1939	407	92.7	22.8	130	30	23

Source: Adamthwaite, Coming of the Second World War, p. 164.

additional cuts might be ordered in his absence. Weygand was extraordinarily influential in France, and his strong opposition could bring down the government, even during the left-leaning cabinets of 1932–34. Weygand was almost always in sharp conflict with the Union des Gauches cabinets, fiercely opposed to efforts at multilateral disarmament, and viewed France's civilian leaders during the period with contempt. His feud with Daladier culminated in the complete collapse in relations between the two men in December 1933, and all of this contributed to the atmosphere that led to the events of February 6.[60]

Weygand was much more comfortable dealing with conservative leaders; he voiced few complaints about civil-military relations in the first quarter of the 1930s (before the union) and saw considerable improvement in relations after the conservatives regained control in 1934 until his retirement in 1935. But in reality this mattered little. The budgetary constraints and pressures that gutted the French military derived from financial orthodoxy, and this, much more than partisan politics, dictated

[60] Robert J. Young, In Command of France: French Foreign Policy and Military Planning, 1933–1940 (Cambridge, MA: Harvard University Press, 1978), p. 37; Philip C. F. Bankowitz, Maxime Weygand and Civil Military Relations in France (Cambridge, MA: Harvard University Press, 1967), pp. 49, 86, 88–89, 95, 104, 151. Bankowitz, sympathetic to Weygand, goes on at length (pp. 168–96) to support the argument that Weygand was not at fault for the events of February 6. For a less sympathetic treatment, see Shirer, Collapse of the Third Republic, pp. 220, 226–27.

the pace of disarmament. Even if the hearts and minds of the French Right were still, in the early 1930s, in favor of a stronger defense and more assertive foreign policy (while the Left still championed multilateral disarmament and pacifism), ultimately, they listened only to their wallets. Military spending was cut sharply in 1930–32, and the cuts continued after the conservatives regained power.[61]

In fact, 1934 represented the low point for French military spending, and the budget featured severe cuts in the purchase of new weapons. In the following year, the second full year of conservative rule, military expenditures finally increased by 200 million francs, an increase of just under 2 percent (German military spending increased by 50 percent from 1934 to 1935, see table 4.2). Spending would have been greater if not for the constraints imposed by high finance. Flandin's new spending program, introduced in 1935, would have raised defense expenditures, before he was forced into retreat by the Bank of France. Even when the government found a way to increase military spending, those measures could be described as "faltering and continuously at the mercy of financial constraints." In 1934 and 1935, for example, the government was able to squeeze in bits of new military spending through the introduction of highly creative accounting techniques. Clearly, however, they were working from within a straitjacket, and there was a limit to how much rearmament could be accomplished solely by juggling the books. And with Laval's efforts at "superdeflation" in late 1935 and early 1936, Flandin's modest efforts were scaled back, and the defense budget was scoured for new sources of financial savings as part of Laval's across-the-board budget cuts.[62]

The contraction of French military spending did more than just homothetically contract France's power; it also affected the nature of French power. This is related to the question of doctrine, which has generated an important debate that is not of central concern here. But the discussion of how the pressures of financial orthodoxy shaped and constrained French strategy can shed light on aspects of that question.

Barry Posen's classic treatment, *The Sources of Military Doctrine*, attributes the adoption of a defensive posture by France to systemic factors. France, intimidated by German strength, saw British participation in any future war as crucial. A defensive doctrine was more in line with Britain's political and military caution—the British would be less likely to support

---

[61] Bankowitz, *Maxime Weygand*, pp. 83, 99, 152; Werth, *Twilight of France*, p. 8; Adamthwaite, *Coming of the Second World War*, p. 26.

[62] Martin S. Alexander, *The Republic in Danger: General Maurice Gamelin and the Politics of French Defense, 1933–1940* (Cambridge: Cambridge University Press, 1992), pp. 56, 58–61; David Kaiser, *Economic Diplomacy and the Origins of the Second World War: Germany, Britain, France, and Eastern Europe, 1930–1939* (Princeton: Princeton University Press, 1980), p. 203; Jackson, *Politics of Depression*, pp. 2 (quote), 108.

a war where France was perceived to be the aggressor. The defensive would also buy time needed to get Britain into the war, and, importantly, shift more of the costs of the conflict onto Britain than would be the case had France pursued an offensive strategy.[63]

Beth Kier, on the other hand, argues that systemic factors are indeterminate, and that the choice of doctrine can be understood only via domestic-level variables—political conflict within France and the distinct organizational culture of the French military. Specifically, Kier argues that opposing forces within French society had competing visions for the military. The Left preferred a force drawn from the general public—a military fully integrated into republican France. The Right preferred a more professional force, and one that stood apart from other elements of French society. The Left won this battle, with the reduction of military service in 1928 from two years to one, a term more conducive to "citizen soldiers" than a highly professionalized service. This had a profound and unintended effect, Kier argues, in that the French military elites could not imagine conducting an offensive war with short-term conscripts. Thus, domestic politics and organizational culture, not systemic constraints, explain French doctrine.[64]

While Posen and Kier disagree on a number of issues, since their chosen variables point in the same direction in this case, it is also possible to view their explanations as complementary.[65] More to the point for the current discussion, both authors leave unexplored a crucial puzzle: why, regardless of doctrine, was France not better prepared for the Second World War? Even if only for defense, why not a stronger and better-equipped defense, especially given the threat? Although solving this riddle is not necessary for the principal goals of both books—explaining doctrine—the question is of great significance. Kier, given her chosen variables, does capture the iron links between domestic politics and foreign policy in interwar France. But she minimizes the cost constraints faced by the military. Posen, on the other hand, is more sensitive to cost consciousness in

[63] Posen, *Sources of Military Doctrine*, pp. 130, 135, 139, 236; see also Robert J. Young, "La Guerre de Longue Durée: Some Reflections on French Strategy and Diplomacy in the 1930s," in Adrian Preston (ed.), *General Staffs and Diplomacy before the Second World War* (London: Croom Helm, 1978); Thomas J. Christensen and Jack Snyder, "Chain Gangs and Passed Bucks: Predicting Alliance Patterns in Multipolarity," *International Organization* 44:2 (Spring 1990), pp. 159–62.

[64] Beth Kier, *Imagining War: French and British Military Doctrine between the Wars* (Princeton: Princeton University Press, 1997), pp. 3, 5, 7, 12, 41, 56, 140.

[65] Posen, for example, argues that decisions made in the 1920s—the introduction of one-year conscription and the construction of fortifications—made "a substantially defensive strategy . . . almost inevitable"; *Sources of Military Doctrine*, p. 119. This is not to deny that there are sharp disagreements between the two authors on important theoretical issues and more broadly in their treatment of the British case.

France, but he explicitly holds domestic politics constant.[66] His systemic emphasis also calls greater attention to France's underresponsiveness in the shadow of the towering German menace, a threat, according to Posen, that was clearly understood by no later than 1934. Yet ultimately, while both tried to buck-pass, and although France faced the more proximate threat, contrary to what systemic pressures would suggest, "the British . . . insured themselves against the worst, the French did not."[67]

France was less well prepared than it could have been because of the ravages of financial orthodoxy. Further, the constraints imposed by orthodoxy introduce yet another reason why French doctrine was defensive. It simply would not have been possible to provide the military hardware necessary for an offensive doctrine and maintain the economic policies demanded by the Bank of France and the French Right.

The cuts and constraints imposed on the defense budget hit hardest on areas that were needed most, such as expensive new weapons programs, and this also would have effectively precluded an offensive doctrine were one so desired. The constant pressures on spending described earlier meant that when new funds were made available, it was unlikely that they would be earmarked for major new systems. The pie was not getting any bigger, and there were only so many slices. A huge chunk went to the Maginot line, a popular and ongoing multiyear project that commenced during the Poincaré years. Funds had been earmarked for the line, and they were largely protected from the budget cutter's ax. Even as the military contracted, other fixed costs for manpower and general upkeep were also essentially invariable. Thus when something had to go, the only place left was new weapons. From the end of 1927 through the middle of 1936, France spent 6 billion francs on fortifications and 3.4 billion on weapons. Finance was the "soft underbelly" of France's defense posture.[68]

The budgetary constraints on French military spending underscore the crucial links between finance, strategy, and politics. There were several reasons why France adopted a defensive posture before the Second World War, but as long as financial interests controlled the purse, an offensive

[66] Kier, *Imagining War*, pp. 49, 52, 83–84; Posen, *Sources of Military Doctrine*, pp. 224, 234. Posen notes that "French domestic politics played a role in French grand strategy that I have not even attempted to analyze," p. 240.

[67] Posen, *Sources of Military Doctrine*, pp. 126, 178 (quote).

[68] Bradford A. Lee, "Strategy, Arms, and the Collapse of France, 1930–40," in Richard Langhorne (ed.), *Diplomacy and Intelligence during the Second World War* (Cambridge: Cambridge University Press, 1985), pp. 59, 63 (quote), 64, 65; Shamir, *Economic Crisis* ("deflationary policies struck a blow at the offensive capabilities of the army"), p. 26; Young, *In Command of France*, pp. 41, 58; see also Kaiser, *Economic Diplomacy*, pp. 203–4; Charles Kupchan, *The Vulnerability of Empire* (Ithaca: Cornell University Press, 1994), pp. 217, 221.

doctrine would not have been possible anyway. In the words of one leading expert on France's armament program, the "domestic fears and interests" of the French Right were consistent with "deflation and with the defensive military strategy." Worse, budgetary constraints prevented France from fielding as effective a defense as it otherwise might have done. Even on defense, military modernization would have greatly enhanced French security. But time and time again, new weapons programs and efforts at modernization were the first, easiest place to find savings from the budget, given the barriers to cuts in other areas.[69]

Fragile Franc, Timid Statesmen

Even in the relatively flush years of the 1920s, those interests in France most sensitive to financial stability saw important links between the vital demands of monetary stability and the limitations this implied for foreign policy. Aristide Briand, foreign minister from 1925 to 1932, famously (or infamously) pursued "Locarno diplomacy," a web of ultimately ill-fated efforts to settle Europe's political struggles and rivalries through a series of treaties, agreements, and understandings. An important motivating factor behind Briand's efforts (and an important source of political support for those policies) was concern for the weakness of the franc. In 1925 and 1926 rampant inflation motivated the search for a political accommodation with Germany; after the Poincaré stabilization in 1926, even the hard-line prime minister, his greatest priority now ensuring the stability of the franc, authorized Briand, if with some skepticism, to continue his efforts to find a broad political understanding with Germany that would keep France secure and thus reduce the need for defense spending. This in turn went hand in hand with the shift to a defensive strategy (and the Maginot line), which, in a more cooperative international environment, would be politically popular and fiscally attractive.[70]

[69] Robert Frankenstein, "The Decline of France and French Appeasement Policies, 1936–9," in Wolfgang J. Mommsen and Lothar Kettenacker (eds.), *The Fascist Challenge and the Policy of Appeasement* (London: George Allen and Unwin,1983), p. 237; Alexander, "In Defense of the Maginot Line," p. 175; Alexander, *The Republic in Danger*, pp. 57, 62; Weber, *The Hollow Years*, pp. 246–47, 254; Adamthwaite, *Grandeur and Misery*, p. 191.

[70] Jon Jacobson and John T. Walker, "The Impulse for a Franco-German Entente: The Origins of the Thoiry Conference, 1926," *Journal of Contemporary History* 10:1 (January 1925), pp. 164–65, 169–70; Edward D. Keeton, "Economics and Politics in Briand's German Policy, 1925–1931," in Carole Fink, Isabel V. Hull, and MacGregor Knox (eds.), *German Nationalism and the European Response, 1890–1945* (Norman: University of Oklahoma Press, 1985), pp. 170, 172, 179; Alexander, "In Defense of the Maginot Line," pp. 172–73; Adamthwaite, *Grandeur and Misery*, pp. 111, 117, 118; see also Jon Jacobson, "The Conduct of Locarno Diplomacy," *The Review of Politics* 34:1 (January 1972), esp. p. 76.

In the 1920s, the case could be made for the search for accommodation, even if motivated by a tight wallet. In the 1930s, however, the commitment to financial orthodoxy inhibited French diplomacy with great consequence, at inopportune moments. For not only were concerns for the franc one of the motivations behind the balanced-budget obsessiveness, but the constant threat that a financial crisis would force the franc off gold paralyzed French leaders and contributed to a conciliatory bias in French foreign policy. In 1933 Governor Moret wrote in the bank's annual report that "the bank is resolved to consent to no measure whatsoever that could again endanger the stability of the franc."[71] This contributed to France's sluggish response to Germany's rearmament, which was clearly understood in France by the end of 1932. Citing the pace of German rearmament, France withdrew from multilateral disarmament negotiations in April 1934. Opponents of the disarmament talks had argued that they inhibited France from embarking upon ambitious new armaments programs, but neither the end of the talks nor the arrival of the new conservative government was accompanied by major new spending.[72]

Rather, just as the Shidehara diplomacy in Japan went hand in hand with financial orthodoxy, adherence to orthodoxy in France required, if not appeasement, something very close to it. It is no coincidence that the Laval superdeflation of 1935 was engineered by "one of the few Frenchmen committed to Franco-German rapprochement." Others would write more plainly that some in France thought that "to defend the franc was more important than national defense."[73] This was not, of course, divorced from material interest. Deflation had been good to high

[71] Mouré, *The Franc Poincaré*, p. 151. This was, of course, the long-held view of the Bank of France. Moreau held that ensuring the convertibility of the franc was the only fundamental role for the bank; he repeatedly emphasized that the bank was a private institution and would not discuss policy with government officials outside of the Treasury. See Moreau, *The Golden Franc*, pp. 128, 513–15, 517–18.

[72] J. Nere, *The Foreign Policy of France from 1914–1945* (London: Routledge and Kegan Paul, 1975), pp. 127, 129–30; Adamthwaite, *Coming of the Second World War*, pp. 27 ("the franc was the Achilles' heel of French Policy"); Bankowitz, *Maxime Weygand*, p. 151; Young, *In Command of France*, p. 53; Shamir argues that France was aware of Germany's secret rearmament efforts as early as 1931, and lodged protests with other states on the matter in multilateral settings (*Economic Crisis*, p. 63); Alexander states that "there was no shortage of information reaching the French high command about Germany's clandestine military build-up between 1930 and 1935," *The Republic in Danger*, p. 46.

[73] Young, *In Command of France*, p. 99 (quote); Werth spoke in person with Laval about his policy of rapprochement; see *Twilight of France*, pp. 33, 35; Shamir, *Economic Crisis*, p. 201 (quote). See also Michael Jabara Carley, "End of the 'Low Dishonest Decade': Failure of the Anglo-France-Soviet Alliance in 1939," *Europe-Asia Studies* 45:2 (1993), p. 305; Alexander, *The Republic in Danger*, p. 73.

finance and to the rentier class more generally. The real value of pensions, for example, rose by 46 percent during the first half of the 1930s.[74] But even these narrow gains came with great risks that would ultimately affect all. Even before superdeflation, in 1934, Paul Einzig underscored the basic choice, writing that "the French nation has to choose between the franc and France." Einzig, who only two years previously had criticized France's overly assertive and obstructionist foreign policy, now urged France to abandon its "fetish" of monetary orthodoxy, devalue, and come to its own defense before it was too late. He feared that France would soon

> be confronted with the dilemma of either sacrificing the franc or exposing herself to the danger of invasion. It is possible that the fanatic adherents of monetary orthodoxy will be sufficiently influential to delay urgent armament expenditure in order to avoid jeopardizing the stability of the franc.[75]

But this was the course France followed until September 1936. Each year leading up to that point France recognized new German challenges and remained passive. In 1933 France was aware that Germany was in violation of the arms limits imposed by the Treaty of Versailles but did nothing in response. A dramatic increase in German military spending in March 1934 did contribute to the withdrawal of France from multilateral disarmament talks but, as noted, had no effect on French policy. On March 16, 1935, Germany took a much bolder step, announcing the reestablishment of compulsory military service. Further, the German army would expand to thirty-six divisions, more than five times the ceiling mandated by the Versailles treaty. Here there was even less room to allow for competing explanations of German behavior. Yet France again stood by passively, aside from raising protests and seeking to stitch together a multilateral response, which came to nothing. The threat of capital flight reinforced the policy of appeasement. In the words of one critic, "Since many

[74] Brendan Browne, *The Flight of International Capital: A Contemporary History* (London: Croom Helm, 1987), pp. 67, 84.

[75] Paul Einzig, *France's Crisis* (London: Macmillan, 1934), pp. viii, ix (quote), 12, 102 (quote), 119; see also Einzig, *Economics of Rearmament*, pp. 98, 99–100. There is a fascinating change of tone in Einzig's work; in *Rearmament*, published in February 1934, Einzig matter-of-factly assumed that France would be forced to abandon deflation in order to rearm. In *Crisis*, published in September, Einzig's tone is more urgent as he realizes that France might stick with orthodoxy, preventing needed rearmament. See also Einzig, *Bankers, Statesmen, and Economists*, pp. 224–25. For Einzig's earlier criticisms of French policy, see Einzig, *Finance and Politics* (London: Macmillan, 1932) and *The Fight for Financial Supremacy* (London: Macmillan, 1931).

capital holders preferred to forget national priorities, and even national defense, for political reasons or out of self-interest, any government was condemned to a certain impotence."[76]

This would have more severe consequences one year later. On March 7, 1936, Germany remilitarized the Rhineland. Not only was this in direct violation of the Treaty of Versailles, it also closed the corridor through which France would have, in theory, come to the defense of its eastern allies. Yet again, France took no action, a policy that has been called "the first capitulation."[77]

Why did France fail to act? Its political and military leadership was not caught by surprise—by January 1936 at the latest France was aware of Germany's intentions, if not the exact timing of the move. The gravity of the situation and the political costs of inaction were also discussed and understood by political and military elites, yet France did not lift a finger in response.[78] Once again, a number of factors involving both domestic and international politics contributed to the outcome. Domestic political conflict continued to paralyze foreign policy, and it also became clear that no foreign power, such as Britain, would participate in military action against Germany. But financial questions were decisive and essentially ruled out the use of force, or even the threat of force. The military had been so weakened by the cuts of the previous five years that it did not have a large standing force capable of swift offensive action.[79] Worse, mobilization was incompatible with the protection of the franc. It would have required devaluation.

This stark fact guaranteed French inaction, because in March 1936 the proponents of orthodoxy still held the reins of power in France. As one student of the crisis observed, "Hitler and the rest of the world knew"

[76] Young, *In Command of France*, p. 37; Nere, *Foreign Policy of France*, p. 152; René Girault, "The Impact of the Economic Situation on the Foreign Policy of France, 1936–9," in Mommsen and Kettenacker, *Fascist Challenge*, p. 223 (quote); see also pp. 214, 216; Shamir, *Economic Crisis*, pp. 133, 211, 215; see also D. C. Watt, *Too Serious a Business: European Armed Forces and the Approach of the Second World War* (Berkeley: University of California Press, 1975), pp. 27, 37, 92–93.

[77] See Piotr Wandycz, *The Twilight of French Eastern Alliances, 1926–1936: French-Czechoslovak-Polish Relations from Locarno to the Remilitarization of the Rhineland* (Princeton: Princeton University Press, 1988), pp. 434–36, 444–45; Kaiser, *Economic Diplomacy*, pp. 197, 207; R.A.C. Parker, "The First Capitulation: France and the Rhineland Crisis of 1936," *World Politics* 8:3 (April 1956), p. 367.

[78] Nere, *Foreign Policy of France*, pp. 186–89; Raphaelle Ulrich, "Rene Massigli and Germany, 1919–1938," in Boyce (ed.), *French Foreign and Defense Policy*, p. 143.

[79] James Thomas Emmerson, *The Rhineland Crisis, 7 March 1936: A Study in Multilateral Diplomacy* (Ames: Iowa State University Press, 1977), pp. 39, 41, 47; Parker, "First Capitulation," p. 371; Shamir, *Economic Crisis*, p. 218. Adamthwaite, *Grandeur and Misery*, p. 203 ("financial and military weakness dictated acquiescence"); see also p. 209.

that the French government would "above all . . . do nothing that would endanger the franc." Even *couverture*, the state of armed readiness that would precede a general mobilization, would have cost thirty million francs a day. This cost, Stephen Schuker argues, although not impossible, would "undoubtedly provoke a run on the franc." Because of the fragility of France's financial position, full mobilization would have led to an immediate "full-scale monetary crisis" and "exposed the virtual bankruptcy of the French treasury and toppled the franc."[80]

Any doubts about this relationship were erased as capital flight and pressure on the franc increased in the few days before it was known that France would not take any strong measures of resistance. On Sunday, March 8, there were rumors that France might use force against Germany, and on Monday the franc came under renewed pressure in international markets. This pressure did not abate until Wednesday, after the announcement that France would act only with multilateral support and within the framework of the League of Nations, which made it clear that there would be no military response to the German provocation.[81] The franc would be defended above all other concerns.

Devaluation and Rearmament

With the arrival of the Popular Front government in June 1936, the elements of financial orthodoxy were sequentially abandoned. Having run on the oxymoronic platform "Neither deflation nor devaluation," reflation came first. The balanced budget no longer guided policy, and this finally allowed for substantial increases in military spending. Within months, this put pressure on the franc, and, when forced to choose between the franc and reflation, the Socialists chose the latter. Indeed it was Blum's announcement of a major new military spending package of 14 billion francs that precipitated the crisis that led to the devaluation. The relaxation of the budget constraint, rearmament, and devaluation went hand in hand.[82]

[80] Emmerson, *The Rhineland Crisis*, p. 78 (quote); see also pp. 105, 111, 247. Stephen Schuker, "France and the Remilitarization of the Rhineland, 1936," *French Historical Studies* 14:3 (Spring 1986), pp. 304, 330, 335 (quotes). Note that Schuker's conclusion is not that France should have devalued and mobilized but that the mistakes that led to March 1936 meant that by then it was already too late, pp. 320, 338.

[81] Browne, *The Flight of International Capital*, pp. 71–72; Schuker, "Remilitarization of the Rhineland," p. 334; Mouré, *The Franc Poincaré*, p. 152; see also "The Repudiation of Locarno," *The Economist*, March 14, 1936, pp. 582–83, and "French Financial Weakness," *The Economist*, March 28, 1936, p. 711.

[82] Martin Thomas, "French Economic Affairs and Rearmament: The First Crucial Months, June-September 1936," *Journal of Contemporary History* 27:4 (October 1992), p. 668; Lee, "Strategy, Arms, and the Collapse," p. 65; Nere, *Foreign Policy of France*,

Until the bitter end, however, the financial community, and the Bank of France, opposed and fought devaluation, even though it was increasingly obvious to most other observers that it was undoubtedly the right and necessary move. *The Economist*, urging devaluation as the only way to resolve France's "extremely virulent and intractable economic malady," noted critically that "the financial interests which support the right are unalterably opposed to devaluation."[83] Nor was there any mystery regarding the link between devaluation and rearmament. Paul Reynaud, a conservative stalwart and former minister of finance, broke with his party and came out publicly for devaluation in 1934, citing the need to rearm and face the German threat. In response, the Bank of France redoubled its efforts, printing and distributing fifty-two thousand copies of its pamphlet "No New Monetary Bankruptcy: The Franc Must Remain the Franc" and secretly financing public lectures and widespread campaigns in the media. Its efforts were successful in slowing the growth in support of devaluation, which was finally visible as 1936 approached, if still virtually unmentionable in the elections of that year.[84]

The link between devaluation and rearmament was underscored by how the devaluation was finally brought about. Instead of simply announcing a change in the franc's value, the measure was dressed up as a currency "realignment," taken in concert with the United States and Great Britain, in a pact known as the Tripartite Monetary Agreement. France was motivated by an effort to provide some foreign cover for the act—still unpopular but ultimately met with resignation—and to ensure that the measure would not be undercut by new rounds of devaluation by the others.[85] The motives of the other parties, and especially the United

---

pp. 195–96. Jackson writes that "broadly speaking, whereas between 1932 and 1936 arms spending had been largely subject to financial and economic policy, between 1936 and 1939 the relationship was reversed"; *Politics of Depression*, p. 207.

[83] "France Wavers," *The Economist*, June 8, 1935, p. 1292; the preferred remedy of finance and the Right, "budget cuts and a high bank rate, while leaving the overvaluation of the franc unsolved, would almost certainly result in an intensification of the already intense economic depression."

[84] M. Paul Reynaud, "The New French Parliament and the Financial and International Situation," *International Affairs* 15:5 (September–October 1936), pp. 705, 708; aware that many might wish to avoid an unnecessary arms race, Reynaud urged his audience at the Royal Institute for International Affairs to understand the difference between "the future attackers and the future attacked," arguing that Germany had made its intentions clear and could be stopped only by a strong and united Britain and France; pp. 710 (quote), 711. On the resistance of the bank, see Mouré, *The Gold Standard*, pp. 58, 181, 209–10, 213–15, 226; see also Mouré, " 'Une Eventualité Absolument Exclude': French Reluctance to Devalue, 1933–1936," *French Historical Studies* 15:3 (Spring 1988), pp. 480, 486–87, 491, 496.

[85] Werth, *Twilight of France*, p. 106; Kenneth Oye, "The Sterling-Dollar-Franc Triangle: Monetary Policy, 1929–37," in Oye (ed.), *Cooperation under Anarchy* (Princeton: Princeton University Press, 1986).

States, are quite illustrative. The United States saw little at stake in the economic merits of the agreement and stuck with the pact long past the point it would have were its concerns truly with nominal function of coordinating exchange rates. Rather, the Americans supported the agreement because they thought that the devaluation of the franc was necessary to allow for needed French rearmament, and because they were looking for a measure that would signal to Germany increased cooperation among the western democracies.[86]

Monetary cooperation had escaped the three western powers as recently as three years previously, with the failed London Economic Conference. But the political landscape had changed quite dramatically in the interim. In the six months prior to the agreement alone, Fascist aggression appeared at every turn: Germany had remilitarized the Rhineland, Italy conquered Ethiopia, and the Spanish Civil War commenced. Britain and the United States were motivated by a desire to support French democracy and rearmament, not by any anticipated economic benefits from the pact. U.S. Treasury secretary Henry Morgenthau, confident that the agreement would not have any significant effect on the U.S. economy, was determined to use international monetary policy for international political purposes. He saw the pact as "a threat to Italy and Germany . . . a notice to the boys—Achtung!"[87]

A mixed bag at best from an economic standpoint,[88] from a political perspective the agreement was successful; devaluation did allow for rearmament. Ironically, as Robert Frankenstein noted, "the Popular Front did more for 'guns' than for 'butter' in France." When the Socialist government was forced to retreat from many of its goals, especially in 1937, social spending took the first hits in order to sustain the maximum

[86] Jonathan Kirshner, *Currency and Coercion: The Political Economy of International Monetary Power* (Princeton: Princeton University Press, 1995), pp. 91–95; see also Shamir, *Economic Crisis*, p. 225.

[87] Harold van B. Cleveland, "The International Monetary System in the Interwar Period," in Benjamin Rowland (ed.), *Balance of Power or Hegemony: The Interwar Monetary System* (New York: New York University Press, 1976), p. 51. On the primacy of political motives for Britain, see Rowland, "Preparing for American Ascendancy: The Transfer of Economic Power from Britain to the United States, 1933–1944," in Rowland, *Balance of Power*, p. 209. On Morgenthau, see Kenneth Oye, *Economic Discrimination and Political Exchange* (Princeton: Princeton University Press, 1992), p. 128 (quote); J. M. Blum, *From the Morgenthau Diaries* (Boston: Houghton Mifflin, 1959), 1:140, 471. See also Ian M. Drummond, *London, Washington, and the Management of the Franc*, Princeton Studies in International Finance 45 (November 1979), pp. 3–4, 32, 53; S.V.O. Clarke, *Exchange Rate Stabilization in the Mid-1930s: Negotiating the Tripartite Monetary Agreement*, Princeton Studies in International Finance 41 (September 1977).

[88] Oye, in "Sterling-Dollar-Franc Triangle," accentuates the positive; much more skeptical are Drummond, in *Management of the Franc*, and Kirshner, in *Currency and Coercion*.

amount of military expenditure. Spending on weapons was two and a half times greater in 1937 than it had been in 1935. Military spending increased even further in 1938, and in 1939 France produced more tanks and planes than did Germany. The rearmament program was substantial and did affect the military balance. But it did not make up for the fact that France was severely handicapped by its late start, and improvements in the readiness of the armed forces did not solve the problem of France's dismal strategic planning.[89]

Additionally, while finance had lost the political battle, it continued to fight the war for financial orthodoxy with those tools that remained at its disposal. Presented with economic constraints in February 1937, Blum was willing to scale back social spending but remained committed to rearmament and would not propose exchange controls. But the government's need to borrow and the ability of money to flee the country "made the Popular Front cabinets . . . prisoners of capital holders." A financial crisis in June forced Blum's resignation, causing a retreat in policy that slowed the economy. Blum returned to power in March 1938, this time proposing further increases in defense spending and, most controversially, exchange controls. As Talbot Imlay has argued, Blum finally acknowledged that "unless capital flight could be prevented, the franc . . . would be at the mercy of capital holders, who had in the past repeatedly put their own interests above those of the nation." But Blum's program was rejected by the Senate Finance Commission, forcing his resignation less than a month after his return to office. His successor, Daladier, took exchange control off the table; although he remained committed to the rearmament effort, these efforts were handicapped by slower growth in 1938 and by repeated rounds of capital flight.[90]

Even in the general context of rearmament, clashes between the government and financial interests over military spending continued. In late 1937 the influential economist and prominent central bank figure Jacques Rueff argued "repeatedly in favor of sacrificing rearmament to orthodox finance." Even in 1938, after the Anschluss, Rueff stated that defense spending for 1938 should be held to its 1937 level. Nor did devaluation

---

[89] Frankenstein, "French Appeasement Policies," pp. 238 (quote), 239; Williamson Murry, *The Change in the European Balance of Power, 1938–1939* (Princeton: Princeton University Press, 1984), pp. 95, 102–3, 106–7; Weber, *The Hollow Years*, p. 173; Anthony Adamthwaite, "France and the Coming of War," in Mommsen and Kettenacher, *The Fascist Challenge*, p. 255; Young, *In Command of France*, pp. 162, 166, 173, 181; Lee, "Strategy, Arms, and the Collapse," pp. 66, 67.

[90] Thomas, "French Economic Affairs," pp. 659–60, 662; Adamthwaite, *Grandeur and Misery*, p. 145 (quote); "investors scared by the Popular Front sold their francs and exported gold," p. 207. Imlay, *Facing the Second World War*, pp. 256 (quote), 262, 264. On exchange control, see also Mouré, *The Franc Poincaré*, p. 243, and Wolfe, *The French Franc*, p. 170.

eliminate all concerns for the franc; it continued to decline and was subject to severe pressure during periods of great international tension (pressures that would have been less intense with capital controls). In May 1938 the franc was devalued for the third time in three years. The gathering momentum toward war did little to alter the preferences of finance. In the following winter, after the Munich crisis, concerns for the franc led the government to cut back its proposed purchase of U.S. aircraft from one thousand to six hundred. In March 1939, in a letter written *after* Germany seized what was left of Czechoslovakia, in violation of the Munich accords, officials in the Ministry of Finance urged Daladier to scale back the "already ruinous level of military spending." In January 1940 the Bank of France, alarmed by the decline in France's gold reserves, called for a reduction in purchases from the United States, contributing to another debate over how many warplanes the country could afford to buy.[91] Technically at war, with the German invasion months away, many in France remained determined to hold on to as much of their money as possible. In the decade leading up to the Second World War, France would have been better off if finance had been less influential.

[91] Jackson, *Politics of Depression*, p. 207 (quote of Jackson regarding Rueff); Frankenstein, "French Appeasement Policies," pp. 241, 245; Young, *In Command of France*, p. 186; Adamthwaite, *France and the Coming of the Second World War*, pp. 163, 200; Alexander, *The Republic in Danger*, p. 138; Imlay, *Facing the Second World War*, pp. 273 (quote), 291–92.

CHAPTER 5

"National Security Rests on the Dollar": The Early Cold War and Korea

The debates about the construction of U.S. foreign policy during the early cold war represent an extraordinarily difficult challenge to the thesis of this book—that finance will be extremely cautious and among the most reluctant of warriors (hot or cold)—for three principal reasons.[1] First, cold-war internationalism was the basis for President Harry Truman's foreign policy, and the political alignment of the period required that support for those ambitious foreign policies come from the financial community's home base: the Northeast. Democrat Truman faced stiff opposition from the Republican Party and, with regard to foreign policy, especially from its influential isolationists of the Midwest and the mountain states. Moreover, even within the president's own party, southern Democrats' commitment to small government and states' rights left them an unlikely source of support for ambitious internationalism. Indeed, as is well and properly understood, the bedrock of political support for internationalism, engagement, European reconstruction, and collective security could be found in the Northeast and especially in states and regions that had commercial and financial interests with transatlantic ties.[2] Moreover, many of the most influential architects of Truman's foreign policy were lawyers and invest-

---

[1] There is a vast literature on the early cold war. For a general overview, see Melvyn Leffler, *A Preponderance of Power: National Security, the Truman Administration, and the Cold War* (Stanford: Stanford University Press, 1993). On early grand strategy with an emphasis on economic debates and constraints, see Michael J. Hogan, *A Cross of Iron: Harry S. Truman and the Origins of the National Security State, 1945–1954* (Cambridge: Cambridge University Press, 1998), and Aaron Friedberg, *In the Shadow of the Garrison State: America's Anti-Statism and Its Cold War Grand Strategy* (Princeton: Princeton University Press, 2000).

[2] Lynn Eden, "Capitalist Conflict and the State: The Making of United States Military Policy in 1948," in Charles Bright and Susan Harding (eds.), *Statemaking and Social Movements: Essays in Theory and History* (Ann Arbor: University of Michigan Press, 1984), pp. 242–44; Thomas Christensen, *Useful Adversaries: Grand Strategy, Domestic Mobilization, and Sino American Conflict, 1947–1958* (Princeton: Princeton University Press, 1996), p. 71; Friedberg, *Garrison State*, pp. 43–44; Hogan, *Cross of Iron*, pp. 5–6, 28; see also David S. McLellan and Charles E. Woodhouse, "The Business Elite and Foreign Policy," *Western Political Quarterly* 13:1 (March 1960), and Ronald J. Caridi, *The Korean War and American Politics: The Republican Party as a Case Study* (Philadelphia: University of Pennsylvania Press, 1968).

ment bankers who had made their fortunes on Wall Street (many would return there) representing internationally oriented firms.[3]

Second, the ideational climate of the postwar period created space for even relatively conservative minds to contemplate economic policies and options beyond the traditional menu offered by classical economics. The abject failure of monetary orthodoxy during the Great Depression, the wartime boom, and lingering concerns that the postwar economy might fall back into stagnation left society (and policy-makers) eager to do whatever was necessary to avoid the mistakes of the past. The rise of the intellectual influence of Keynesian economics at this time also shaped debates and expanded conceptions of what could and could not be considered "sound" economic policy. More subtly, early postwar Keynesians tended to marginalize the significance of monetary policy for the health of the economy as a whole.[4]

Finally, the early cold war itself represents a hard case for any theory that anticipates hearing the voice of constraint. At this time the United States was enormously—if not unprecedentedly—powerful as its economy roared ahead during the war that ravaged the productive capabilities of all of the other great powers in the system. The dollar was unrivaled and rock solid; concerns were widespread for its scarcity,[5] not its relative weakness, while the once mighty British pound survived on the life support of inconvertibility and looming devaluation; yet still it was the world's second most important currency. At the same time, it was unthinkable that America would have fought total war to ensure the unconditional surrender of the Fascist powers only to yield the stage to Stalin's Soviet Union. Given the sacrifices of the war, and the profound anticommunism deeply embedded in American society, "we can't afford it" seems

[3] Walter Isaacson and Evan Thomas, *The Wise Men: Six Friends and the World They Made* (New York: Simon and Schuster, 1986), pp. 112, 119, 350, 381, 571, 574; Eden, "Capitalist Conflict and the State," pp. 236–37. For a more ambitious claim linking the narrow economic interests (of firms and states and the preferences of their elected representatives) and internationalist foreign policy preferences, see Benjamin Fordham, *Building the Cold War Consensus: The Political Economy of U.S. National Security Policy, 1949–51* (Ann Arbor: University of Michigan Press, 2001), esp. pp. 4, 44, 77, 87, 95, 186.

[4] James L. Sundquist, Bertram R. Gross, Leon H. Keyserling, and Walter S. Salant, "The Employment Act of 1946," in Francis H. Heller (ed.), *Economics and the Truman Administration* (Lawrence: Regents Press of Kansas, 1981), p. 108; see also Seymour Harris (ed.), *The New Economics: Keynes' Influence on Theory and Public Policy* (New York: Alfred A. Knopf, 1952), and Karl Brunner and Allan H. Meltzer, *Money and the Economy: Issues in Monetary Analysis* (Cambridge: Cambridge University Press, 1993), p. 15.

[5] See, for example, Richard N. Gardner, *Sterling-Dollar Diplomacy* (Oxford: Oxford University Press, 1956), pp. 295, 308, 331; but see also the prescient, posthumous Keynes on the dollar shortage, "The Balance of Payments of the United States," *The Economic Journal* 56 (June 1946), pp. 172–87.

like an unlikely cry to be heard in the face of perceived Russian aggression, especially as the stakes seemed to be raised with each passing year from 1947 to 1950.

Yet despite all of this—political alliances, economic interests, permissive ideologies, preponderant power, and the gripping tenor of the early cold war—finance tenaciously clung to its core and unchanging macroeconomic preferences above all else. Financial interests were deeply skeptical of international institutions and costly commitments and opposed to increases in military spending. For most of the late 1940s, Truman and his conservative economic advisers fought to keep a lid on military spending, to the applause of the financial community. With the outbreak of the Korean War, and subsequently with China's intervention, the administration departed from this policy, as it revised upward the magnitude and imminence of the threat posed by global communism. At each of these points—the outbreak of the war and the expansion of the war—finance moved aggressively to seize control of monetary policy and ensure that no matter what, inflation would be kept low. To the financiers, inflation posed a greater threat to America than did Stalin.

In this chapter I consider each of these elements in turn. I first briefly review finance's opposition to the International Monetary Fund and the Marshall Plan. I then consider the budget debates of the 1940s and the financial community's opposition to increased defense spending, even as the cold war steadily intensified. In two subsequent sections I look closely at finance on the offensive: the bankers' instigation of a fight over monetary policy at the start of the Korean War and the full seizure of monetary authority in the wake of the Chinese entry into the war.

THE INTERNATIONAL MONETARY FUND AND THE MARSHALL PLAN

The opposition of the financial community to both the International Monetary Fund (IMF) and the Marshall Plan is not as inconsistent as it might appear at first glance. Certainly finance did eagerly envision a recovering, capitalist Europe, an open, thriving international economy, and an outward-oriented U.S. foreign economic policy designed to support those goals. What the community rejected, however, were the particular means chosen to try to achieve those ends. While to its framers the International Monetary Fund was an institution designed to encourage openness, ameliorate short-term balance of payments crises, and oversee the smooth functioning of the international monetary system, to those already in the business of global banking the institution might just as easily look like a scheme to interfere with market forces, coddle debtors, fuel inflation, and generally step on the toes of those who knew better.

Indeed, even scholars who have attempted to trace much of cold war U.S. foreign policy back to domestic economic interests acknowledge the opposition of the big banks to the IMF.[6] Thus, while it is unsurprising to learn that Robert Taft and the Republican isolationists in Congress opposed the creation of the fund, it is important to note as well the vehement opposition of the New York banking community. The American Bankers Association, the Federal Reserve Bank of New York (and its influential governor, Allan Sproul), and the *Wall Street Journal* all fought against the creation of the institution, and repeated efforts to find compromise provisions that would placate them failed.[7] The universal nature of the opposition is notable as well. In the words of one participant in the debates at the time, the leading New York bankers "condemned the fund." This included Leon Fraser, president of the First National Bank of New York, and Russell Leffingwell of Morgan Stanley, who dismissed the proposed IMF as a "dream child" designed to support unrealistic exchange rates.[8] As the president of the American Bankers Association (and vice chairman of the National City Bank of New York) told Congress plainly, "We think that the fund should not be created." It was too costly and unlikely either to lend on a sound basis or guarantee that U.S. interests would be protected.[9]

Perhaps even more notable is the opposition of the financial community to the Marshall Plan. The bold initiative can be seen (beyond the short-run humanitarian aspect) from either a realist or a revisionist perspective

[6] See, for example, Fred Block, *The Origins of International Economic Disorder: A Study of United States International Monetary Policy from World War II to the Present* (Berkeley: University of California Press, 1977), pp. 52–53.

[7] John Morton Blum, *From the Morgenthau Diaries: Years of War, 1941–1945* (Boston: Houghton Mifflin, 1967), pp. 427, 432; Robert A. Pollard, *Economic Security and the Origins of the Cold War, 1945–1950* (New York: Columbia University Press, 1985), p. 16; Eric Helleiner, *States and the Reemergence of Global Finance: From Bretton Woods to the 1990s* (Ithaca: Cornell University Press, 1994), pp. 39–44; Miles Kahler, "Bretton Woods and Its Competitors: The Political Economy of Institutional Choice," in David M. Andrews, C. Randall Henning, and Louis Pauly (eds.), *Governing the World's Money* (Ithaca: Cornell University Press, 2002), pp. 53, 54, 56.

[8] Raymond F. Mikesell, "The Bretton Woods Debates: A Memoir," *Essays in International Finance* 192 (March 1994), International Finance Section, Princeton University, p. 43 (quote); Ron Chernow, *The House of Morgan: An American Banking Dynasty and the Rise of Modern Finance* (New York: Atlantic Monthly Press, 1990), p. 518; Armand Van Dormael, *Bretton Woods: Birth of a Monetary System* (New York: Holmes and Meier, 1978), pp. 241, 244–45, 247–48, 255, 257.

[9] W. Randolph Burgess, "A Bretton Woods Formula," *Banking: Journal of the American Bankers Association* 37:11 (May 1945), pp. 33, 34, 35; see also Allan H. Meltzer, *A History of the Federal Reserve*, vol. 1, *1913–1951* (Chicago: University of Chicago Press, 2003), pp. 629, 724; Thomas G. Paterson, *Soviet-American Confrontation: Postwar Reconstruction and the Origins of the Cold War* (Baltimore: Johns Hopkins University Press, 1973), p. 150.

as an effort to help rehabilitate the struggling economies of western Europe so that capitalism and democracy could thrive in Britain and on the Continent, which would enhance the strategic and long-run economic goals of the United States.[10]

Various members of the Truman administration were undoubtedly motivated by differing combinations of humanitarian, strategic, and far-sighted economic concerns. But in making the case to the American people, Truman emphasized the security issue. In his October 1947 radio address to the nation, the president warned, "The most imminent danger exists in France and in Italy. If these countries collapse and the people succumb to totalitarian pressures, there will be no opportunity for them or for us to look forward to their recovery so essential to world peace."[11] Truman's instincts were correct, as it took the Communist coup in Czechoslovakia in February 1948 to ensure enough Republican votes in Congress to pass the Marshall Plan in March.[12]

But none of these strategic, humanitarian, or potential long-run economic prospects could sell the financial community on what looked to its members like little more than a massive handout. Worse, and of paramount concern, the sudden transfer of truly massive amounts of American purchasing power to the dollar-starved Europeans carried with it the threat of inflation. Early on in the debate, the American Bankers Association warned that "the Marshall Plan provides an automatic guarantee of continued inflation," indeed, of "advancing hordes of inflation." With reference to lend-lease and the British loan as unhappy precedents, and deriding the "European Shopping List," the association doubted that "any conceivable amount of American help will cause existing European socialism to be replaced by greater private capitalism" and concluded that "many thinking Americans" will wonder "just what lasting benefits we can expect from the fulfillment of Europe's requests" and whether "this Marshall Plan sacrifice is worth undertaking."[13]

Opposition to the plan was heated and consistent. In February the president of the association wrote, "Most of us believe that a substantial part

---

[10] See Michael Hogan, *The Marshall Plan: America, Britain, and the Reconstruction of Western Europe* (Cambridge: Cambridge University Press, 1987), esp. pp. 443–44; Fred Block, "Economic Instability and Military Strength: The Paradoxes of the 1950 Rearmament Decision," *Politics and Society* 10:1 (1980), pp. 43, 45, 49; see also Leffler, *Preponderance of Power*, pp. 157–64, 182–92.

[11] Harry S. Truman, *Memoirs: Years of Trial and Hope, 1946–1952* (New York: Doubleday, 1956), p. 117; see also pp. 111–21; see also Dean Acheson, *Present at the Creation: My Years at the State Department* (New York: Norton, 1969), pp. 229–34.

[12] Hogan, *Cross of Iron*, pp. 90, 94–95; Pollard, *Economic Security*, p. 151.

[13] "The Uncharted Course for the Future," *Banking* 40:5 (November 1947), p. 31; "The European Shopping List," *Banking* 40:5 (November 1947), p. 39.

of Europe's troubles can be corrected with a combination of sound money and hard work," and its journal continued to publish critical essays. Nor did the Marshall Plan's political and economic successes—grudgingly acknowledged—change this fundamental perspective. Rather, the approach was to highlight problems, emphasize pessimistic projections, and question the entire enterprise. In mid-1949 the director of the Bankers Trust Company of New York argued that the Marshall Plan amounted to "coddling socialism" and that it was "very doubtful whether we are doing the British a favor," since despite the noble goals of the European Recovery Program, its achievements had allowed the British Socialists to claim that their economic approach had been successful.[14]

In sum, with regard to two flagship political undertakings designed to defend global capitalism and ensure American participation and leadership in an open, outward-oriented international economy, the financial community stood opposed to both. While this seems counterintuitive at first glance, a distinction between ends and means resolves the apparent puzzle. The ends envisioned by the Marshall Plan and the International Monetary Fund were certainly in accord with the interests of finance, but the debate from their perspective was never a question of supporting an open international economic system; rather it was about the appropriate means to achieve those ends.[15] And the means mattered more, since, to a large extent, they reflected first principles: low inflation, limited government, sound money. Similarly, as the cold war heated up, finance took seriously the threat from Soviet communism, but in facing that challenge it never lost sight of the primacy of those first principles.

THE BUDGET BATTLES AND THE EARLY COLD WAR

Truman came to the presidency as a staunch fiscal conservative, with a deeply held, almost puritanical commitment to balanced budgets, sound

---

[14] "The Anti-Inflation Program of the American Bankers Association," *Banking* 40:8 (February 1948), p. 33; see also, for example, "The Coming Adventures of ERP," *Banking* 40:8 (February 1948), pp. 52–53; "Broad Ramifications of ERP," *Banking* 41:4 (October 1948), p. 50; "Dim View of Post ERP Outlook," *Banking* 41:8 (February 1949), p. 50; Fred I. Kent, "Are We Coddling Socialism Abroad, Too?" *Banking* 41:12 (June 1949), p. 33.

[15] Finance, sticking to its orthodox guns, envisioned an open international system based on strict adherence to classical liberal principles, rather than the "embedded liberalism" envisioned by the framers of the postwar international economic institutions. See Mark Blyth, *Great Transformations: Economic Ideas and Institutional Change in the Twentieth Century* (Cambridge: Cambridge University Press, 2002); Helleiner, *States and the Reemergence of Global Finance*, p. 39, and John Ruggie, "International Regimes, Transactions and Change: Embedded Liberalism in the Postwar Economic Order," *International Organization* 36:2 (Spring 1982), pp. 393–96.

money, and low inflation. His economic advisers were similarly minded. Secretary of the Treasury John Snyder, an intimately trusted confidant, was a fiscal conservative, as were Budget Directors James Webb and Frank Pace. Another influential voice was Edwin Nourse, first chairman of the newly formed Council of Economic Advisors. Nourse, sixty-three years old when he took the job, had been president of the American Economic Association and was widely respected by his fellow economists. Truman and Snyder were fiscal conservatives by instinct—Nourse preached financial orthodoxy with the confident authority of a professional, in a language recognizable and reassuring to the financial community.[16]

As the cold war emerged in 1946 and even as it crystallized in 1947, Truman was able to keep military spending down, proposing a defense budget of $11.8 billion for fiscal year 1947, with further cuts projected for each of the following fiscal years. The context of these cuts, postwar demobilization, should be understood; indeed, in historical perspective defense spending remained very high (it stood at $1.8 billion in 1940). Additionally, the Republicans in Congress, briefly ascendant after the 1946 elections, were eager to scale back both taxes and spending, which would require even deeper cuts to military spending.[17] And the financial community could still complain, with *Banking* providing a platform in March 1947 for the proposal to immediately cut federal spending by 20 percent and the observation that the proposed defense budget is *"not the minimum or even essential"* amount that must be spent. Nevertheless, in 1946 and 1947, Truman was able to anticipate continued reductions in both defense spending and total federal spending; the cold war did not yet present agonizing choices between national security and fiscal rectitude.[18]

---

[16] Oral History Interview with John W. Snyder, Truman Presidential Museum and Library, April 10, 1968, p. 560; Oral History Interview with Frank Pace Jr., Truman Presidential Museum and Library, January 17, 1972, p. 5, January 22, 1972, p. 5; Oral History Interview with Leon H. Keyserling, Truman Presidential Museum and Library, May 10, 1971, p. 20, May 19, 1971, pp. 9, 14; Hugh S. Norton, *The Employment Act and the Council of Economic Advisors, 1946–76* (Columbia: University of South Carolina Press, 1977), p. 104; Edward S. Flash Jr., *Economic Advice and Presidential Leadership: The Council of Economic Advisors* (New York: Columbia University Press, 1965), pp. 20, 21; Hogan, *Cross of Iron*, p. 69.

[17] Christensen, *Useful Adversaries*, p. 46; Warner R. Schilling, "The Politics of National Defense: Fiscal 1950," in Warner Schilling, Paul Y. Hammond, and Glenn H. Snyder, *Strategy, Politics and Defense Budgets* (New York: Columbia University Press, 1962), pp. 29, 30; Hogan, *Cross of Iron*, p. 86. Behind the formidable armor of Truman's fiscal conservatism beat the heart of a social liberal; within balanced budgets Truman hoped to find the resources necessary to expand domestic spending in support of the Fair Deal. Ultimately, Truman's domestic ambitions had to be sacrificed to support the bipartisan cold war coalition—this is the principal argument of Hogan's *Cross of Iron* and is also an important theme in Fordham's *Building the Cold War Consensus*.

[18] Rosewell McGill, "We Can't Afford this Budget," *Banking* 39:9 (March 1947), p. 29 (emphasis in original); Robert Donovan, *Conflict and Crisis: The Presidency of Harry S*

The events of 1948, however, would prove more challenging. The Communist coup in Czechoslovakia in February was an important psychological blow—the republic that had symbolized the hopes of Wilsonian self-determination in the twenties and the signature failure to resist fascism in the 1930s now seemed to reflect the darkest interpretation of Soviet motives. If the Soviet threat in the near term was military as well as political, then the United States faced considerable gaps in its ability to resist. A brief "war scare" followed, with significant implications for the defense budget. On March 17, speaking before a joint session of Congress convened for the occasion, Truman castigated the Soviet Union as a "growing menace" to freedom in Europe, condemning its "ruthless" action in Czechoslovakia and serial support of aggression against other states. By the end of the month, NSC-7 concluded that "the ultimate objective of Soviet-directed world communism is the domination of the world" and compared Stalin to Hitler. Tensions were also mounting over Berlin, and in June the Russians sealed off the city, to be countered by the drama of the airlift.[19]

The Pentagon asked for an additional $8.8 billion to meet the Soviet threat, a figure that "stunned" Truman, who had been warned by Nourse on March 24 that increased government spending might unleash rampant inflation. Truman responded that "we must be very careful that the military does not overstep the bounds from an economic standpoint domestically" and authorized a $3 billion increase. At the same time, he made plain that $15 billion should be understood as the maximum he was willing to allocate for defense.[20] Budget Director Webb was an important source of support for this policy, and among Truman's senior advisers, only Secretary of Defense James Forrestal was sympathetic to some further increases in military spending. Nourse thought that even the $3 billion threatened the economy, sharing the financiers' view that "industrial power" and "adequate capital supply" (two things threatened by a big weapons buildup) were the true foundations of American national security.[21]

Truman, 1945–1948 (New York: Norton, 1977), p. 261; Paul G. Pierpaoli, *Truman and Korea: The Political Culture of the Early Cold War* (Columbia: University of Missouri Press, 1999), pp. 17, 18.

[19] Donovan, *Conflict and Crisis*, p. 357; Truman, *Years of Trial and Hope*, p. 242 (quote); see also pp. 241–43, 120–30. NSC-7 is reprinted in Thomas Etzold and John Lewis Gaddis (eds.), *Containment: Documents on American Policy and Strategy, 1945–50* (New York: Columbia University Press, 1978), pp. 164–69.

[20] This is often referred to as $14.4 billion, as $600 million was set aside for the stockpiling of raw materials. Note also that this figure does not include foreign assistance.

[21] Hogan, *Cross of Iron*, pp. 103 (quote), 109 (Truman quote), 110; Edwin G. Nourse, *Economics in the Public Service: Administrative Aspects of the Employment Act* (New York: Harcourt, Brace, 1953), p. 486; Lester H. Brune, "Guns and Butter: The Pre-Korean War Dispute over Budget Allocations," *American Journal of Economics and Sociology* 48:3

The Joint Chiefs of Staff, however, thought the ceiling was simply incompatible with the basic needs of American security and, beset by irretrievably bitter interservice rivalries, refused even to produce a program based on the $15 billion limit. Forrestal sought the middle ground, warning that at $15 billion, national security could not be assured, and he urged the president to consider the compromise figure of $17.5 billion. But Truman and the economizers would not budge. Nourse lectured the military planners that any increase in defense spending would have unacceptable inflationary consequences, arguing that current levels were already so high that the economy had reached a critical point where "relatively small changes ... [would] have decisive influence" and might "cause long term damage" to the economy. Truman dismissed Forrestal's appeals, agreeing only to permit a new Policy Planning assessment of Soviet intentions and statement of U.S. strategic objectives (which would become NSC-20/4, the gloomy successor to NSC-7). But increases in defense spending were not forthcoming. As Forrestal wrote, Truman was "determined not to spend more than we take in in taxes. He is a hard money man if I ever saw one."[22]

If anything, toward the end of 1948 Truman was looking to reduce the defense burden, not add to it. Inflationary pressures were building, and Truman ran for reelection as an inflation fighter, which meant keeping the lid on spending. In the same month that he approved NSC-20/4, Truman commented at a press conference that he hoped to be able to reduce the military budget considerably, since "the country could not go on spending $14–15 billion a year for defense." After his surprise reelection (and the return of Democratic control of Congress), Truman directed Nourse to head an interdepartmental anti-inflationary task force, and in January he submitted a budget that reaffirmed the defense ceiling and sought new taxes (which Congress would not provide). In March Truman named the ambitious, bullying, and austerity-minded Louis Johnson to replace the more hawkish Forrestal at defense.[23]

(July 1989), p. 360; Melvyn P. Leffler, "The American Conception of National Security and the Beginnings of the Cold War, 1945–48," *The American Historical Review* 89:2 (April 1984), p. 376; Joseph Stag Lawrence, "Capital Markets and National Defense: The Backbone of American Military Security Is Industrial Power," *Banking* 40:10 (April 1948), pp. 33, 34 (quotes).

[22] Walter Mills (ed.), *The Forrestal Diaries* (New York: Viking Press, 1951), pp. 492, 500, 509, 536–37 (quote); Nourse, *Economics in the Public Service*, pp. 490 (quote), 494 (quote); Friedberg, *Garrison State*, p. 103; Hogan, *Cross of Iron*, pp. 161, 163, 171; Leffler, "American Conception of National Security," p. 377. NSC-20/4 is reprinted in Etzold and Gaddis, *Containment*, pp. 203–11.

[23] Craufurd D. Goodwin and R. Stanley Herren, "The Truman Administration: Problems and Policies Unfold," in Craufurd D. Goodwin (ed.), *Exhortation and Controls: The Search for a Wage-Price Policy, 1945–1971* (Washington, DC: Brookings Institution, 1975), p. 60;

In the spring of 1949, it was increasingly apparent that the economy was slowing, and the danger was now recession, not inflation. The slowdown in economic activity put pressure on the budget, and with tax increases off the political table, Truman instinctively reached for the budget ax. Writing to the National Security Council (NSC) on July 1, he explained that "levels contemplated for military and international aid programs in fiscal year 1950 are substantially above the levels we can hope to maintain consistent with a sound fiscal and economic program." Truman ordered that all defense and aid programs be reevaluated, and Pace drew up plans for detailed cuts of a little over $5 billion from these programs. Responding in late September, the NSC resisted, citing "grave risks" to U.S. military capabilities, and sought to recapture up to $2 billion of the proposed cuts. In response, Nourse fired off a memo to the council, warning that the deficits implied by the NSC's request "would have such adverse effects on the functioning of the domestic economy so as to threaten total national security." With Johnson cracking the whip, the economizers again held sway, and the defense ceiling was lowered to $13.5 billion.[24]

But even as these cuts were being enforced, the unrelenting intensification of the cold war meant that the defense debates had not been settled for good. In September Truman announced to the nation that the Russians had successfully tested a nuclear weapon, ending the American monopoly and pulling away the security blanket that had implicitly covered the gap between U.S. military commitments and capabilities; in October China, the world's most populous nation, fell to the Communists. Both events were not just real blows but also psychological ones that heightened fears and set off acrimonious domestic debates, and on January 31, 1950, Truman authorized the strategic review that would lead to NSC-68.[25]

Truman's staffing choices in his second administration, with the exception of the switch from Forrestal to Johnson, afforded greater influence to those who felt that the United States should—and could—increase its

---

Schilling, "Politics of National Defense," pp. 46, 48, 100; Friedberg, *Garrison State*, p. 104; Robert J. Donovan, *Tumultuous Years: The Presidency of Harry S Truman, 1949–1953* (New York: Norton, 1982), pp. 22–23, 58–59; Snyder, Oral History, July 10, 1968, p. 746.

[24] Bert G. Hickman, *Growth and Stability of the Postwar Economy* (Washington, DC: Brookings Institution, 1960), p. 71; Craufurd and Goodwin, "The Truman Administration," p. 63; *U.S. Department of State, Foreign Relations of the United States [FRUS] 1949*, vol. 1, *National Security Affairs, Foreign Economic Policy* (Washington, DC: U.S. Government Printing Office, 1976), pp. 350–52 (Truman); 353–55 (Pace); 368, 391, 393 (NSC); 394–95 (Nourse); Pierpaoli, *Truman and Korea*, pp. 20–21.

[25] Paul Y. Hammond, "NSC-68: Prologue to Rearmament," in Schilling, Hammond, and Snyder, *Strategy, Politics and Defense Budgets*, pp. 285, 292; Samuel F. Wells Jr., "Sounding the Tocsin: NSC 68 and the Soviet Threat," *International Security* 4:2 (Autumn 1979), pp. 117, 119; Robert Jervis, "The Impact of the Korean War on the Cold War," *Journal of Conflict Resolution* 24:4 (December 1980), p. 576.

defense spending. Dean Acheson succeeded Marshall as secretary of state, and in the summer he urged George Kennan, director of policy planning, to bring Paul Nitze on board. Unlike Kennan (and Marshall), Acheson and Nitze shared the view that the Russians presented a military (as opposed to a primarily political) challenge, and by January 1950 Kennan was out and Nitze assumed his position.[26] Nitze also cultivated a relationship with Leon Keyserling of the Council of Economic Advisors (CEA). At the CEA, the Keynesian, growth-oriented Keyserling had an ally in John Clark, thus presenting a two-to-one challenge to an increasingly frustrated Nourse. Relations at the council had never been smooth, and by 1949 its members were bitterly divided. Nourse, holier than the pope, pressed for ever further cuts, unwilling to abide the budget deficits generated by the soft economy. He viewed Keyserling's growth-oriented theories unsound, thought his highly visible public profile inappropriate for the apolitical mandate of the council, and chafed at the increasing bureaucratic influence of a man twenty-five years his junior. Nourse left the government in November, resigning over the budget issue, unable to tolerate the "unduly complacent" position adopted by the council's majority. Keyserling ultimately replaced him.[27]

Keyserling and Nitze were natural allies. Nitze's political assessment was that a dramatic increase in military spending was necessary to meet the Soviet threat, and Keyserling's economic thinking held that the economy had the potential for considerably more robust expansion. In the context of that expansion, larger military spending could easily be accommodated. Keyserling's proclivities led him to prefer spending on domestic programs, but he had opposed efforts to balance the budget on the back of the defense department, deriding Nourse, Webb, and Johnson's efforts "on the economy binge" in that regard.[28]

The drafting of NSC-68 represented yet another opportunity to shake Truman from his conservative economic instincts. The international situation looked grim. Nourse was out, and Pace was gone too—Pace

[26] Acheson, *Present at the Creation*, pp. 347, 373; Hammond, "Prologue to Rearmament," p. 287; Hogan, *Cross of Iron*, pp. 276, 293.

[27] Flash, *Economic Advice*, p. 24; Brune, "Guns and Butter," pp. 362–63, 366; Nourse, *Economics in the Public Service*, pp. 231, 279 (quote). See also Edwin G. Nourse and Bertram M. Gross, "The Role of the Council of Economic Advisors," *American Political Science Review* 42:2 (April 1948), and Bertram M. Gross and John P. Lewis, "The President's Economic Staff during the Truman Administration," *American Political Science Review* 48:1 (March 1954).

[28] Paul Nitze, "NSC-68 and the Soviet Threat Reconsidered," *International Security* 4:4 (Spring 1980), p. 173; Isaacson and Thomas, *The Wise Men*, p. 496; Keyserling, Oral History, May 10, 1971, p. 19 (quote); Friedberg, *Garrison State*, p. 110. On Keyserling's economic thought, see W. Robert Brazelton, *Designing US Economic Policy: An Analytical Biography of Leon H. Keyserling* (New York: Palgrave, 2001).

told Truman that the gap between his and Keyserling's economic ideologies was insurmountable—and Acheson outmaneuvered Johnson, freezing him out of the process. Written in February and March, the document presented to Truman (and a furious Johnson) was an olympian dissertation, though it did take as its point of departure the themes and analysis recognizable from NSC-20/4. The rhetoric of NSC-68 painted the cold war and the Soviet threat in the starkest terms imaginable, and in substance called for a rapid buildup of U.S. military strength. The argument was clear: "Budgetary considerations will need to be subordinated to the stark fact that our very independence as a nation may be at stake."[29]

On April 12 Truman ordered that the document be referred to the National Security Council for further study, with a particular interest in ascertaining more clearly its budgetary implications. Truman had good reason to be cautious. The economy had rebounded from the brief, shallow recession of 1949, and the threat of inflation was again a concern as the economy approached capacity. A May 8 memo from the Budget Bureau to the National Security Council offered a scathing critique of NSC-68, lambasting the document as vague and simplistic and raising, in that spirit, twenty-eight antagonistic questions within the space of two pages. Emphasizing the risk to the economy of large military expenditures, the memo reminded council members that "security rests in economic as well as military strength." At a press conference that same week, Truman stated that fiscal year 1952 would see a contraction in military spending. In early June Defense Secretary Johnson was singing a similar tune.[30]

Truman's June 25 decision to intervene in the Korean War ended the continuing debate over NSC-68. Although it would not meet with Truman's formal approval until September 30, the budgetary die was cast. Military spending would increase, and not just to fight the Korean War but more generally to confront the global Soviet threat. Within one year, defense spending would more than triple, soaring upward of $50 billion. Truman still hoped to keep the budget balanced and avoid inflation; and, sticking to his conservative guns, he was determined to fight the war on a pay-as-you-go basis. But Korea was a watershed moment, and Truman had thrown in his lot with those who would unleash massive amounts of

[29] Pace, Oral History, January 22, 1972, p. 5, February 17, 1972, p. 9; Hammond, "NSC-68," pp. 298, 324; Acheson, *Present at the Creation*, pp. 373–79. NSC-68 is reprinted in Etzold and Gaddis, *Containment*, pp. 385–442 (quote p. 435).

[30] Hammond, "NSC-68," pp. 327, 330; Wells, "Sounding the Tocsin," pp. 131, 137, 138; Hickman, *Growth and Stability*, pp. 78, 79; "Comments of the Bureau of the Budget [on NSC-68]," *FRUS 1950*, 1:298–306 (305 quote); Pierpaoli, *Truman and Korea*, pp. 26–29; Pollard, *Economic Security*, p. 239.

military spending.[31] Nourse, out of government, now felt free to enter the public debate. Fearful as ever of inflation, the former CEA chair was alarmed by the "new military strains" that were the result of the "extreme" and "fantastically ambitious" reactions to the Soviet threat in the wake of the Korean War. Such policies "jeopardize the solvency of the monetary system" and risk bringing about "a contagion of fear" about the dollar. Peace, as soon as possible, was essential. "We cannot," he lectured, "simply plunge into a military commitment that makes us feel most secure. . . . National security rests on the dollar, the government bond, and the price index just as much as it does on the tank, the atom bomb, and the radar net."[32]

But Nourse could do little more than shout from the sidelines. Finance, no longer adequately protected by Truman's policies, had to get into the game. The implications of the deteriorating international situation had made the financial community nervous even before the surprise of Korea. "While the cold war is attracting all the headlines, the future of the American public is perhaps more seriously jeopardized by . . . the deficits of the Federal Government," warned Joseph Stagg Lawrence, the vice chairman of New York's Empire Trust Company. "The financial community . . . is in the process of becoming its first victim."[33]

THE KOREAN WAR AND THE FIRST REASSERTION OF THE BANKERS

There was no "prewar" debate about Korea. The attack from the North was unexpected, and it very quickly became clear that without U.S. intervention, the South would be lost. To a man, Truman and his advisers interpreted the invasion as a challenge from the Soviet Union that had to

---

[31] There is considerable debate over whether Truman would have approved NSC-68 had the Korean War not settled the issue. The evidence is persuasive that the outbreak of the Korean War was decisive. See Friedberg, *Garrison State*, pp. 107–14; Acheson, *Present at the Creation*, p. 420; Hogan, *Cross of Iron*, pp. 266, 304; Donovan, *Tumultuous Years*, p. 242; Jervis, "The Impact of the Korean War," pp. 578, 580; Pollard, *Economic Security*, pp. 223, 240, 242. Especially compelling is Friedberg's argument that without Korea, "a 30 percent increase in military expenditures was plausible; a 300 percent increase was not" (*Garrison State*, p. 155); see also Wells, "Sounding the Tocsin," p. 139; Pierpaoli, *Truman and Korea*, p. 30. Fordham insists that the administration was committed to NSC-68 regardless of Korea (*Cold War Consensus*, pp. 55, 60–62, 72); Christensen argues that the full rearmament program was not politically possible until after China's entry into the war (*Useful Adversaries*, pp. 169, 180, 190); see also Hogan, *Cross of Iron*, pp. 307, 311.

[32] Edwin G. Nourse, *The 1950s Come First* (New York: Henry Holt and Company, 1951), pp. 124, 144, 146, 157, 158, 166 (quotes); see also pp. 114, 138, 143, 149, 160, 165.

[33] Joseph Stagg Lawrence, "Deficits Rain or Shine," *Banking* 42:12 (June 1950), p. 33.

be resisted. As one evocative account described, "There were no doves in Washington's inner circle that night." Broader political support was also remarkable; in the first two weeks of the crisis, twenty-two Republican senators took to the floor to speak to the issue. All supported intervention, as did the party's most recent presidential nominee, Governor Thomas E. Dewey, and its next nominee, General Dwight Eisenhower.[34] Of course, political and public support was egregiously fickle, and when setbacks occurred—with GIs huddled in the Pusan Perimeter or retreating in the face of China's intervention—partisan dissent emerged. But the country rallied broadly around the two big consequential decisions—intervention and, subsequently, the advance across the thirty-eighth parallel—decisions that were made quickly, with little dissent, and certainly with no time for a grand national debate. Moreover, Truman and his advisers sought no wider war. As Treasury Secretary Snyder wrote, "We did not want to get involved with a principal nation, don't you see—it would be devastating, financially [and] economically." But in the heady days after MacArthur's stunning Inchon landing, and especially given the domestic political context (the withering McCarthyite attacks on the "soft-on-communism" administration that "lost China"), stopping at the thirty-eighth parallel was politically inconceivable; even the *New York Times* called for the push to reunite Korea.[35]

In the absence of a prewar debate, finance never had the opportunity to speak to the question of Korean intervention. But the financial community could—and did—react to the new realities it implied. While Truman and Snyder were focused on the stability of America's finances as they stared down the possibility of World War III, the bankers became obsessed with defending the dollar. They were concerned with the prospects for wartime inflation (and the price index did spike at the start of the war, the result of a surge in consumer spending), and as a result of the war they instigated a confrontation with the administration to shift the locus of monetary power from Washington politicians back to New York bankers. Key figures in this confrontation were Allan Sproul, the powerful governor of the Federal Reserve Bank of New York, Thomas McCabe, the chairman of the Federal Reserve Board, and board member (and former chairman) Marriner Eccles. Sproul, McCabe, and Eccles were supported in their efforts by the broader financial community, the financial press, and some

[34] Pace, Oral History, January 22, 1972, p. 17; Snyder, Oral History, March 26, 1969, p. 1302; Isaacson and Thomas, *The Wise Men*, p. 507 (quote); Donovan, *Tumultuous Years*, pp. 203, 205; Ronald James Caridi, "The G.O.P and the Korean War," *Pacific Historical Review* 37:4 (November 1968), pp. 424–25.

[35] Caridi, "The G.O.P and the Korean War," pp. 426, 429, 431; Snyder, Oral History, March 26, 1969, p. 1307 (quote); Isaacson and Thomas, *The Wise Men*, pp. 526, 527, 532; Donovan, *Tumultuous Years*, p. 277; Christensen, *Useful Adversaries*, p. 152.

allies in Congress, including especially Paul Douglas, the Chicago economist and past president of the American Economic Association, who was
elected to the Senate from Illinois in 1948.

The members of the Federal Reserve Board were profoundly allergic to
even the hint of inflation. In reference to the 1950s, one scholar observed
that their "fundamental abhorrence" of inflation led to discussions that
were "so fervent and the predictions so dire that it is hard to believe that
inflation was actually very low." From the end of the Second World War
(when most of the country was fixated on the concern that the economy
might slip into postwar recession) through September 1951, the Federal
Reserve reported to Congress that it engaged in twenty-five actions designed to influence economic activity: twenty-two restrictive and three
expansionary—the latter three all during the period March–September
1949. With the exception of the brief 1949 recession, the Fed was using
every lever at its disposal to fight inflation.[36]

The problem for the Fed in June 1950 was that those levers had been
stretched near to their limits. Contributing to this was the modest political
cachet of the Federal Reserve System after the Second World War. From
1914 to 1928, U.S. monetary policy was virtually run out of the hip pocket
of Benjamin Strong, who left the Bankers Trust Company to become the
first governor of the Federal Reserve Bank of New York. After Strong's
death, the Fed's management of monetary policy during the Great Depression was seen, most charitably, as unhelpful. Subsequently, during World
War II, Chairman Eccles agreed to "the peg": the Federal Reserve would
support (that is, buy) government securities at whatever rate was needed to
keep the long-term interest rate fixed at 2.5 percent, thus ensuring adequate
financing for the war effort.[37] After the war, the continuation of the peg
damped the power of the inflation-fighting tools at the Fed's disposal. The
system has three mechanisms for fighting inflation. It can increase *reserve
requirements* for member banks, it can raise the *discount rate* (the rate at
which the system lends to member banks), and it can engage in *open market operations* (the buying and selling of short- and long-term government
securities). In each case, the system felt hamstrung. Reserve requirements
were increased, but they offered a modest and blunt tool.[38] Open-market

[36] Joint Committee on the Economic Report, "Monetary Policy and the Management of
the Public Debt," 82nd Cong., 2nd sess. (Washington, DC: U.S. Government Printing Office, 1952), pp. 222–23; Christina D. Romer and David H. Romer, "A Rehabilitation of
Monetary Policy in the 1950s," *American Economic Review* 92:2 (May 2002), p. 121
(quotes); see also p. 126.

[37] On the Fed, see Meltzer, *History of the Federal Reserve*; on Strong, see Lester Chandler,
Benjamin Strong, Central Banker (Washington, DC: Brookings Institution, 1958).

[38] In 1948 the board had raised reserve requirements to the extent of their authority; in
August 1948 Congress granted the Fed the right to raise the ceiling further. Joint Committee,
"Monetary Policy," p. 360.

operations were limited by the commitment to support the price of government bonds: for long rates, by the formal peg; for short rates, by informal understanding. The Treasury and the Fed coordinated policy on short-run rates, and the system would buy (or theoretically sell) short-term bonds to support the price and thus set the short-term rate. These policies in turn left little wiggle room for changes in the discount rate that would be compatible with the existing rate structure.

Throughout the early postwar period, the Federal Reserve chafed at the restrictions of the arrangement, and would have preferred the freedom to pursue even more restrictive policies than it did. The requirement to purchase long-term government bonds at par, Eccles argued, forced the system to be an "engine of inflation"; and his complaints contributed to Truman's decision to abruptly "fire" (not reappoint to the chair) a stunned Eccles in 1948, replacing him with McCabe. And there were some voices in support of greater Fed independence—Senator Douglas held hearings that lent those voices a stage.[39] But before Korea, the Fed was cautious. While the big New York commercial banks and insurance companies favored a more aggressive interest rate posture (and certainly Sproul was sympathetic to their position), in the rest of the country there was little support for higher rates outside the financial community, and the general understanding that higher interest rates would increase bank earnings would have made a very tough political sell even tougher.[40]

Everything changed with Korea. All of the participants—who otherwise recall the details and implications of meetings differently, and who each claimed to be the offended party—agree on this point. According to Sproul, the most aggressive of the central bankers, "Up to the time of the Korean Crisis, the Federal Reserve was content to carry on a holding operation." His main antagonist, Snyder, agrees, noting that while the New York Fed had consistently pressed for a faster rise in short-term rates, coordination between the Treasury and the Fed on rate increases was successful. "Up to Korea, our disagreements had generally been relatively minor."[41]

[39] Sydney Hyman, *Marriner S. Eccles: Private Entrepreneur and Public Servant* (Stanford: Stanford University Graduate School of Business, 1976), p. 334; Robert P. Bremner, *Chairman of the Fed: William McChesney Martin Jr. and the Creation of the American Financial System* (New Haven: Yale University Press, 2004), pp. 73–74; Donald F. Kettl, *Leadership at the Fed* (New Haven: Yale University Press, 1986), pp. 62–63. Daniel S. Ahearn, *Federal Reserve Policy Reappraised, 1951–1959* (New York: Columbia University Press, 1963), p. 19; on the Douglas hearings, see also "Government Bond Support Politics," *Banking* 42:7 (January 1950), pp. 46, 48.

[40] Herbert Stein, *The Fiscal Revolution in America: Policy in Pursuit of Reality*, 2nd rev. ed. (Washington, DC: AEI Press, 1996), pp. 245, 246; Meltzer, *History of the Federal Reserve*, pp. 580–82.

[41] Allan Sproul, "The 'Accord': A Landmark in the First Fifty Years of the Federal Reserve System," *Monthly Review of the Federal Reserve Bank of New York* (November 1964);

For the Truman administration in the early days of the Korean War, the security situation, and its uncertainty, was paramount. As Snyder explained, "When aggression broke out in Korea, the Treasury visualized the possibility of a third world war." This was not hyperbole. While the NSC did not think a global war was imminent, it also warned in August that "events of the past few weeks could be interpreted as the first phase of a general Soviet plan for global war," and greater attention and planning were urgently needed to anticipate U.S. responses to possible Russian attacks in various parts of the world. The Joint Chiefs of Staff took a similar position. For Snyder at the Treasury, it was clear that "a decisive and critical period in the life of the Nation had been reached." Thus, while the Treasury had agreed to short-term interest rate increases in response to requests by the Federal Reserve in February, May, and June, in the midst of a national emergency, financial stability and confidence in the solvency of the government were crucial. This required across-the-board stability in interest rates.[42]

But for the financial community, the imminent threat was not the prospect for a larger war but the inflationary consequences of the current one. In the months approaching the Korean War, the Fed was already concerned about the expanding economy. As Sproul observed, the economy was "rapidly recovering" when the war "transformed the tone and tempo of American economic life." Inflation jumped ahead, driven by consumer spending (probably due to fresh memories of wartime scarcities); but behind the spending spree loomed higher wholesale prices, and the prospective costs of the war suggested another wave of inflationary pressures to come. Sproul pressed for an increase in short-term rates, both to combat inflation and also, as a senior staff economist at the time re-

---

reprinted in Lawrence S. Ritter (ed.), *Selected Papers of Allan Sproul* (New York: Federal Reserve Bank of New York, 1980), p. 69 (quote); Snyder, "Responses to the Joint Committee," February 12, 1952, in Joint Committee, "Monetary Policy," p. 66; see also Oral History, May 7, 1969, pp. 1146 (coordination between the Treasury and the Fed was "going along splendidly, until the Korean invasion took place," p. 1147). On the decisiveness of Korea, see also Clay J. Anderson, *A Half Century of Federal Reserve Policymaking, 1914–1964* (Philadelphia: Federal Reserve Bank of Philadelphia, 1965), pp. 104, 105, 150; A. Jerome Clifford, *The Independence of the Federal Reserve System* (Philadelphia: University of Pennsylvania Press, 1965), pp. 231–32; Ahearn, *Federal Reserve Policy,* p. 19; Bremmer, *Chairman of the Fed,* p. 74; Kettl, *Leadership at the Fed,* pp. 68–69; Stein, *Fiscal Revolution,* p. 262.

[42] Snyder, responses to Joint Committee, p. 66 (quote), 67 (quote); Meltzer, *History of the Federal Reserve,* p. 681; NSC, "The Position and Actions of the United States with Regard to Possible Further Moves in Light of the Korean Situation," August 25, 1950, *FRUS* 1 (1950), pp. 375, 378 (quote), 384, 386; memo from the Joint Chiefs to Secretary of Defense Johnson, "Statement of United States and Allied War Objectives in the Event of Global War," August 22, 1950, *FRUS* 1 (1950), pp. 390, 391; see also Clifford, *The Independence of the Federal Reserve System,* p. 230.

called, to "reestablish the earlier dominant position of the New York Fed" as it was when Governor Strong ran the institution in the 1920s.[43]

From the start of the war through the middle of August, Secretary Snyder and Chairman McCabe went back and forth on the issue of the short-term rate, largely talking past one another on security and inflation. On July 10 McCabe and Sproul discussed the inflationary implications of the war with the members of the Federal Open Market Committee (FOMC), and the committee sent Snyder a letter highlighting its concerns in this regard on July 13. Snyder's reply was as forceful as it was unsatisfactory to the committee's members, reiterating what he had told McCabe on June 26. "During the present stage of the emergency," he wrote, maintaining confidence "is of the utmost importance." Rates were not to change.[44] The committee responded on July 31 with a letter that reemphasized the need to combat inflation in the light of mounting defense expenditures. This led to a "spirited discussion" between McCabe and Snyder at a face-to-face meeting on August 10. Snyder was "irritated" with press reports of possible increases to the short-term rate and stated that personally he saw "no reason" for such a move. That very afternoon, the Treasury secretary stressed, he had attended a meeting of the National Security Council, and "at this time there is no way of knowing what might come out of the Korean situation." McCabe emphasized the concerns of the committee, but when it became clear that Snyder would not budge, he stated simply that he would report the conversation to the committee. In retrospective accounts Snyder insisted that he and McCabe had an understanding that rates would be held, at the very least until after the next round of issues the Treasury planned to float.[45]

Things came to a head on Friday, August 18, when Sproul challenged the committee to shoulder its responsibility given the "dangerously infla-

[43] Sproul, " 'The Accord,' " pp. 57 (quote), 58; Bert G. Hickman, "The Korean War and United States Economic Activity, 1950–1952," *National Bureau of Economic Research Occasional Paper* 49 (1955), pp. 5, 21, 28; Meltzer, *History of the Federal Reserve*, p. 684; Hyman, *Marriner S. Eccles*, p. 341; on bankers' concerns more generally, see "A Time to Watch Our National Step," *Banking* 43:3 (September 1950), p. 44; on Sproul, see Robert L. Hetzel and Ralph F. Leach, "The Treasury-Fed Accord: A New Narrative Account," *Federal Reserve Bank of Richmond Economic Quarterly* 87:1 (Winter 2001), p. 35.

[44] Federal Reserve Board, "Minutes of the Federal Open Market Committee and Its Executive Committee, 1950," Monday, July 10, 1950, pp. 106–8; Friday, July 21, 1950, pp. 117, 118 (quotes), 120; see also Snyder, "Responses to the Joint Committee," p. 67. The Federal Open Market Committee (FOMC) consisted of twelve members: the seven members of the board of governors, the president of the Federal Reserve Bank of New York, and four of the remaining eleven bank presidents, who served on a rotating basis. The executive committee (Ex Com) consisted of McCabe, Sproul, Eccles, and two other members.

[45] Federal Reserve Board, Minutes, Friday, August 18, 1950, pp. 131 (quotes), 132 (quotes); Snyder, Oral History, May 7, 1969, p. 1467.

tionary situation." He argued, "If we don't act . . . the purchasing power of the dollar is bound to decline further and drastically." Eccles followed with a statement of strong support, emphasizing the inflationary dangers of likely expansions in military expenditures even greater than those already announced by the administration. Foreshadowing the possibility of a fight, the influential former chairman also noted that the Fed had some support in Congress, naming Senator Douglas, among others. After some discussion, the FOMC unanimously approved Sproul's motion that open-market operations be adjusted to allow the one-year rate to increase from 1¼ percent to 1³/8 percent.[46]

McCabe and Sproul then went to Snyder's office to inform him of the shift in Fed policy that would cause the short-term rate increase. Moreover, it was also announced that the Federal Reserve Bank of New York (which was swiftly followed by all of the other reserve banks) would increase its discount rate from 1½ percent to 1³/4 percent, the first such increase in two years. A statement released to the press that evening announced that the change would be effective at the start of business on Monday. According to Snyder, "This was a body blow . . . a real shock," given the "very clear understanding" he had with McCabe that rates would be held. In his view, the change of heart was the result of a power play by Sproul, who was being urged on by the New York banking community to assert the primacy of the Federal Reserve Bank of New York over the conduct of monetary policy.[47]

Snyder stewed for a while and then called McCabe later that day to inform him that the Treasury was going to proceed with its own announcement that it would offer, as originally planned, a new refunding issue for September and October securities at the same rate (1¼ percent) as the June–July refunding. McCabe replied that such an announcement would be obviously inconsistent with the Fed's public measures, causing considerable confusion in the market. But neither side would blink, and the dueling announcements did cause instability in the markets and satisfied neither the Treasury nor the Fed. The FOMC was not willing to simply let the market collapse for the new Treasury issue and thus stepped in to buy the new securities at the rate now unattractive to the private sector.

[46] Federal Reserve Board, Minutes, Friday, August 18, 1950, pp. 135 (quote), 136 (quote), 137–39, 143–44. At McCabe's initiative, the committee also decided that should the situation arise, the Fed would not allow a new Treasury issue to fail. Rather, it would if necessary purchase the new issue and try to offset the purchase through the sale of other government securities held by the Fed (pp. 147–48).

[47] Federal Reserve Board, Minutes, August 18, 1950, pp. 147, 149; Snyder, Oral History, May 7, 1969, pp. 1448 (quotes), 1468–69; Sproul, "Letter to Robert Stevens, Chairman of the Board of Directors, Federal Reserve Bank of New York, August 28, 1950," reprinted in Ritter, *Selected Papers of Allan Sproul*, p. 74.

At the same time, it sold other government securities from its portfolio, in support of its policy to let the market rate rise. As for the Treasury, since, as Snyder observed, due to the actions of the Fed "short term rates on outstanding issues of government securities were allowed to reach levels inconsistent with the rate on the refunding offering of the Treasury," private investors redeemed over $2 billion in bonds to the Treasury, causing a "significant financing failure of the Federal Government."[48]

The fight over the short-term rate simmered and then heated up again a month later, as Sproul urged the committee on September 27 to bump up short-term rates once more, given that "inflationary pressures are strong." It was agreed that letting the short-term rate increase further was appropriate, given the "dangerously inflationary" prospects since Korea, especially if the country was "moving into a garrison economy." McCabe and Sproul arranged to meet with Snyder to discuss the issue. There had been no contacts whatsoever between the Treasury and the Fed since Snyder's phone call of August 18, but the conversation picked up where it had left off. The chairman and vice chairman reported back to the committee that Snyder was "emphatic" in his opposition to any further increase in the short-term rate.[49]

The committee was not eager to defy the Treasury again, and, despite Sproul's suggestion that interest rates be raised immediately, the FOMC split the difference by authorizing the executive committee to raise short-term rates but not to act until they had pursued further discussions with the secretary of the Treasury. Another meeting was arranged. On October 5 Snyder and other Treasury officials argued that inflationary trends were abating; McCabe and Sproul countered that the FOMC unanimously favored a rate hike. Snyder, possibly playing for time, asked for a brief delay. That evening, back at the Fed, Sproul moved that the rates be increased immediately. Eccles supported the motion, but McCabe preferred to move cautiously, and his position held sway in the executive committee. Four days later (Monday, October 9) Snyder called McCabe, twice, and argued "very forcibly" against any change in short-term rates. On Wednesday the eleventh the FOMC voted to effect open-market operations that would raise short-term interest rates by another $1/8$, to 1.5 percent; the Fed also announced a 2 percent increase in member banks' reserve re-

[48] Snyder, "Responses to the Joint Committee," pp. 70, 72; Alfred H. Williams (president of the Federal Reserve Bank of Philadelphia), "Responses to the Joint Committee," pp. 680–81; Sproul, " 'The Accord,' " p. 59; Meltzer, *History of the Federal Reserve*, pp. 692–93. On "confusion and selling" in August due to the "much publicized" disagreement between the Treasury and the Fed, see "Responses by Government Securities Dealers," in Joint Committee, "Monetary Policy," pp. 1252, 1256–59, 1266, 1268 (quotes).

[49] Federal Reserve Board Minutes, Wednesday, September 27, 1950, pp. 159 (quote), 162 (quote), 166–67; Thursday, September 28, 1950, pp. 171, 173 (quote), 174, 175 (quote).

quirements at the same time. In informing the Treasury, the committee wrote that despite some signs that inflation might be abating, underlying inflationary pressures "will be accelerated by increasing Government expenditures as the rearmament program really begins to bring its huge demands on our economy."[50]

After the late September–early October episode, the fight over short-term rates petered out. There were a number of reasons for this. First, with long-term rates pegged at 2.5 percent, there were limits to how far the short-term rate could rise without undermining the overall interest rate structure—and the Fed gave repeated assurances that it remained committed to the peg at this time. Second, after the short-term rate reached 1.5 percent, President Truman took the opportunity to meet with McCabe and Sproul personally and express his concern about the situation, a bold action that considerably raised the political stakes. Third, there was reason to believe that inflationary pressures had been easing— the inflationary pressures of the early Korean War were caused almost exclusively by consumer spending, which was driven by expectations and very responsive to news about the war. In August the war news was bad; in late October and November the news was good and spending abated.[51]

This last issue was very likely decisive. For not only did consumers listen to the war news, the financial community did as well. The mid-August confrontation initiated by the Fed took place during the darkest days of the early war effort—the bloody and uncertain defense of the Pusan Perimeter. But September 15 saw the Inchon landing, and only a few days after the FOMC authorized the second rate hike, Seoul was liberated. By mid-October U.S. troops were advancing into North Korea, and in November there was good reason to be optimistic that the war would come to a swift and successful conclusion. Nothing could have been as reassuring to the financial community, which had little taste for protracted military adventures. From the start Eccles had been leery of the Korean campaign—tellingly, in later years he would be actively opposed to the Vietnam War, outspoken as early as 1965 in his concerns for

---

[50] Federal Reserve Board Minutes, Thursday, September 28, 1950, pp. 177, 180; Thursday, October 5, pp. 189–91; Wednesday, October 11, pp. 193 (quote), 200, 205, 208 (quote); see also Meltzer, *History of the Federal Reserve*, p. 695.

[51] As the committee wrote to Snyder, "We can assure you that these actions will not affect the maintenance of the 2½ per cent rate for the outstanding longest term Government bonds." Federal Reserve Board Minutes, Wednesday, October 11, 1950, p. 209; see also p. 201; Wednesday, September 27, pp. 165–66; Thursday, September 28, p. 180; Stein, *The Fiscal Revolution in America*, pp. 265–67; Hickman, "The Korean War and United States Economic Activity," pp. 2, 3, 28; Joint Committee on the Economic Report, "The Economic and Political Hazards of an Inflationary Defense Economy," 82nd Cong., 1st sess. (Washington, DC: U.S. Government Printing Office, 1951), p. 5; James Tobin, "Monetary Restriction and Direct Controls," *Review of Economics and Statistics* 33:3 (August 1951), p. 197.

the dollar and inflation. Sproul too was an opponent of the Vietnam War, similarly distressed about its financial implications. In the hopeful days of November 1950, Eccles wrote an essay for *Fortune* magazine, calling for inflation fighting, defense of the dollar, and a more cautious foreign policy. Eccles went so far as to call for the post–Korean War recognition of China, a passage that he was asked to delete and refused. The United States had 6 percent of the world's population and limited resources, Eccles reminded his readers; it was important that America recognize the economic limits to its power. The American Bankers Association saw the relationship between economics and security even more concisely: "Communism and Inflation," the association resolved at its 1950 annual convention, were "Twin Threats."[52]

The Expansion of the War and the Treasury-Fed "Accord"

The prospect that the war might be winding down took considerable pressure off both interest-rate and debt-management issues. On November 22, just to be on the safe side, the Treasury preannounced its December and January refunding operations, and, in contrast to the August fiasco, the initial market response to the issue was orderly and favorable. But just three days later hundreds of thousands of Chinese troops surprised MacArthur's forces in North Korea, and on November 28 MacArthur announced that the allies now faced "an entirely new war." The war was not going to end soon. In fact, it had considerably expanded, and it was not implausible to imagine that global war could soon follow. Consumer spending surged again, especially for durable goods, causing a new jump in the price index. More government spending was also on the horizon, as the widening of the war ended any lingering debate about the need for a massive rearmament program. In mid-December UN forces were still retreating; the first Marine division was almost completely encircled, and 55 percent of Americans polled thought that World War III was at hand. On December 15 Truman addressed the nation on television and the following day officially declared a national emergency and the formation of several new government agencies (such as the Office of Defense Mobilization) to help stabilize and manage the economy in the context of war and rearmament.[53]

[52] Hyman, *Marriner S. Eccles*, pp. 339, 341, 402, 410–16, 419; Ritter, *Selected Papers of Allan Sproul*, pp. 19, 43; Marriner S. Eccles, "The Defense of the Dollar: A Pay-as-You-Go Program to Keep Our Freedom during Rearmament," *Fortune* (November 1950); "Communism and Inflation: Twin Threats," *Banking* 43:5 (November 1950).

[53] Hetzel and Leach, "The Treasury-Fed Accord," pp. 39–40; Meltzer, *History of the Federal Reserve*, p. 696; Pierpaoli, *Truman and Korea*, pp. 42 (quote), 43, 46, 49; Hogan,

While U.S. entry into the Korean War had created considerable discomfort for the financial community, the economic implications of China's intervention were even more dire and raised the stakes considerably. As one survey of prominent bankers at the time concluded, "Within a matter of months the explosive impact of the rearmament program will begin to strike the American Economy." That meant, of course, "that the United States will be menaced by strong inflationary forces." Thus, while once again there was no "debate" over China's entry into the Korean War, there certainly could be a response to the new realities. The character of that response emerged less than a week after China's intervention transformed the nature of the war: on December 1 a story appeared in the *New York Herald Tribune* suggesting that there was now "open speculation" as to whether the Federal Reserve would continue to support the long-term government bonds.[54] Throughout the fight over short-term rates, the Fed repeatedly affirmed its commitment to the peg, and thus to the ultimate subordination of the Fed to the Treasury of control over the long-term rate. But with the war expanding and rearmament on the way, the bankers would see it necessary to seize control of monetary policy.

President Truman took notice of the *Tribune* story and called Chairman McCabe at his home to discuss it with him. According to McCabe, the story "seemed to have upset the President very much," and Truman urged continued support of the peg. Days later, McCabe received a note from the president, who had cut out the article and included it with his letter. Truman called the situation "very dangerous," and urged "that the Federal Reserve Board should make it perfectly plain to the open market committee and the New York Bankers that the peg is stabilized." It was vital that "the Board . . . realize its responsibilities and not allow the bottom to drop from under our securities. If that happens that is exactly what Mr. Stalin wants." McCabe responded in writing on December 9, and the two men met on the eighteenth. In each instance McCabe was reassuring but ultimately vague on the Fed's long-term commitment to the peg.[55]

But conflict was unavoidable. Once again, the administration and the bankers had different perspectives on how best to protect the national interest. Secretary Snyder, calling on the precedent established during World War II, was "deadly opposed to enter into a war of unknown di-

Cross of Iron, pp. 345–48; Christensen, *Useful Adversaries*, p. 190; Flash, *Economic Advice and Presidential Leadership*, pp. 62–63, 97; Brazelton, *Designing U.S. Economic Policy*, p. 41; Hickman, *Growth and Stability*, p. 83; B. C. Roberts, "Wage Stabilization in the United States," *Oxford Economic Papers* 4:2 (July 1952), pp. 149–50.

[54] "Groping for an Inflation Damper," *Banking* 43:6 (December, 1950), p. 36 (quote); Federal Reserve Board, "Minutes of the Federal Open Market Committee and Its Executive Committee, 1951," January 31, 1951, p. 9 (quote).

[55] Federal Reserve Board, Minutes, January 31, 1951, pp. 9 (quotes), 11, 12.

mensions on a rising interest rate not knowing what it would cost us." But the bankers were just as anxious to avoid fighting a war in a way that threatened the dollar. McCabe and Sproul met with Snyder on January 3 and voiced their concerns about "present inflationary advances" and projected "tremendous armament expenditures"; they argued that given these conditions, the present interest rate structure was not sustainable.[56] Snyder listened but offered no response. The administration had its hands full, to say the least, and was not interested in measures that might upset confidence in government bonds just then. As McCabe and Sproul met with Snyder, Seoul was falling to the advancing Communists and U.S forces were continuing their pitched retreat down the Korean peninsula. NSC memos assessing world politics were describing a "war of survival" that was not going well at the moment. On January 15 the Joint Chiefs reported that the country was facing "one of the greatest dangers in its history," with realistic prospects that UN forces would be defeated in Korea and the possibility of a global war with the Soviet Union for which the United States was not adequately prepared. Two days later, McCabe met with Truman and Snyder at the White House, where the president reiterated that his "chief concern is the maintenance of the 2–1/2 per cent rate on these bonds" and argued that uncertainty about the Fed, more than anything else, was unsettling the markets, points driven home again by Snyder. Now it was McCabe's turn to return the noncommittal silence he had recently received.[57]

The next day, Snyder gave a speech before the New York Board of Trade. He discussed the importance of avoiding inflation and emphasized the need to raise taxes in order to fight the war. Fiscal conservatives Truman and Snyder were of one mind on these points. They would avoid the mistakes of World War II and adopt a pay-as-you-go policy that would keep the budget in order and prevent inflation. This was a constant theme of the administration, and on this point finance was in agreement (though with a preference for even deeper cuts in domestic spending).[58] But Snyder

[56] Snyder, Oral History, May 28, 1969, p. 1626 (quote), 1627; Federal Reserve Board Minutes, January 31, 1951, pp. 4 (quotes), 5, 6.

[57] "Report to the NSC by the Chairman of the National Security Resources Board," January 11, 1951, *Foreign Relations of the United States, 1951*, vol. 1, *National Security Affairs, Foreign Economic Policy* (Washington, DC: U.S. Government Printing Office, 1979), pp. 7 (quote), 12; Memo by Joint Chiefs, "Review of the World Situation," January 15, 1951, ibid., pp. 63 (quote), 65, 67; Federal Reserve Board Minutes, January 31, 1951, pp. 12 (quote), 13.

[58] Meltzer, *History of the Federal Reserve*, pp. 632, 700; Snyder, Oral History, May 7, 1969, p. 1482; May 28, 1969, p. 2642; Snyder, "The Treasury and Economic Policy," in Heller (ed.), *Economics and the Truman Administration*, p. 30; Donovan, *Tumultuous Years*, p. 326; Goodwin and Herren, "The Truman Administration," pp. 67, 71; "How Far Can We Pay as We Go?" *Banking* 43:8 (February 1951), pp. 129–30, 157.

also spoke forcefully in support of the peg, and he phrased his words so that it appeared that the Fed had been consulted (and approved of) this position. McCabe was furious and spoke directly to the president of his "astonishment" at the content of the speech.[59]

Snyder, focused on the Korean War ("We'd seen two world wars develop from lesser incidents") and convinced that the "whole thing" boiled down to a power play by Sproul and the New York Fed to advance the interests of the banking community and "get the control of finance back in New York," was trying to end the interest rate controversy once and for all. But the Fed pushed back. On January 22, at the New York Banking Association, Sproul gave a guarded speech that was interpreted (as intended) in the press as challenging the Treasury position. Eccles was less guarded in public comments days later, and on January 29, their talk was backed up by action. While reaffirming its support of the peg, the Fed altered its open-market operations to allow the price of long-term bonds to fall from $100^{22}/_{32}$ to $100^{21}/_{32}$—still above par, and with the same effective interest rate. But the three-cent drop was unmistakably "an open challenge to the Treasury," and one that got Snyder's attention.[60]

The next day the White House called the Fed and asked for an immediate—and unprecedented—meeting between the president and the entire Federal Open Market Committee. At four o'clock on January 31 Truman addressed the committee at the White House. He stressed three themes. First, "The present emergency is the greatest this country has ever faced." Second, he was determined to pay for the defense effort with taxes and gave each member of the committee a copy of *The Federal Budget in Brief* to elaborate the specifics of his plan. Third, confidence in government securities must be rock solid for the duration of the defense emergency, both to ensure that military mobilization was not "jeopardized" and to present "a united front against communism." Truman was clearly talking about the peg, and Federal Reserve officials, at the White House in the presence of their commander in chief, did not explicitly contradict him. But neither did they pledge their support, agreeing instead to "protect the government credit" and to increase contacts between the Treasury and the Fed to better coordinate efforts at ensuring that confidence, about which there were likely to be differences of opinion.[61]

[59] Federal Reserve Board Minutes, January 31, 1951, p. 13 (quote); Snyder, "Responses to the Joint Committee," p. 73; Sproul, " 'The Accord,' " p. 59.

[60] Snyder, Oral History, May 7, 1969, pp. 1477, 1478 (quotes); May 28, 1969, pp. 1624–25 (quote); Sidney Hyman (ed.), *Beckoning Frontiers: Public and Personal Recollections of Marriner S. Eccles* (New York: Alfred A. Knopf, 1951), pp. 484–86; Federal Reserve Board Minutes, January 31, 1951, pp. 2–3, 20; Hetzel and Leach, "The Treasury-Fed Accord," p. 44 (quote).

[61] Federal Reserve Board Minutes, January 31, 1951, pp. 15, 16–17, 19, 24.

The committee then retreated to the Fed to sort out what had just happened and to get down on paper an internal memorandum of their understanding of what had transpired at the meeting and what had been agreed to (nothing). But at noon the next day, the White House released statements to the press that the "Federal Reserve Board has pledged its support to President Truman," and "the market for government securities will be stabilized at present levels and . . . these levels will be maintained during the present emergency." This was followed by a letter from Truman to McCabe, stressing the president's deep concern over the international situation and repeating his understanding of McCabe's "assurance" on interest rates. McCabe of course did not believe any assurance had been extended, and matters were complicated further when the president's letter was released to the press.[62]

Truman understood he was playing hardball, noting in his memoirs, "I felt I had a duty as well as a right to use every available resource to make sure of the success of the defense program." He maintained that the FOMC members had voluntarily pledged their support for the duration of the Korean War at the January 31 meeting, but also explained that "it was my duty to keep the financial capital of the United States in Washington." This would, as Truman correctly noted, "not be an easy task." Eccles, furious at Truman's media offensive, countered with one of his own and leaked to both the *Washington Post* and the *Washington Star* the Fed's internal memorandum summarizing the White House meeting, which contradicted the president's version. At an emergency meeting of the FOMC, Eccles explained that he had acted on his own initiative and had "no regrets." With reference to the war and rearmament, he argued, "There is going to be nothing for us to protect in this country unless we are willing to do what is necessary to protect the dollar."[63]

The conflict was spilling out into the open. The financial press supported the Fed, which seized the initiative and drafted letters to both the president and the Treasury, pressing more explicitly for a change in the long-term rate. The letter to Snyder was hand delivered at the start of a confrontational meeting on February 8 where McCabe and Snyder traded charges about who had mistreated whom. On substance, there was "quite a discussion" during which Snyder remained opposed to any action at this time, in favor of giving the markets some time to settle down. The FOMC considered rattling the cage more vigorously by letting long-term

---

[62] Ibid., p. 27; Federal Reserve Board Minutes, February 6–8, 1951, p. 36.

[63] Truman, *Years of Trial and Hope*, pp. 44, 45 (quotes); Federal Reserve Board Minutes, February 6–8, 1951, pp. 35, 41, 49 (quotes), 51; Hyman, *Recollections of Marriner S. Eccles*, pp. 490–91, 494; see also Richard H. Timberlake, "The Tale of Another Chairman," *Federal Reserve Bank of Minneapolis—The Region* (June 1999).

bonds drift down closer toward par, but the case for delay was strengthened when Snyder entered the hospital days later for an eye operation, which would put him out of commission for approximately two weeks.[64]

At this time Snyder's congressional allies picked up the ball, with Senators Burner Maybank, A. Willis Robertson, and Joseph O'Mahoney calling McCabe and urging that the committee agree to a two-week delay and withdraw its letter to the president. McCabe quickly polled the executive committee and acceded to the former but not the latter. O'Mahoney subsequently wrote to McCabe arguing that the Treasury-Fed conflict was playing into the hands of the "Soviet dictators" and it was "imperative" that during the Korean crisis "there should be no conflict" between the two agencies.[65]

But congressional allies could be found on both sides. Senator Douglas and his colleagues had been holding hearings on monetary policy and inflation that provided a platform for the Federal Reserve and the financial community more broadly. Congressional hearings explored the "inflationary defense economy" and emphasized the "subversive dangers of inflation." Witnesses from the banking community stressed the need to raise taxes and cut nondefense spending; the American Bankers Association thought that economies could be found in defense production and foreign assistance as well. (Eccles testified that he favored a cap of $50 billion for both defense spending and foreign assistance.) The committee's report concluded, "Inflation is the great danger that the United States faces, and it is the best weapon of international communism." To the applause of the New York bankers, Douglas took to the floor himself in February and delivered a powerful speech in support of the Fed and thus higher interest rates. Regarding the praise lavished upon him by the financial community for his efforts, the senator later recalled, "They thought the policy was sound, but their belief stemmed from economic self-interest."[66]

Truman was an avid poker player, and he knew a losing hand when he saw one. The president's popularity was eroding, and the Treasury would

[64] Federal Reserve Board Minutes, February 6–8, 1951, pp. 67 (quote), 68–70, 72; February 14, pp. 78–79; Meltzer, *History of the Federal Reserve*, p. 702; Clifford, *The Independence of the Federal Reserve System*, p. 241.

[65] Federal Reserve Board Minutes, February 14, 1951, pp. 79–80, 83, 85.

[66] Joint Committee on the Economic Report, "The Economic and Political Hazards of an Inflationary Defense Economy," 82nd Cong., 1st sess. (Washington, DC: U.S. Government Printing Office, 1951), pp. 2 (quote), 11, 17, 21, 35, 41, 51, 52 (quote), 56, 95; Paul H. Douglas, *In the Fullness of Time: The Memoirs of Paul H. Douglas* (New York: Harcourt Brace Jovanovich, 1971), pp. 332–33, 334 (quote); according to Nourse, the Douglas subcommittee "contributed importantly" to the outcome of the dispute; Edwin G. Nourse, *Economics in the Public Service: Administrative Aspects of the Employment Act* (New York: Harcourt, Brace, 1953), p. 443; see also Kettl, *Leadership at the Fed*, p. 71 and passim.

not win if the battle was decided in Congress, where the Democrats (with Douglas among them) held a razor-thin 49–47 advantage in the Senate. In the media Eccles's parry had caused Truman's press release gambits to backfire—even the *New York Times* lambasted the president for his attempts to strong-arm the Fed. Nor were Truman's direct discussions with potentially friendly bankers any more fruitful. On February 10 Truman wrote to Russell Leffingwell of the Morgan Bank that he could not "understand why the bankers would want to upset the credit of the nation in a national emergency" and that he would stop them if he could. But Leffingwell was opposed to the peg as well. And on the fifteenth, the Council of Economic Advisors, which had strongly supported the Treasury's position, told Truman that there "must be an end" to the conflict— the greatest danger now derived from the "continuing uncertainty and undermining of confidence" that the public dispute itself was causing.[67]

With the emboldened Fed rebuffing the administration's efforts to drag out deliberations over monetary policy, the modest extension of Snyder's hospital stay proved fortuitous. Now that the FOMC was insisting on an immediate resolution to the dispute, Snyder authorized his deputies, most notably William McChesney Martin, to negotiate with Fed officials. Martin was familiar with the issues, and although he clearly expressed the administration's concern for stability in the government's finances during the grave national security crisis, the former president of the New York Stock Exchange—and son of a former Federal Reserve Bank president— was also more sympathetic to the committee's perspective on interest rates. Perhaps most important, he carried none of the baggage that would have made it difficult for Snyder to negotiate a good-faith agreement with McCabe and Sproul. Still, suspicion between the Treasury and the Fed was such that even with Martin at the helm, the negotiations were lengthy, detailed, and elaborate, with repeated calls for clarification of minutiae that are all the more remarkable in retrospect since the parties were essentially "negotiating" over one issue: who would ultimately dictate monetary policy.[68]

The "accord," communicated to the public in a brief, bland press release on March 4, handed that authority squarely to the Fed. Ultimately, the administration had been backed into a corner, and thus Snyder grudgingly gave his "unsmiling support to a smiling Bill Martin." All the com-

[67] Stein, *The Fiscal Revolution*, p. 274; Bremner, *Chairman of the Fed*, p. 75; Hyman, *Marriner S. Eccles*, p. 349; Chernow, *House of Morgan*, pp. 490, 491 (quote); Flash, *Economic Advice and Presidential Leadership*, p. 79 (quotes).

[68] Snyder, "Responses to the Joint Committee," p. 73; Snyder, Oral History, May 7, 1969, p. 1472; Federal Reserve Board Minutes, February 14, 1951, pp. 83, 86; February 26, 1951, pp. 94, 97; March 1–2, 1951, pp. 110, 113, 118–19, 120–23, 126–27, 139, 142–44; Bremner, *Chairman of the Fed*, pp. 4, 76–77, 82.

mittee had really committed to was an "orderly" transition, although this issue was indeed taken very seriously by the Treasury in wartime. The Treasury also insisted on the right to state, separately, that the accord was "not inconsistent" with Snyder's January 18 speech and, extracting a final pound of flesh, demanded McCabe's resignation (his current term would have ended in 1956). Martin was appointed to replace him and, despite some initial concerns that as Snyder's former deputy he would be too sympathetic to the administration, Martin as chair lived up to his reputation as an inflation hawk and well represented the Fed's preference for a restrictive monetary policy. The accord was "a severe defeat" for the Treasury—as Sproul would later boast, it was "only an accord by courtesy," which provided "a bridge over which the Treasury could retreat."[69]

TAKING CARE OF BUSINESS

Almost immediately after the announcement of the accord, inflation suddenly ceased to be a significant problem and would remain low for the remainder of the war. There are still differences of opinion as to how decisive the accord was in ending the inflation. It is widely agreed that both inflationary spikes associated with the war were driven by surges in consumer spending motivated by expectations about the economic consequences of the war and especially by concerns about shortages. Some argue that the failure of shortages to materialize changed expectations and thus contributed to the end of the inflation; others insist that the accord was decisive (preventing the expansion of credit and a monetary accommodation for consumer demand); still others hold that the combination of temporary price controls coupled with the monetary credibility afforded by the accord were needed to break the back of inflationary

[69] Bremner, *Chairman of the Fed*, pp. 78 (quote), 79; Federal Reserve Board Minutes, March 1–2, 1951, pp. 138–39, 145–46; March 3, 1951, pp. 156–58; Snyder, Oral History, May 7, 1969, p. 1473; Bernard Katz, *Biographical Dictionary of the Board of Governors of the Federal Reserve* (New York: Greenwood Press, 1992), pp. 195, 197, 327 (see also Andrew F. Brimmer, "Andrew F. Brimmer Remembers William McChesney Martin Jr.," *Federal Bank of Minneapolis—the Region* [September 1998]); J. S. Fforde, *The Federal Reserve System, 1945–1949* (Oxford: Clarendon Press, 1954), p. 338 (quote); Allan Sproul, "Letter to Murry J. Rossant, February 10, 1963," in Ritter (ed.), *Papers of Allan Sproul*, pp. 86 (quote), 87 (quote). According to Keyserling, Truman "caved in" to the bankers (Oral History, May 19, 1971, p. 5); see also Herbert Stein, "Monetary Policy and the Management of Public Debt," *American Economic Review* 45:5 (December 1952), p. 866; Stein, *The Fiscal Revolution in America*, pp. 275, 277; Meltzer, *History of the Federal Reserve*, pp. 708, 710, 712; Hetzel and Leach, "The Treasury-Fed Accord," pp. 49–52; Kettl, *Leadership at the Fed*, pp. 74–75.

expectations.[70] The resolution of this debate is not of concern here; rather, of central interest is the behavior of finance during the crisis.

The influence of finance was at a low ebb in the late 1940s, having been eroded by the death of Benjamin Strong, the Great Depression, the New Deal, and the Second World War. Already skeptical of the government's role in the new internationalism and anxious about the costs of the emerging cold war, the inflationary threat posed by Korea—with its assurance of a major arms buildup and the real possibility of a wider war—was uniformly understood by the financial community to pose a pressing threat to its vital interests. Given its sudden nature, neither the outbreak nor the expansion of the war could be extensively debated, but actions could be taken to defend those interests—and they were, at critical junctures. At the start of the war, the bankers moved to gain control of monetary policy. With the widening of the war, they seized it.

Especially after China's entry into the war made it clear that there would be no quick, successful termination of the conflict, concerns for the dollar—and the need to retake monetary policy—became critical. In mid-January, whether it was McCabe firing off memos to the director of Defense Mobilization or Eccles testifying before Congress or campaigning in the editorials of the American Bankers Association, the bankers spoke with one voice: in the shadow of Korea and rearmament, there could be no greater domestic policy priority than defending the integrity of the dollar. The final move against the peg would quickly follow.[71]

The collective sigh of relief that emanated from finance afterward was audible. Not just Federal Reserve officials (like the board of directors of the Federal Reserve Bank of Boston, who submitted, unsolicited, a vituperative collective letter against the Treasury's "easy money"), but private bankers and securities dealers who testified before the Monetary Policy Committee in Congress overwhelmingly supported the elimination of the peg. Among the bankers, such as those from National City Bank (New York), First National Bank (St. Paul), Riggs National Bank (Washington, D.C.), Bank of America (San Francisco), and First National Bank (St.

[70] Joint Committee, "Inflationary Defense Economy," p. 5; Norton, *The Employment Act*, p. 109; Meltzer, *History of the Federal Reserve*, p. 684; Donovan, *Tumultuous Years*, p. 327; Pierpaoli, *Truman and Korea*, p. 100; Hickman, "The Korean War," p. 26; Hickman, *Growth and Stability*, p. 91; Milton Friedman and Anna Schwartz, *A Monetary History of the United States, 1857–1960* (Princeton: Princeton University Press, 1963), pp. 598, 621 (see also Milton Friedman, "Comments on Monetary Policy," *Review of Economics and Statistics* 33:3 [August 1951], pp. 187, 191); Hugh Rockoff, *Drastic Measures: A History of Wage and Price Controls in the United States* (Cambridge: Cambridge University Press, 1984), pp. 177–78, 186–87.

[71] Federal Reserve Board Minutes, February 6–8, 1951, pp. 42, 49, 53; Hetzel and Leach, "The Treasury-Fed Accord," p. 44; "1951: A Scene in Black and White," *Banking* 43:7 (January 1951), p. 33.

Louis), the principal complaint was that the peg should have been abandoned even sooner. Support for the independence of the Federal Reserve generally was, if anything, even more vehement.[72]

Resurgent finance not only ensured that inflation would remain low during the Korean War but also played an important role in inhibiting the expansion of the war and in containing any additional increases in military spending. In September 1951, as the war continued, the American Bankers Association raised new concerns for the inflationary consequences of defense spending and complained bitterly that the British Loan and the Marshall Plan were sold to the American people on the argument that without them the United States would be forced "to spend scores of billions annually and become a semimilitary state," dreaded outcomes that had nevertheless become reality. At its annual convention the following month, the association expressed support for a strong defense and commended the administration's efforts to balance the budget and three rounds of tax increases. But it insisted that any further taxes would be "destructive," and thus spending must be cut across the board, including for defense and foreign aid. "We cannot safely allow the military alone to determine military spending," the association formally resolved. For the bankers, the dollar came first. "Our economic strength is now threatened," they explained, and "economic weakness could undermine our security."[73]

As noted, after the accord the financial community was able to achieve many of its objectives, such as limiting the war and moderating defense spending. It should be clear, however, that numerous other important factors contributed to these outcomes. (The preferences of finance did not determine that the Korean War would be limited.)[74] Like the U.S. forces in Korea, the isolationists, antistatists, and budget cutters back home, initially routed and thrown off balance, were able to regroup, rally, and reestablish firm lines of resistance to higher taxes and government spend-

---

[72] Of the thirty responses reproduced in the committee's report from bankers in sixteen states, only three small provincial banks supported the peg, typically out of concern for and moral obligation to holders of older bonds. All the big banks strongly supported the accord; twenty-two wished it had been done sooner. Many securities dealers, although supportive of the accord, were critical of the management of the change. See Joint Committee, "Monetary Policy," pp. 838–44, 845 (quote), 1160–67, 1205–17, 1273–79.

[73] "Impact of the Defense Program," *Banking* 44:3 (September 1951), pp. 39–41, 108 (quote); "Defense . . . Inflation . . . Spending . . . Credit," *Banking* 44:4 (October 1951), p. 73.

[74] Similarly, while defense spending was contained in the name of economic rectitude and, after peaking in 1953, declined notably more or less for the rest of the decade, military expenditures nevertheless remained higher than what finance would have preferred. Finance had a distinct vision of the national interest and how best to pursue that vision, rooted in its macroeconomic preferences.

ing. It was also Truman's preference to fight a "limited war" in Korea, and by the end of 1951 the president was planning to "stretch out" spending on the military buildup. Eisenhower was even more conservative on each of these fronts.[75]

This was not the only plausible trajectory for U.S. policy. Keyserling in particular thought that the economy could (and should) accommodate considerably more defense spending in support of a more assertive foreign policy posture. But Keyserling's star was fading. While the council did urge the president to settle the Treasury's dispute with the Federal Reserve, Keyserling was unhappy with the outcome and "irked" by his marginalization in the process that produced it. In the fall he stood opposed to slowing down military spending, which he attributed to the "pressures of the businessmen" concerned with inflation. "Inflation is a bad thing and should not be underestimated," Keyserling wrote to Truman in a long memo arguing against the stretch-out. "But it would seem to me highly dangerous to be concerned so exclusively with inflationary dangers as to underestimate Communist dangers." In later years he would put it more bluntly: "I was against those who were using exaggeration of the damage done by inflation to justify the stretch-out, e.g., 'Inflation is a greater danger than Stalin.' "[76]

But not everybody agreed with him.

[75] Friedberg, *Garrison State*, p. 115; Hogan, *Cross of Iron*, pp. 364–65.

[76] W. Robert Brazelton, "Retrospectives: The Economics of Leon Hirsch Keyserling," *Journal of Economic Perspectives* 11:4 (Autumn 1997), p. 194; Brazelton, *Designing US Economic Policy*, pp. 2, 28, 57, 150; Flash, *Economic Advice and Presidential Leadership*, pp. 82, 83 (quote), 92 (quote); Keyserling, Oral History, May 19, 1971, pp. 3 (quote), 4; Leon Keyserling, "Economic Implications of the Security Program," *FRUS*, 1951, vol. 1, October 16, 1951, p. 231; Keyserling to Truman, *FRUS 1951*, vol. 1, November 2, 1951, pp. 245–55 (p. 251 quote).

CHAPTER 6

Taking One for the Team?
Finance and the Falklands War

On April 2, 1982, Argentina invaded and seized the Falkland Islands, much to the surprise of the rest of the world.[1] General unfamiliarity with the Falklands was certainly understandable. A vestige of the British Empire, the islands were home to well over half a million sheep as well as about eighteen hundred "Kelpers," many of whom were sixth-generation descendants of nineteenth-century British settlers. But for at least as long as there had been a British presence on the islands, Buenos Aires retained a counterclaim to sovereignty over the real estate three hundred miles off its coast, which was in Argentina known (and, after the invasion, rechristened) as the Malvinas. Also seized at this time were South Georgia, seven hundred miles still farther to the east, and the South Sandwich Islands beyond them. These inhospitable rocks were administered from the Falklands and were occasionally home to small scientific survey teams—but were strategically important from the perspective of the specialist's game of Antarctic geopolitics.

Yet if most could be forgiven for being caught unaware by the Argentinian invasion, the government of Prime Minister Margaret Thatcher could not—and arguably should not—be so easily absolved. The dispute with Argentina had been an often-salient irritant to successive British governments since the mid-1960s, and the most recent high-level negotiations between the two sides (a month before the invasion, in New York) had reached an acrimonious conclusion. While Argentina had talked tough in the past, the Thatcher government failed to recognize the real threat of invasion and, once alerted to that threat, failed to deter Argentina from

---

[1] For more on the Falklands, see Lawrence Freedman and Virginia Gamba-Stonehouse, *Signals of War: The Falklands Conflict of 1982* (Princeton: Princeton University Press, 1991). Good journalistic accounts include those by Paul Eddy and Mahnus Linklater with Peter Gillman, *The Falklands War* (London: Andre Deutsch, 1982), and Max Hastings and Simon Jenkins, *The Battle for the Falklands* (New York: Norton, 1983). On the crisis as seen from Argentina, see Oscar Raul Cardoso, Ricardo Kirschbaum, and Eduardo van der Kooy, *Falklands—the Secret Plot* (Surrey, UK: Preston, 1987), and Jimmy Burns, *The Land That Lost Its Heroes* (London: Bloomsbury, 2002). For an account sympathetic to the Argentinean perspective, see Virginia Gamba, *The Falklands War: A Model for North-South Crisis Prevention* (Boston: Allen and Unwin, 1987).

acting. Without warning, British territory had been seized, and British subjects were under the occupation and rule of foreign military dictators. In an effort to set things right, the prime minister dispatched a fleet eight thousand miles from home to take the islands back.

With the fleet sailed Thatcher's political future. As a consequence of this, the Falklands War provides a case that would appear to press the limits of the theory of this book beyond the breaking point. Because for the City of London—the square mile that was home to Britain's powerful financial services sector (a hub of banking and insurance companies and of exchange and equity markets)—the arrival of Mrs. Thatcher in 1979 marked nothing less than a return from the wilderness. Beginning in 1964, with the end of thirteen years of Tory rule, the City—conservative to its bones—had been forced to endure fifteen years of Labour's economic management, interrupted only briefly by a weak and wobbly Tory government that offered little respite in terms of public policy; additionally, the years 1964–79 were characterized by economic distress, ever higher inflation, and chronic crises of sterling. The Tory victory in 1979 did not simply return the Conservatives to office; it handed the reins of power to a revolutionary movement within the party that had taken its leadership in 1975. The determination of the new leadership was most clearly evident in the prime minister's unflinching commitment to sound money, which meant that she had been willing to bear whatever burdens necessary—and they proved to be substantial—to wring inflation out of the British economy.

There was no substitute for Thatcher. Certainly it would be a nightmare for the City if the whole government came tumbling down and Labour returned to power. But even a change of leadership within the Tory party would almost certainly yield a prime minister, and a government, markedly less committed to those policies that the financial community held dear. Moreover, as wars go, this one promised to be strictly limited. Argentina could not strike at Britain, and the British fleet had little capacity for and even less interest in attacking the South American mainland. No other country was remotely likely to enter the conflict. The entire war would amount to assembling the fleet, steaming south while diplomacy intervened, and, if necessary, attempting to retake the islands, successfully or not.

In sum, the Thatcher government could not survive inaction, and the war promised to be limited. It would seem to be a moment for the financial community to "take one for the team" and, despite its pacific instincts, support the limited war that would save the Thatcher government. And yet, surprisingly, finance still flinched. In a war that was vastly popular throughout the country (and a remarkable military success), the City was one of the few lonely voices of dissent—a remarkable illustration of how deeply ingrained is the bankers' aversion to war.

The resort to war over the Falklands was abetted by serious blunders committed by each side—in Britain, a failure of deterrence, in Argentina a fundamental misreading of the likely consequences.[2] But the roots of the conflict were much deeper, and repeated efforts to find a mutually acceptable resolution proved unsuccessful. A contributing factor was that each side was in no doubt as to the self-evident rectitude of its position, despite the fact that the tangled web of claims and counterclaims to the islands went back hundreds of years and left neither party with an airtight case. The British boasted of discovering the Falklands in 1592 and first landing there in 1690, but the initial settlement, in 1764, was by the French, who designated the islands Les Malouines (from which the name Malvinas derives); the British established a settlement soon after. For the next fifty years the islands were a pawn of European power politics; Spain superseded France's position and wrestled with the British for control, though eventually each side withdrew its settlers (but not its claims). In 1829 Argentina, which by that time was independent of Spain, established a small garrison, to the protests of the British government, which, in 1833, expelled the two dozen Argentine soldiers it encountered and established a permanent settlement. The strength of the British case rests on self-determination—by 1982 the Kelpers and their descendants had been there for 150 years and overwhelmingly preferred to remain under British rule; Argentina's case derives from the principle of decolonization—as the rightful inheritor of Spain's colonial position.[3]

Argentina never withdrew its claim to sovereignty over the islands, but despite the occasional saber rattling, the dispute remained on the back burner until 1965, when, in the context of the decolonization movement, the UN General Assembly approved Resolution 2065, urging Britain and Argentina to resolve the conflict peacefully. The following year negotia-

---

[2] Richard Ned Lebow, "Miscalculation in the South Atlantic: The Origins of the Falklands War," in Robert Jervis, Richard Ned Lebow, and Janice Gross Stein, *Psychology and Deterrence* (Baltimore: Johns Hopkins University Press, 1985), pp. 89, 110–11; "The Misjudgments That Led to the Falklands War," *The Economist*, June 19, 1982, p. 41. (Note that *The Economist* supported the use of force to retake the islands if diplomacy failed, on the principle of not rewarding aggression and in the context of cold war credibility.)

[3] On these issues, see Julius Goebel Jr., *The Struggle for the Falklands: A Study in Legal and Diplomatic History* (New Haven: Yale University Press, 1927), and Peter Beck, "The Anglo-Argentine Dispute over Title to the Falkland Islands: Changing British Perceptions on Sovereignty Since 1910," *Millennium* 12:1 (Spring 1983); Christopher Bluth, "The British Resort to Force in the Falklands/Malvinas Conflict of 1982: International Law and Just War Theory," *Journal of Peace Research* 24:1 (March 1987), esp. pp. 6–7; Joseph S. Tulchin, "The Malvinas War of 1982: An Inevitable Conflict That Never Should Have Occurred," *Latin American Research Review* 22:3 (1987), p. 126; Fritz L. Hoffmann and Olga Mingo Hoffmann, *Sovereignty in Dispute: The Falklands/Malvinas, 1493–1982* (Boulder, CO: Westview Press, 1984).

tions commenced and continued off and on for the next sixteen years, often interrupted by instability in Argentinean domestic politics. The negotiations followed a disheartening pattern. The British Foreign Office, bowing to the realities of geography and the constraints of British resources, sought to find a way to increasingly enmesh the islands and Argentina, hoping that over time this would pave the way for a transfer of sovereignty that respected the wishes of the Kelpers. But these efforts—most notably in the 1968 "memorandum of understanding" and the Communications Agreement of 1971—ran into difficulties from all sides when presented to the public. The Kelpers simply preferred to remain British, and the small but formidable "Falklands Lobby" in Parliament left prime ministers unwilling to spend political capital on an obscure political problem eight thousand miles away. On the other side Buenos Aires remained intransigent and suspicious of half measures that would not lead to the prompt recognition of Argentinean sovereignty. By the late 1970s Labour saw little hope of a settlement but held the view that Argentina would not invade the islands as long as negotiations were perceived to be "serious," and thus played for time. The Tories ultimately proved either unwilling or unable to sustain the charade, and on March 2, 1982, the Argentinean Foreign Ministry rejected the bland communiqué released at the end of the New York talks. Instead, Argentina now reserved the right to "employ other means" if clear and prompt progress on sovereignty was not forthcoming.[4] Within a month a desperate military regime rolled the dice on an invasion, and what had been a modest diplomatic sideshow became a crisis that would completely dominate British politics for the next three months.

This chapter proceeds in four parts. First, it considers the logic behind finance's preferences—why it made sense for British bankers to be wary of military adventurism, but also why the City had a considerable incentive to set these concerns aside this time and rally around the prime minister. This discussion provides crucial context for the position of finance in this case; it also provides yet another window on the distinct way in which finance conceptualizes the national interest. Second, it considers the view from Argentina—an interruption of the linear narrative but one that offers something of a case within the case, or more accurately given the setting, an illuminating "shadow case" (as described later). The chapter then considers the crisis as it unfolded: the invasion, the diplomatic efforts

---

[4] Michael Charlton, *The Little Platoon: Diplomacy and the Falklands Dispute* (London: Basil Blackwell, 1989), pp. 29–30, 36, 45–46, 53, 68; Hastings and Jenkins, *Battle for the Falklands*, pp. 14, 21–22; Burns, *The Land That Lost Its Heroes*, pp. 43, 45, 52, 57, 67; Peter Carrington, *Reflections on Things Past: The Memoirs of Lord Carrington* (London: Collins, 1988), p. 348.

to avoid war, and the military confrontation; the final section looks more closely at the reaction of the British financial community in the context of the domestic debate on the crisis.

WAR AND THE CITY

The City of London had good reasons to be nervous about the financial implications of going to war over the Falklands. The twenty-five years leading up to the crisis served lesson after lesson as to the intimate (and disheartening) relationship between Britain's financial distress and its global ambitions. While Britain had faced the hard realities of realigning its extensive international position with its diminished economic circumstances since the end of the Second World War, the limits of British power and the constraints of financial fragility were brought into stark relief with the humiliation of the Suez Crisis in 1956.

On October 31 of that year, British and French forces attacked Egypt with the stated goal of seizing the Suez Canal, but with the additional goal of causing the overthrow of Egypt's president Gamal Abdel Nasser, with whom the Europeans had been clashing for some time over a variety of issues and who had nationalized the canal in July, considerably raising the stakes in that confrontation. But on November 6, just days short of victory, and to the great dismay of the French, Britain called a halt to the operation. Harold Macmillan, chancellor of the exchequer (and to that point one of the most forceful proponents of the Suez adventure), informed his cabinet colleagues that a run on the pound, which he claimed was "viciously orchestrated" in Washington, had become overwhelming and the country did not have adequate reserves to save the currency on its own. Moreover, the Americans made clear that they would block Britain's ability to seek help from the International Monetary Fund (IMF). On the other hand, if (and only if) the British agreed to an immediate cease-fire and prompt withdrawal from the Suez Canal zone, the United States would facilitate IMF support and provide additional emergency financial relief of its own.[5]

---

[5] Jonathan Kirshner, *Currency and Coercion: The Political Economy of International Monetary Power* (Princeton: Princeton University Press, 1995), pp. 64–70; Harold Macmillan, *Riding the Storm (Memoirs, 1955–1959)* (New York: Harper and Row, 1971), p. 164 (quote). See also Diane B. Kunz, *The Economic Diplomacy of the Suez Crisis* (Chapel Hill: University of North Carolina Press, 1991); Lewis Johnman, "Defending the Pound: The Economics of the Suez Crisis, 1956," in Anthony Gorst, Lewis Johnman, and W. Scott Lewis (eds.), *Post-war Britain, 1945–64: Themes and Perspectives* (London: Pinter Publishers, 1989); Howard J. Dooley, "Great Britian's 'Last Battle' in the Middle East: Notes on Cabinet Planning during the Suez Crisis of 1956," *International History Review* 11:3 (August

Britain caved in, bringing down Prime Minister Anthony Eden along the way, and the entire affair was a formative experience for a generation of British politicians, who came away with an instinctive sensitivity to the economic limits of British power and impossibility of sustaining a major military operation into the teeth of American opposition. Margaret Thatcher would remember it this way: "Our most painful experience of the country's reduced circumstances was the failure of the Suez expedition in 1956. This was the result of political and economic weakness rather than military failure, because the government withdrew a victorious force from the Canal Zone in response to a 'run on the pound' encouraged by the US government."[6]

Avoiding confrontation with the United States, if occasionally irritating, was well within British means; coping with economic weakness would prove more challenging. In the 1950s, both before and after the Suez Crisis, the *Financial Times*—the voice of the City of London—repeatedly argued that Britain was carrying an excessive defense burden relative to its economic capacity and post–World War II power.[7] This burden would become a defining problem for Labour prime minister Harold Wilson and his defense minister, Denis Healey, from 1964 to 1967 (and beyond). Wilson and Healy were sincerely committed to retaining Britain's military role "East of Suez" (principally in Malaysia, Singapore, and the Persian Gulf); and this was also important to the Americans, who saw the British presence as indirectly supporting the Vietnam War. More generally, the United States also valued the role Britain played as its only ally with worldwide political and military commitments. President Lyndon Johnson considered sterling's weakness a "major foreign policy concern" and was eager to take steps that would take the pressure off the British currency and thus "sharply reduce the danger of sterling devalua-

---

1989); and Jeffrey Pickering, *Britain's Withdrawal from East of Suez: The Politics of Retrenchment* (London: Macmillan, 1998), p. 90. It should be noted that the extent to which the United States caused the distress of the pound is difficult to establish, and, further, Macmillan's behavior has been questioned. Some argue that either Macmillan failed to alert the cabinet to Britain's financial fragility before the invasion (Johnman, "Defending the Pound," p. 179) or he overstated the nature of the crisis at the November 6 meeting (Kunz, *Economic Diplomacy of the Suez Crisis*, pp. 131, 132). But all agree that financial fragility (coupled with U.S. opposition) forced British capitulation, that reserve losses for November were unsustainable, and that the United States insisted on British withdrawal as the precondition for American help (see, for example, Kirshner, *Currency and Coercion*, pp. 70–72; Dooley, "Great Britain's Last Battle," pp. 516–17; Johnman, "Defending the Pound," p. 176; Kunz, *Economic Diplomacy*, pp. 139–40, 143, 152–53).

[6] Margaret Thatcher, *The Downing Street Years* (New York: Harper Collins, 1993), p. 8.

[7] David Kynaston, *The Financial Times: A Centenary History* (New York: Viking, 1988), pp. 246, 262.

tion or . . . British military disengagement east of Suez." But economic pressure on the East of Suez commitment was unrelenting, both as a strain on the budget and as a direct and indirect source of pressure on sterling, which staggered from crisis to crisis throughout the period.[8]

From 1965, the East of Suez question was the subject of increasing debate in Britain. Defense spending was the second-largest item in the budget, and with almost half of British forces stationed overseas, the cost in foreign exchange of supporting them was equivalent to 40 percent of the trade gap—two facts that could hardly fail to escape attention in the wake of sterling crises in the autumn of 1964 and again in the summer of 1965. Wilson's response was to cut defense spending without addressing overall military posture, a tightrope that could be negotiated only for so long as big choices loomed about aircraft carriers and expensive fighters that would be decisive one way or the other. In 1965 averting one's eyes to these tensions made some sense as emergency financial support from the United States was extended with the understanding that Britain would neither abandon any of its overseas commitments nor devalue sterling.[9]

With the February 1966 defense review the rope frayed further, as defense cuts would hollow out British overseas capacities. This led to protests from the opposition but not the electorate—Labour extended its majorities in the March elections, and even the *Financial Times* strayed a bit from the political reservation, stating its preference for Tory leader Edward Heath but noting that "in terms of cutting down defence commitments in the East to match resources, the clear potential edge went to Labour." Unfortunately for Wilson, the honeymoon was short-lived—a new sterling crisis forced still another round of defense cuts accompanied by a deflationary economic package and a wage and price freeze. Publicly the East of Suez commitment remained untouched, but the cumulative effect of the defense cuts and increasing dissent from within Labour (given austerity at home) forced Wilson and Healey to anticipate the inevitable.[10]

[8] Phillip Darby, *British Defense Policy East of Suez, 1947–68* (London: Oxford University Press, 1973), p. 293; Michael Chichester and John Wilkinson, *The Uncertain Ally: British Defence Policy, 1960–1990* (Aldershot, Hampshire: Gower, 1982), pp. 9–10; Jeremy Fielding, "Coping with Decline: US Policy toward the British Defense Reviews of 1966," *Diplomatic History* 23:4 (Fall 1999), pp. 633–37, 645; "Memorandum from President Johnson to Secretary of the Treasury Fowler," *Foreign Relations of the United States: 1964–1968*, vol. 7, *International Monetary and Trade Policy* (Washington, DC: U.S. Government Printing Office, 1998), p. 173.

[9] C. J. Bartlett, *The Long Retreat: A Short History of British Defense Policy, 1945–70* (London: Macmillan, 1972), pp. 197, 215; Andrew J. Pierre, "Britain's Defense Dilemmas," *Proceedings of the Academy of Political Science* 29:2 (November 1968), pp. 65–67; Fielding, "Coping with Decline," p. 642.

[10] Kynaston, *The Financial Times*, p. 326 (quote); Clive Ponting, *Breach of Promise: Labour in Power, 1964–1970* (London: Hamish Hamilton, 1989), p. 55; Darby, *British De-*

The following year, 1967, featured the blows that would finally burst the sterling piñata. Yet another defense white paper finally outlined a phased withdrawal from Singapore, Malaysia, and Aden. British forces would be cut in half by 1971 and gone completely by 1977. Some pretense was maintained regarding Britain's other positions within the small principalities of the Persian Gulf (of particular concern to the Americans), but these fig leaves were swept aside by the financial crisis that led to sterling's devaluation on November 17. The devaluation itself would increase the burden of Britain's overseas defense bill by £50 million—and Chancellor of the Exchequer Roy Jenkins insisted on a fundamental reassessment of defense policy. Thus not only was defense spending cut further (eliminating the F-111 strike aircraft purchase that had been spared by the previous abandonment of an aircraft carrier), but the timetable for withdrawal from East of Suez was accelerated and would be complete by the end of 1971. This met with vigorous opposition from the Tories at the time, and when the conservatives took power in 1970, there was hope in some quarters that the decision would be reversed. But faced with sluggish growth, promised tax cuts, and the need to fight inflation, the Conservatives could not escape the same financial constraints that had plagued Labour, and the new posture was retained.[11]

With the East of Suez question settled, and with the devaluation of sterling (and the subsequent demise of the Bretton Woods fixed exchange rate system and the general transition to floating exchange rates), some of the tension in the defense-finance dilemma abated. But Britain's defense spending still remained relatively high, and the pound remained vulnerable to external pressure. Labour's 1975 defense review centered around the concept of reducing the defense burden from 5.5 percent of GNP to 4.5 percent, saving £4,700 million over the next decade. Debate on these changes was muted by the 1976 financial crisis, during which Britain was forced to seek help from the IMF, which insisted on further cuts to domestic spending. An additional £300 million was squeezed from the military, despite a direct protest from the chiefs of staff to the prime minister.[12]

---

fense Policy, pp. 283, 304; Pickering, *Britain's Withdrawal,* pp. 150–52, 157; Fielding, "Coping with Decline," pp. 634–36, 651.

[11] Michael Dockrill, *British Defense Policy Since 1945* (Oxford: Basil Blackwell, 1988), pp. 94–95, 97, 101, 103; J. C. Hurewitz, "The Persian Gulf: British Withdrawal and Western Security," *Annals of the American Academy of Political and Social Science* 401 (May 1972), pp. 107, 114; Chichester and Wilkinson, *The Uncertain Ally,* pp. 20, 23, 31–32; Bartlett, *The Long Retreat,* pp. 223–24, 254–55, 260.

[12] Kathleen Burk and Alec Cairncross, *Goodbye, Great Britain: The 1976 IMF Crisis* (New Haven: Yale University Press, 1992), pp. 20, 78, 105; Dockrill, *British Defense Policy,* pp. 104, 106, 107; Chichester and Wilkinson, *The Uncertain Ally,* pp. 47–48, 53; "Britain's Defensive World Role," *The Economist,* November 24, 1979, p. 27.

In sum, the experiences of the previous quarter-century—especially the drop-of-the-hat vulnerability of sterling to crisis and the chronic and inherent contradictions between Britain's overseas ambitions and its financial solvency—certainly helps explain why British financiers would be leery of embarking on the Falklands adventure in 1982. But they also had, uncharacteristically for finance, a good self-interested reason for looking past those concerns—saving Margaret Thatcher.

Fight the War, Keep the Woman?

The warm relationship between Margaret Thatcher and the City of London was a function of politics, not personalities. Thatcher, always and before anything the self-made daughter of a shopkeeper, had little personal affinity for the complacent sons of privilege who ruled the City; as for the old bankers, their attitudes toward women were more characteristic of 1879 than 1979, and they liked it that way. Yet "that woman" was the best thing that had happened to the City in fifty years, and there were three good reasons to rally to her defense. First, the prime minister was in the process of leading Britain from an era of socialism and high inflation to financial orthodoxy and liberalization; second, Thatcher was especially vulnerable on the Falklands issue; third, if she fell, from the perspective of the interests of the City, there was no good alternative.

Thatcher's Revolution

Margaret Thatcher became leader of the Conservative Party not as the heir apparent to Edward Heath, prime minister from 1970 to 1974, but rather as the leader of a minority band of revolutionaries within the Tory party. These upstarts thought the party had lost its way, and in both government and opposition had accommodated rather than opposed British socialism. For years the dissident movement within the party had been growing, and by the mid-1970s, a cornerstone of their agenda, supported by allies in the academy, the financial press, and the City, was "monetarism." In practice, Thatcher and her political allies (and certainly their supporters in the City) were less interested in the technical attributes of monetarism than in what it stood for—the commitment, as the paramount element of economic strategy, to stamp out inflation from the British economy through a package of measures that began first and foremost with targeting the growth of the money supply. This concept gained considerable currency even during the Labour governments of 1975–79, which felt the need to announce monetary targets in order to accommodate the "obsession of the financial markets and the press" with the management of the money supply and with monetarist ideas more generally.[13]

In 1975, inheriting a divided party many of whose members were dismayed at the prospect of a "right-wing takeover," Thatcher moved cautiously in creating her shadow cabinet. Established insiders were retained in prominent roles; most notably, Heath ally William Whitelaw was named deputy leader and shadow home secretary. The financial community was properly supportive. More than happy to see Heath go, quick to lecture Labour on the need to reduce public spending and tighten the money supply, and appreciative of the Tories' new direction, the City was, however, initially somewhat guarded in its enthusiasm for Mrs. Thatcher. Nevertheless, this early caution did not obscure obvious interests, and the *Financial Times* was unqualified in its support in the election of 1979, urging that the choice was "clear cut and potentially historic" and that the Thatcher program "must be given a chance." The markets rallied in anticipation of the comfortable Tory victory that occurred on May 3.[14]

Even with victory, Thatcher still ruled a party in which she represented a minority faction. John Nott, given the trade portfolio, counted himself among the five or six radical Tories in a cabinet with twenty-three ministers; the majority he dismissed as "diplomats" and "managers." Yet the prime minister moved swiftly and with purpose, focusing on "the evil of inflation" and holding the conviction that "there was no hope for the country unless inflation was destroyed by strict monetarist measures." Key ministers shared her passion; Geoffrey Howe, the new chancellor of the exchequer, pledged "absolutism against inflation." Beyond the commitment to tight money and higher interest rates, the Tory manifesto also called for steep cuts in income taxes (while raising consumption taxes) and reductions in government spending and borrowing. The talk of revolution had not been empty.[15]

---

[13] On the dissent, see Thatcher, *Downing Street Years,* pp. 7, 13; Geoffrey Howe, *Conflict of Loyalty* (New York: St. Martin's Press, 1994), pp. 39, 82; John Nott, *Here Today, Gone Tomorrow: Reflections of an Errant Politician* (London: Politicos, 2002), pp. 138, 146–48. On monetarism, see Gordon Pepper, *Inside Thatcher's Monetarist Revolution* (London: Macmillan, 1998), p. 30 (note that Pepper also edited the influential *Greenwell Monetary Bulletin*, the monetarist watchdog newsletter than began publication in June 1972); Burk and Cairncross, *Goodbye, Great Britain,* pp. xiii, 144–45, 158, 161 (quote).

[14] Hugo Young, *One of Us: A Biography of Margaret Thatcher* (London: Macmillan, 1989), p. 101; Howe, *Conflict of Loyalty,* p. 92 (first quote); William Whitelaw, *The Whitelaw Memoirs* (London: Aurum Press, 1989), pp. 140, 142, 144, 149; David Kynaston, *City of London,* vol. 4, *A Club No More, 1945–2000* (London: Chatto and Windus, 2001), pp. 519, 548, 579; Kynaston, *The Financial Times,* pp. 404–5, 434, 437 (quote), 439 (quote).

[15] Nott, *Here Today, Gone Tomorrow,* p. 173 (quote); Thatcher, *Downing Street Years,* pp. 26–27, 33, 36 (quote); Carrington, *Reflections on Things Past,* p. 275; Howe, *Conflict of Loyalty,* pp. 109, 136, 161 (quote); Young, *One of Us,* pp. 138, 144, 148, 193.

The rhetoric was sharp and the pace dizzying—exchange controls, for example, were simply abolished overnight, a long-promised deregulation that gave Thatcher the "greatest personal pleasure." Despite the fact that the Tory manifesto had been public knowledge for years, there was nevertheless something close to a collective gasp in most of Britain in response to the swift and dramatic nature of the policy changes. At the same time, the new program was "music to the City's ears." This is not surprising. Of course, the gentlemen of the City were sympathetic to reduced taxes and less government, but they also benefited directly from the enhanced business brought about by the end of exchange control and later by Thatcher's privatization program. Between 1981 and 1984, as London shed ninety thousand manufacturing jobs, forty-five thousand jobs were created in the financial sector. Among the bankers, the only concern to be heard about Thatcher's policies was not whether they were wise but whether she could see them through.[16]

This was a reasonable concern. The previous Tory government reversed course in the face of stiff economic winds, and Thatcher's deflationary medicine collided with a global recession, generating considerable economic distress in Britain. In 1980 inflation remained stubborn, unemployment was rising, and the money supply proved embarrassingly difficult to manage (sparking internal debates about monetary targets and whether trying to rein in an elusive "M3" was actually overshooting monetary tightness from the perspective of "M0"). But Thatcher pushed ahead, and Howe unveiled a tough budget that included the Medium Term Financial Strategy, which outlined the aggressive policy of reigning in the money supply.[17]

Some ministers within Thatcher's own cabinet, known derisively as "wets" because they were soft on economic strategy, began to speak out in public against the prime minister, and with unemployment reaching

[16] Thatcher, *Downing Street Years*, p. 44 (quote); Howe, *Conflict of Loyalty*, pp. 136, 163; Kynaston, *City of London*, pp. 579, 580, 581 (quote), 588, 590; Richard Roberts and David Kynaston, *City State: A Contemporary History of the City of London and How Money Triumphs* (London: Profile Books, 2002), pp. 21, 92, 166. It should be noted (see these same sources) that the City was taken aback by the suddenness of the removal of exchange controls, and this shock to the Old Boys was one source of Thatcher's satisfaction—she thought them complacent. Similarly, the Bank of England (which had employed 750 workers in its exchange control department) was taken aback by Thatcher's bluntness; some members of the bank also grumbled at the Medium Term Financial Strategy, which seemed to encroach on the bank's autonomy. These early bumps underscore the lack of personal affinity between Thatcher and the City, but the broader political harmony could not have been greater.

[17] Young, *One of Us*, pp. 198–200, 202–3; Thatcher, *Downing Street Years*, pp. 50, 53–54, 95–96, 126; Nott, *Here Today, Gone Tomorrow*, pp. 191–92; see also W. Greenwell & Co., *Monetary Bulletin*, no. 125, December 1981, and no. 129, March 26, 1982.

two million and rising still, the Conservative Party conference in October 1980 was a difficult one in which opposition from the wets emerged as more organized and increasingly vocal. One cabinet minister, Ian Gilmour, later described the budget as "a savage fiscal squeeze" designed to "satisfy the City that the Thatcherites were still being tough." Certainly the City was one of the few places where the Tory agenda was popular; the *Financial Times* held that "if the Government can stick to the strategy outlined, this was an historic occasion." Still, the strategy had yet to deliver, even on inflation, as the real economy staggered.[18]

Yet unlike Heath, who initiated his "U-turn" when unemployment hit one million, Thatcher relished the opportunity to declare "this Lady's not for turning." In 1981 she formally tapped Professor Alan Walters to assume the role of her "personal economic advisor." Walters, a monetarist and an inflation hawk, put great stock in credibility and sought "to convince the financial markets once and for all that it was a reforming government, determined to get inflation down." He had a hand in the formation of Thatcher's most controversial budget, unveiled in March 1981, which featured still more spending cuts into the teeth of the deep recession. The measures were wildly unpopular in Britain and were publicly condemned in a circular promoted and signed by 364 economists. But the City stood by the prime minister—the *Financial Times* praised the government for its courage and insisted that Thatcher's strategy was "broadly preferable to the alternatives put forth by its opponents." The only complaint to be heard from the editors of Greenwell's *Monetary Bulletin* was that the spending cuts did not go far enough; they responded to the "widely criticized" budget with a reminder that it "has always been stressed that cutting a deeply ingrained inflationary process would be painful."[19]

With unemployment approaching the impossible figure of three million, things came to a head in July at an acrimonious cabinet meeting described by Thatcher as the most bitter of her premiership—"the whole strategy was at issue." With much of the cabinet in revolt, rather than make a U-turn, Thatcher purged the wets, dismissing some, reassigning others, and dumping party chair Lord Thorneycroft (who had recently

---

[18] Ian Gilmour, *Dancing with Dogma: Britain under Thatcherism* (London: Simon and Schuster, 1992), pp. 18–20, 25 (quote); Young, *One of Us*, p. 205; Thatcher, *Downing Street Years*, pp. 129–30; Kynaston, *The Financial Times*, p. 456 (quote).

[19] Young, *One of Us*, pp. 209, 212, 214 (Walters quote), 216; Alan Walters, *Britain's Economic Renaissance: Margaret Thatcher's Reforms, 1979–1984* (New York: Oxford University Press, 1986), esp. p. 4; Thatcher, *Downing Street Years*, pp. 122, 126, 135, 137–38; Howe, *Conflict of Loyalty*, pp. 197, 201, 203, 208–9; Kynaston, *City of London* (support for Howe's "obstinate, unrelenting budget"), p. 586; Kynaston, *The Financial Times*, pp. 458, 461 (quote); W. Greenwell & Co., *Monetary Bulletin*, no. 116, March 1981, "The Budget" (quotes).

described himself as a "rising damp"), replacing him with loyalist Cecil Parkinson. The purge was widely critiqued, criticism that was only compounded by a further increase in interest rates, tough choices that nevertheless met with the "solid backing of the financial community." There would be no U-turn.[20]

Thatcher's Achilles' Heel

Thatcher's commitment to financial orthodoxy knew virtually no limit. This meant that although she assumed leadership with the purpose of "again asking the Conservative Party to put its faith in freedom and free markets, limited government and strong national defense," choices would have to be made if circumstances dictated that all good things could not go together. Thatcher had always advocated a strong military and ran on a platform of increased defense spending, a promise on which she delivered in 1979, much to the enthusiasm of the defense establishment. But as the economy slowed and then stagnated, the goal of greater military spending was increasingly at odds with the government's financial strategy. Chancellor Howe, in his unrelenting search for budgetary savings, saw the Ministry of Defense as "recidivist over-spenders," and in 1980 Defense Minister (and notorious wet) Francis Pym was able to extract another increase in defense spending only after a bitter row with the Treasury, and even then only by threatening to resign.[21]

That victory would prove to be Pym's last. As the recession deepened, free spending at Defense was incompatible with the government's spending and borrowing targets, and some programs would have to be jettisoned if there was to be any hope of keeping the economic strategy afloat. Thatcher moved Pym from Defense (he would become leader of the House) and replaced him with the financially savvy and economy-minded Nott, convinced that defense "would have to be cut back if we were to keep within any kind of financial discipline." With little expertise in defense, Nott was seen as Thatcher's hatchet man, a "treasury stooge . . . interested in controlling the money."[22]

[20] Thatcher, *Downing Street Years*, pp. 147–48, 149 (quote), 150–52; Cecil Parkinson, *Right at the Center: An Autobiography* (London: Weidenfeld and Nicolson, 1992), p. 173 (quote); Howe, *Conflict of Loyalty*, pp. 227, 228 (quote), 229–30; Gilmour, *Dancing with Dogma*, pp. 28, 38.

[21] Thatcher, *Downing Street Years*, p. 15 (quote); Howe, *Conflict of Loyalty*, pp. 144–45, 189 (quote); Francis Pym, *The Politics of Consent* (London: Hamish Hamilton, 1984), p. 105; Daniel K. Gibran, *The Falklands War: Britain versus the Past in the South Atlantic* (Jefferson, NC: McFarland, 1998), pp. 123–25; Chichester and Wilkinson, *The Uncertain Ally*, pp. 63, 66; Dockrill, *British Defense Policy*, pp. 111–12.

[22] Thatcher, *Downing Street Years*, pp. 125, 131, 249, 250 (quote); Young, *One of Us*, p. 210, 266; Peter Calvert, *The Falklands Crisis: The Rights and the Wrongs* (New York:

Nott would subsequently be accused of "going native" and guarding the military against the accountants at Treasury ("they would have been happy for everything to be sold to square their books"), but initially he lived up to initial expectations, producing the enormously controversial 1981 defense review. Rather than trim at the margins, Nott evaluated Britain's entire defense posture, refocusing it toward a Eurocentric, cold war–oriented posture. While all the services would face cuts (as well as reductions in projected growth, which upset planning), the navy bore the brunt of them. The future navy would have fewer large surface ships and focus instead on anti-Soviet submarine warfare. The military was unhappy, and Chief of Staff Admiral Lord Lewin furious; he saw no logic to the cuts other than "this driving thing of saving money." Navy Minister Keith Speed went public with his dismay but neither survived the process nor derailed the project.[23]

But Thatcher's choice of orthodoxy over defense was one of the reasons she was distinctly vulnerable in the Falklands affair. For one casualty of Nott's budget ax was the HMS *Endurance*. A modestly armed ship that carried twenty marines and a few helicopters, the old icebreaker cost only £3 million a year for the navy to run, but with the desperate search for savings every little bit helped, and from a military standpoint, the *Endurance* was expendable. From a political standpoint, however, as Britain's only armed presence in the South Atlantic, it was not. Foreign Secretary Lord Carrington considered the vessel crucial to British deterrence with regard to the Falklands, and he wrote Nott on three separate occasions urging that the decision to retire the ship be reversed or at least postponed. Captain Nicholas Barker of the *Endurance* was even more alarmed; he informed his superiors (and the press) that in Argentina the decision was seen as a "deliberate political gesture," an indication of Britain's fading commitment to the region. Former prime minister James Callaghan raised similar concerns directly to the prime minister in Parliament on February 9 and was rebuffed on the grounds of financial necessity. Even though three hundred members of Parliament signed a letter in support of keeping the ship at sea for at least one more season, Nott and Thatcher stood their

---

St. Martin's Press, 1982), p. 69; Nott, *Here Today, Gone Tomorrow,* pp. 199, 201, 204, 210 (quote); "Battle Stations for Defence," *The Economist,* June 26, 1982, p. 18; Hastings and Jenkins, *Battle for the Falklands,* p. 80.

[23] Nott, *Here Today, Gone Tomorrow,* p. 240 (quote); "Next Round in the Budget Battle," *The Economist,* July 3, 1982, p. 29; Charlton, *The Little Platoon,* pp. 139–40, 144, 146, 148 (Lewin quote); "Marshall Thatcher Believes in Discipline, Even if the Admirals Don't," *The Economist,* May 23, 1981, p. 29; "Britain's Battle of the Budget," ibid., p. 14; Christopher Coker, "Less Important Than Opulence: The Conservatives and Defence," Institute for European Defence and Strategic Studies, Occasional Paper 34 (1988), pp. 8, 29, 33, 47–48.

ground, and there was little dissent within the cabinet—as Chancellor Howe recalled, "It was certainly not for Treasury ministers to make the opposite case."[24]

Yet after the invasion the decision was widely seen as a colossal blunder. Even the *Franks Report*, the official government inquiry into the Falklands affair widely derided as a whitewash, concluded that the withdrawal of the *Endurance* was "inadvisable" and should have been rescinded, given the deteriorating situation in 1981.[25] The debacle directly implicated the prime minister and, worse, was a mistake that was part of a larger pattern of her failure to deter an invasion. Thatcher was warned repeatedly—and explicitly by Carrington as early as October 12, 1979— that the Argentineans would invade the islands if they did not perceive that negotiations were proceeding in good faith. And Argentina did lodge a formal protest regarding the lack of progress in July 1981. By February 1982 Captain Barker of the *Endurance* was convinced an invasion was in the cards and dispatched warnings to London expressing his concerns.[26]

Thatcher, however, did not act on these warnings; in fact, at bottom, she had no Falklands policy. On the international front she had bigger fish to fry, such as Rhodesia; also, importantly, she viewed the Foreign Office with some suspicion and thought ministers there tended to be overly sensitive to the concerns of foreign interests at the expense of British ones. Thatcher was thus somewhat tone-deaf to warnings and advice that sounded from this quarter. But the Foreign Office understood that after fifteen years of negotiations, the practical choices on the Falklands had finally boiled down to two: either abandon the negotiations and move to a policy of "fortress Falklands" or explore further the possibility of a "leaseback" solution (some sort of Argentinean sovereignty and British administration), an imperfect concept that was essentially the only way forward (Carrington, Pym, Nott, and Howe, for example, favored leaseback).[27]

---

[24] *Falkland Islands Review: Review of a Committee of Privy Counselors*, the Rt. Hon. the Lord Franks, Cmnd. 8787 (London: HMSO, 1983) (known as *The Franks Report*), pp. 33, 34; Nicholas Barker, *Beyond Endurance: An Epic of Whitehall and the South Atlantic* (London: Leo Cooper, 1997), pp. 3, 20, 75 (quote), 76, 300; G. M. Dillon, *The Falklands, Politics and War* (New York: St. Martin's Press, 1989), p. 36; Carrington, *Reflections on Things Past*, pp. 359–60; Nott, *Here Today, Gone Tomorrow*, pp. 254–55; Howe, *Conflict of Loyalty*, p. 245 (quote).

[25] *Franks Report*, p. 78 (quote); see also Barker, *Beyond Endurance*, pp. 233–36; Dillon, *The Falklands, Politics and War*, p. 54.

[26] Charlton, *The Little Platoon*, p. 182; Arthur Gavshon and Desmond Rice, *The Sinking of the Belgrano* (London: Secker and Warburg, 1984), p. 10; Carrington, *Reflections on Things Past*, pp. 351, 357; Hastings and Jenkins, *Battle for the Falklands*, p. 42; Barker, *Beyond Endurance*, pp. 1, 116, 127, 224, 232.

[27] Carrington, *Reflections on Things Past*, pp. 285, 352, 354; Dillon, *The Falklands, Politics and War*, pp. 20, 229, 231; Charlton, *The Little Platoon*, pp. 68, 70, 71, 73; Howe,

Thatcher instead chose to do nothing and thus left herself exposed to charges that she had invited the invasion. Fortress Falklands was simply inconceivable; it would have involved a huge investment, building up a military base eight thousand miles from home while defense everywhere else faced cuts. But on leaseback, Thatcher was equally clear: she "disliked this proposal." When Nicholas Ridley, the Foreign Ministry official responsible for the islands, returned from the Falklands with a report proposing leaseback, Thatcher's negative response was vehement; she was opposed to even a cabinet-level discussion. On December 2, 1980, Ridley was allowed to present his ideas to Parliament, where he was unceremoniously hung out to dry, subject to savage cross fire from the Falklands lobby and point scorers from the opposition; not one member of the government rose to his defense. With leaseback dead, the British now brought nothing to the negotiating table save blatant stalling.[28]

The Bankers' Dilemma

Thus on April 2, 1982, Thatcher was a uniquely vulnerable figure. While the economy was finally showing some initial signs of life—and the budget presented in March was the first since 1979 not viewed as draconian—unemployment was still at three million, and three difficult years into her term, the prime minister was an unpopular and divisive figure.[29] With news of the invasion, an uproarious House of Commons met in an emergency Saturday session for the first time since the Suez Crisis. It did not go well. Nott's defensive and combative performance in particular was seen as disastrous. Obviously, the right wing was furious; headlines even in the conservative press screamed of "humiliation" and "shame." As Thatcher well understood, "There was no doubt the Party's blood was up: nor was it just John Nott they were after."[30]

The Left was, if anything, angrier still. Certainly political opportunism was a factor, but there was more. It was as if the pent-up frustrations of twenty-five years of decline had finally burst and unleashed a torrent of anger upon the prime minister and her cabinet. Labour's big guns landed haymaker blows, and the prime minister was reeling. Denis Healey spoke

---

Conflict of Loyalty, p. 245; "What Happens When a Lady Falls Out with Her Diplomats," *The Economist*, November 27, 1982, p. 25.

[28] Thatcher, *Downing Street Years*, pp. 175 (quote), 176; Young, *One of Us*, pp. 259–60; "The Misjudgments That Led to the Falklands War," p. 41; Dillon, *The Falklands, Politics and War*, pp. 25, 27, 31–32; Charlton, *The Little Platoon*, pp. 74–76, 182–83.

[29] Howe, *Conflict of Loyalty*, pp. 209, 241, 244; Walters, *Britain's Economic Renaissance*, pp. 91–94; Kynaston, *City of London*, p. 587; Young, *One of Us*, pp. 241, 245–46.

[30] Eddy and Linklater, *The Falklands War*, pp. 98 (quotes), 99–100; Thatcher, *Downing Street Years*, p. 185.

of "inexplicable errors of action and judgment that led to the Government betraying their duties to the Falkland Islanders." Former prime minister Callaghan, a veteran of previous Falklands negotiations, noted, "The government was warned time after time about this"; going for the jugular, he added: "I cannot conceive of a more naïve invitation to a military dictator to invade than to say there are other, higher claims on our defence budget." Surveys showed that 80 percent of the public blamed the government; and although Britons would soon rally around Thatcher's bold initiative to retake the islands, in one poll, as late as April 14, she earned the dubious distinction of "worst Prime Minister in history," crushing perennial "favorite" Neville Chamberlain by a margin of 48 to 12 percent.[31]

There is some academic debate as to how important the "Falklands factor" was in Thatcher's big electoral victory in 1983. While most studies (as well as almost all politicians and observers at the time, including Thatcher herself) support the view that the military victory (and Thatcher's wartime leadership) contributed crucially to the electoral fortunes of the prime minister and her party, a minority have argued that absent the Falklands, the improving macroeconomic environment would on its own have ensured Thatcher's reelection.[32] While this issue is debatable, it is not the relevant counterfactual for the choice faced by the financial community in 1982. The question was not, "Absent the Falklands crisis, would Thatcher have won re-election?" Rather, it was, "Given the Argentinean invasion, what were the likely consequences for Thatcher?"

On this question the answer is clear. However risky the operation might be, Margaret Thatcher's political future depended on her setting right, in her response to the invasion, the disgrace of presiding over the Falklands humiliation. For the Tories, according to party chair Parkinson, if the government failed to respond forcefully to the attack, "We could have certainly written off the next election."[33] For Thatcher the stakes

[31] House of Commons, *The Falklands Campaign: A Digest of Debates in the House of Commons, 2 April to June 1982* (London: HMSO, 1982), pp. 24, 29 (quote), 36 (quote), 39, 50; Dillon, *The Falklands, Politics and War*, p. 120 (polls); Freedman and Gamba-Stonehouse, *Signals of War*, p. 121.

[32] Brian Lai and Dan Reiter, "Rally 'Round the Union Jack? Public Opinion and the Use of Force in the United Kingdom, 1948–2001," *International Studies Quarterly* 49:2 (June 2005), pp. 255–56, 264; "Will Her Luck Hold?" *The Economist*, October 2, 1982, p. 13; David Sanders, Hugh Ward, David Marsh, and Tony Fletcher, "Government Popularity and the Falklands War: A Reassessment," *British Journal of Political Science* 17:3 (July 1987); Harold Clarke, William Misher, and Paul Whiteley, "Recapturing the Falklands: Models of Conservative Popularity, 1979–83," *British Journal of Political Science* 20:1 (January 1990); Thatcher, *Downing Street Years*, p. 265.

[33] Andrew Dorman, Michael D. Kandiah, and Gillian Staerk (eds.), "The Falklands Seminar: A Gathering of the Senior Commanders and Politicians Who Directed the Course of

were even higher—many doubted whether she could survive a negotiated settlement. Some Conservatives worried that she might drag the
party down with her, and there was considerable talk of a Suez-like maneuver, whereby the prime minister would be jettisoned but the party
would survive.[34]

In short, finance faced the following choice: support the prime minister,
which meant an assertive response that carried the clear risk of limited
war, or stick with war aversion above all else. There were good reasons
why the City feared a military confrontation—and its possible implications for the budget, inflation, and sterling. But giving in on the Falklands
meant losing Thatcher, which would result in one of two unattractive
alternatives: a Labour government or a new Tory leadership. Certainly
the former was wholeheartedly unpalatable. The City had an "atavistic
anti-Labour attitude," and the animosity ran deep and both ways; most
members of the Labour party regarded the City as an "implacable
enemy." The mutual disdain and distrust went back decades, if not longer,
and recent experiences did nothing but deepen the chasm. Wilson, who
once accused the Bank of England of "cooking the books" in support
of the Tories, promised during the 1974 election campaign to end the
"anarchy" in the City. The *Financial Times* was openly hostile to the Labour governments of the seventies, a posture that reflected a virtual bun-
ker mentality in the City more broadly.[35]

But if a return to Labour was unacceptable, the prospect of a new Tory
leadership offered few attractions. The conventional wisdom held that
Francis Pym, who had "a lack of enthusiasm for [Thatcher's] strict economic policies," would be her successor; there was further speculation
that if tapped, he would bring Gilmour and Heath into leadership positions.[36] A more notorious troika of wets could scarcely be found, nor did

Events of the Falklands War of 1982," Strategic and Combat Studies Institute, Occasional
Paper 46 (June 5, 2002), p. 22 (Parkinson quote); Lawrence Freedman, *Britain and the
Falklands War* (Oxford: Basil Blackwell, 1988), pp. 4, 104; Freedman and Gamba-Stone-
house, *Signals of War*, p. 156; Young, *One of Us*, pp. 258, 264, 265, 268.

[34] See for example Barry May, "Iron Lady's Career Rides with the Royal Armada," *The
Globe and Mail*, April 10, 1982, p. 15; "British Politics: Off on the Wrong Foot," *The
Economist*, April 10, 1982, p. 22; "City Peers through Its Telescope," *Financial Times*, April
10, 1982, p. 24; Peter Riddell, "Tribal Loyalties among the Tories," *Financial Times*, April
15, 1982, p. 19.

[35] Roberts and Kynaston, *City State*, p. 16 (quote); Kynaston, *City of London*, pp. 295
(quote), 296, 493 (quote), 494 (quote), 495, 552, 554; Kynaston, *The Financial Times*, pp.
385, 401, 402.

[36] "Winners in the War at Westminster," *The Economist*, May 15, 1982, p. 33; William
Borders, "Right Wing Rumblings an Issue for Mrs. Thatcher," *New York Times*, May 14,
1982, p. 10 (quotes); May, "Iron Lady's Career Rides," p. 15; Riddell, "Tribal Loyalties,"
p. 19.

this escape the City's notice. Pym, pushed out from Defence for free spending, thought "that 'monetarism' has encouraged a disproportionate emphasis on inflation" and very much saw himself as the standard-bearer for the liberal wing of the Tory party. Gilmour was even wetter; in his view "everything about the Medium Term Financial Strategy turned out to be mistaken," and the party's relationship with the "City of London, . . . an enthusiastic acolyte of Thatcherite economics," was too cozy.[37]

Yet despite these implications, while the public rallied broadly behind Margaret Thatcher, as I will discuss in greater detail later, finance would not.

THE VIEW FROM ARGENTINA

The decision of Argentina's governing military junta to seize las Islas Malvinas provides a unique opportunity to look at the politics of a crisis from both sides of the conflict. As Argentina shares the history of the dispute (as discussed earlier) and the diplomatic and military narrative (see below), weaving together these elements with an interlude that considers the view from Argentina offers something of an attractive "shadow case," an additional, promising setting for the exploration of the politics of finance and war.

However, Argentina does not offer a full-fledged case or an opportunity for a straightforward test of the central argument of this book. There was no significant contemporaneous debate about the Malvinas,[38] and thus no posturing by various interest groups, for two reasons. First, there was no opportunity for actors to weigh in on the merits of the invasion—the decision was made in extraordinary secrecy—and only a handful of people knew of the plan before it was executed. Second, there simply was no open domestic political discussion in Argentina, either before the invasion or during the months of crisis that followed. The military dictatorship was oppressive and extraordinarily ruthless, and it comprehensively permeated virtually all aspects of civil society. Media outlets, for example, were state-run, or knew enough to censor themselves, or were subject to swift retribution if they were not adequately circumspect.

Yet considered as a shadow case, the Argentinean experience has much to offer, including some intriguing (analytical) parallels with Britain: the

---

[37] Pym, *The Politics of Consent*, pp. x, 6–8, 14 (quote), 131–33, 148; Gilmour, *Dancing with Dogma*, pp. 22 (quote), 25, 29–31, 59, 73 (quote); "City Peers through Its Telescope," p. 24.

[38] And given that the invasion failed and the junta was subsequently removed, vilified, and disgraced, the retrospective memoirs of participants are likely to be even less trustworthy than usual.

prior support of the financial community for an unpopular government, the immense popularity of the decision to use force, and the financial implications of the war. Pursuing these strands will shed more light on key questions of this inquiry.

The Long Trip to the Brink

Argentina's famously difficult economic history in the twentieth century—before the First World War it was among the world's prosperous nations—was of a kind with its troubled political history.[39] The republic suffered its first military coup in 1930, and for the next fifty-two years the military dominated politics—of the twenty-four presidents during that half-century, thirteen were civilian, and every one of them was interrupted by military intervention. The only reelected government was that of Juan Perón, who governed from 1943 to 1955 (with a brief interlude in 1945, when he was imprisoned by the military). Perón was a charismatic populist with close ties to labor, and although the former colonel governed as a civilian, he nevertheless militarized the society and devoted considerable resources to defense.[40]

Perón fell to a coup in 1955, but the next eighteen years of intermittent weak civilian government and unpopular military rule (usually stepping in to curb the influence of Peronist trade unions) served only to enhance his image in exile, and he triumphantly (if somewhat anachronistically) returned in 1973, assuming the presidency after seven years of military rule. But Perón's reprise was marred by increasingly violent conflict between his leftist and rightist supporters; the crisis was compounded by the old man's death in 1974, which left the presidency in the untested hands of his third wife, Isabel. In the wake of increasing political violence, Isabel was removed in a bloodless coup in March 1976. Perón's ouster was enthusiastically supported by industry, landowners, and especially finance; but with leftist groups waging a full-scale guerrilla war against the army in the north, politically motivated murders in the cities, and mounting economic distress and labor unrest, it should be noted that a broad cross section of society viewed the return of the military with some relief.[41]

---

[39] On Argentina's long economic decline, see Gerardo Della Paolera and Alan M. Taylor (eds.), *A New Economic History of Argentina* (Cambridge: Cambridge University Press, 2003), and Carlos F. Diaz Alejandro, *Essays on the Economic History of the Argentine Republic* (New Haven: Yale University Pres, 1970).

[40] Guillermo A. Makin, "The Military in Argentine Politics, 1880–1982," *Millennium* 12:1 (Spring 1983), p. 53; Burns, *The Land That Lost Its Heroes*, pp. 13–14.

[41] Makin, "The Military in Argentine Politics," pp. 57–59; Paul G. Buchanan, "The Varied Faces of Domination: State Terror, Economic Policy, and Social Rupture during the Argentine 'Proceso,' 1976–81," *American Journal of Political Science* 31:2 (May 1987), p.

That relief would prove short-lived. The new military regime under the leadership of General Jorge Videla introduced a radical military project known as the Proceso de Reorginization Nacional. The Proceso had three principal goals: to destroy the leftist insurgency (and allied subversives), restructure the economy along liberal, free market lines, and transform society to finally eliminate Peronism. These goals would be achieved through a dramatic expansion of the military's reach, accompanied by an orgy of state-sponsored violence and terror. The legislature was disbanded, the judiciary was placed under military control, and all political parties and activities were outlawed. Cabinet ministries were filled exclusively with soldiers (with the exception of finance); basic legal rights were suspended and unions outlawed, their assets seized by the state. Media censorship was universal, and art, literature, or any expression deemed subversive was banned. TV stations, banks, and even ballet companies found themselves under the authority of newly appointed military masters.[42]

The army's strategy was not subtle—one of Videla's commanders remarked that to win the internal war, the military would "have to kill 50,000 people: 25,000 subversives, 20,000 sympathizers, and we will make 5,000 mistakes." Within a few years, the army was successful in defeating the guerrillas in the northern provinces, but the climate of terror throughout the country did not abate. As General Videla explained, "A terrorist is not just someone with a gun or a bomb but someone who spreads ideas that are contrary to Western and Christian civilization." The junta, aided by paramilitary death squads, continued in its effort to remake Argentinean society. Perceived enemies of the regime, especially journalists, lawyers, psychiatrists, students, and professors, were targeted in the "dirty war" of kidnappings, systematic torture, undocumented imprisonment, murder, and "disappearance." Ten thousand were killed, tens of thousands disappeared, countless more were tortured, and an even larger number fled the country.[43]

The regime showed a similar if less bloody single-mindedness in its efforts to remake the economy. New finance minister José Martínez de

---

338. Latin America Bureau, *Falklands/Malvinas: Whose Crisis?* (London: Latin America Bureau, 1982), p. 66.

[42] William C. Smith, *Authoritarianism and the Crisis of the Argentine Political Economy* (Stanford: Stanford University Press, 1989), p. 224; Buchanan, "The Varied Faces of Domination," pp. 352, 355, 360, 362, 365; Burns, *The Land That Lost Its Heroes*, pp. 80, 86, 94–95.

[43] Smith, *Authoritarianism and the Crisis*, pp. 1, 232 (quote); Latin America Bureau, *Falklands/Malvinas*, p. 67 (quote); Buchanan, "The Varied Faces of Domination," pp. 368–69, 371, 373; Simon Collier, "Argentina: Domestic Travail, International Censure," *International Affairs* 57:3 (Summer 1981), p. 478; Juan E. Corradi, *The Fitful Republic: Economy, Society and Politics in Argentina* (Boulder, CO: Westview Press, 1985), pp. 115–16.

Hoz, armed with degrees from Harvard and Oxford, well-known and popular in global banking circles, embarked on an all-out effort to recast Argentina's economy along orthodox, monetarist lines. Wages were frozen (real wages fell by 50 percent in 1976), spending was slashed, and monetary policy became severe; regulations, tariffs, and subsidies were scaled back; and government employees were shed (there were 200,000 fewer on the federal payroll by 1980). The program was met with cheers from the international financial community—the IMF and private syndicates extended loans, and foreign investors were enthusiastic.[44] Not surprisingly, the measures caused considerable economic dislocation and distress in Argentina—this was to be expected in any event. But even though Martínez de Hoz could point to some successes—economic conditions were improving in 1977 and there were signs of improvement after a terrible 1978—by the end of the decade support for more of his bitter medicine from agriculture and industry, and certainly from the general public, diminished considerably.[45]

The junta faced a very difficult period in 1980. With the dirty war declared over and won, the regime searched for a new foundation of legitimacy, a quest that was seriously complicated by a major financial crisis in April. The default of the Banco de Intercambio Regional, the republic's largest private bank, generated waves of aftershocks that rumbled through the economy. The economy remained unsettled through March 1981, when General Videla (along with Martínez de Hoz) was scheduled to step down as leader of the junta. The armed forces, previously united by their paramount commitment to the dirty war, now eyed the economy nervously and squabbled over various succession issues. General Roberto Viola, a moderate, emerged from the infighting, though his plans for political and economic reform were opposed by many in the military. Viola included seven civilians in his cabinet and made overtures to the main political parties, the Peronists and the Radicals; his finance minister, Lorenzo Sigaut recalls "profound dissent between the outgoing and incoming administrations in economic, political and social matters."[46]

[44] Guido di Tella and Carlos Rodriguez Braun (eds.), *Argentina, 1946–83: The Economic Ministers Speak* (New York: St. Martin's Press, 1984), pp. 22, 151, 153; Buchanan, "The Varied Faces of Domination," pp. 357–58, 362–63; Burns, *The Land That Lost Its Heroes*, p. 85.

[45] Smith, *Authoritarianism and the Crisis*, pp. 1, 224, 236; Corradi, *The Fitful Republic*, pp. 123, 134; Gibran, *The Falklands War*, pp. 60, 62; Calvert, *The Falklands Crisis*, p. 53.

[46] Di Tella and Braun, *The Economic Ministers Speak*, pp. 25, 175, 181, 182 (quote), 189; see also Martínez de Hoz's criticism of Viola on p. 178; Gerardo L. Munck, *Authoritarianism and Democratization: Soldiers and Workers in Argentina, 1976–1983* (University Park: Penn State University Press, 1998), p. 120. Burns, *The Land That Lost Its Heroes*, p. 126; Makin, "The Military in Argentine Politics," p. 62.

Viola's initial reforms did not resolve the growing economic distress; rather, the recession seemed to be deepening, inflation was galloping to triple digits, and the budget deficit soared. A financial crisis in June was the third in as many months, and the foreign exchange markets were in panic. The government seemed helpless to stop the bleeding; foreign reserves plunged—over $300 million was lost in a single day. Viola's hardline opponents in the military were restless and in search for a way out of the mess.[47]

The Decision to Invade

In November 1981 over 100,000 people took to the streets of Buenos Aires to protest military rule; behind the scenes, routine changes in the three-man junta that stood behind the presidency posed an even greater threat to Viola. General Leopoldo Galtieri, the hard-drinking and ambitious head of the army, was joined by the powerful admiral Jorge Anaya as well as the commander of Argentina's third service, Air Force General Basilio Lami Dozo. Galtieri and Anaya met in early December to discuss their shared concern for the state of the economy and the future of the armed forces. They viewed Viola's soft economic politics with contempt, his political reforms with alarm. The army and navy leaders, like many officers in Argentina's military, had developed a "Nuremberg mentality"; they feared that if there was a return to civilian rule, they would be held accountable for crimes against humanity given their actions during the dirty war. Galtieri sought Anaya's support for a move against Viola, a coup that would install Galtieri as president *and* permit him to retain his position as the army chief on the junta. Anaya, who had already been nursing a plot to land commandos on South Georgia, agreed, with one condition: the Malvinas must be recaptured by Argentina within a year, that is, before 1983, the 150th anniversary of British occupation.[48]

Reclaiming the islands was an ambition at the core of Argentinean national identity, but it was always the navy that was most eager to turn those dreams into action, most recently in 1977, when Anaya had been ordered to draw up invasion plans by his then-boss Admiral Massera, plans that were tactfully set aside by General Videla, who suspected a navy power play. But now the army and navy were on the same page. A

---

[47] Latin America Bureau, *Falklands/Malvinas*, pp. 73–74; Buchanan, "The Varied Faces of Domination," pp. 375–76; Gibran, *The Falklands War*, p. 63.

[48] Burns, *The Land That Lost Its Heroes*, pp. 126, 128–30; Cardoso, Kirschbaum, and Van der Kooy, *The Secret Plot*, pp. 17, 25–26; Hastings and Jenkins, *Battle for the Falklands*, pp. 46, 48; Guillermo A. Makin, "Argentine Approaches to the Falklands/Malvinas: Was the Resort to Violence Foreseeable?" *International Affairs* 59:3 (Summer 1983), p. 398; Makin, "The Military in Argentine Politics," pp. 61–62.

triumphant return of the Malvinas would provide cover for one final round of economic austerity and wipe clean the military's dirty hands; Galtieri dreamed of ruling for ten years and easily agreed to Anaya's bold scheme. Viola was ousted on December 18, and Galtieri was sworn in on the twenty-second; Lami Dozo was informed of the invasion decision a week later. The more cautious air force man offered no objection.[49]

The new leadership embarked on a highly visible project to address Argentina's economic woes. Galtieri dismissed Viola's entire cabinet and brought in Roberto Alemann as the new economic minister. A strict monetarist, Alemann held the view that the only reason Martínez de Hoz's policies failed to work was that they were not applied strictly enough. Upon assuming office, he unleashed an ambitious deflationary package that cut the peso loose and left it to float, targeted the money supply, froze public sector wages (which hit home, given the very high inflation), raised indirect taxes, and sharply cut government spending across the board— including (where Martínez de Hoz could not go) projected cuts to the defense budget.[50]

Well out of the public view, Galtieri and Anaya worked on the secret element of their daring blueprint to recast the foundation of Argentinean politics. Two weeks before the invasion, fewer than ten men in the republic knew of the plans, and those involved were sworn to "absolute" secrecy. No civilians were in the loop; Foreign Minister Nicanor Costa-Méndez "did not discuss the possibility with the junta" before March 22. Argentina's new senior diplomat had assumed office with the understanding that negotiations with the British were to be given priority over other issues, such as the Beagle Channel dispute with Chile. The two controversies were not unrelated. The Latin neighbors were at the brink of war over the border issue in 1978, when papal intervention ruled in Chile's favor, serving the Argentineans another dish of bitter frustration that they hoped a triumph in the Malvinas would wash away.[51]

Absolute secrecy was essential for the junta's strategy. Well aware of Britain's defense review of 1981 and its pressure on spending and cuts to

[49] Carlos J. Moneta, "The Malvinas Conflict: Some Elements for an Analysis of the Argentine Military Regime's Decision-Making Process, 1976–82," *Millennium* 13:3 (Winter 1984), p. 318; Munck, *Authoritarianism and Democratization*, pp. 126, 139–40; Burns, *The Land That Lost Its Heroes*, pp. 109–10; Corradi, *The Fitful Republic*, p. 79.

[50] Cardoso, Kirschbaum, and Van der Kooy, *The Secret Plot*, p. 2; Smith, *Authoritarianism and the Crisis*, p. 244; Hugh O'Shaughnessy, "Buenos Aires Tries to Slim Public Sector," *Financial Times*, January 15, 1982, p. 5; Hastings and Jenkins, *Battle for the Falklands*, p. 47; Calvert, *The Falklands Crisis*, p. 55.

[51] Cardoso, Kirschbaum, and Van der Kooy, *The Secret Plot*, pp. 3, 51–52, 53 (quote), 58, 65; Charlton, *The Little Platoon*, pp. 101, 110 (Costa-Méndez quote); Burns, *The Land That Lost Its Heroes*, pp. 116, 135, 157; Freedman and Gamba-Stonehouse, *Signals of War*,

the navy, the invasion date was set for sometime after mid-May. A relatively bloodless lightning strike—after the *Endurance* was gone, with the navy cuts under way, and the fearsome South Atlantic winter about to begin—was designed to present Britain with a fait accompli. If the British suspected an invasion was coming, they could reinforce their modest garrison of marines on the islands and, worse, dispatch submarines that might cripple the landing force.[52]

Ironically, it was Anaya who compromised this plan, by moving ahead, at the same time, with his scheme to covertly establish a permanent presence on South Georgia by inserting Argentinean commandos into a party of legitimate civilian scrap metal workers (there to salvage an old whaling station) and then subsequently establish a military base on the island in April, when the *Endurance* was scheduled to visit Brazil. This was a blunder—the two operations were incompatible—but Anaya orchestrated each scheme in secrecy, so no one in the navy knew of both operations. It is conceivable that the South Georgia operation was Anaya's insurance policy, forcing the junta's hand over the Malvinas, but the evidence suggests that the admiral simply blundered; most likely he assumed that the scheme would go unnoticed or unchallenged by the British.[53]

Receiving reports that an Argentinean flag had been raised by the "scrap metal workers," the British government interpreted the events as another flare-up of the South Atlantic cat-and-mouse game (most recently played on the South Sandwich Islands in 1977). Already planning a firm riposte to Argentina's strident "unilateral declaration" released after the February Falklands talks, the British responded with stern diplomatic warnings and on March 20 ordered the *Endurance* toward South Georgia with tentative instructions to remove the small Argentinean party, estimated to include about ten men. These measures, combined with media rumors that British submarines might be on the way in response to the South Georgia crisis, took the junta by surprise and inadvertently lit the fuse. For there were also armed marines on South Georgia, under the command of Lieutenant Carlos Astiz, the notorious "white angel of

---

pp. 105–6, 109; Felipe Sanfuentes, "The Chilean Falklands Factor," in Alex Danchev (ed.), *International Perspectives on the Falklands Conflict* (New York: St. Martin's Press, 1992).

[52] Charlton, *The Little Platoon*, p. 109; Hastings and Jenkins, *Battle for the Falklands*, p. 48; *Franks Report*, pp. 75, 77; Burns, *The Land That Lost Its Heroes*, p. 144.

[53] Burns, *The Land That Lost Its Heroes*, pp. 150, 154–55, 172; Cardoso, Kirschbaum, and Van der Kooy, *The Secret Plot*, pp. 61–62; Barker, *Beyond Endurance*, p. 128. Anaya still felt the need to lie about the South Georgia operation in a confidential jailhouse interview with his friend, U.S. admiral Harry Train, commander-in-chief, Atlantic Command, in December 1984. See the comments by Train in Miller Center of Public Affairs, Oral History Project, "The Falklands Roundtable," May 15–16, 2003, final edited transcript, pp. 15–16; see also Charlton, *The Little Platoon*, pp. 115, 118.

death" from the torture chambers of the Naval Mechanics School (another example of how the participants in the invasion plans, from Galtieri on down, were men deeply implicated in the dirty war looking to rehabilitate their reputations). Thus any encounter with the *Endurance* would be bloody, and then British reinforcements and, worse, submarines, would certainly be on their way, removing the element of surprise from and greatly complicating the Malvinas operation.[54]

With confrontation in the South Atlantic now on the front page of newspapers and debated in the House of Commons, the junta first stalled, to keep the *Endurance* at bay, and within a few days (on March 26) reached the inevitable conclusion: the Malvinas operation would have to be executed immediately. Two days later the invasion fleet sailed, though not until March 31 did the British fully understand that their destination was not South Georgia.[55] In Argentina all eyes were on the streets of Buenos Aires, not the South Atlantic, where growing public opposition to the regime had led to a general strike and, on March 30, to a massive public demonstration—the largest since the final days of Isabel Perón in 1976. At the time, it was often asserted that the March demonstrations forced the regime into a diversionary war. This was clearly not the case, but nevertheless the decision for war, reached in December, was made for domestic political reasons: to wipe the slate clean and reinvent the nature of military rule in Argentina, which had otherwise reached a dismal dead end.[56]

Taking One for El Equipo? The Financial Implications of the Malvinas War

The military regime hoped that recapturing the Malvinas would wipe the slate clean and rally domestic support that would carry it on the shoulders of an exuberant public from the overwhelming burdens of an ugly past to a new and promising future. In the early weeks at least, if anything,

[54] Freedman and Gamba-Stonehouse, *Signals of War*, pp. 56–58; Hastings and Jenkins, *Battle for the Falklands*, p. 55; Moneta, "The Malvinas Conflict," pp. 319, 322; Buchanan, "The Varied Faces of Domination," p. 370; Burns, *The Land That Lost Its Heroes*, pp. 102, 168, 170.

[55] Cardoso, Kirschbaum, and Van der Kooy, *The Secret Plot*, pp. 71, 72, 75; Burns, *The Land That Lost Its Heroes*, pp. 171–72, 176; Charlton, *The Little Platoon*, p. 114; Freedman and Gamba-Stonehouse, *Signals of War*, pp. 63, 67–68, 98.

[56] On the fundamental domestic imperatives, see, for example, Makin, "The Military in Argentine Politics," pp. 62–65; Munck, *Authoritarianism and Democratization*, p. 145; Latin America Bureau, *Falklands/Malvinas*, p. 79; Gibran, *The Falklands War*, pp. 69–70. John Arquilla and Maria Moyana Rasmussen, in "The Origins of the South Atlantic War," *Journal of Latin American Studies* 33 (2001), pp. 739–75, illustrate the limits of a simple diversionary argument based solely on the March 30 demonstrations.

their expectations were exceeded. The massive crowds that days before had dodged police batons and worse to call for an end to military rule now filled the air with cheers. As with the reaction of the British public, the conflict touched a nerve that released the pent-up frustrations of the time, in this case stemming from economic misery, political horror, and, over the Beagle Channel, thwarted international ambition. As one journalist in Buenos Aires reported, the invasion "forged an unprecedented unity in a country characterized by the divisiveness of its political and economic system." The euphoria of the crowds reflected the "unlimited support" of everyone from fascist politicians and the most conservative elements of the church to the Communist Party and left-wing human rights activists—and most everyone in between. The media were unquestioning, public reputations were rehabilitated, and at the ceremony for the swearing in of the governor of the Malvinas, leaders of political parties and trade unions stood in solidarity with the military officers who had recently been at war with their brethren. The only downside from the perspective of the junta—and this would come back to haunt them—was that having crawled so far out on this ledge, there was precious little space for retreat or compromise. Strict censorship served only to paint the regime further into a corner. The Argentinean public was served a steady diet consisting solely of good (and greatly exaggerated) news from the war front; when one news report suggested that supplies on the islands might be inadequate, the paper that published it was shut down.[57]

The financial community needed no reason to rally around the junta; they had always been among the regime's most loyal supporters. In 1976 the bankers were at the forefront of the large collection of interests celebrating the demise of Mrs. Perón and her labor-based coalition, which was associated with ruinous inflation and ambitious financial "reforms" that were heavy on regulations and state intervention in the banking system. Finance had traditionally supported the military's frequent interventions in Argentina's domestic politics, as the soldiers usually arrived to kick out labor and the Left and tended to pursue free-market, inflation-fighting policies. In particular, the appointment of Martínez de Hoz, with his orthodox pedigree and international cachet, met with the applause of both the domestic and the international banking community—and his

---

[57] Alejandro Dabat and Louis Lorenzano, *Argentina: The Malvinas and the End of Military Rule* (trans. Ralph Johnstone) (London: Verso, 1984), pp. 76, 83, 105 (quote), 106; Simon Collier, "The First Falklands War? Argentinean Attitudes," *International Affairs* 59:3 (Summer 1983), p. 460; Jimmy Burns, "Falklands Adventure Unites a Country in Search of Its Identity," *Financial Times*, April 21, 1982, p. 4 (quote); Eddy and Linklater, *The Falklands War*, pp. 119, 215; Cardoso, Kirschbaum, and Van der Kooy, *The Secret Plot*, p. 102; Burns, *The Land That Lost Its Heroes*, pp. 179, 188, 238–39, 261; Lebow, "Miscalculation in the South Atlantic," p. 110.

finance-friendly reform and liberalization packages did not disappoint them. Even in the difficult days of early 1981, finance remained loyal to the conservative junta while others in big business seemed to slip a safe political distance away—which is not surprising given that the financial sector's share of the GDP grew from 1976 to 1981 (part of which, of course, was attributable to industrial decline). These instincts were subsequently vindicated with the appointment of Alemann and the return to strict monetary orthodoxy after the unfortunate Viola interlude.[58]

But the war was another matter. Despite the enormous popularity of the invasion (and despite the absence of any sort of public debate), financial leaders were "among the few who opposed the invasion from the outset."[59] And for good reasons. Certainly the Malvinas affair and its international political fallout raised some potential complications for Argentina's relations with the international financial community. More concretely, the war would be costly; even before the attack, the inability to control defense spending had undermined Martínez de Hoz's blueprints for economic reform, a problem Alemann had been keen to redress upon becoming finance minister. Especially after the confrontation with Chile in 1978, defense spending had increased markedly under military rule. This profligacy "was largely responsible for the crucial reversal in the trend of the fiscal deficit and also for the increase in the external debt," which in turn, according to Martínez de Hoz, were "mainly responsible" for the struggles with inflation.[60]

War would compound those problems and introduce a host of additional ones. Not surprisingly, then, in "the midst of effervescent nationalism and self-congratulatory jingoism . . . the tense public manner of Sr. Roberto Alemann . . . stuck out like a sore thumb." His entire program—including spending cuts (featuring a 10 percent cut in military spending), tight money, the freely floating peso—was at once swept away, and the

---

[58] Di Tella and Braun (eds.), *The Economic Ministers Speak*, pp. 18, 25–26, 153–54; Makin, "The Military in Argentine Politics," pp. 58, 61; Smith, *Authoritarianism and the Crisis*, p. 255; Guido di Tella, *Argentina under Perón, 1973–76: The Nation's Experience with a Labour-Based Government* (New York: St. Martin's Press, 1983), pp. 11–12, 98–99, 101, 105, 118; Hector Schamis, "The Political Economy of Currency Boards: Argentina in Historical Perspective," in Jonathan Kirshner (ed.), *Monetary Orders* (Ithaca: Cornell University Press, 2003), pp. 132–34; Latin America Bureau, *Falklands/Malvinas*, pp. 66–67, 82; Corradi, *The Fitful Republic*, p. 133.

[59] Carlos J. Moneta, "The Malvinas Conflict," in Heraldo Munoz and Joseph Tulchin (eds.), *Latin American Nations in World Politics* (Boulder, CO: Westview Press, 1984), p. 129 (quote).

[60] Di Tella and Braun, *The Economic Ministers Speak*, pp. 24 (quote), 171 (Martínez de Hoz quote); Latin America Bureau, *Falklands/Malvinas*, p. 70; Dabat and Lorenzano, *The Malvinas and the End of Military Rule*, p. 93; Burns, *The Land That Lost Its Heroes*, pp. 89–90.

economy minister was forced instead into taking measures that would "undermine the very principles on which his economic program" was founded. Even a successful war effort would irretrievably set back orthodox economic policymaking, and this prospect "badly frightened the previously all-powerful financial sector." For industry, on the other hand, which during successive rounds of liberalization had seen its star fade vis-à-vis finance, the war brought increased political influence.[61]

Finance's fears were well founded. The government was promptly forced to suspend foreign exchange transactions and impose a fiat exchange rate for the limited currency trades that new regulations permitted. Panic withdrawals from the banking system forced Alemann to reduce minimum reserve requirements and abandon money supply targets. Within weeks galloping monetary expansion was financing war preparations and keeping banks afloat. A jump in gasoline taxes pushed an additional ripple of price increases throughout the economy, ending whatever slim hopes remained of bringing inflation below triple digits for 1982— the opposite of what Alemann had envisioned as he put the finishing touches on his budget just before the invasion. As a consequence of the crisis, the economy was increasingly regulated, isolated, and inflationary. On April 21 foreign companies were no longer permitted to remit profits or repatriate investments. Ubiquitous black markets undermined the official value of the peso; bowing to reality, in early May, a devaluation moved the official rate from 11,500 pesos to 14,000 pesos per dollar, but on the street (and in neighboring Uruguay) the dollar traded for 20,000.[62]

Over the course of the crisis, finance's worst fears were confirmed; increasingly it became clear that, win or lose, after the war Alemann would be forced out of office and a new direction in economic policy (less financial orthodoxy, more government intervention) would be undertaken. With each passing week, Argentina's industrialists were becoming more assertive in their complaints against what they called the "excessively monetarist policies of the military junta"; and after years of relative political marginalization, finally industry was given assurances from the junta that it was time to abandon the Hoz-Alemann formula that had led to

[61] Jimmy Burns, "Crisis Upsets Argentina's Economic Plans," *Financial Times*, April 8, 1982, p. 4 (quotes); Smith, *Authoritarianism and the Crisis*, p. 246 (third quote).

[62] Jimmy Burns and Andrew Whitley, "Hopes for Falklands Peace Efforts Improve," *Financial Times*, April 17, 1982, p. 1; Andrew Whitley, "Embargo Buffets Shaky Argentine Economy," *Financial Times*, April 22, 1982, p. 6; Jimmy Burns, "Highly Strung City Lives on Its Nerves," *Financial Times*, May 22, 1982, p. 2; "Falklands Crisis Is Continuing to Threaten Argentina's Financial System," *Latin American Weekly Report*, May 1, 1982, p. 4; "Argentina Devalues Peso 17%," *Globe and Mail*, May 6, 1982, p. 13; "Argentina," *Latin American Weekly Report*, May 7, 1982, p. 6; "Argentine Economy: Steady as She Sinks," *The Economist*, May 15, 1982, p. 28.

the contraction of domestic industry.[63] In sum, for the vast majority of Argentineans, the reclaiming of the Malvinas was a celebrated national triumph; for the bankers, it was a disaster.

CRISIS, DIPLOMACY AND WAR

Finance Minister Roberto Alemann was not alone in finding his world turned upside down by the junta's surprise invasion. Margaret Thatcher and her government staggered under the force of the blow. On Tuesday, March 31, 1982, Defense Minister Nott informed Thatcher that Argentina's fleet was indeed heading to the Falklands, as opposed to South Georgia. That day, at a crisis meeting of the cabinet, the prime minister consulted with Admiral Sir Henry Leach, chief of the naval staff, who assured her that (assuming planned cuts to the navy were put on hold) a formidable task force could be assembled, but retaking the islands by force would be a challenging and dangerous operation. Thatcher also contacted President Ronald Reagan in the hope that he could persuade the Argentineans to call off the invasion before it was too late. The Reagan administration, having reversed President Jimmy Carter's policy of isolating Argentina for its human rights abuses, had cultivated close ties with the military government and with Galtieri in particular.[64]

But Galtieri managed to dodge Reagan's phone call for almost a full day, and when finally the two leaders spoke they talked past each other over the course of an hour-long late-night rambling discussion. By the time the conversation took place, it was probably too late to stop the operation; moreover, while the massive ongoing protests in the streets of Buenos Aires had not been the proximate cause of the invasion, they confirmed the junta's view that only through a heroic national triumph could the regime possibly survive. The next morning Argentine troops landed in Port Stanley. The news was reported on the London morning TV shows, but not until 6 p.m. did Nott and Foreign Secretary Carrington

[63] "Argentina: All Change on the Economic Front," *Latin American Weekly Report*, April 23, 1982, p. 11; Hugh O'Shaughnessy, "Argentine Industry Postpones Attack on Government Policy," *Financial Times*, May 12, 1982, p. 4 (quote); Hugh O'Shaughnessy, "Industry Attacks Galtieri's Monetarism," *Financial Times*, May 13, 1982, p. 4; Hugh O'Shaughnessy, "Pressure for Foreign Debts Freeze," *Financial Times*, June 2, 1982, p. 4; "Argentina: Economic Team Fights It Out," *Latin American Weekly Report*, June 4, 1982, p. 11.

[64] Freedman and Gamba-Stonehouse, *Signals of War*, pp. 123–24; Burns, *The Land That Lost Its Heroes*, pp. 143, 285–87, 289; David Lewis Feldman, "The United States Role in the Malvinas Crisis, 1982: Misguidance and Misperception in Argentina's Decision to Go to War," *Journal of Interamerican Studies and World Affairs* 27:2 (Summer 1985), pp. 2, 3; Latin America Bureau, *Falklands/Malvinas*, p. 81; *Franks Report*, p. 81.

emerge to confirm the disaster. The special Saturday session of Parliament was announced, as was the formation of the British task force. Thatcher had secured the full support of her cabinet for the task force, polling members individually with an eye toward linking their fate with hers, but for the moment this made little difference. As one study explained, the government simply "could not face the parliament the following day without a task force." The alternative was resignation.[65]

Even with the announcement of the task force, as discussed above, when Thatcher took her place in the House, "contempt rolled like thunder from the benches around her." Politicians of all stripes (and the public at large) spoke of support in a time of crisis but also expressed, vehemently, condemnation of the government for its failed policies, impotent deterrence, and national humiliation. Scorn rained down on Carrington and Nott. The foreign minister did not survive the onslaught, and he tendered his resignation (despite the fact that given his warnings, others, including Thatcher, were more culpable; nevertheless he hoped to take the hit for the team). But that would not be enough. As the *Financial Times* observed, "The central political issue, now that Lord Carrington has resigned, is not the future and influence of Mr. Nott, but that of the Prime Minister herself, assuming that she can survive tomorrow's renewed debate in the Commons."[66]

As British ships left port to the cheers of well-wishers, the specter of Munich was routinely invoked in support of the need to stand up to aggressive dictators. Thatcher's only hope of redemption rested in setting things right. The *Daily Mail*, which insisted that Argentina must be forced from the Falklands, captured the prevailing sentiment: "If she flinches, if this bold venture fizzles out in vainglorious bathos, Margaret Thatcher, her government, and the Tory party will be sunk." But Thatcher did not and would not flinch. Her diplomats in New York secured an impressive (and somewhat surprising) political victory; Ambassador Anthony Parsons shepherded Resolution 502 through the Security Council with a commanding 10–1–4 vote. The British-penned resolution demanded an immediate end to hostilities and the unconditional withdrawal of Argentinean forces.[67]

[65] Hastings and Jenkins, *Battle for the Falklands*, pp. 75–76, 77 (quote); Young, *One of Us*, p. 268.

[66] Hastings and Jenkins, *Battle for the Falklands*, p. 78 (first quote); Carrington, *Reflections on Things Past*, pp. 368, 370; Nott, *Here Today, Gone Tomorrow*, pp. 265–67; Freedman, *Britain and the Falklands War*, pp. 84, 93; House of Commons, *The Falklands Campaign*, pp. 1, 4; Charlton, *The Little Platoon*, pp. 64–66; "After Lord Carrington," *Financial Times*, April 6, 1982, p. 14 (second quote).

[67] Christoph Bluth, "Anglo-American Relations and the Falklands Conflict," in Danchev, *International Perspectives on the Falklands Conflict*, p. 209; Lebow, "Miscalculation in the South Atlantic," p. 117; Freedman and Gamba-Stonehouse, *Signals of War*, p. 128; Robert

On the home front, the prime minister formed the Overseas Defense Committee, South Atlantic (ODSA), which became known as the war cabinet. The other members were Nott, Deputy Prime Minister Whitelaw, Foreign Minister Pym, and party chair Cecil Parkinson. Thatcher appointed Pym to succeed Carrington as a matter of political necessity; the relationship was a difficult one for both of them. Parkinson, considerably more junior than the others, had been groomed by Thatcher and previously worked under Nott. He was added essentially to ensure that the prime minister could expect to be in the majority, anticipating some dissent from Pym and former Heath protégé Whitelaw. In practice Whitelaw was steadfastly loyal to the prime minister, and she greatly valued his counsel. Lord Lewin, the chief of defense staff, participated in the deliberations of the War Cabinet as a nonvoting member; his contributions to the cabinet (and to the prime minister) could not easily be overestimated.[68]

Noticeably absent from the war cabinet was Geoffrey Howe, the chancellor of the exchequer, or any representative of the Treasury, for that matter. The slight did not go unnoticed by Howe, nor was it unintentional. Following the personal advice of venerable party elder (and Suez veteran) Harold Macmillan, Thatcher kept the Treasury uninvolved. Before the crisis, even with the easing of the government's austerity in 1982, "no department was having a worse time with the Treasury than the Ministry of Defence." But with the sailing of the task force, money would not be an object—Thatcher was briskly dismissive of any questions regarding the costs of the operation directed at her by members of Parliament.[69]

The disregard for financial constraint was welcomed by those who would lead the war effort. One British general remarked years later, "One of the reasons why we won the war was that there was no one from the Treasury on the War Cabinet," a joke that nevertheless reflected attitudes at the time. Thatcher "never regretted following Harold Macmillan's advice. We were never tempted to compromise the security of our forces for

---

Harris, *Gotcha: The Media, the Government and the Falklands Crisis* (London: Faber and Faber, 1983), pp. 38–39 (*Daily Mail* quote); Anthony Parsons, "The Falklands Crisis in the United Nations, 31 March–14 June 1982," *International Affairs* 59:2 (Spring 1983), p. 169.

[68] Thatcher, *Downing Street Years*, pp. 4, 27, 187; Young, *One of Us*, pp. 104, 235, 266, 269, 273; Nott, *Here Today, Gone Tomorrow*, p. 285; Whitelaw, *The Whitelaw Memoirs*, pp. 143, 201–2, 204; Parkinson, *Right at the Center*, pp. 192–93, 197–98; Dorman, Kandiah, and Staerk, "The Falklands Seminar," p. 63. Nott had come to defense as a budget cutter and "not a hawk by nature," but increasingly as defense minister and especially with the war, he saw it as his "responsibility to give every possible support to the military" (Nott, *Here Today, Gone Tomorrow*, p. 285 [quotes]; Young, *One of Us*, p. 270).

[69] Howe, *Conflict of Loyalty*, p. 246; Alistair Horne, *Harold Macmillan*, vol. 2, *1957–1986* (New York: Penguin, 1989), pp. 621–22; Hastings and Jenkins, *Battle for the Falklands*, p. 53 (quote); House of Commons, *The Falklands Campaign*, p. 70.

financial reasons." Nott was pleased that "money was never mentioned and the institutionalized negativism of the Treasury was avoided." Nott probably anticipated problems from the Treasury because he harbored financial concerns of his own. He was convinced that "had we a fixed exchange rate during the Falklands crisis, the financial pressures would have been very similar to those during Suez." The ghosts of Suez would haunt the war cabinet, especially in the first month of the crisis. According to the defense minister, "Whitelaw, Lewin and I, in the early stages, thought Suez, Suez, Suez in many of our waking hours."[70]

Suez signified not only the financial limits of British power but also the threat that the Americans might yet undermine the British position. These fears were heightened by the initial U.S. reaction to the crisis. The Americans at first adopted a position of neutrality so that they could serve as mediators between their quarreling allies. Privately, the U.S. position was more complex. The administration was first incredulous and then horrified at the thought of Britain and Argentina going to war over some obscure, icy islands in the South Atlantic. In an era of heightened cold-war tensions, Britain was a bedrock NATO ally, and the Reagan administration had put considerable effort into developing its relationship with Argentina, which was emerging as an anti-Communist partner in Central American conflicts. Nevertheless, with the exception of UN ambassador Jeane Kirkpatrick, who was sympathetic to Argentina's position and thought it in the U.S. national interest to remain neutral, the private sympathies of the president and his key advisers were with the British. The U.S. hope was thus to prevent the conflict and remain friendly with both sides. But even during the period of American neutrality and mediation, Secretary of Defense Caspar Weinberger provided important military support to the British via preexisting channels of cooperation, including access to U.S. and NATO stocks of Sidewinder missiles and aviation fuel.[71]

It would take the British fleet weeks to reach the Falklands, which provided a window of opportunity for negotiations. U.S. Secretary of State Alexander Haig embarked on an arduous round of "shuttle diplomacy" between London and Buenos Aires; his efforts were followed by those of the government of Peru and finally the UN secretary general. In each case,

---

[70] Dorman, Kandiah, and Staerk, "The Falklands Seminar," p. 64 (quote); Thatcher, *Downing Street Years*, p. 188 (quote); Nott, *Here Today, Gone Tomorrow*, pp. 74–75, 242, 246 (quote), 247 (quote).

[71] "America's Falklands War," *The Economist*, March 3, 1984, p. 23; Alexander Haig, *Caveat: Realism, Reagan and Foreign Policy* (New York: Macmillan, 1984), pp. 266, 268; Jeane J. Kirkpatrick, "My Falklands War and Theirs," *The National Interest* 18 (Winter 1989/90), pp. 13, 14, 17, 19; Miller Center of Public Affairs, "The Falklands Roundtable," pp. 5, 7, 10 (comments by Kirkpatrick and Weinberger); Nott, *Here Today, Gone Tomorrow*, pp. 270–71; Feldman, "The United States Role in the Malvinas," pp. 5, 18.

the features of a negotiated settlement centered around variations of three basic themes: the stopping or slowing of the task force and the withdrawal of Argentinean forces; joint interim administration of the islands including some international presence; and mutual commitment to a clear, prompt timetable for a resolution of the final status of the disputed territory. At times the negotiations seemed close to success, largely due to movement by the British, who showed flexibility on issues such as how the wishes of the Kelpers would be considered; but in retrospect, the junta would not sign off on any agreement that did not guarantee Argentinean sovereignty (thus presuming the outcome of the final status talks), which was simply more than the British were willing to cede.[72]

Haig traveled first to London, where "it was clear that the survival of Mrs. Thatcher's government was at stake." He was impressed with the firmness of the prime minister and with the strong and broadly held sentiments that unified her war cabinet and the public at large. But there were subtle and important divisions as well. Despite Haig's private assurances in London (and in Washington to British ambassador Nicholas Henderson) that there would be no repeat of Suez, Thatcher was irritated by the American fence-sitting and saw little to negotiate about. She was opposed to any concessions that would appear to reward aggression. The balance of the war cabinet, Parliament, and most of the public generally was more receptive to a negotiated settlement that would involve considerable concessions short of immediately ceding sovereignty. Thus, although it was Thatcher's belief that only a military victory or an unconditional Argentinian withdrawal was necessary to restore British honor (or perhaps to save her premiership), she needed to retain the support of her cabinet and the public and avoid the animosity of the Americans, and thus through gritted teeth she acceded to negotiations and concessions that she found unnecessary and distasteful.[73]

If in London Haig found a small window of opportunity, in Buenos Aires he was confronted with a house of mirrors—negotiations there were protracted, tortuous, and often bitter. Foreign Minister Costa-Méndez appeared to negotiate in good faith, but eventually it was all too clear that he spoke only for himself; on two occasions he presented Haig

---

[72] Haig, *Caveat*, pp. 271, 273–74, 293; Parkinson, *Right at the Center*, pp. 200–201; Dillon, *The Falklands, Politics and War*, p. 143; Hastings and Jenkins, *Battle for the Falklands*, pp. 107–8; Burns, *The Land That Lost Its Heroes*, p. 206; Bluth, "Anglo-American Relations," p. 212.

[73] Haig, *Caveat*, pp. 265 (quote), 272–73; Thatcher, *Downing Street Years*, pp. 195, 197, 199; Nott, *Here Today, Gone Tomorrow*, pp. 286–87, 291–92; Nicholas Henderson, "Case Study in the Behavior of an Ally," *The Economist*, November 12, 1983, pp. 32, 33; Dorman, Kandiah, and Staerck, "The Falklands Seminar," p. 26; Freedman and Gamba-Stonehouse, *Signals of War*, pp. 170–71, 182–84, 216.

with papers—to be read only when the secretary was airborne—that retreated from earlier concessions. Galtieri was drunk on the cheers of the massive crowds (and possibly more) that continued to rally in support of the invasion; even in more sober moments, progress was limited by the hopelessly complex decision-making process of the junta. Admiral Anaya was invariably unyielding and less than diplomatic; more important, his intransigence accurately reflected the fact that despite the hopes and mood swings that would characterize the marathon negotiating sessions, at bottom the junta instinctively knew that it had painted itself into a corner and would not likely survive any outcome that did not guarantee Argentinean sovereignty.[74]

Unable to produce a common text, Haig's final gambit was to present both Britain and Argentina with his own proposal, which he developed (much to Thatcher's irritation) in consultation with Pym, who was determined to explore every imaginable option that might avoid armed conflict. Pym returned to London in support of the Haig proposals, but Thatcher was vehemently opposed, describing them as "totally unacceptable" and tantamount to "conditional surrender." As a way around the impasse, Nott suggested the strategy of waiting first to hear Argentina's reaction and then, if it was positive, present the proposals to Parliament for their consideration. The war cabinet agreed to this compromise and was spared further grief when Argentina rejected the proposals. According to Thatcher, she "could not have stayed as Prime Minister had the War Cabinet accepted Francis Pym's proposals. I would have resigned." Instead, with the junta's rejection, on April 30 President Reagan branded Argentina as the aggressor, declared it to be responsible for the diplomatic impasse, and finally sided openly with the British.[75]

The conflict now escalated. Due to logistical necessity and out of deference to Haig, Britain had refrained from major military actions (even as its submarines shadowed key Argentinean warships), although British forces did recapture South Georgia on April 25.[76] But with the failure of

[74] Haig, *Caveat*, pp. 274–76, 279–83, 286, 288; Cardoso, Kirschbaum, and Van der Kooy, *The Secret Plot*, pp. 140, 144, 154–55, 175, 178–79; Eddy and Linklater, *The Falklands War*, p. 149; Charlton, *The Little Platoon*, pp. 166, 172–74; Freedman and Gamba-Stonehouse, *Signals of War*, pp. 181, 193–95, 200–204, 210, 213–14; Hastings and Jenkins, *Battle for the Falklands*, pp. 108–10.

[75] Haig, *Caveat*, pp. 290–92; Nott, *Here Today, Gone Tomorrow*, pp. 245, 286, 292–93; Thatcher, *Downing Street Years*, pp. 203–4, 205–6 (quotes), 208 (quote), 211–12; Parkinson, *Right at the Center*, pp. 202–3; Dorman, Kandiah, and Staerk, "The Falklands Seminar," p. 29; Freedman and Gamba-Stonehouse, *Signals of War*, pp. 216–17, 232–34, 236–37; Hastings and Jenkins, *Battle for the Falklands*, pp. 138–39.

[76] After some very anxious moments caused by an unforgiving Antarctic storm, British forces recaptured the island after a two-hour battle, taking almost two hundred prisoners under the command of Lieutenant Astiz; the notorious "white angel of death" was relatively

American mediation and key elements of the fleet now within striking distance of the Falklands, war became a reality. On May 1, British Vulcan bombers (supported by a fleet of in-flight tankers) flew all the way from Ascension Island in the mid-Atlantic to bomb the runway at Port Stanley; more proximate carrier-based aircraft also participated in the attack. British ships bombarded Argentinean positions, inflicting casualties, and during the racket teams of British special forces slipped onto the Islands. The following day the submarine HMS *Conqueror* torpedoed Argentina's cruiser *General Belgrano,* and the ship was lost along with 368 of her sailors. Two days later, on May 4, HMS *Sheffield* was set ablaze by an air-launched Exocet missile; twenty British sailors lost their lives and the ship subsequently sank. Military engagements at sea and on the Falklands continued throughout the month.[77]

Efforts to find a negotiated solution continued at this time as well— Peruvian president Fernando Belaúnde Terry picked up almost immediately where Haig left off, pitching a simplified version of the final American proposal. The Peruvian effort was suspended by Argentina after the sinking of the *Belgrano* but subsequently resumed.[78] Despite the fact that

---

quick to raise the white flag when confronted by trained British soldiers. Burns, *The Land That Lost Its Heroes,* pp. 340–41; Thatcher, *Downing Street Years,* p. 205; Nott, *Here Today, Gone Tomorrow,* p. 303; Freedman and Gamba-Stonehouse, *Signals of War,* pp. 223–24.

[77] Duncan Anderson, *The Falklands War, 1982* (Oxford: Osprey Publishing, 2002), pp. 43–45; Douglas Kinney, *National Interest/National Honor: The Diplomacy of the Falklands Crisis* (New York: Praeger, 1989), pp. 323–25; Eddy and Linklater, *The Falklands War,* pp. 150, 156.

[78] It has been often suggested that the war cabinet ordered the sinking of the *Belgrano* in order to undermine the Peruvian effort, charges that gained some momentum thanks to the extremely poor job the government did in explaining the attack, efforts riddled with errors and confusion. (See, for example, Gavshon and Rice, *Sinking of the Belgrano;* also sympathetic are Cardoso, Kirschbaum, and Van der Kooy, *The Secret Plot,* pp. 225–28.) However, the evidence overwhelmingly fails to support this contention. Space constraints prevent a comprehensive discussion, but the *Belgrano* was indeed a threat to the fleet, the attack was consistent with Britain's formal public international warnings of April 23, and from a military perspective the attack was successful—after *Belgrano,* the Argentinean navy retreated to home waters for the remainder of the conflict. As for the Peruvian proposals, they were essentially the same deal that the junta had just turned down, and it is virtually impossible that any possible progress on that front could have been communicated from Peru, through Pym in Washington, and on to the war cabinet in London in time to affect the decision to allow the *Conqueror* to act. Moreover, it is not likely that such information would have changed the outcome; from a military perspective the decision was an obvious one—as was understood in Washington and Buenos Aires as well as in London. Finally, the HMS *Superb* already had standing orders to sink the Argentinean aircraft carrier *25 de Mayo;* had *Superb* not lost track of its prey, an even bigger enemy vessel would have been hit absent any new action from the war cabinet. See Dillon, *The Falklands, Politics and War,* pp. 149–50, 152–54, 194–96, 202–9, 213–14, 219, 221; House of Commons, Third Report of the Foreign

the sinking of the *Sheffield* increased British flexibility, the negotiations followed the same pattern as before. Public support remained high, but political pressure on Thatcher to exhaust every possible diplomatic solution increased; the prime minister was forced repeatedly to extend concessions she found personally objectionable but were satisfactory even to many of her supporters.[79] At each crucial moment Argentinean intransigence saved Thatcher from having to accept the half a loaf for which she had little appetite. On May 5 the full cabinet agreed to accept a version of the Peruvian proposals, but these were subsequently rejected by Argentina; a final round of negotiations were orchestrated by UN Secretary General Javier Peréz de Cuéllar. Again, largely to assure domestic supporters (and, importantly, the Americans) that Britain had gone the extra mile for peace, on May 17 UN Ambassador Parsons delivered a final British proposal. But despite the urgings of Jeane Kirkpatrick, who thought it "a very generous proposal" they were "lucky to be offered," the junta turned it down.[80]

On May 21 British forces landed at San Carlos, on the far side of East Falkland from Port Stanley. During the landing, ships were especially vulnerable from the air, and over the course of the next four days waves of attacks from the air exacted a heavy toll—the HMS *Ardent*, *Antelope*, and *Coventry* were all lost, and others were damaged. In a separate engagement the container ship *Atlantic Conveyer* was also sunk. The pilots of Argentina's air force fought with remarkable bravery, and it could eas-

---

Affairs Committee, Session 1984–85, *Events of the Weekend of 1–2 May 1982* (London: HMSO, 1985), pp. xii–xiii, xxii–xxiv, xxxiii, 48, 176–77; Dorman, Kandiah, and Staerk, "The Falklands Seminar," pp. 31–33; Charlton, *The Little Platoon*, pp. 211–13, 215–17; Burns, *The Land That Lost Its Heroes*, pp. 210–11; Henderson, "Case Study in the Behavior of an Ally," pp. 34–36; Parkinson, *Right at the Center*, p. 204; Nott, *Here Today, Gone Tomorrow*, pp. 273, 308–9; Whitelaw, *The Whitelaw Memoirs*, p. 207.

[79] Even *The Economist*, for example, supported the Peruvian proposals and subsequently advanced its own formula, which it acknowledged would require "heavy prices for both sides to pay. Particularly for Mrs. Thatcher." "Time Runs Out," *The Economist*, May 1, 1982, p. 25; "Mayday in the South Atlantic," *The Economist*, May 8, 1982, p. 25; "Let Them Go In?" *The Economist*, May 15, 1982, p. 15 (quotes). On the Peruvian plan, influence of the *Sheffield*, and Thatcher's general irritation with the constant pressure to negotiate and personal opposition to various proposals, see House of Commons, *The Falklands Campaign*, pp. 208–9, 211, 223, 242; Thatcher, *Downing Street Years*, pp. 209, 213, 217–18, 223; Young, *One of Us*, p. 277; Parkinson, *Right at the Center*, p. 205; Whitelaw, *The Whitelaw Memoirs*, p. 208; Dillon, *The Falklands, Politics and War*, pp. 157, 159; Kinney, *National Interest/National Honor*, p. 18; Eddy and Linklater, *The Falklands War*, p. 168.

[80] Parsons, "The Falklands Crisis in the United Nations," pp. 173–74; Charlton, *The Little Platoon*, pp. 207–8, 218–19; Freedman and Gamba-Stonehouse, *Signals of War*, pp. 293–95, 300–304, 310–11; Hastings and Jenkins, *Battle for the Falklands*, pp. 165–68, 171, 173; Kirkpatrick, "My Falklands War," p. 14; Miller Center of Public Affairs, "The Falklands Roundtable," p. 9 (Kirkpatrick quotes).

ily have been much worse. After the twenty-fifth, however ("one of the worst nights of the war," according to Thatcher, and with the outcome in doubt), British forces were well established, and three days later they scored a major victory in the bloody battle for Goose Green. After Goose Green British victory was presumed; nevertheless, the continuing fighting was brutal and fierce. Though fewer, there were still terrible losses at sea (on June 8 fifty men died when HMS *Sir Galahad* was lost), and the deeply entrenched defensive positions at Port Stanley were yet to be breached.[81]

In the last stages of the campaign, British troops advanced on the capital as Thatcher and her diplomats resisted calls for a cease-fire from the UN and pleas from the Reagan administration (still concerned about the fallout in Latin America) for "magnanimity" in victory. The prime minister thought such confidence premature and told President Reagan on May 31 that she saw little reason to "snatch diplomatic defeat out of the jaws of military victory." On June 13 British forces began their final assault on Port Stanley; resistance from Argentina's army collapsed rather quickly, and the Argentineans surrendered two days later. In London Thatcher emerged triumphant and was cheered in the House of Commons, while anger on the streets of Buenos Aires forced the resignation of Galtieri and his cabinet on June 17. Within days the remnants of the junta were dissolved as the army assumed full power and promised a restoration of civilian rule.[82]

THE DEBATE IN BRITAIN

As her biographer neatly summarized, "Just as defeat would have destroyed her, victory elevated Mrs. Thatcher to a new level of public esteem." That Britons hailed their prime minister in the wake of her triumph—one of the few clear cases where war did produce a sustained "rally-around-the-flag" effect—should not obscure the fact that as as-

---

[81] Anderson, *The Falklands War, 1982*, pp. 48–49, 54–56, 60; Eddy and Linklater, *The Falklands War*, pp. 183, 199, 201, 205–7, 217, 231; Hastings and Jenkins, *Battle for the Falklands*, pp. 228–29, 267–68; Burns, *The Land That Lost Its Heroes*, pp. 372, 376, 378, 382; Nott, *Here Today, Gone Tomorrow*, p. 312; Thatcher, *Downing Street Years*, pp. 225–26, 227 (quote), 278; Miller Center of Public Affairs, "Falklands Roundtable," p. 31; Dorman, Kandiah, and Staerk, "The Falklands Seminar," p. 36.

[82] Thatcher, *Downing Street Years*, pp. 229, 230 (quote); Henderson, "Case Study in the Behavior of an Ally," pp. 38, 41; Parsons, "The Falklands Crisis in the United Nations," p. 176; Whitelaw, *The Whitelaw Memoirs*, p. 209; Parkinson, *Right at the Center*, p. 209; Freedman and Gamba-Stonehouse, *Signals of War*, pp. 246–48, 352, 395, 400, 412; Anderson, *The Falklands War, 1982*, pp. 57, 87.

signing blame gave way to dealing with the problem, the public was very strongly supportive of Thatcher's efforts to restore British honor even when the outcome was uncertain. William Whitelaw recalled that despite having served in the heroic days of World War II, he was nevertheless "amazed by the surge of patriotic spirit" brought about by the Falklands affair; the country was remarkably unified and even swept up by a wave of nationalism not typically associated with the stoic British image. The government's hand was strengthened by the fact that its opposition was more or less limited to the strangest of bedfellows—a minority faction within the Labour Party, and the City of London. This did not suggest in the slightest that the prime minister was home free; it was her mess, and she had to clean it up. "The future of Mrs. Thatcher," Peter Riddell of the *Financial Times* observed, "is dependent on what would be generally regarded as a successful outcome."[83]

The United Home Front

The government enjoyed remarkable support for its Falklands policy in the Parliament, among the public, and in the media. The Tories favored action, and thus a majority at least was ensured; Labour was largely supportive as well, its posture a marriage of opportunism and sincerity. Having made the political calculation to attack Thatcher where she seemed weakest, for sleepwalking into national humiliation, they could not easily oppose a forceful response at the same time. Additionally, in their bones most Labour politicians felt the same burning outrage as did the rest of the British public. Its leadership in Parliament, therefore, assumed something of a watchdog role. More nervous about the use of force, less threatened by a compromise solution, and suspicious that Thatcher was spoiling for a fight even if there was a plausible deal to be had, the party leadership supported the government's basic policies throughout while subjecting them to rigorous challenge and scrutiny. Exchanges were at times sharp, with the government's prewar failures routinely evoked. Members found they could get under the prime minister's skin by heaping praise on Pym's herculean efforts to find a negotiated solution. But despite their differences, on some basic issues (such as no presumption of sovereignty before Argentinean withdrawal) Labour shared the government's position. And most Labourites agreed with the sentiments of one opposition member,

---

[83] Young, *One of Us*, p. 280 (quote); Lai and Reiter, "Rally 'Round the Union Jack?" pp. 256, 264; Whitelaw, *The Whitelaw Memoirs*, p. 205 (quote); Dillon, *The Falklands, Politics and War*, p. 233; Peter Riddell, "Pym Wins Backing on Falklands Diplomacy," *Financial Times*, April 8, 1982, p. 18 (quote); see also Anderson, *The Falklands War, 1982*: the junta "imposed on the Thatcher government a choice between victory or political death," p. 88.

who mused, "It is clear that one of two governments are at risk . . . I have very little cause to admire the present Administration here, but in the national interest and to avoid further international ignominy one hopes that the Buenos Aires government collapses rather than ours." More profound dissent was heard from Tony Benn, who led a faction of the Labour Party that steadfastly opposed the war. But as a minority within a minority, his group was vastly outnumbered and had little influence on the course of events.[84]

Broad parliamentary support reflected the public sentiment. Once the task force left port, public mood shifted from anger at the government to support for Thatcher and the fleet. Opinion polls captured a steady growth of support for the prime minister, her party, and their approach to the Falklands. There was a small wobble after the *Sheffield* was lost—satisfaction slipped from 76 percent to 71 percent before rebounding—but this was the point when even the government's knee seemed to buckle slightly. Other than that, the government went from strength to strength, and the public expressed more rather than less confidence in Thatcher's leadership as war approached.[85]

The media were largely behind the government as well, often enthusiastically, and at times to a degree that was little short of embarrassing. The fiercely competitive tabloids trafficked in jingoist sensationalism—the lonely exception was the *Daily Mirror*, which had always been closely associated with the Labour Party. The *Mirror* condemned the Argentinian invasion but concluded in an April 5 editorial that "military revenge is not the way to wipe it out" and favored a negotiated settlement. The quality newspapers were more responsible than the heady tabloids but still very supportive of the government. Witness the *Times*'s banner headline "We Are All Falkland Islanders Now"; similar sentiments filled the pages of the *Daily Telegraph*. Indeed, the only serious paper (other than the *Financial Times*, about which more later) to oppose the government was the *Guardian*. The mood was such that when the BBC's effort to engage in relatively objective reporting stood out from the general tone of other TV newscasts, it not only was deemed traitorous by the tabloids

[84] House of Commons, *The Falklands Campaign*. For examples of support from Labour, see pp. 89 (quote), 94, 99, 104 ("The opposition share all the Government's objectives"), 156, 281–82, 299, 301; its emphasis on negotiations, pp. 127, 152, 154, 174, 242; critique of past blunders, pp. 81, 98, 155; and Benn and his allies, pp. 95, 129, 140 (an especially bitter exchange with Thatcher), 163.

[85] "We Like It So Far," *The Economist*, April 24, 1982, p. 29; "Satisfaction Peaks," *The Economist*, May 8, 1982, p. 31; "Rally Round the Tory Flag," *The Economist*, May 29, 1982, p. 26; Freedman, *Britain and the Falklands War*, pp. 82, 94–95; Dillon, *The Falklands, Politics and War*, pp. 125, 135–36.

but incurred the public wrath of sniping Tory backbenchers—and the prime minister herself—in the House of Commons.[86]

The City Sulks

The City of London was unable to share the country's enthusiasm for a forceful response to Argentina's invasion of the Falkland Islands. Invariably cautious about the use of force, Thatcher's campaign seemed like the wrong war in a ridiculous place at the worst possible time. Obviously the costs of war (and the uncertainties that would inherently accompany it) were unwelcome as always. But in the spring of 1982, after years of painful austerity, a military adventure—even a successful one—seemed certain to upset the finally emerging economic recovery. Perhaps worst of all, despite the obvious facts that the unprovoked invasion was outrageous and the unsavory military junta entirely in the wrong, the bankers, well trained to discount sunk costs, saw no logic in nor any British interests at stake that would justify risking war to get the islands back—save possibly the survival of the Thatcher government. Nor could the financiers understand how the game was worth the candle; if successful, Britain would have no choice but to adopt in victory the "Fortress Falklands" posture that had been previously rejected as a strategically absurd budget-busting white elephant.

The Bank of England had an unhappy war. Irritated by Thatcher's order to freeze Argentina's assets in London, which it thought encroached on its autonomy and would undermine the City's reputation as a financial center, the bank was also charged with protecting the pound for the duration of the crisis.[87] This challenge was successfully met—as Nott suspected, contra Suez the floating exchange rate could absorb some of the pressure and, importantly, absent the commitment implied by a fixed rate, there was no obvious threshold that the bank was forced to defend and around which speculators' expectations could converge. Nevertheless, the pound did come under considerable pressure, falling within days of the

---

[86] Valerie Adams, *The Media and the Falklands Campaign* (New York: St. Martin's Press, 1986), pp. 10, 148; Harris, *Gotcha*, pp. 13, 38, 40, 43, 44 (quote), 53, 76–80; Glasgow University Media Group, *War and Peace News* (Philadelphia: Open University Press, 1985), p. 21; see also Derrick Mercer, Geoff Mungham, and Kevin Williams, *The Fog of War: The Media on the Battlefield* (London: Heinemann, 1987); *Times*, April 5, 1982, (headline); Eddy and Linklater, *The Falklands War*, p. 214; Freedman, *Britain and the Falklands War*, p. 89; Dillon, *The Falklands, Politics and War*, pp. 122–23. Hastings and Jenkins see more nuanced public and press sentiment, *Battle for the Falklands*, pp. 135–36.

[87] "Tremors from the Falklands," *Financial Times*, April 6, 1982, p. 16; Burns, *The Land That Lost Its Heroes*, p. 182; see also "Bankers and Realpolitik," *Financial Times*, April 19, 1982, p. 14.

attack to four-and-a-half-year lows against the dollar. The bank was able to stem the decline with massive interventions in the market. Having survived the initial blow, sterling stabilized, but it would invariably come under pressure whenever war seemed more likely (and would strengthen when negotiations seemed to advance), and the Bank of England intervened, often heavily and considerably running down its reserves, to support the currency whenever necessary throughout the crisis.[88]

Indications of the deep distress of the City could also be seen in the behavior of the stock market. Drawing conclusions about "market sentiment" by looking at stock returns is a tricky business and should be evaluated with this in mind. Even though the Falklands crisis was the dominant news story for the duration of the crisis, obviously other factors still affected share prices. Additionally, on a day-to-day basis, the war "news" itself must be considered judiciously; working assumptions and even rumors competed with the available information of distant battles and closed-door negotiations in setting market sentiment. Finally, over the longer course of events even greater caution is called for, as establishing baseline expectations of what the general trend should otherwise have been is not unproblematic; for what it is worth, most observers anticipated that 1982 would be a bull year on the London market.

With these qualifications in mind, however, given the brief duration of the crisis and the way it dominated the news, the crisis offers a laboratorylike setting unique for this book and rare in history—and the pattern of market behavior does contribute to understanding, if somewhat indirectly, the attitude of the City. Throughout the crisis, all news sources, regardless of their general political leanings or editorial positions on the war, reported market movements in the same way: the approach of war was associated with falling shares; when the prospects for peace seemed brightest, stocks rebounded. Market distress was attributed not solely to the costs and dislocations of war but also to uncertainty and dismay that disaster would lead to the fall of the Thatcher government. As *The Economist* recounted, "The market's reaction to the Argentine invasion was to tumble to its (then) biggest one day fall of the year . . . breakdown of the United Nations peace

---

[88] *Greenwell's Monetary Bulletin*, no. 134, June 1982; Latin America Bureau, *Falklands/ Malvinas*, p. 90; "Boost for Metals as Falklands Crisis Weakens Sterling," *Metal Markets*, April 9, 1982, p. 272; "Sterling in Sharp Fall Against Dollar," *Financial Times*, April 6, 1982, p. 1; David Marsh and John Moore, "Sharp Fall in Sterling," *Financial Times*, April 7, 1982, p. 1; "Sterling at 4½ Year Low," *Financial Times*, April 7, 1982, sec. 2, p. 30; Colin Millham, "Counting on the Fleet," *Financial Times*, April 13, 1982, sec. 2, p. 26; "Sterling Shows Late Fall," *Financial Times*, April 15, 1982, sec. 2, p. 40; David Marsh, "Reserves at Three-Year Low," *Financial Times*, May 6, 1982, p. 8; Hugh O'Shaughnessy and Elinor Goodman, summary of Bank of England interventions during crisis, *Financial Times*, June 3, 1982, p. 1.

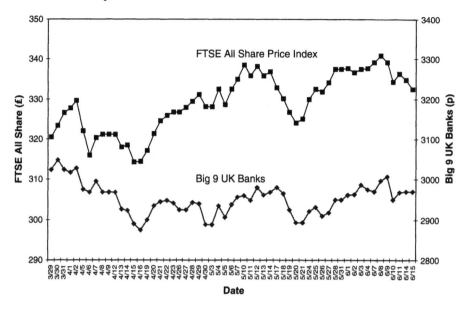

talks caused an even bigger drop in May." On the other hand, "When a peaceful settlement seemed possible and before interest rates were raised to support sterling, the index was within touching distance of its all time high."[89] This conventional wisdom is confirmed by figure 6.1.

Figure 6.1 shows the behavior of two stock indices during the crisis. The first is the FTSE "All Share" index, the broadest possible measure of the stock market. The FTSE All Share and the FT30 index (which behaved similarly) were the two measures commonly used as shorthand for the performance of "the market." The second, "Big 9 Banks" (BANKS), is an index I constructed for this book. It measures the combined movement of the "Big Four" British banks (Barclays, Lloyds, Midland, and National Westminster), along with five of the next-largest British banks.[90] I include it here to hone in on the interests of the financial community and to make

[89] "The City Waits to Win the Peace," *The Economist*, May 29, 1982, p. 87; "British Markets in Turmoil," *New York Times*, April 7, 1982, p. D1; "Falklands Crisis Takes Its Toll on Market Sentiment," *Financial Times*, April 6, 1982, sec. 2, p. 28; "Markets Show Growing Concern over Falklands," *Financial Times*, April 16, 1982, p. 1; "Pym Takes Peace Plan to US," *Financial Times*, April 21, 1982, p. 1; "Firmer Trend Continues as Market Pins Hopes on Peaceful Solution," *Financial Times*, April 22, 1982, p. 34; "The Other Campaign," *Financial Times*, May 1, 1982; "Falkland Islands Crisis Stifles Stock Exchange Business," *Financial Times*, May 6, 1982, p. 14; "Markets Make Progress as Hopes of Peaceful Solution to Falklands Crisis Revive," *Financial Times*, May 13, 1982; Freedman, *Britain and the Falklands War*, pp. 87–88.

[90] Bank of Scotland, Grindlays, Kleinwort, Royal Bank of Scotland, and Schroeder's.

sure that bank stocks did not behave anomalously in the context of broader market trends from which the conventional wisdom on the Falklands and market sentiment was derived. Both indices follow the same general contours and are consistent with six phases of war news: (1) they fall steeply with the invasion; (2) they recover as Haig's peace initiatives seem to gain traction; (3) they briefly slip and stagger with the end of American mediation and the losses of the *Belgrano* and *Sheffield*; (4) they recover again as negotiations appear to make progress; (5) they collapse with the failure of the UN talks; and (6) they rebound once more as the success of the San Carlos landing indicates the final stages of the war, British victory, and Thatcher's triumph. Notably, bank stocks not only conformed to this general pattern but also underperformed the market as a whole—they were slower to recover their losses, and all told did moderately worse from start to finish. This is confirmed by a closer look at the data (which find the BANKS index even more sensitive to war news than the general indices) and supported by a modest statistical test.[91] Part of this is can be attributed to the fact that the All Share index included companies that stood to gain from the war, such as defense industries and defense-related firms in electronics. Unlike the banks, defense stocks outperformed the market over the course of the crisis.[92] In any event, the bottom line remains that while sensitive to the limitations inherent in reading market sentiment, the movements of the indices are consistent with the view that for the City, in terms of the stock market in general and bank equities in particular (and sterling's bumpy ride), the eruption of the crisis and the march toward war were unwelcome visitors.

Finance Dissents

The City did not suffer in silence. In a nation where the media overwhelmingly supported the prime minister, the *Financial Times*—the "City's Vil-

---

[91] The day-to-day data confirm that, as *The Economist* and other news sources reported, when the Falklands news dominated the headlines, the market indices (and the BANKS index) moved lockstep in the anticipated direction. Probing further, I looked at the behavior of the indices on all the days of the crisis (up to the San Carlos landing) and compared stock movements with "news" on the war. All the indices performed inversely with the likelihood of war, and the BANKS index appears more sensitive to war news than the FTSE All Share (or the FT30). Fisher's Exact Test for nonrandom associations between two categorical variables yields the p-value of .0003 for the BANKS index and the somewhat more modest but still statistically significant .046 for the FTSE All Share (and .034 for the FT30). "News" was derived from coding front-page stories from the *London Times* (in some cases cross-checked against other sources); this was compared with that day's closing share prices. I thank Geoff Wallace for help in constructing the data set and Nick Winter for help with the tests.

[92] "A Firm Defence of Profits," *Financial Times*, June 23, 1982, p. 18; "British Electronics: The Spoils of War," *The Economist*, July 3, 1982, p. 66.

lage Newspaper"—which had stood by Thatcher, almost alone, during the darkest days of economic despair, steadfastly opposed the government's response to the Falklands crisis. "Jingoism Is Not the Way" was the headline of its first editorial on the subject, which hit the stands the day the nation cheered its departing fleet. While other papers talked of humiliation and shame, the *Financial Times* stressed that "no substantial British interest was involved" and warned that "the results of negligence cannot be undone by something near panic." Fearing the uncertain consequences of escalation, the paper also reminded its readers that even if the risky military adventure was successful, "the problem of the Falkland Islands would not disappear." These points were hammered home the following day, when the paper reasserted, "No vital British interest is involved." As the rest of the country was scrambling to find the surest way of getting the Falklands back, the *Financial Times* was already trying to get rid of them: "Our long-term aim must still be to disengage from this remote area." The cost of war was simply prohibitive, both in terms of pounds spent and inflation risked. The paper was appalled that the government might "sacrifice its central achievements to this deplorable side show." The priorities of the City could not be more distinct from those who cried Munich:

> If the aim of our actions is to show that aggression has an unacceptable cost, then we must remember that resisting aggression has a cost too. This means some unpalatable fiscal decisions. The sooner they are faced, the sooner the Government will be seen to have reasserted its central policies, and the sooner both Ministers and Opposition are likely to sober up from the potentially dangerous wave of jingoism which now threatens the true national interest.[93]

The *Financial Times* was consistent and relentless in its opposition. Its principal arguments were that the islands were not worth fighting for, that a negotiated outcome even at the cost of considerable concessions was essential to solving the underlying problem of the unsatisfactory prewar status quo; and it repeatedly lambasted the government for failing to articulate its political objectives or any sort of postwar vision. Simply reasserting sovereignty, it lectured, was "a response, not a strategy," which did nothing to resolve the "longstanding historical anomaly" of the status of the Falklands.[94]

---

[93] "Jingoism Is Not the Way," *Financial Times*, April 5, 1982, p. 14 (quotes); "After Lord Carrington," *Financial Times*, April 6, 1982, p. 14 (quotes); Roberts and Kynaston, *City State*, p. 180 ("village paper").

[94] "After Lord Carrington," p. 14 (quote); "Diplomacy to the Rescue," *Financial Times*, April 13, 1982, p. 16.

The need for more diplomacy was the paper's most consistent theme, from beginning to end. As the Haig mission approached its unsuccessful conclusion, it stated plainly, "The government has not yet made the case" for war, and urged that the dispute be referred to the International Court of Justice and that the British propose to place the Falklands under UN trusteeship. "Our reservations remain the same," which, on April 29, included the costs of the war and the absence of a strategy in victory.[95] The paper drew much criticism for its oppositional stance, to which it retorted, "Bankers and diplomats" are often "suspected of being wobbly on patriotism" because "neither group is equipped to realize our dreams . . . they deal in realities." And reality required that the dispute be resolved through politics, not force. The *Financial Times* greeted military success as the best moment for a "magnanimous gesture," any prospects for negotiations requiring that "military activities should be restrained," and the failure of talks—even as Argentina's rejection of Britain's final UN proposal touched the hair trigger of the San Carlos landing (and thus as the editorial hit the stands British troops were hitting the beaches)—meant that "the strategy of limited military activity while keeping open all diplomatic channels should survive."[96] Even as Britain advanced toward victory, the paper sought a compromise solution, critical of the government's decision to "exclude the possibility of a negotiated settlement before . . . an Argentine surrender," hoping still for a settlement, like UN trusteeship, that "recognizes the economic and geopolitical realities of the Falklands." A week before the white flag was raised over Port Stanley, the *Financial Times* was still berating Thatcher for taking "entirely the wrong approach," repeating again its position that "military action by itself leads in totally the wrong direction unless it is coupled with reasonable long term diplomatic and political aims."[97]

Even more remarkable about the contrary position of the *Financial Times* was that the paper was under no illusions regarding the likely consequences for Thatcher if its preferred Falklands policy was adopted. The

[95] "Diplomacy to the Last," *Financial Times*, April 27, 1982, p. 16 (quotes); "A Question of Proportion," *Financial Times*, April 29, 1982, p. 18; see also Malcolm Rutherford, "An Awful Lot of Ifs," *Financial Times*, April 23, 1982, p. 23; "Putting the Falklands in Trust," *Financial Times*, April 28, 1982, p. 28.

[96] "Bad Days for Formal Dress," *Financial Times*, April 17, 1982, p. 20 (quotes); "Reverting to Diplomacy," *Financial Times*, May 5, 1982, p. 18; Ian Davidson, "Falklands: Time to Be Generous," *Financial Times*, May 5, 1982, p. 19 (quote); "A Weekend of Waiting," *Financial Times*, May 8, 1982, p. 14; "Keeping Open the Channels," *Financial Times*, May 21, 1982, p. 16.

[97] "The Future of the Islands," *Financial Times*, May 26, 1982, p. 18 (quotes); "The Terms of the Peace," *Financial Times*, June 2, 1982, p. 14; "The Need to Be Reasonable," *Financial Times*, June 7, 1982, p. 20 (quotes); also notable for the tenor of its criticism is David Marsh's "War Images and Real Life," *Financial Times*, May 7, 1982, p. 1.

paper's political editor reported the widespread belief that "Mrs. Thatcher has staked her future on expelling the Argentines from the Falklands and that any failure or climb-down might force her out of office." Even within her own party, many thought that only by retaking the islands could the government survive the political fallout from its failure to anticipate the invasion. This, for the paper, was a cause for alarm, not a call for support. In its editorials, the *Financial Times* went so far as to describe "two governments, rather than simply the Argentine aggressors, driven to extremes by their internal weakness."[98]

If forced to choose between peace and Thatcher, the *Financial Times* would choose peace. The bottom line was a familiar one. The City stood behind the prime minister when she, alone, could deliver monetary orthodoxy. Now it was Thatcher herself who threatened it. Observing as did others that after three hard years, the government's two key policy targets, the inflation rate and the money supply, were finally "performing more satisfactorily than at any time since the election," it was this hard-fought victory that war might transform into bitter defeat. The good economic news was "completely obliterated by the alarming build-up of military and political tension over the Falkland islands" and might yet undermine "the whole of the government's economic policies" and "choke off the incipient economic recovery." The loyalties of the paper (and the City) slipped out in a news item reporting on quiet dissent from the "new monetarist Right" in the Tory party. "This group shares the Prime Minister's view of the economy but tends to take a more pragmatic line on international affairs . . . privately, some wonder what Britain is doing so close to a full scale military conflict in the South Atlantic." This was certainly the very public position of monetarist champion Samuel Brittan, who used his column in the *Financial Times* to oppose the war and remind readers, "Patriotic belligerence has its costs—most important in human lives, but also in economic resources," especially for an economy just "beginning to turn the corner."[99]

As it did invariably, the *Financial Times* reflected the mood of the City—and of finance more generally. At the start of the conflict, *The Econ-*

---

[98] Peter Riddell, "Pledge on Funding of Falklands Operation," *Financial Times*, April 10, 1982, p. 1 (quote); Peter Riddell, "Sense of Crisis Pervades London," *Financial Times*, April 5, 1982, p. 1; "After Lord Carrington," p. 14 (quote); "The Fleet Gets Nearer," *Financial Times*, April 21, 1982, p. 20.

[99] "A Question of Confidence," *Financial Times*, April 10, 1982, p. 12 (quotes); Elinor Goodman, "The Unpalatable Option," *Financial Times*, May 14, 1982, p. 8 (quote); Samuel Brittan, "The Falklands: The Price to Be Paid," *Financial Times*, April 8, 1982, p. 17 (quotes); see also Brittan's *Financial Times* columns "There Are No Cheap Wars," April 26, 1982, p. 19; "Stop the Killing, Straight Away," May 6, 1982, p. 19; and "Dissent on the Falklands," May 26, 1982, p. 19.

omist acknowledged that "No good . . . will come to London's banking centre from this" and thus predicted that Thatcher would "come under increasing pressure" from her traditional constituents, "particularly in the City of London." Concerns about rising defense expenditures were widely reported, as were frustrations that crisis-related inflationary pressures and interest rate hikes needed to defend the pound were pulling the rug out from the monetarist strategy just as it was about to pay dividends. The City's powerful insurance companies were also frustrated by the war's disruption to their business and were banned from paying out any Argentinean claims. Globally financiers around the world were aghast at the anachronistic outbreak of hostilities, though as the weeks passed, the sense of crisis faded from international markets. British bankers were less fortunate. Toward the end, as the UN negotiations collapsed, *The Economist* reported, "Nowhere is the impending invasion of the Falklands less popular than in the City of London." Fortunately, from the British perspective, finance's greatest fears were not realized.[100]

Even though victory came more easily than could have been expected, some of the unfortunate consequences predicted by the *Financial Times* and other cost-conscious critics of the war did come to pass. In particular, absolute military victory did give way to an expensive "Fortress Falklands" posture; more generally, Thatcher's commitment to restraining defense spending did not survive the war. On top of the costs of the war and replacement of lost equipment, each estimated to cost in excess of £1 billion, over the following years, the annual costs of maintaining the Falklands garrison would prove even more expensive. Not surprisingly the *Financial Times* feared that the military might now gain the upper hand "in the constant battle with the Treasury over defense spending" and continued to urge the government to seek a political settlement that recognized the "logic of geography." But finally finance was not alone; many of the war's supporters acknowledged the "breathtaking expense of the Falklands garrison." Even short, successful, and limited wars can carry a high price tag.[101]

[100] "By Jingo if We Can," *The Economist*, April 10, 1982 (first quotes); Steven Rattner, "Falkland Issue Imperils Recovery, British Fear," *New York Times*, April 9, 1982, sec. 2, p. 29; "Falkland Island Crisis Leaves UK Defense Budget in Tatters," *The Globe and Mail*, May 13, 1982, p. 15; "The Monetary Trap," *The Economist*, April 17, 1982, p. 32; David Lascelles, "Anxious US Banks Caught in Crossfire," *Financial Times*, May 7, 1982, p. 4; "Finance: Business as Usual," *Latin America Weekly Report*, May 14, 1982, ("bankers were initially horrified"), p. 2; "The City: Slouching Off to War," *The Economist*, May 22, 1982, p. 28 (last quote).
[101] Freedman, *Britain and the Falklands War*, pp. 66, 88; Gibran, *The Falklands War*, pp. 121, 129, 132, 136; Dillon, *The Falklands, Politics and War*, pp. 235, 242; "The Peace Has to Be Won," *Financial Times*, June 16, 1982, p. 16; "Waiting for Recovery," *Financial Times*, June 19, 1982, p. 16 (quote); "A Plan for the Falklands," *Financial Times*, September

The opposition of the British financial community to Thatcher's forceful Falklands strategy confirms once again the central argument of this book, that within societies, finance will be among those most reluctant to risk war. (And Argentina's experience provides yet another example of why it feels that way.) Yet there is a modest anomaly to be puzzled through in this instance; after all, the thesis is not that finance opposes war as an ironclad law, full stop, but rather as a very strong general tendency, and this case was chosen with the anticipation that it would probably illustrate an exception to the general rule. Given the importance of Thatcherism to the City, and the likelihood that war, if necessary, would be limited, why did finance not set aside its natural instincts and, if through gritted teeth, join with the vast majority of the public and support the prime minister?

Speculations that suggest an answer center on first principles, which, in this case, boil down to a commitment to financial orthodoxy. At bottom, the bankers' commitment to peace is a function of macroeconomic preferences, not some international political theory. In this case, even a small Falklands war threatened to bust budgets, rekindle inflation, and destabilize the pound, in sum, upset the monetarist revolution—just as it appeared to be on the verge of showing results. British finance certainly had reason to be especially gun-shy about foreign adventurism, a generation that stretched from the Suez debacle through decades of bitter debates about budgets and overseas force posture, all under the shadow of endemic inflation and financial fragility. The City, it should be recalled, also had little personal affinity for the prime minister. Given this context, perhaps the bankers (not that they thought with one mind) made the calculation that Thatcher might go, but with three years of austerity under their belts, the Tory wets who took over might build upon rather than jettison all those hard-fought gains, and that this would be better than risking it all on an unnecessary war.

14, 1982, p. 16 (quote); "Overdoing the Falklands," *Financial Times*, June 16, 1982, p. 12; "The Next Stage: Britain's Garrison," *The Economist*, June 12, 1982, p. 29; "The Problems of the Peace," *The Economist*, June 19, 1982, p. 55; "Mrs. Thatcher Leads—Will Mr. Alfonsin Follow?" *The Economist*, December 17, 1983, p. 12 (quote).

CHAPTER 7

Speculations: Finance, Power Politics, and Globalization

The principal hypothesis of this book is that financial communities within states are extremely cautious about war and policies that risk war because of the consequences of such actions for macroeconomic stability. Marxists have this flat wrong, liberals miss much by lumping finance with other groups in a pluralist model of the state, and realists fail to account for the important implications of a malleable and contested national interest.

The cases considered in the previous chapters provided strong support for this hypothesis. These cases were also particularly well suited to evaluating the main claims of this book. Sharing the necessary prerequisites—a truly "prewar" setting in which there was opportunity to debate national security strategy—each episode featured distinct characteristics and, with the partial exception of interwar France, offered clean "tests." Particular a priori attributes of each case made them distinctly and especially attractive for this book, but, crucially, I had no prior knowledge of the preferences of finance in each case. Thus, this project has been able to implement Kindleberger's "partial equilibrium" approach and to consider "how general are [political] theorems or laws, how well they fit case 2 if they fit case 1 neatly."[1] Moreover, each case study offered more than a single, static observation of "caution" or "war opposition." In every episode, the preferences of the financial community were traced over a number of years and in some cases decades, and dealt with numerous decision points and topics of debate. Throughout each period, and at crucial moments, the financial community repeatedly and consistently spoke cautiously on questions of war and peace, and for the reasons hypothesized.

The Spanish-American War was (from a theoretical perspective) an attractive case to consider in that it isolated the preferences of finance from the larger business community; it was a relatively risk-free war from the perspective of its ultimate military outcome (thus separating out "prudence" from caution); and it had been presented by radical scholars as an illustration of how finance was the "taproot" of imperialism and war. Yet

---

[1] Charles P. Kindleberger, *The Life of an Economist* (Oxford: Basil Blackwell, 1991), p. 194 (quote); see also Charles P. Kindleberger, *Economic Laws and Economic History* (Cambridge: Cambridge University Press, 1989), pp. ix–xi.

the financial community opposed the war despite enormous support for the conflict from the general population and from other interest groups; and its strong stance was actively and consistently expressed in the years leading up to the conflict. Finance's opposition to war with Spain over Cuba echoed its even lonelier condemnation of President Cleveland's confrontation with Britain over the Venezuela Boundary Dispute and anticipated its profound dismay at the outbreak of the First World War. This was the reaction of bankers elsewhere, as well. As noted in chapter 1, financial centers throughout Europe viewed the outbreak of the Great War as an unmitigated catastrophe.

Interwar Japan offered especially clean tests of the book's main argument, and a closer look at the turning points of 1931 and 1937 revealed major defeats for Japanese finance at each moment when the China war was expanded. The bankers' caution was not simply limited to opposing expansionism in China: finance had been wary of Japan's adventurism in World War I and its immediate aftermath; in the 1920s finance had championed arms control, international cooperation, and the Shidehara diplomacy; and for as long as possible during the 1930s, Japan's financial community fought to hold down defense spending. More often than not, finance won in the twenties and lost in the thirties.

A sustained commitment to monetary orthodoxy would have inhibited Japan's expansionism, but this does not mean that caution is always the best course of action. In fact, in a dangerous world, overly cautious policies may be disastrous (and at other times simply suboptimal). This flip side of the equation was illustrated in the same era, half a world away, where orthodoxy contributed to France's unfortunate response to the rising German threat. Once again, the expression and pursuit of finance's preferences (in this instance, the consequences of monetary orthodoxy) was not a one-time thing. Rather it contributed, from the 1920s, to the search for an accommodation with Germany; to the choice of a defensive military strategy; to inaction over the remilitarization of the Rhineland and appeasement more generally; and, right until the war, to the inhibition of rearmament. As noted in chapter 1, monetary orthodoxy had less of an iron grip on British policy in the 1930s; but the preferences of the British financial community also fit the mold, and the City of London was an important supporter (and practitioner) of appeasement.

The position of finance in American national security debates after the Second World War offered a particularly hard case for the argument of this book. Given the crucial role the Northeast played as a pillar of support for Truman's internationalism (contra powerful isolationist opposition), the extraordinary preponderance of the U.S. economy and the dollar in the world economy, the emergence of the Soviet threat, and the rise of Keynesian thinking, conditions would have appeared ripe for the financial community to shed its traditional predispositions and stand up in favor of Truman's more ambitious, assertive foreign policies. But it did not. American financiers were not only greatly concerned about the inflationary consequences of the Korean War and its expansion, but they also opposed the Marshall Plan and the International Monetary Fund, and they expressed constant alarm about the level of military spending, both before and during the Korean War. For finance, regardless of the imperatives of domestic politics, economic fashion, or international threat, national security rested on the dollar—there was no greater danger than the risk of inflation.

The primal and unshakable commitment of finance to macroeconomic stability was dramatically illustrated during the Falklands War. While the United States in the early cold war offered a "hard case," the Falklands episode was selected with the anticipation that it might press the theory beyond the breaking point and offer an exception to the general rule. Margaret Thatcher was a savior to the City of London; the alternatives to her leadership—the Tory wets or, unspeakably, Labour—were very unattractive to the bankers; and without her limited war, the prime minister would fall. Yet the City, virtually alone, stood against the Falklands adventure, just as, with somewhat lower stakes, British finance in the 1950s and 1960s repeatedly broke ranks with the Tories over defense and foreign policy issues. In all cases, the City urged that Britain's international posture and foreign and defense policies be reined in to reflect its reduced financial capacity. Additionally, when considering the Falklands crisis as a "shadow case" viewed from the perspective of Buenos Aires, the evidence strongly suggests that the preferences of the members of Argentina's financial community were remarkably parallel to those of their British counterparts.

In sum, the cases I considered have provided strong support for the book's principal hypothesis and have offered a variety of settings across which the nature and foundation of financial caution have been explored. They have also illustrated how different groups within societies can have markedly distinct visions of the national interest and of how to best advance that interest. This concluding chapter continues in three parts. First, it considers the "international variable"—the way in which international financial markets can function as a more abstract representation of the preferences of finance—and how that can affect international relations. Second, it explores the question of when finance will "win"; or, more accurately, when the financial community will be relatively more influential, and thus when it will be more likely to see its counsel of caution heeded. Finally, a more speculative section builds on these discussions by considering the influence of financiers and financial globalization on contemporary world politics.

THE INTERNATIONAL VARIABLE

The cases I considered in this book have focused largely on domestic politics and debates. In chapter 1, however, I noted that the "appeasing bankers" argument also implies a notable and similarly generalizable international variable. Given that war or policies that appear to risk war are associated with a much greater likelihood of macroeconomic disorder, international financial markets—that is, the consequences of the cumulative sentiments of uncoordinated market actors—will approach with great caution those states that seem to be headed on a bellicose path. As a result, states must be alert to the fact that by choosing a more assertive or ambitious national security strategy or military confrontation, they may be "punished" by international financial markets, principally via capital flight, pressure on the exchange rate, and greater difficulty in borrowing abroad—in terms of both supply (finding willing lenders) and price (an interest rate premium). National leaders confronting international political crises will thus likely not only hear calls for caution from their domestic financial community but will also face pressures, often considerable pressures, to appease international finance.

Concerns for international financial consequences have been present in each of the cases discussed in this book. The New York financial community opposed the Spanish-American War for a host of reasons, but the Venezuela Boundary Dispute touched more directly upon another, very sensitive, nerve: the prospect of conflict with the world's primary international financial center. In addition to their instinctive aversion to the risk of war, leading bankers expressed explicit concerns about how confrontation with Britain threatened both capital flight and the ability of the United States to borrow money on European markets.[2] Japan's expansion of the war in China not only was opposed by its financial community but was also reflected (unfavorably) on international financial markets. From September 1931, after the Manchurian Incident heralded the expansion of Japan's military ambition in China, a "large-risk premium" on Japanese bonds emerged in the London market. In foreign currency trading more generally, the yen routinely fell on news of war (most notably with a sharp fall on January 29, 1932, the day after Japan's attack on Shanghai) and tended to appreciate on rumors of peace.[3]

---

[2] "Opinions on the Situation," *Wall Street Journal*, December 21, 1895, p. 1; see also *Commercial and Financial Chronicle*, December 28, 1895, p. 1.

[3] Takatoshi Ito, "News and the Dollar/Yen Exchange Rate, 1931–1933: The End of the Gold Standard, Imperialism, and the Great Depression," *Journal of the Japanese and International Economies* 7 (1993), pp. 110, 119, 128, 130; Toshiki Tomita, "Direct Underwriting of Government Bonds by the Bank of Japan in the 1930s," Nomura Research Institute, *NRI Papers* 94 (September 1, 2005) p. 3 (quote).

In the interwar period, the appeasement policies of both Britain and France, supported by finance, were reinforced by pressures imposed by international financial markets. Throughout the era, French policies were constrained by domestic capital fleeing the country; at crucial moments, such as in the period immediately following Germany's remilitarization of the Rhineland, the franc came under considerable foreign pressure as well, creating an important disincentive to a more assertive response. In Britain rearmament and defense spending took place under the heavy shadow of concerns that at some threshold, more defense spending would be counterproductive to British security because it would undermine the credibility of Britain's commitment to sound finance, and with that the value and stability of the pound and London's position as an international financial center. British leaders, even those not intimately associated with the financial community, viewed Britain's financial credibility as nothing less than the "fourth arm of defense." Consequently they were alert and sensitive to warning indicators such as balance-of-payments problems and outflows of gold, and viewed these as red flags that cautioned against government spending and financial impiety.[4]

Remarkably, even the United States during the early cold war was sensitive to how defense spending and related budget deficits might undermine international confidence in the dollar—and this at a time when the greenback was the world's only major convertible currency, and the prominent concern about the dollar was that it was too scarce.[5] More readily understandable was the concern of the City of London about the reaction of international financial markets to the Falklands venture (and certainly the international market reaction was felt in Buenos Aires, which was forced to retreat behind a wall of exchange controls in an effort to stem capital flight and a collapse in the value of the peso). Sterling, after all, had taken a considerable beating in foreign-exchange markets throughout the post-

[4] "French Franc Suffers Extensive Decline on German Move," *Wall Street Journal*, March 9, 1936, p. 7; see also "French Recovery Faces New Obstacle in Rhineland Episode," *Wall Street Journal*, March 9, 1936, p. 1; J. L. Richardson, "New Perspectives on Appeasement: Some Implications for International Relations," *World Politics* 40:3 (April 1988), pp. 298–300; Paul Kennedy, " 'Appeasement' and British Defence Policy in the Inter-war Years," *British Journal of International Studies* 4 (July 1978), pp. 167–68, 175–66; R.A.C. Parker, "Economics, Rearmament and Foreign Policy: The United Kingdom before 1939; A Preliminary Study," *Journal of Contemporary History* 10:4 (October 1975), pp. 637–38, 642–43, 645.

[5] Thomas J. Christensen, *Useful Adversaries: Grand Strategy, Domestic Mobilization, and Sino-American Conflict, 1947–1958* (Princeton: Princeton University Press, 1996), p. 43; Albert O. Hirschman, "Disinflation, Discrimination, and the Dollar Shortage," *American Economic Review* 38:5 (December 1948), pp. 886, 888; Seymour E. Harris, "Dollar Scarcity: Some Remarks Inspired by Lord Keynes' Last Article," *Economic Journal* 57 (June 1947), pp. 165–66, 171.

war era. Most famously, market pressure on the pound during the Suez operation was decisive in forcing the British to abandon that effort.[6]

However, while market "opposition" to military adventurism can be confidently anticipated, this does not tell us "how much" international financial pressure will be exerted, nor does it tell us how affected states will choose to react to that pressure. During the Suez crisis, for example, Britain was both more economically vulnerable and more politically sensitive to financial crisis than was France. These differences were crucial in explaining why Britain pulled the plug on the operation while France urged that the campaign be allowed to continue.[7] Once again, as with the analysis of the preferences of domestic finance, the international variable can be understood only from a partial equilibrium perspective.

Several factors affect how states will react to pressure emanating from international financial markets. Such market pressure behaves like a structural variable that acts as a systemic constraint on the proclivity of states to initiate war or to pursue bellicose and ambitious foreign policies.[8] But that constraint is not, by any means, absolute or irresistible; rather it reflects the costs and opportunity costs of pursuing policies that are antagonistic to the "preferences" of financial markets. The magnitude of those costs depends on the extent of financial globalization (at high levels, greater opportunities are forgone and avenues for foreign pressure broader) and the role that access to international finance plays in the economy in question (small, open, developing economies risk more by flouting

---

[6] Kendall W. Stiles, "Argentina's Bargaining with the IMF," *Journal of Interamerican Studies and World Affairs* 29:3 (Autumn 1987), p. 61; Everett G. Martin, "Argentina: Facing the Financial Facts," *Wall Street Journal*, April 23, 1982, p. 31; Howard J. Dooley, "Great Britain's 'Last Battle' in the Middle East: Notes on Cabinet Planning during the Suez Crisis of 1956," *International History Review* 11:3 (August 1989), pp. 516–17; "Britain Defends the Pound," *New York Times*, December 6, 1956, p. 36; Russell Baker, "Britain Granted 1.3 Billion Credit by World Fund," *New York Times*, December 11, 1956, p. 1.

[7] Jonathan Kirshner, *Currency and Coercion: The Political Economy of International Monetary Power* (Princeton: Princeton University Press, 1995), pp. 77–80.

[8] The level of financial globalization is not purely a structural variable, in that the degree of financial openness in the international system is greatly influenced by the choices of powerful states. (Compare this with the distribution of power in the international system—great powers do not get to "decide" whether the system will be bipolar or multipolar.) Yet it is reasonable to consider the level of global capital mobility as if it were a structural variable because those choices are reinforcing (that is, it is difficult to re-create general closure once enough states have opted for openness); additionally, for most states most of the time the level of global capital mobility is manifested as a common, exogenous, external pressure over which they have no control. See David Andrews, "Capital Mobility and State Autonomy: Toward a Structural Theory of International Monetary Relations," *International Studies Quarterly* 38 (1994), pp. 193–218. On the central role of state decision making, see Eric Helleiner, *States and the Reemergence of Global Finance: From Bretton Woods to the 1990s* (Ithaca: Cornell University Press, 1994).

finance than do large, insular economies). Even if states act to defend themselves and contain these costs by unilaterally restricting their own interactions with international financial markets, and even if these measures are successful, they nevertheless cannot escape the opportunity costs represented by the benefits foreclosed by their actions. The opportunity costs of closure remain a function of the level of financial globalization (how large and interconnected global financial markets are) and the structure of the domestic economy.[9]

This suggests that periods of high financial globalization will present states, and especially small, open, developing states, with an important inhibitor to aggressive foreign politics. Yet again, it must be stressed that these pressures are not deterministic. This is illustrated by Malaysia's response to the Asian financial crisis in 1998. At perhaps the high-water mark of post–World War II financial globalization, Malaysia, a small, internationally oriented economy, opted to impose exchange controls in response to the crisis, to the nearly universal and vehement condemnation of western countries (especially the United States), international institutions (such as the IMF), and, perhaps most dangerous of all, credit-rating agencies. Nevertheless, the Malaysian economy performed well after the imposition of the controls, and subsequently the government was able to scale back those controls in a manner and timing of its choosing.[10] It is certainly possible that had Malaysia abandoned financial orthodoxy not in the name of weathering an arguably exogenous economic crisis but rather in the pursuit of an open-ended military adventure, it would have faced even greater pressure from international financial markets, and even more daunting and costly challenges in defending itself via exchange controls. But the general point is clear: financial globalization creates disincentives to war, but it will not prevent war from taking place. Thus the question is one of understanding how (and under what conditions) the international variable functions, which in turn raises more general issues regarding the influence of finance in debates about national security strategy.

[9] For a general discussion of opportunity costs in the context of economic closure, see Jeffry Frieden and Ronald Rogowski, "The Impact of the International Economy on National Economies: An Analytical Overview," in Robert Keohane and Helen Milner (eds.), *Internationalization and Domestic Politics* (Cambridge: Cambridge University Press, 1996), pp. 32–33.

[10] Rawi Abdelal and Laura Alfaro, "Capital and Control: Lessons from Malaysia," *Challenge* 46:4 (July/August 2003), pp. 36–53; Mahani Zainal-Abidin, "Implications of the Malaysian Experience on Future International Financial Arrangements," *ASEAN Economic Bulletin* 17:2 (2000), p. 135; Akira Ariyoshi et al., "Capital Controls: Country Experiences with Their Use and Liberalization" (International Monetary Fund Occasional Paper 190, 2000), pp. 30–31, 97, 113; Kanitta Meesok et al., "Malaysia: From Crisis to Recovery" (International Monetary Fund Occasional Paper 207, 2001), p. 50.

When Does Finance Win?

The question of how and under what circumstances the international variable will serve to inhibit states' aggressive inclinations raises the larger question of when finance will "win"—that is, when its counsel of caution will be heeded. A casual glance at the cases discussed in this book might leave the impression that finance never wins; after all, each episode ended in war. But that would be misleading. As discussed in the introduction, the universe of cases considered to evaluate the appeasing bankers hypothesis was limited to cases where war occurred to ensure that these were unambiguously prewar episodes. That finance ultimately lost in these cases is not news. Moreover, even in these prewar settings, finance often wielded considerable influence and on many occasions got what it wanted. In steadfastly opposing the quick and easy Spanish-American War, New York bankers were not able to sweep back the tide of overwhelming public support and the temptation implied by the changing balance of power. But the U.S. financial community was in fact disproportionately influential in the 1890s, especially given its position in the developing American economy at the time.[11] Japan's financiers were routed in the 1930s, but they met with great success in the 1920s, securing the highly contested Washington and London Naval Treaties. In France, with unfortunate consequences, the champions of monetary orthodoxy won almost every battle, even if they were ultimately unable to avoid the war. As the cold war heated up, the U.S. financial community was successful in seizing control of monetary policy, and it was on the winning side of the debates about keeping the Korean War limited and about reining in high levels of defense spending in the 1950s. Finally, step by step, British finance won the day on defense issues in the 1950s, 1960s, and 1970s. Indeed, had Argentina's invasion of the Falklands occurred in 1983, after just one more year of economy-induced reductions to British defense posture and force structure, finance would have won this debate too, as Thatcher would almost certainly not have had the means at her disposal to even attempt to retake the islands by force. In sum, finance often wins; the question is when and why.

In considering the issue of when finance will be more successful in debates about national security strategy, two qualifications must be explicit. First, to ask "when will finance win" is not, for this book, to predict when

---

[11] See, for example, Alexander D. Noyes, "The Financial Record of the Second Cleveland Administration, II," *Political Science Quarterly* 12:4 (December 1897), pp. 561–88; Matthew Simon, "The Morgan-Belmont Syndicate of 1895 and Intervention in the Foreign Exchange Market," *Business History Review* 42:4 (Winter 1968), pp. 392–93, 396, 411; Elmer Ellis, "Silver Republicans in the Election of 1896," *Mississippi Valley Historical Review* 18:4 (March 1932), pp. 532–34.

war will be prevented. That would imply a theory of war and would suggest that finance always opposes war. However, for reasons elaborated in chapter 1, the partial equilibrium approach adopted here does not engage in the enterprise of predicting war. Moreover, the main argument of this book is not that "finance always opposes war" but rather that finance will, virtually invariably, be among the most cautious voices in domestic debates within states in prewar settings. But this does not preclude the possibility that there may be some wars that finance does indeed support (or, in some cases, reluctantly come around to supporting at the end of the day).[12] Recasting, then, the question "when does finance win" can be considered as "when will the financial community be most influential?"

A second qualification is that it is important to reemphasize that there is nothing "good" about the preferences of finance. The financial community prefers peace not out of the goodness of its heart but as a residual of its self-interested macroeconomic policy preferences. Moreover, finance may be wrong on the politics—sometimes caution is the wrong strategy; and on foreign policy questions more generally, the interests of the bankers may be distinct from, and at times oppositional to, the national interest.[13] Finally, finance may even be wrong on the economics. That is, the domestic macroeconomic preferences of the financial community—such as very low inflation and adherence to strict monetary orthodoxy—may be good for the bankers but suboptimal for society as a whole, and result in slightly lower (and differently distributed) domestic economic growth. On the international side, while onerous barriers to the flow of productive capital are certainly costly and inefficient, unlimited financial globalization may also be suboptimal, imparting a deflationary bias on the international economy, imposing inappropriate uniformity on states' macroeconomic policies, and increasing the likelihood of international financial crises.[14] Note that the resolution of these debates (on the relative economic merits of finance's preferred policies) does not affect the arguments of this book, which is concerned solely with the implications of finance's preferences and its efforts to advance them. Rather they serve as a reminder that the appeasing bankers hypothesis is agnostic on the economic merits of the preferences of finance and, if anything, suggests that finance

---

[12] Efforts to falsify this argument, then, would concentrate on accumulating instances where finance was leading the charge for war or was at least near the head of the pack.

[13] On this issue, see Benjamin J. Cohen, *In Whose Interest? International Banking and American Foreign Policy* (New Haven: Yale University Press, 1986).

[14] Jonathan Kirshner, "The Political Economy of Low Inflation," *Journal of Economic Surveys* 15:1 (January 2001), pp. 41–70; Richard N. Cooper, "Should Capital Controls Be Banished?" *Brookings Papers on Economic Activity* (1999), p. 1; Thomas D. Willett, "International Financial Markets as Sources of Crisis or Discipline: The Too Much Too Late Hypothesis," Princeton Essays in International Economics 218 (May 2000).

is overly, as opposed to optimally, cautious in its vision of national security strategy.

With these two caveats in mind, it is possible to address the question of when the financial community will be more likely to achieve its goals. Three sets of factors are crucial in setting the playing field: international, domestic, and ideological.

International Factors. The influence of domestic financiers (and, as something of a prima facie parameter, of international financial markets) will be greatly affected by the nature of the international financial economy. As mentioned earlier, high levels of financial globalization will raise the costs and opportunity costs of closure, and these costs will also provide ammunition for those arguing against the use of force. It is no accident, for example, that both Germany and Japan embarked upon military adventurism in the wake of the collapse of the international financial economy. In Japan's case, had its return to the gold standard not been so spectacularly ill-timed—and had Britain not been knocked off gold as Japan was struggling with its own restoration—finance would have found its domestic political power enhanced.

Germany's experience also illustrates how global financial closure strengthened the hand of the expansionists. In the mid-1930s Germany used elaborate schemes to insulate itself behind a wall of exchange controls from the pressures of the international financial system, which allowed it to pursue uninhibited rearmament and to orchestrate politically motivated economic relations with its eastern European neighbors. But the Nazis did not simply abandon the international economy and impose exchange controls. Initially, the German financial retreat was defensive, with measures introduced in August 1931, in response to the collapse of Austria's Creditanstalt bank and the international financial crisis that swept across Europe. These devices then became overtly politicized and integrated into Nazi grand strategy in 1934. But it was the collapse of the international financial economy years earlier that put these mechanisms in place (and that made the small states of eastern Europe susceptible to Germany's politically motivated exchange-clearing schemes).[15]

Thriving, open international financial markets provide an environment that nurtures bankers' preferred policies. They also strengthen the hand of domestic finance—figuratively, allowing them to point to the interna-

---

[15] Frank C. Child, *The Theory and Practice of Exchange Control in Germany* (The Hague: Martinus Nijhoff, 1958), pp. 3, 133–34, 150–54; Howard S. Ellis, *Exchange Control in Central Europe* (Cambridge, MA: Harvard University Press, 1941), pp. 166, 212, 290; Arthur Schweitzer, "The Role of Foreign Trade in the Nazi War Economy," *Journal of Political Economy* 57:4 (1943), pp. 322–24.

tional example (and to warn of the punishing costs of deviation); and also literally, if they can reach out to friends abroad, when such friends are available. Once again the case of interwar Japan illustrates this well. In the 1920s Japanese financiers such as Inoue Junnosuke found important allies abroad, including the powerful New York Federal Reserve chair Benjamin Strong and Thomas Lamont, the head of J. P. Morgan. American international bankers, eager to support their Japanese counterparts and encourage liberalism and openness in Japan, not only extended credit to the Japanese government but used their influence to help ensure that Japan's political concerns would be reflected in international negotiations, such as the Washington Naval Treaty. Of course, having friends in high places offers no guarantees and is to some extent dependent upon the opportunities presented by international finance. After all, Lamont's two "best friends" in Japan, Inoue and Takuma Dan (Mitsui's liberal internationalist), were assassinated one month apart in 1932. For Karl Polanyi, there was nothing surprising in "the dominating influence of the international bankers on the twenties, nor in their eclipse in the thirties," as each reflected the prospects suggested by the international financial environment of their respective decade.[16]

Domestic Factors. Finance's competition for influence also takes place in a domestic setting, which is defined by both an economic and a political context. The economic context speaks mainly to the role of finance in the economy, as well as to the nature of the economic system in question. In command-style economies including Communist, Fascist, and to a somewhat lesser extent authoritarian states that rely on illiberal controls to distribute economic rents to political allies, finance is more likely to be politically marginalized. And in large, insular states, especially those where a considerable percentage of the population is engaged in economic activity that is divorced from the monetary economy, finance is again likely to be less influential than in small, open economies actively engaged with the international financial system.

One way to conceptualize the role of finance in the economy is to consider a "life cycle" model of national economies, in which states evolve from insular economies to developing debtors to industrial economies to "mature creditors." From this perspective, developing debtors, due to

[16] David L. Asher, "Convergence and Its Costs: The Failure of Japanese Economic Reform and the Breakdown of the Washington System, 1918–1932" (PhD diss., St. Anthony's College, Oxford University, 2002), pp. 188, 130–34, 137, 139; Edward M. Lamont, *The Ambassador from Wall Street: The Story of Thomas W. Lamont, J. P. Morgan's Chief Executive* (Lanham, MD: Madison Books, 1994), pp. 157, 195–96, 236–37, 311 (quote); Karl Polanyi, *The Great Transformation: The Political and Economic Origins of Our Time* (Boston: Beacon Press, 1957 [1944]), pp. 199 (quote), 212.

their need for access to loans from abroad, and mature creditors, where financial services account for a larger share of the economy, will be more sensitive to the preferences of finance than will insular and industrial economies. In "mature" capitalist economies, with notable regularity, the financial sector tends to become larger and increasingly prominent. Charles Kindleberger neatly captured the organic quality of this widespread observation, arguing that "interest in international finance may itself be an early sign of aging, like the first lock of gray hair." According to Robert Gilpin, the increasing importance of the financial sector is an important contributing factor to the relative decline of great powers compared with their more industrially oriented up-and-coming challengers. This "aging" of the structure of the economy was a dilemma with which Keynes wrestled in the 1920s, before his focus shifted from the problems of the sluggish British economy to the more general crisis of capitalism during the global depression of the 1930s. In the 1920s Keynes wrote (and spoke) extensively of the sluggish performance of British industry, and of how the interests of the powerful British financial services sector diverged from the "national" economic interest. More than simply a question of the return to gold, the preferences and behavior of British finance tended to exacerbate and reinforce the problems associated with Britain's struggling industries, especially compared with their overseas competitors.[17]

Without getting to the bottom of the various strands of these debates, it is safe to conclude, for the present discussion, that "leading" or "mature" or "advanced" capitalist economies will tend to have relatively large and influential financial sectors. Such states, therefore, from a partial equilibrium perspective, should be *more* sensitive to the preferences of finance (and thus to financial caution) than other states, and in particular as compared with those rivals that are at a somewhat earlier stage of economic development. Additionally, international creditors will be

---

[17] Charles Kindleberger, "The Aging Economy," in *Historical Economics: Art or Science?* (Berkeley: University of California Press, 1990), p. 240 (quote); see also Kindleberger, *World Economic Primacy* (New York: Oxford University Press, 1996); Robert Gilpin, *U.S. Power and the Multinational Corporation: The Political Economy of Direct Foreign Investment* (New York: Basic Books, 1975), pp. 44, 64–65, 77, 91–93; see also Gilpin, *War and Change in World Politics* (Cambridge: Cambridge University Press, 1981); John Maynard Keynes, "Home versus Foreign Investment," *The Nation and Athenaeum*, August 21, 1924, reprinted in Elizabeth Johnson and Donald Moggridge (eds.), *The Collected Writings of John Maynard Keynes* [JMK] (London: Macmillan, 1971–89), 14:285; Keynes, "The Return towards Gold," *The Nation and Athenaeum*, February 21, 1925 (*JMK* 9, p. 198); Keynes, "The British Balance of Trade, 1925-7," *The Economic Journal* 37 (December 1927), pp. 558, 565; Keynes, "The Question of High Wages," *The Political Quarterly*, January–March 1930 (*JMK* 20, p. 9); Keynes, *A Treatise on Money II: The Applied Theory of Money* (*JMK* 6 [1930], pp. 168–69).

particularly invested in international financial openness and international political stability.[18]

The British experience offers insights into those cases where the home country issues "international currency," that is, where the home currency is widely used by foreigners, as reserves, or a unit of account, or even an exchange mechanism. Here there is another "cycle" at work: when such countries (and currencies) are at the height of their power, they are likely to be exceptionally exempt from international financial constraints on their policy choices. At the center of a monetary system, liabilities accumulated by such states will be denominated in their own currency—thus balance-of-payments pressure and the ability to borrow will be less pressing and come more easily than they will for virtually all other countries that have to borrow in foreign currency. The "key" currencies of such leading powers also are more likely, initially, to enjoy the halo effects of prestige and presumptions of stability, which can further extend the discretion such states can enjoy before being called to task for profligacy by international financial markets.

On the flip side, however, if this once great power faces relative economic and political decline, and if the international use of its currency is reduced, then such a country will be especially vulnerable to international financial pressures. What was once the ability to assume that one's currency will be held and used abroad will become known as an "overhang" problem—what to do with all that excess currency out there now looking for a new safe haven. In this setting, concerns for the perceived stability and prestige of the currency become acute, and the finances of the country in question face greater scrutiny. This contributed to Britain's capitulation at Suez and to its economic struggles (and grand strategy dilemmas) of the 1960s, pathologies of economic management that Susan Strange referred to as the "top currency syndrome."[19]

Finally on the domestic front, partisan politics can also affect how influential finance will be, although history suggests a strong paradoxical element to this relationship. Typically, but not exclusively, the financial community will be aligned with conservative political parties, and the interests of finance are more likely to be represented when such parties are in power. But that sensitivity might not translate into commensurate

[18] See, for example, Paul Kennedy, "Strategy versus Finance in Twentieth-Century Britain," *International History Review* 3:1 (1981), pp. 44–61.

[19] Susan Strange, *Sterling and British Policy: A Political Study of an International Currency in Decline* (London: Oxford University Press, 1971), esp. pp. 298–309, 317, 322–25; see also Benjamin J. Cohen, *The Future of Sterling as an International Currency* (New York: St. Martin's Press, 1971) pp. 144–47, 171–74, 245–46, and Robert Z. Aliber, "The Costs and Benefits of the U.S. Role as a Reserve Currency Country," *Quarterly Journal of Economics* 78:3 (August 1964), esp. pp. 442–50.

influence on questions of war and peace. Conservative leaders tend to serve the interests of finance on economic issues, but upon making the decision to embark upon the path to war, they may rely on the advice of other confidants. In any event, there will be times when a rightist administration chooses to embark on a risky foreign strategy. In those instances, it is more likely that finance may bark, but not bite, given the political alternatives. And international markets will be more tolerant of conservative adventurism given that such a government will enjoy greater credibility for financial rectitude. Thus the paradox is that left-wing governments, which are less likely to count the bankers among their key political allies, will tend to be more constrained in their foreign policy choices by the dictates of sound finance than their conservative counterparts. In the domestic arena, financial opposition will be more aggressive and less inhibited against a left-wing administration, with actions (such as capital flight) backing up harsh words. Internationally, leftist governments, whose economic policies are viewed with suspicion, will more quickly feel the constraint of admonishing financial markets.[20]

Prevailing Economic Ideology. The economic beliefs of members of the financial community are remarkably constant; in every era, in every country, the same tenets of "sound finance" are shared. But among other actors within and across nations, the prevailing economic ideology can change—financial orthodoxy can come in and out of fashion, and this variable, interacting with both the domestic and the international factors just discussed, has a powerful effect on the extent to which the preferences of finance will prevail. John Lewis Gaddis has argued that changes in economic ideologies, and in particular the willingness of different administrations to tolerate deviations from financial orthodoxy, were influential in shaping changes in the tactics and disposition of U.S. grand strategy during the cold war.[21]

Ideology and changes in ideology are tricky to measure, but differences in beliefs regarding the range of legitimate macroeconomic policies clearly

[20] The cases from this book offer a number of illustrations and intriguing counterfactuals. Certainly the rearmament efforts in the late 1930s by the Popular Front in France were undermined by the flight of domestic capital and by the skepticism of international markets. In the Falklands crisis, the fact that the pound remained reasonably steady under pressure was due to the floating exchange rate, timely interventions by the Bank of England, and the limited nature of the conflict. But had a Labour government been in power and embarked upon a similar course of action, pressure on the pound would probably have been even greater.

[21] John Lewis Gaddis, *Strategies of Containment: A Critical Reappraisal of Postwar American National Security Policy* (New York: Oxford University Press, 1982), pp. 354–56 and passim.

exist across nations, within nations across time, and in distinct global eras as well—and these differences matter. In the West, "acceptable" levels of inflation were lower in the 1950s and 1990s than they were in the 1960s and 1970s (and typically lower, for example, in Germany than in Italy). Orthodoxy was more likely to prevail before the Great War than it did in the interwar period; the post–World War II international order of "embedded liberalism" (1948–73) was much more tolerant of deviations from financial orthodoxy than the contemporary system of globalized finance. In the current era, then, the financial constraint will be more acutely felt, not simply because of the dismantling of capital controls and the tremendous growth in the scale of exchange markets (though these are very important) but also due to ideology. Contemporary markets not only equilibrate national and international prices (states with higher-than-average inflation rates see their exchange rates depreciate) but can punish those that deviate from the set of policies which are currently seen as legitimate (resulting in a greater depreciation than could be explained by the higher inflation rate).[22]

APPEASING BANKERS IN CONTEMPORARY INTERNATIONAL POLITICS

Armed with these expectations, it is possible to speculate about how the preferences of domestic financial interests and the influence of international financial markets will affect contemporary international politics. The contemporary international setting is one of breathtaking financial globalization and a rather broad consensus of the singular legitimacy of financial orthodoxy: low inflation, vigilance against inflation, limited deficits, sustainable debts, and capital deregulation (if with somewhat less crusading zeal after the Asian financial crisis). Although high levels of financial globalization are neither novel nor irreversible (and economic ideology can also change), these elements appear to be well-entrenched fixtures of the current international system and present constraints that all states face.[23] What distinguishes how this will affect

[22] John Gerard Ruggie, "International Regimes, Transactions, and Change: Embedded Liberalism in the Post-war Economic Order," *International Organization* 36:2 (1982), pp. 379–415; G. John Ikenberry, "A World Economy Restored: Expert Consensus and the Anglo American Post-war Settlement," *International Organization* 46:1 (Winter 1992), pp. 289–321; Ilene Grabel, "Ideology, Power and the Rise of Independent Monetary Institutions in Emerging Economies," in Jonathan Kirshner (ed.), *Monetary Orders: Ambiguous Economics, Ubiquitous Politics* (Ithaca: Cornell University Press, 2003); see also Louis W. Pauly, *Who Elected the Bankers? Surveillance and Control in the World Economy* (Ithaca: Cornell University Press, 1997), esp. pp. 30, 33, 37, 85.

[23] Harold James, *The End of Globalization: Lessons from the Great Depression* (Cambridge, MA: Harvard University Press, 2001). Many scholars call attention to the high level

various countries, then, and how acutely they will feel the influence of these relatively robust international pressures will depend on the domestic economic and political differences among them. This suggests distinct consequences for mature capitalist economies, more insular giants, small states, and the United States.

Mature Capitalist Economies. The dispositions of the advanced economies of Europe and of Japan are suggestive of a strong sensitivity to financial interests and related pressures. The leading states of the European Union have large and influential financial sectors, and Europe's commitment to financial orthodoxy is virtually unrivaled. Further, the institutional design of the euro imparts a deflationary bias to macroeconomic management, and its collective governance inhibits the bold leadership that a strong, single voice might provide, inhibiting the exploitation of any expansionist opportunities that might be suggested by the role of the euro as international reserve currency, if in fact the Europeans were inclined to embark upon a more ambitious international path.[24]

Japan is somewhat similarly situated (though, of course, with obvious differences). It is the case that Japanese leadership, especially in the wake of the Asian financial crisis, has been much more receptive than either the United States or Europe to the idea that some forms of capital controls might be appropriate in order to reduce the risk of financial crisis and provide space for states to pursue heterogeneous strategies of capitalist development. But in practice, Japan's macroeconomic policies are influenced both by its large financial sector and by very cautious and rigid institutions of monetary governance, which contributed to the persistence of the country's long deflationary episode that extended from the 1990s into the twenty-first century.[25]

---

of financial globalization before World War I; Michael Bordo, Barry Eichengreen, and Douglas Irwin, in "Is Globalization Today Really Different Than Globalization a Hundred Years Ago?" *Brookings Trade Forum, 1999*, argue that contemporary financial globalization is more significant now than it was then.

[24] Rawi Abdelal, *Capital Rules: The Construction of Global Finance* (Cambridge, MA: Harvard University Press, 2006), chapter 4: "The Paris Consensus: European Unification and the Freedom of Capital"; Benjamin J. Cohen, "Global Currency Rivalry: Can the Euro Ever Challenge the Dollar?" *Journal of Common Market Studies* 41:4 (2003), pp. 584–88; Kathleen McNamara and Sophie Meunier, "Between National Sovereignty and International Power: What External Voice for the Euro?" *International Affairs* 78:4 (2002), p. 850.

[25] Saori N. Katada, "Japan and Asian Monetary Regionalization: Cultivating a New Regional Leadership Role after the Asian Financial Crisis," *Geopolitics* 7:1 (Summer 2002), pp. 87, 97; Christopher W. Hughes, "Japanese Policy and the East Asian Crisis: Abject Defeat or Quiet Victory?" *Review of International Political Economy* 7:2 (April 2000), pp. 241–42; William Grimes, *The Unmaking of the Japanese Miracle: Macroeconomic Politics, 1985–2000* (Ithaca: Cornell University Press, 2001), esp. pp. 211–14; see also Jennifer

It is possible to imagine scenarios in which Europe or Japan could change its spots, such as a dramatic reversal in financial globalization and a reorientation of the world economy along more regional lines. Europe and Japan then might find themselves at the center of monetary systems, from which they could take advantage of the longer leash provided to issuers of key currency and the less financially forbidding postglobalized international economic environment. This combination of events, however, seems highly unlikely, or at least much less likely than other plausible futures. Thus, the application of the appeasing bankers perspective to contemporary Europe and Japan suggests factors that powerfully reinforce foreign policy dispositions of caution that already are fairly well established in these states.

More Insular Giants. In contrast to western Europe and Japan, states like India, Russia, and China have (to varying degrees across these dimensions) much less well developed financial services sectors, ambivalent attitudes toward financial liberalism, and large internal markets of which significant segments are detached from the global financial economy.[26] The national security strategies of these countries are therefore among the least likely to be constrained by appeasing bankers at home or abroad. Compared with others, these states will have one less restraint on foreign policy adventurism and enjoy a strategic advantage in any confrontations they might have with states more sensitive to the preferences of finance.

Russia and India have most of these characteristics, while China, an emerging great power, has them all. At its current stage of development, China's economy is dominated by a booming industrial sector and a vast insular interior; its fragile, sheltered, and inefficient banking system is not yet ready for prime time. And despite its economic liberalization and dramatic integration into the international economy, China remains a one-party state, and that party is the Chinese Communist Party, which, if it deemed it necessary, would not be inhibited by the protestations of its bankers or from interfering with the market. This is eminently the case in the financial sector, where, despite international pressure, China has retained both a fixed exchange rate and capital controls. The government, not without reason, has placed a great premium on exchange rate stability and has approached financial liberalization with great caution—well aware of the fragility of its banks, and wrestling with the management of

---

Amyx, *Japan's Financial Crisis: Institutional Rigidity and Reluctant Change* (Princeton: Princeton University Press, 2004).

[26] Anne O. Kruger and Sajjid Z. Chinoy (eds.), *Reforming India's External, Financial and Fiscal Policies* (Stanford: Stanford University Press, 2003); Erik Berglöf et al., *The New Economy of Russia* (Cambridge, MA: MIT Press, 2003), pp. 106–20.

its unbridled economy, exchange rate stability has provided a welcome policy anchor.[27]

China, therefore, is virtually immune to domestic and international financial constraints on its national security strategy decisions, or at least as uninhibited by these forces as a state in the contemporary international system can possibly be. In potential confrontations with a country like the United States or Japan, China will have one less reason, and its adversaries one more reason, to be cautious and accommodating. This is not to predict that China *will* become aggressive. (While there are theories of international relations that would predict this, to date there is good evidence that China will continue to pursue its strategy of "peaceful rise.")[28] Rather, the conclusion is that *if* China embarks on a path of more assertive foreign policy, compared with other states China will be less inhibited by appeasing bankers. Adventurism would still come with costs—the question is one of the relative size of those costs and the sensitivity of the government to the consequences of bearing them. Through the lens of this analysis, China faces fewer barriers to aggression than many of its potential adversaries.

Small States in World Financial Markets. In stark contrast to China and other insular giants, most developing states are profoundly affected by the combination of financial globalization and the ideological consensus on orthodoxy. Small developing states are in great need of external finance, more open to financial flows, and highly vulnerable to the rapid, sudden movements of capital across borders. Contemporary financial globalization has, probably with even greater force and consequence, recreated the pressures for conformity that existed in the late nineteenth

---

[27] Eswar Prasad, Thomas Rumbaugh, and Qing Wang, "Putting the Cart before the Horse? Capital Account Liberalization and Exchange Rate Flexibility in China" (IMF Policy Discussion Paper, January 2005), pp. 3–4, 7; Ronald I. McKinnon, *Exchange Rates under the East Asian Dollar Standard* (Cambridge, MA: MIT Press, 2005), pp. 10–11, 129–30, 151–53; Morris Goldstein, "Adjusting China's Exchange Rate Policies," Institute for International Economics (Working Paper 04/1, 2004), pp. 3, 26, 30.

[28] On why rising powers are likely to challenge the existing international order, see Gilpin, *War and Change*; on China more specifically, see John Mearsheimer, *The Tragedy of Great Power Politics* (New York: Norton, 2001), pp. 400–402. On the prospects for "peaceful rise," see Avery Goldstein, *Rising to the Challenge: China's Grand Strategy and International Security* (Stanford: Stanford University Press, 2005) esp. pp. 177, 193, 202, 211; Alastair Iain Johnston, "Is China a Status Quo Power?" *International Security* 27:4 (Spring 2003), p. 47; and Robert Ross and Zhu Feng (eds.), "The Rise of China: Theory and Practice" (ms in progress). More agnostic are Aaron Friedberg, "The Future of U.S.–China Relations: Is Conflict Inevitable?" *International Security* 30:2 (Fall 2005), esp. p. 39, and Thomas Christensen, "Fostering Stability or Creating a Monster: The Rise of China and U.S. Policy toward East Asia," *International Security* 31:1 (Summer 2006), pp. 81–126.

century, when adherence to the gold standard represented a "good housekeeping seal of approval." In that previous golden age of capitalism, Polanyi (though he was somewhat ambivalent regarding the attitude of *haute finance* toward war that was limited exclusively to the periphery) argued that finance "acted as a powerful moderator in the councils and policies of a number of small sovereign states." Loans and their renewal "hinged . . . upon good behavior."[29] In the present era, the "good behavior" of small states is constantly evaluated by credit-rating agencies, which determine the ease with which states can borrow and reinforce the ideological consensus that punishes deviant behavior.[30]

Small developing states, therefore, risk considerable costs when contemplating aggression. Yet at the same time, *within* small states, participants in the illicit economy, entrepreneurs of political violence, criminal gangs, separatist and insurgent groups, and terrorist organizations are unaffected by the concerns of the financial community. These irregular but often highly organized armed forces operate outside the visible, monitored, and regulated international system. Once established, irregular forces are able to sustain themselves by plunder, various criminal enterprises, and cash remittances from loosely affiliated transnational workers. These unsupervised financial lifelines are often enhanced by alliances with networks of apolitical criminal gangs and money launderers.[31]

Financial globalization (and the processes of globalization more generally) thus serves both to undermine the political authority of small developing states and to provide opportunities and safe havens for stateless entrepreneurs of organized violence that operate outside of normal financial networks. By shifting the balance of power and recasting incentive structures, financial globalization (unintentionally) contributes to an in-

---

[29] Karl Polanyi, *The Great Transformation: The Political and Economic Origins of Our Time* (Boston: Beacon Press, 1957 [1944]), p. 14 (quote); Polanyi suggests that finance is more tolerant of war between small states than it is of great power war, which was the "chief danger" (pp. 14–15); Michael D. Bordo and Hugh Rockoff, "The Gold Standard as a 'Good Housekeeping Seal of Approval,' " *Journal of Economic History* 56:2 (June 1996), pp. 389–428.

[30] Ilene Grabel, "The Political Economy of 'Policy Credibility': The New Classical Macroeconomics and the Remaking of Emerging Economies," *Cambridge Journal of Economics* 24:1 (2000), pp. 1–19; Abdelal, *Capital Rules*, chapter 7: "A Common Language of Risk: Credit Rating Agencies and Sovereigns"; see also Timothy Sinclair, *The New Masters of Capital: American Bond Rating Agencies and the Politics of Creditworthiness* (Ithaca: Cornell University Press, 2005), pp. 136–47.

[31] Peter Andreas, "The Clandestine Political Economy of War and Peace in Bosnia," *International Studies Quarterly* 48 (2004), pp. 29–51; Michael T. Klare, "Waging Post-Industrial Warfare on the Global Battlefield," *Current History* (December 2001), pp. 434–35; Philip Cerny, "Terrorism and the New Security Dilemma," *Naval War College Review* 58:1 (Winter 2005), 11–33. Douglas Farah, *Blood from Stones: The Secret Financial Network of Terror* (New York: Broadway Books, 2004).

crease in insurgency, civil war, and an environment in which international terrorist organizations find it easier to operate. Thus if financial globalization produces disincentives for traditional interstate war, it might, at the same time, produce strategic responses from political actors that increase the likelihood of intrastate violence and irregular forms of warfare.[32]

The View from the Top. At the center of the global financial economy sits the massive, peerless United States. The U.S. dollar serves as the world's currency (as well as its principal reserve asset and, in many corners of the world, the local money of choice). The American economy is robust, diverse, institutionally rich, and enormous: nearly three times the size of the next-largest economy (Japan) and about twice the size of the combined economies of Germany, France, and Britain. U.S. military preponderance is overwhelming and unprecedented. America comes close to spending as much on defense as the rest of the world combined, and its leadership in military technology (and lack of threatening neighbors) magnifies its relative strength and the breadth of its military prerogative. Since the collapse of the Soviet Union, the United States has been further uninhibited, given the absence of anything approaching a peer competitor in the international system.[33]

Given these attributes, the United States, especially since the end of the cold war, has been uniquely unconstrained by financial pressures. The U.S. economy is so large that even with huge post–9/11 increases, American defense spending, while truly massive in an absolute sense ($454.1 billion in 2004, $493.6 billion in 2005), as a percentage of gross domestic product, remains near post–World War II lows (3.9 percent in 2004, 4.0 percent in 2005). In the absence of neighboring threats and peer competitors, the United States can throw its weight around more cavalierly than any other state; at the center of the international financial system, the United States can more easily finance its military operations; and despite the fact that its financial services sector is large and influential, these circumstances afford American political leaders considerable insulation

[32] Mary Kaldor, *New and Old Wars: Organized Violence in a Globalized Era* (Stanford: Stanford University Press, 2001), pp. 2, 3, 9, 90, 110; Jonathan Kirshner (ed.), *Globalization and National Security* (New York: Routledge, 2006); see also John Mackinlay, *Globalization and Insurgency* (London: International Institute for Strategic Studies, Adelphi Paper 352, 2002), p. 27.

[33] *OECD in Figures: Statistics on Member Countries* (Paris: OECD, 2005), pp. 13–14. U.S. military spending accounted for 47 percent of world military spending in 2004. *SIPRI Yearbook 2005: Armaments, Disarmament, and International Security* (Stockholm: Almquist and Wiksell, 2005), chapter 8. For an entrée into the burgeoning literature on the implications of American preponderance, see G. John Ikenberry (ed.), *America Unrivaled: The Future of the Balance of Power* (Ithaca: Cornell University Press, 2002).

from concerned bankers. If the United States appeared to be ramping up for major war with a serious military competitor, the government might get an earful of antiwar protestations from the financial community (and then some), just as financiers everywhere have appealed to their governments in the past. But the United States could *double* its current level of defense spending and still spend less than it did during the Vietnam War or the Korean War (9.5 percent of GDP in 1968, 13 percent in 1953). Even spending at levels equivalent to the peak years of the Reagan buildup (from 1983 to 1987, about 6.1 percent of GDP) would reflect a 50 percent increase from 2005's military outlays.[34]

Of course, over time, these advantages will recede. And that will present new challenges for the United States, if and when the dollar begins to play a somewhat reduced international role. Then the "dollar overhang" of American currency abroad will require attention that will inhibit, rather than extend, American power and influence, for all the reasons discussed in this book. There are, from this perspective, two likely futures for the dollar. A scenario emphasizing relative continuity envisions the United States artfully managing its macroeconomic affairs and thus maintaining the international attractiveness of the dollar. In this future, the dollar retains its current international position for an indefinite period, if only by default—due to inertia, American political and economic stability, the ungainliness of the euro, and Sino-Japanese political rivalry in Asia. Even in this placid scenario, eventually, if gradually, the relative preponderance of the dollar will fade and present some new financial constraints on the United States, especially if the euro gels, Japan rebounds, and China (and India?) continues to emerge.

A second vision anticipates a much more turbulent future, pointing to the significant clouds currently on the horizon, threatening storms that could fundamentally transform the sensitivity of the United States to financial constraints on its national security strategy. America's macroeconomic house is not in order. Its ability to enjoy the benefits of providing the world's currency depends on the continued willingness of foreigners to use and hold dollars, which in turn is a function of a widely shared confidence in the value and stability of the greenback. But guesses about the future value of the dollar and, just as important, guesses about what other people are guessing about its future value are based on expectations regarding the internal and external price of the dollar—the inflation rate and the exchange rate.

[34] "Historical Budget Data" (Congressional Budget Office, January 26, 2006), tables 8 and 9 (http://www.cbo.gov/budget/historical.pdf; accessed March 3, 2006); Jeffrey Chamberlin, "FY2005 Defense Budget: Frequently Asked Questions," *CRS Report for Congress* (Congressional Research Service, July 12, 2004), pp. 28–29; James L. Clayton, "The Fiscal

There are good reasons to be concerned about each of these parameters. Guesses about the inflation rate are informed by a number of considerations, but the large, sustained U.S. federal budget deficits warn of the threat of future inflation. Even more plainly, the massive imbalances in American external accounts suggest that the dollar is considerably overvalued.[35] Beyond these indicators is the larger question of whether the U.S. current account position is sustainable. American trade deficits have spent the early twenty-first century shattering record after record, surpassing $700 billion in 2005; and as a percentage of GDP, the U.S. current account deficits reached annual levels at or above 5 percent—by a considerable amount the highest levels in U.S. history. Total U.S. net external liabilities, about 25 percent of GDP in 2005, are projected to reach 50 percent in 2015 and 100 percent by 2030. For developing countries, 40 percent is the level often used as a "crisis threshold"—the point at which the imbalance will trigger a financial crisis. Obviously, for a variety of reasons, the United States will be able to sustain external deficits longer and at higher levels than would a developing country. But there is no good reason to believe that the United States can sustain ever widening deficits indefinitely.[36]

Compounding this further is the paradox that because the U.S. dollar has been so attractive, there is an enormous amount of dollars held abroad. (Japan, China, Taiwan, and South Korea hold well over a *trillion* dollars; many others, including Saudi Arabia, also have significant dollar reserves.)[37] Thus if there was a spark, somewhere, that touched off a fi-

---

Cost of the Cold War to the United States: The First Twenty-Five Years, 1947–1971," *Western Political Quarterly* 25:3 (September, 1972), pp. 379, 393.

[35] A common estimate is that the dollar is overvalued by about 30 percent. See C. Fred Bergsten and John Williamson (eds.), "Dollar Adjustment: How Far? Against What?" (Institute for International Economics, Special Report 17, November 2004), and C. Fred Bergsten and John Williamson (eds.), *Dollar Overvaluation in the World Economy* (Washington, DC: Institute for International Economics, 2003).

[36] Maurice Obstfeld and Kenneth Rogoff, "The Unsustainable US Current Account Position Revisited" (National Bureau of Economic Research, Working Paper 10869, October 2004), pp. 1, 5, 7, 18; Michael Mussa, "Sustaining Growth While Reducing External Imbalances," in C. Fred Bergsten (ed.), *The United States and the World Economy* (Washington, DC: Institute for International Economics, 2005), pp. 175–76, 186, 194–95, 201–3; William R. Cline, *The United States as a Debtor Nation* (Washington, DC: Institute for International Economics, 2005), pp. 3, 66, 85, 99, 154, 168–71, 275–77; Sebastian Edwards, "Is the U.S. Current Account Deficit Sustainable? And If Not, How Costly Is Adjustment Likely to Be?" (National Bureau of Economic Research, Working Paper 11541, August 2005), pp. 2–3, 11–12, 26, 40–42.

[37] It is sometimes suggested that states like China might threaten to dump their dollar holdings as an act of political coercion against the United States, but this is unlikely, as it would not be in China's interest to see a sudden collapse in the dollar. A dollar crisis, like most financial crises, would be fueled by thousands of uncoordinated, individually rational

nancial crisis implicating the dollar, given the state of underlying expectations about its future value and the number of greenbacks out there, a tidal wave of dollars could flood the market. In the aftermath of this much larger crisis, the United States would find itself, suddenly, in a very different international financial position. It would certainly not look like Britain after the fall of sterling—the comparison between the two economies more broadly is remote. But some monetary similarities would be notable. America would at once be confronted with the burdens of its own dollar overhang. No longer given the benefit of the doubt, its macroeconomic management would be subject to intense scrutiny in international financial markets. Its ability to borrow from foreigners (that which has fueled its twenty-first-century federal deficits) would be reduced, or at least more expensive, and possibly arranged to protect lenders from dollar devaluation. And, finally, its deviations from financial rectitude would be punished. In this future, under the watchful eye of the bankers, given the pressures that would be felt to cut government spending (and the country's latent isolationist disposition), paying hard cash for foreign military adventurism and half of the world's defense spending might seem like dispensable luxuries.

---

decisions to get out of the dollar in anticipation of further dollar decline, decisions that would be self-fulfilling. If anything, the fact that a large percentage of dollars and dollar liabilities is held by governments is relatively stabilizing, as governments are less sensitive to profit motives in managing their reserves. For similar reasons, the idea that the United States went to war in Iraq to protect the international role of the dollar is at best a red herring; the fate of the dollar lies in the hands of anonymous investors, not coercible governments; and the Iraq war has, as would be anticipated, made the international role of the dollar marginally less secure, not more secure.

Index

Milton Keynes UK
Ingram Content Group UK Ltd.
UKHW040747180824
447095UK00001B/65